FROMMER'S
EasyGuide
TO
FLORENCE & TUSCANY

By
Stephen Brewer & Donald Strachan

Easy Guides are ✦ Quick To Read ✦ Light To Carry
✦ For Expert Advice ✦ In All Price Ranges

FrommerMedia LLC

Published by
FROMMER MEDIA LLC

Copyright © 2015 by Frommer Media LLC. All rights reserved. No part of this publication may be repro-
duced, stored in a retrieval system, or transmitted in any form or by any means, electronic, mechanical,
photocopying, recording, scanning or otherwise, except as permitted under Sections 107 or 108 of the
1976 United States Copyright Act, without the prior written permission of the Publisher. Requests to the
Publisher for permission should be addressed to support@frommermedia.com.

Frommer's is a registered trademark of Arthur Frommer. Frommer Media LLC is not associated with any
product or vendor mentioned in this book.

ISBN 978-1-62887-112-8 (paper), 978-1-62887-113-5 (e-book)

Editorial Director: Pauline Frommer
Editor: Lorraine Festa
Production Editor: Heather Wilcox
Cartographer: Andrew Murphy
Cover Design: Howard Grossman

For information on our other products or services, see www.frommers.com.

Frommer Media LLC also publishes its books in a variety of electronic formats. Some content that
appears in print may not be available in electronic formats.

Manufactured in the United States of America

5 4 3 2 1

CONTENTS

ABOUT THE AUTHORS

Stephen Brewer has been savoring Italian pleasures ever since he sipped his first cappuccino while a student in Rome many, many years ago (togas had just gone out of fashion). He has written about Italy for many magazines and guidebooks and began spending many happy days at a house outside Cortona long before a neighbor decided to write a book about the town. He remains transported in equal measure by the Campo in Siena, the Piero della Francesca frescoes in Arezzo, the facade of the Duomo in Orvieto, and all the countryside in between.

Donald Strachan is a travel journalist who has written about Italy for publications worldwide, including "National Geographic Traveller," "The Guardian," "Sunday Telegraph," CNN.com, and many others. He has also written several Italy guidebooks for Frommer's, including "Frommer's Easy Guide to Rome, Florence, and Venice." For more information, see www.donaldstrachan.com.

ABOUT THE FROMMER'S TRAVEL GUIDES

For most of the past 50 years, Frommer's has been the leading series of travel guides in North America, accounting for as many as 24 percent of all guidebooks sold. I think I know why.

Although we hope our books are entertaining, we nevertheless deal with travel in a serious fashion. Our guidebooks have never looked on such journeys as a mere recreation, but as a far more important human function, a time of learning and introspection, an essential part of a civilized life. We stress the culture, lifestyle, history, and beliefs of the destinations we cover and urge our readers to seek out people and new ideas as the chief rewards of travel.

We have never shied from controversy. We have, from the beginning, encouraged our authors to be intensely judgmental, critical—both pro and con—in their comments, and wholly independent. Our only clients are our readers, and we have triggered the ire of countless prominent sorts, from a tourist newspaper we called "practically worthless" (it unsuccessfully sued us) to the many rip-offs we've condemned.

And because we believe that travel should be available to everyone regardless of their incomes, we have always been cost-conscious at every level of expenditure. Although we have broadened our recommendations beyond the budget category, we insist that every lodging we include be sensibly priced. We use every form of media to assist our readers and are particularly proud of our feisty daily website, the award-winning Frommers.com.

I have high hopes for the future of Frommer's. May these guidebooks, in all the years ahead, continue to reflect the joy of travel and the freedom that travel represents. May they always pursue a cost-conscious path, so that people of all incomes can enjoy the rewards of travel. And may they create, for both the traveler and the persons among whom we travel, a community of friends, where all human beings live in harmony and peace.

Arthur Frommer

THE BEST OF FLORENCE & TUSCANY

As the cradle of the Renaissance, Tuscany—and its easygoing neighbor, Umbria—boast some of the world's most captivating art and architecture, from the sublime sculpture of Michelangelo to paintings by Botticelli and Leonardo, to rural hilltop towns and the noble *palazzi* of Florence. Yet Tuscany isn't all churches and palaces and galleries. These are regions of lush landscapes, the snow-capped Apennine mountains, and olive groves and vineyards that produce prized oils and famous wines. Every drive or country walk is a photo-op waiting to happen.

The artistic treasures of **Florence** have been dragging visitors to the city for hundreds of years—its show-stopping cathedral dome, giant "David," and Uffizi are genuine bucket-list attractions. The picturesque, narrow streets of **Siena** and **San Gimignano** ooze medieval history, while **Pisa**'s Leaning Tower is a curiously unsettling sight, however many times you've seen pictures of it. It's straightforward to add a side trip into Umbria, for the Basilica di San Francesco in **Assisi** and one of Italy's marquee painting collections at the Galleria Nazionale, in cosmopolitan **Perugia.**

The most cherished pastime of most Italians is eating. If the weather is fine and you're dining outdoors, perhaps with a view of a medieval church or piazza, you'll find the closest thing to food heaven. But there's no genuine "national" cuisine here—and even within Tuscany and Umbria, each city has its own recipes handed down through generations. Food is always a joy, whether you dine in one of the fine *osterias* of Florence, or just grab a crisp, fatty *porchetta* sandwich at a weekly Umbrian farmers' market. Try the olive oil—it's like sipping liquidized olives straight off the tree (and it's famously low in acidity). Sample the gelato in Florence, Baci chocolates in Perugia, and **Prato**'s crunchy biscuits, *cantuccini.* Then there's the wine: not just the **Chianti,** but the mighty Brunellos of **Montalcino,** Sagrantino from **Montefalco,** and subtle white wines of Orvieto that once took pride of place at the Roman emperor's table.

Central Italy's complex recorded history begins with the Etruscans, a heritage best explored today in **Volterra** and Orvieto, and at the civic museum in **Cortona.** The legacy of painter Piero della Francesca is preserved in **Arezzo**'s San Francesco church and a fine museum in **Sansepolcro.** The region's contemporary culture is best represented by the eclectic **Spoleto Festival** and **Perugia**'s annual jazz fest, as well as the bars and nightlife along Florence's Left Bank.

Tuscany and Umbria are fairly compact, too. You can see a lot of both regions in a fairly short space of time, should you need to move fast. Of course, this is Italy: It's always better to move as slowly as you dare. *Buon viaggio!*

THE best AUTHENTIC EXPERIENCES

o **Enjoying aperitivo, Tuscan-style:** These days *aperitivo* means more than just a pre-dinner drink: Bars in Siena, Pisa, and Florence offer rich buffets of finger food, pasta, salads, cured meats, and *pizzette,* for free, with that drink (usually 6–8pm).

o **An Evening Stroll in Perugia:** Perugia's broad Corso Vannucci is perfect for the early-evening stroll Italians everywhere turn out for—the *passeggiata.* It's the time to see and be seen, to promenade arm in arm with your best friend dressed in your best duds. The crowd flows up the street to one piazza and then turns around and saunters back down to the other end. When you tire of meandering, take a break to sip a glass of Umbrian wine or nibble Perugia's fine chocolates in one of the classy cafes lining the street. See "Perugia" in chapter 8.

o **Sampling the Porchetta Sandwich:** Take a suckling pig, debone, roll, spit and roast over a wood fire, with a sumptuous stuffing of garlic, rosemary, and fennel. Then carve and serve on a crusty roll for 2.50€. Can it get any better than this? Available at weekly markets, including in Spoleto.

o **Slowing Down to Italy Pace:** Nothing happens quickly here: Linger over a glass of wine from the Tuscan hills, slurp a gelato made with seasonal fruit, enjoy the evening *passeggiata* just like the locals. And they call it Slow Food for a reason.

THE best RESTAURANTS

o **Ora d'Aria, Florence:** For all its historic location in an alleyway behind Piazza della Signoria, Florence's best dinner spot is unshakably modern. Head chef Marco Stabile gives traditional Tuscan ingredients a fresh (and lighter) makeover. Even if you can't stretch to a table, take a walk down the medieval lane to watch the kitchen staff at work through a picture window. See p. 61.

o **Antica Locanda di Sesto, near Lucca:** The food in the northern part of Tuscany is quite different to that elsewhere in the region, making more liberal use of pulses like *farro* (emmer or spelt) and Sorano beans. Everything you'll eat at this roadside inn in the Serchio valley is freshly made on the premises, and dishes rely on seasonal and foraged ingredients, or produce from the owner family's nearby farm. Park right outside or ride the bus north from Lucca. See p. 153.

o **La Tana del Brillo Parlante, Massa Marittima:** Italy's smallest Slow Food–endorsed dining room is also one of Tuscany's best. Don't expect haute cuisine and stuffy waitstaff: The strictly local and seasonal menu is prepared with skill, and delivered with rustic informality at a price that will make you glow. See p. 150.

o **Acquacheta, Montepulciano:** The open flame grill takes center stage right across southern Tuscany, but nowhere more than at Montepulciano's quintessential cellar steakhouse. Cramped tables, one set of cutlery to last the whole meal, and a chef doing the rounds armed with his meat cleaver are all part of the charm. Order your *bistecca alla fiorentina* by weight, wash it down with house red drunk from a beaker, and soak up the experience. See p. 168.

o **Antica Osteria l'Agania, Arezzo:** On any given night at least half of Arezzo seems to be packing into the two floors of these plain, brightly lit dining rooms, where all of the pastas are homemade from organic ingredients, produce is market fresh, and the meats are sourced from local farms. See p. 182.

THE best HOTELS

o **Continentale, Florence:** Echoes of *la dolce vita* fill every sculpted corner of this modern hotel, and rooms are flooded in natural light. If you want to relax away from your 1950s-styled bedroom, there are day beds arranged by a huge picture window facing the Ponte Vecchio, and on the roof, La Terrazza is Florence's best gathering spot for evening cocktails. See p. 55.

o **La Dimora degli Angeli, Florence:** You walk a fine line when you try to bring a historic *palazzo* into the 21st century, and this place walks it expertly. Rooms are split over two floors, with contrasting characters—one romantic and modern-baroque in style; the second characterized by clean, contemporary lines and Scandinavian-influenced design. All are affordable. See p. 54.

o **NUN Assisi Relais & Spa Museum, Assisi, Umbria:** A dramatic change of pace from Assisi's heavily medieval aura is in full force here, a contemporary redo of a centuries-old convent. Guest quarters are all white surfaces and bursts of bright colors, accented with stone walls and arches. Downstairs are hedonistic pleasures the veiled former tenants could never have dreamed of—two pools, saunas, steam rooms, and a state-of-the-art spa. See p. 210.

o **Villa Zuccari, Montefalco, Umbria:** You'll feel like a guest in a noble Italian country house at Villa Zuccari, an old family estate outside the Umbrian wine village of Montefalco. Lounge on your own large terrace, in the palm-shaded garden surrounding a pool. Welcoming communal areas are filled with books and pottery. See p. 211.

o **San Michele, Cortona, Tuscany:** Many hotels in Italy occupy old palaces, but few do so as seamlessly and comfortably as the accommodations at the San Michele, in a 15th-century *palazzo* in the center of Cortona. Some of the high-ceilinged guest rooms are frescoed and paneled, others have views over the valley below, and a choice few have their own terraces. See p. 191.

THE best FOR FAMILIES

o **Climbing Pisa's Wonky Tower:** Are we walking up or down? Pleasantly disoriented kids are bound to ask as you spiral your way to the rooftop viewing balcony atop one of the world's most famous pieces of botched engineering. Pisa is an easy day trip from Florence, if that's how you want to see it. Eight is the minimum age for heading up its *Torre Pendente* or Leaning Tower. See p. 162.

o **A Trip to an Artisan Gelateria:** Fluffy heaps of gelato, however pretty, are built with additives, stabilizers, and air pumped into the blend. Blue "Smurf" or bubble-gum-pink flavors denote chemical color enhancement, and ice crystals or grainy texture are telltale signs of engineered gelato—so steer clear. Authentic artisan *gelaterie* produce good stuff from scratch daily, with fresh ingredients and less bravado. See p. 69 for our favorites in **Florence;** in Siena, we love **Kopakabana** (p. 128).

o **Orvieto from Below:** Young spelunkers bored with museums will enjoy guided tours of Orvieto's Grotte della Rupe, **Orvieto Underground,** taking in natural caverns 15m (45 ft.) below Orvieto's Santa Chiara convent. The caverns, reached by a steep climb up and down 55 steps and along a narrow rock-hewn passage, have variously been used as Etruscan houses, water wells, ceramic ovens, pigeon coops, quarries, and cold storage used during the many centuries before the fridge came to Umbria. See p. 224.

o **Patrolling the Battlements of a Tuscan Castle:** Tuscans spent a lot of their history fighting each other, and have left behind many a noble ruin. These sturdy fortifications have a magical way of tugging kids into the Middle Ages. Wannabe knights can wander round the walls and scale a ladder to the highest turret at the *fortezza* in **Montalcino** (p. 173), and stand watch in the lookout towers of **Monteriggioni** (p. 135), from which soldiers once kept an eye out for Florentine troops.

o **Getting Gruesome at Florence's Zoology Museum:** For grisly viewing, with a dose of morbid fascination, teens should book in a trip to the **Museo Zoologia "La Specola"** on Florence's south bank. If the Room of Skeletons doesn't creep them out, the dissected wax bodies and mockups of plague-infested Florence surely will. See p. 90.

THE most OVERRATED

o **Ponte Vecchio, Florence:** Sorry, lovers, but this isn't even the prettiest bridge in Florence, let alone one of the world's great spots for romantics. It's haphazard by design, packed at all hours, and hemmed in by shops that cater mostly to mass tourism. For a special moment with a loved one—perhaps even to "pop the question"—head downstream one bridge to the Ponte Santa Trínita. Built in the 1560s by Bartolomeo Ammanati, its triple-ellipse design is pure elegance in stone. At dusk, it is also one of Florence's best spots to take a photo of the Ponte Vecchio . . . if you must. See p. 83.

o **San Gimignano, Tuscany:** This little town is sometimes nicknamed the "medieval Manhattan," and from the distance, as you approach across rolling countryside, the dozen remaining towers do indeed appear like skyscrapers. Once inside the gates, the town is a beautifully preserved time capsule. But Manhattan comes to mind, too, because visitors cram its narrow lanes shoulder to shoulder, laying asunder the medieval aura you've come to savor. Stay here overnight, to experience it at dusk or the early morning, to really capture the atmosphere you came to find. See chapter 6.

undiscovered TUSCANY

o **Drinking your Coffee *al Banco*:** Italians—especially city dwellers—don't often linger at a piazza table sipping their morning cappuccino. For them, a *caffè* is a pit stop: They order at the counter (*al banco*), throw back the bitter elixir, and continue on their way, reinforced by the hit of caffeine. You will also save a chunk of change drinking Italian style—your coffee should cost at least 50 percent less than the sit-down price.

o **Abbey of San Galgano:** Sitting in a grassy meadow on the banks of the River Merse about 40km (25 miles) southwest of Siena may be the most enchanting spot in Tuscany, with two magical ingredients: the mossy ruins of a once-great church and a saintly hermitage that is the setting for Italy's own "Sword in the Stone" legend. See p. 135.

○ **Driving the Back Roads of the Crete Senesi and Val d'Orcia:** It's never clear to us why the spectacular winding roads southwest of Siena—past Asciano and San Giovanni d'Asso, and further south to the balcony-like ridges around Pienza— aren't the most heavily trafficked in all Tuscany. They are as gloriously empty as the landscape they survey, a rolling terrain punctuated by farmhouses and dotted with cypress stands. Such is the beauty of the scenery that you'll still find the going slow, however: Every new bend in the road reveals another photo stop as essential as the last. See chapter 7.

○ **Dining at a Southern Tuscan Grill:** They like their meat properly reared and cooked plain and simple on the flame grill right across southern and eastern Tuscany. Look out especially for beef sourced from white Chianina cattle and pork from the Cinta Senese breed of pig. See chapter 7.

○ **Florence's Vegetarian Dining Scene:** The days when you had to be a carnivore to fully enjoy a meal in the Tuscan capital are long gone. Modern menus at **iO** (p. 68) and **Vagalume** (p. 67) are populated with veggie dishes to match any appetite. There's memorable vegan and vegetarian cuisine at **Brac** (p. 67). And vegans, as well as celiacs, are looked after by the organic menu at **Vivanda** (p. 68).

THE best MUSEUMS

○ **Galleria degli Uffizi, Florence:** This U-shaped High Renaissance building designed by Giorgio Vasari was the administrative headquarters, or *uffizi* (offices), for the dukes of Tuscany when the Medici called the shots round here. It's now the crown jewel of Europe's art museums, housing the world's greatest collection of Renaissance paintings, including icons by Botticelli, Leonardo da Vinci, Michelangelo, and many, many others. Recent developments to create the "New Uffizi" have seen the inauguration of galleries dedicated to Mannerism, baroque art, and the Uffizi's large collection of art by foreign painters, including Rembrandt, El Greco, and Velázquez. See p. 76.

○ **Santa Maria della Scala, Siena:** The building is as much the star as the collections. This was a hospital from medieval times until the 1990s, when it was closed and frescoed wards, ancient chapels and sacristy, and labyrinthine basement floors were gradually opened up for public viewing. See p. 133.

○ **Galleria Nazionale, Perugia:** Umbria's National Gallery boasts more Peruginos than it knows what to do with. It also has one of the masterpieces of his teacher, Piero della Francesca, the "Polyptych of Sant'Antonio," with its Annunciation scene of remarkable depth. Duccio, Arnolfo di Cambio, Fra' Angelico, and Gentile da Fabriano add to one of Italy's weightiest regional collections. See p. 204.

○ **Museo Etrusco Guarnacci, Volterra:** One of Dodecapolis's ancient centers, Volterra has a medieval core still surrounded in places by the old Etruscan town walls. The best section encompasses the 4th-century-B.C. Porta all'Arco gate, from which worn basalt gods' heads gaze mutely over the valley. The Museo Etrusco Guarnacci here houses hundreds of funerary caskets and the "Shadow of the Evening," a tiny bronze youth of elongated grace. Its remarkable collection of Etruscan funerary urns and other artifacts is dusty, poorly lit, and devoid of a lot of English labeling, but is nonetheless a joyful celebration of this culture that flourished before the Golden Age of Greece and laid many of the foundations for the Roman Empire. See p. 145.

○ **Museo Nazionale del Bargello, Florence:** Past early Michelangelo marbles and Giambologna bronzes, the main attraction at the primary sculpture museum of the

Renaissance is a room full of famous works that survey the entire career of Donatello, in his time rightly considered the greatest sculptor since antiquity. See p. 79.

THE best FREE THINGS TO DO

o **Basking in the Lights of the Renaissance:** At dusk, make the steep climb up to the ancient church of San Miniato al Monte in Florence. Sit down on the steps and watch the city begin its daily twinkle. See p. 92.

o **Visiting a Monastery:** Should the urge to lead a monk's life ever strike, or if you simply want to retreat from the world for an hour or two, you'd be hard-pressed to find better places than the lonely abbeys of **Sant'Antimo** and **Monte Oliveto Maggiore,** both close to Montalcino. A visit to Sant'Antimo can be accompanied by the strains of Gregorian chant and the scent of incense wafting over surrounding fields. The cloisters at Monte Oliveto Maggiore are decorated with frescoes by Luca Signorelli and Il Sodoma. See p. 174 and 175.

o **Going off the Path in Assisi:** Who would've thought you could find a primal Umbrian country experience close to well-touristed Assisi? Get up early to hike into the wooded mountains of Monte Subasio to St. Francis's old hermitage. After a morning spent in contemplation with the monks and wandering the state parkland, head back to town. See chapter 8.

THE best ARCHITECTURAL LANDMARKS

o **Brunelleschi's Dome, Florence:** It took the genius of Filippo Brunelleschi to work out how to raise a vast dome over the huge hole in Florence's cathedral roof. Though rejected for the commission to cast the bronze doors of the Baptistery, Filippo didn't sulk. He went away and became the city's greatest architect, and the creator of one of Italy's most recognizable landmarks. See p. 75.

o **The Gothic Center of Siena:** The shell-shaped Piazza del Campo stands at the heart of one of Europe's best-preserved medieval cities. Steep, canyonlike streets, icons of Gothic architecture like the Palazzo Pubblico, and ethereal Madonnas painted on gilded altarpieces transport you back to a time before the Renaissance. See chapter 6.

o **Piazza Pio II, Pienza:** Plans to make tiny Pienza into the "ideal Renaissance city" never got very far. But what's here—a stage-set piazza, an Austrian-influenced Duomo, and a papal palace—show off a refined and sophisticated urban plan in which spaces and perspectives were designed to reflect Renaissance ideals of rationality and humanism. See p. 171.

THE best ACTIVE ADVENTURES

o **Biking Lucca's Walls:** The elegant Republic of Lucca is still snuggled comfortably behind its 16th-century walls, ramparts so thick they were converted into a city park—a tree-lined promenade running a 5km (3-mile) loop around the city rooftops. A bicycle is the preferred mode of transportation in Lucca, and you'll be in good company as you tool under the shade past parents pushing strollers, businessmen walking their dogs, and old men at picnic tables in their 40th year of a never-ending card game. See "Lucca" in chapter 6.

o **Taking the Thermal Waters in Rapolano:** Soaking isn't the most strenuous exercise, admittedly, but you can splash around enough in the large thermal pools at Rapolano, 38km (23 miles) southeast of Siena, to make your session into a bit of a workout. The hot-spring–fed bathing establishments are open on some weekend nights, providing a memorable under-the-stars experience. See p. 136.

o **Hiking Up to Cortona's Renaissance Castle:** It's all uphill along a tortuous, stepped ascent to **Fortezza Medicea di Girifalco,** built in 1556. When you get there, views over central Tuscany and south into Umbria from the four surviving bastions reward your climb. See p. 193.

THE best NEIGHBORHOODS & SMALL TOWNS

o **The Left Bank, Florence-style:** Most Florentines have abandoned their *centro storico* to the visitors, but south of the Arno in the areas of Oltrarno, San Frediano, and San Niccolò, you'll find plenty of action after dark. Slurp a gelato by the Arno at **La Carraia** (p. 69) and drink until late at **Volume** (p. 100).

o **Volterra, Tuscany:** Proud Volterra has been important in western Tuscany since the Etruscan era. From its magnificent rocky promontory, the ocher city surveys the sometimes wild, vast countryside surrounding it. Volterra is still home to workshops where artisans craft the native alabaster into translucent souvenirs. See "Volterra" in chapter 6.

o **Cortona, Tuscany:** This stony hill town is no longer big enough to fill its medieval walls, but it still has its first-rate civic museums with paintings by Fra' Angelico and local boys Luca Signorelli and Pietro da Cortona. The restaurants serve steak from the famed Chianina cattle, raised in the valley below, where several Etruscan tombs hint at the city's importance in a pre-Caesar Tuscany. See "Cortona" in chapter 7.

o **Gubbio, Umbria:** This ancient Umbrian stronghold (and home of the truffle) is like the last outpost of civilization before the wilderness of the high Apennines. The central piazza cantilevers over the lower town like a huge terrace. The square is bounded on one end by a mighty palace, all sharp stone lines and squared-off battlements. Inside is a cluttered archaeological museum and the same echoey medieval atmosphere that pervades the entire town. See "Gubbio" in chapter 8.

THE ART masterpieces

o **Lorenzo Ghiberti's Gates of Paradise, Battistero, Florence:** In 1401, young Ghiberti won a sculpture competition to craft the doors of Florence's Baptistery. Fifty-one years later, he completed his second and final set, boosting the Gothic language of three dimensions into a Renaissance reality of invented space and narrative line. Art historians consider that 1401 competition to be the founding point of what we now call the Renaissance. Michelangelo looked at the doors and simply declared them "so beautiful they would grace the entrance to Paradise." See p. 71.

o **Michelangelo's "David," Galleria dell'Accademia, Florence:** The Big Guy, the perfect Renaissance nude, masterpiece of sculpture, and symbol of Tuscany itself. See p. 87.

The Art Masterpieces | THE BEST OF FLORENCE & TUSCANY

○ **Giotto's "Life of St. Francis," Basilica di San Francesco, Assisi:** This fresco cycle shocked the painting world out of its Byzantine stupor and thrust it full tilt on the road toward the Renaissance. Giotto perhaps did more groundbreaking work in this one church than any other single painter in history, bringing a realism, classicism, a concept of space and bulk, and pure human emotion that parlayed humanist philosophy into paint. See p. 212.

○ **Masaccio's "Trinità" and the Cappella Brancacci, Santa Maria Novella and Santa Maria del Carmine, Florence:** The greatest thing since Giotto: Masaccio not only redefined figure painting with his strongly modeled characters of intense emotion and vital energy, but also managed to be the first painter to pinpoint precise mathematical perspective and create the illusion of depth on a flat surface. The world's first perfecter of virtual reality. See p. 86 and 93.

○ **Giovanni Pisano's Pulpit of St. Andrew, Sant'Andrea, Pistoia:** For more than a century, the search for Gothic perfection in stone seemed almost to be a private Pisano family race. Here Giovanni's 1301 sculpted hexagonal pulpit outshines father Nicola, and is the commanding work of the genre, crammed with emotional power and narrative detail. See p. 114.

○ **Filippo Lippi's "Life of St. John the Baptist," Duomo, Prato:** A restoration of this dazzling fresco cycle has brought the city of Prato some of the recognition (and visitors) it deserves. Lippi's depiction of the "Dance of Salome" is possibly a portrait of the amorous monk's mistress, Lucrezia Buti, and certainly one of the iconic images of the early Renaissance. See p. 108.

○ **Piero della Francesca's "Resurrection of Christ," Museo Civico, Sansepolcro:** Piero's dead-on geometric perspective and exquisitely modeled figures helped make this haunting work the model for all later depictions of the risen Christ. This is quite possibly the only fresco whose reputation as the "best painting in the world" actually saved it from bombardment during World War II. See p. 187.

○ **Duccio di Buoninsegna's "Maestà," Museo dell'Opera Metropolitana, Siena:** The genre-defining painting of the Virgin Mary in majesty, surrounded by saints, was carried through the streets of Siena in triumph when it was unveiled in the early 14th century. See p. 132.

FLORENCE & TUSCANY IN CONTEXT

As the cradle of the Renaissance, Florence has an abundance of blockbuster architecture and artistic masterpieces—as do most of the smaller cities that dot the Tuscan countryside, such as Arezzo, Pisa, and Lucca. This profusion of art is the direct result of historic rivalries between the region's cities dating back to the medieval era. Various noble and merchant families spent centuries trying to outdo each other with shows of artistic wealth; they often competed to see who could procure the most elaborate and grandest artistic masterpieces, from the most celebrated artists and architects they could lay their hands on. Today we are left with vivid reminders of those historic rivalries: an artistic treasure trove in nearly every city, and even hamlet, in this region.

While historically the intercity rivalry boiled over into countless wars, today it persists in other forms: clashes between soccer fans, graffiti sprayed on *palazzo* walls (*"Pisa merda"* is a favorite vulgar phrase of vandals from Livorno), and throughout the tourism sector at every level.

What would Tuscany be today had these rivalries never existed? Brunelleschi might have continued to work as a goldsmith, instead of crowning Florence's cathedral with his revolutionary dome. Donatello might have eked out an existence as a stonemason, and Michelangelo might have chiseled away in anonymity on his father's marble quarries, instead of becoming the legendary artists that produced some of Italy's most extraordinary works of art.

FLORENCE & TUSCANY TODAY

Tuscany primarily relies on two economic resources: tourism and the land—which are inextricably linked. Visitors come to see Tuscany's peerless art, of course, but also to sample the food and fine local wines, and take in landscapes that look like they have been Photoshopped. The economy of Florence (and even more so, of neighbor Prato) is also driven by a booming fashion and textile industry. Indeed, Tuscany is one of the richest parts of Italy, with GDP per capita well above the European average. Its economy is far bigger than nations such as Bulgaria and Croatia, and U.S. states such as Maine, New Mexico, or Kansas.

eating YOUR WAY AROUND TUSCANY

The genius of Tuscan cooking is in its simplicity. Fancy sauces aren't needed to hide the food because Tuscans use pure, strong flavors and the freshest of ingredients. The great dishes are in fact very basic: tomatoes tossed with local olive oil, famously low in acidity; homemade ribbons of pasta in hare sauce; game or free-range meats grilled over wood coals; beans simmered in earthenware pots.

The classic Tuscan appetizer is an **antipasto misto,** which simply means "mixed appetizer." It often entails *affettati misti* and *crostini misti,* both of which can be ordered alone as well. The former is a plate of sliced cured meats and salami, like *prosciutto* (salt-cured ham), *capocollo* (meaty pork salami), and *finocchiona* (*capocollo* spiked with fennel seeds). **Crostini** are little rounds of toast spread with various pâtés, the most popular being *di fegatini* (chicken liver flavored with anchovy paste and capers) and *di milza* (spleen), though you'll also often get mushrooms or tomatoes or a truffle paste.

Another popular appetizer is simple **bruschetta,** a slab of rustic bread toasted on the grill, rubbed with a garlic clove, drizzled with extra-virgin olive oil, and sprinkled with coarse salt—order it *al pomodoro* for a pile of cubed tomatoes and torn basil leaves added on top. In summer, you'll also see **panzanella,** a kind of cold salad made of stale bread soaked in cold water and vinegar mixed with diced tomatoes, onions, and basil, all sprinkled with olive oil.

For *primo* (first course), among the **zuppa** or **minestra** (soup), top dog is **ribollita,** literally "reboiled," because it's made the day before and reheated before serving. It's a chunky soup closer to stew than anything else. The principal ingredients are black cabbage, bean purée, and whatever vegetables *Mamma* taught you to add in, all poured over stale peasant bread. It's traditionally a winter dish.

Pasta is the most famous Italian *primo,* and in Tuscany the king is **pappardelle alla lepre** (very wide egg noodles in a strong-flavored sauce of wild hare). Every town has its own name for the simple homemade pasta that's basically durum wheat mixed with water and rolled between the hands into chewy, fat spaghetti: From Siena southward, it's usually called **pici** or **pinci.** Other typical pasta dishes include **strozzapreti,** "priest stranglers," because clerics would supposedly choke on these rich ricotta-and-spinach dumplings (sometimes called *gnudi*—nude, since they're

---

Mass tourism loves Tuscany and always will. Florence is an essential stop on almost every Italy tour, and the region is comfortably the country's most famous—sometimes the only one foreigners know by name. However, as in most of the Western world, the global financial crisis—known here as the *crisi*—had a disastrous effect on the economy, causing the deepest recession since World War II. As a result, 2011 and 2012 saw Italy pitched into the center of a European banking crisis, which almost brought about the collapse of the euro currency. The effects here were felt most strongly in Siena, where the world's oldest bank, Monte dei Paschi, needed a bailout in 2013 just to survive. Though the *crisi* had an impact on the region's tourism, visitor numbers to Florence dropped by less than 2 percent over the 2 worst years (2008 and 2009), and a recovery is well under way, driven in large measure by fast-growing visitor numbers from China and Russia. Several Florence hoteliers reported booming bookings through 2014.

basically ravioli filling without the clothing of a pasta pocket).

Tuscans are unabashed carnivores, and the main course *(secondo)* is almost always meat, usually grilled. Italians like their grilled meat as close to raw as rare can get, so if you prefer it a bit more brown, order your bistecca *ben cotta* (well done, which just might get you something close to medium). The mighty **bistecca alla fiorentina** is traditionally made from thick T-bone steak cut from the sirloin and enveloping the tenderloin of the snow-white muscular cattle raised in the Chiana valley, in southeast Tuscany. This is grilled over wood coals, then brushed with extra-virgin olive oil and sprinkled with cracked black pepper. So simple, so good. The steaks average 1 to 2 inches thick and weigh about 3 to 4 pounds.

More everyday secondi include **grigliata mista** (mixed grill that may include sausage, chicken, and steak), **arista di maiale** (slices of roast pork loin, sometimes with a meat stuffing), and any wild game, especially **cinghiale** (wild boar), which is often cooked *in umido* (stewed with tomatoes). A **lombatina di vitello** is a simple veal chop, prepared in myriad ways. Tuscans also make widespread use of **baccalà,** salt-cured cod they soften in water before cooking, often *alla livornese* (with tomatoes, white wine, and olive oil).

Tuscans are nicknamed *mangiafagioli* (bean-eaters) by other Italians, and **fagioli** here, the Italian word for beans in general, almost invariably means white cannellini beans. However, a simple plate filled with nothing but *fagioli* or **fagioli in fiasco,** cooked al dente and swimming in olive oil, is somehow divine. For something zestier, order **fagioli all'uccelletto,** beans stewed with tomatoes, garlic, and sage.

Tuscany's best sweet is the dreamy **gelato,** a dense Italian version of ice cream, which you should ideally get at a proper *gelateria* and not in a restaurant—see p. 69 for Florence's best gelato artisans. **Cantuccini,** or *biscotti di Prato* in that town most famed for them, are the Tuscan variant on twice-baked hard almond crescent cookies, usually eaten by dunking them in a small glass of the sweet vin santo. **Panforte** is a very dense fruitcake. (One of Siena's specialties, *pan pepato,* is its medieval predecessor, with spices including black pepper added into the sweetness.) A **castagnaccio** is a dense cake made of chestnut flour and topped with pine nuts.

Politically, Tuscany is a stronghold of Italy's center-left Democratic Party, forming with Umbria, Emilia-Romagna, and Le Marche the so-called "Red Quadrilateral" of Italian politics. In 2014, Matteo Renzi swapped his job as left-wing mayor of Florence to become Italy's youngest prime minister at age 39, heading a center-left coalition. One of his first major interventions was to force through the abolition—from 2015—of Italy's *province.* This layer of government, between *comune* (town or city) and *regione* (region—for example, Tuscany), has been deemed one bureaucracy too far for the 21st century. Whether the reforms will be implemented in full, or watered down somehow, or even abandoned, remains to be seen: This is Italy, after all, where change comes slowly, yet governments come and go rapidly.

A tradition of liberal government, combined with strong financial motivations to protect natural resources, has helped fuel a strong environmental movement in Tuscany. With a greater emphasis on sustainability, the regional government has generated tough traffic laws, reinforced strict zoning standards, and built bicycle paths. Ironically, tourism can have detrimental effects on the environment and vitality of the cities and regions that vie for it. Today Florence's historic core caters almost entirely to tourists, driving locals to move to the suburbs and rent out their historic homes. (The recent boom in San Frediano's Left Bank nightlife and dining scene is in some ways a response to this.) And although the region strives for sustainability, sometimes those well-meaning efforts backfire. For example, when pedestrian-only zones started being erected across Italy's city centers over a decade ago, the plans were met with cheers. Yet today, those pedestrian-only zones have interrupted traffic flow, and have unwittingly exacerbated an already horrible traffic problem. Car parking is a political hot potato.

One gastronomic trend to watch out for as you travel is the growth in popularity of artisanal beer, even here in the home of wine, and especially among the young. Although supermarket shelves are still stacked with mainstream brands Peroni and Moretti, smaller stores and bars increasingly offer craft microbrews. Italy had fewer than 50 breweries in 2000. That figure was well over 400 by 2013, and rising fast. You'll even find quality beers on the hallowed racks of the occasional wine cantina.

THE MAKING OF FLORENCE & TUSCANY

Etruscans & Romans (9th C. B.C.– A.D. 5th C.)

Although Neanderthals, ancient *Homo sapiens,* and Paleolithic and Bronze Age humans left some of their bones and tools lying about, things really didn't start getting lively in central Italy until the **Etruscans** rose to power.

One theory is that the Etruscans came from modern-day Turkey, and arrived in central Italy in the late 9th or early 8th century B.C. The fact that their language isn't Indo-European but appears similar to some Aegean dialects helps confirm this theory, but there are others who feel the Etruscans may have risen from native peoples in central Italy. Whatever the case, these Etruschi, or Tuschi, formed the basic cultural-political force in the region that's now named for them, Tuscany.

Much of what little remains to tell us of the Etruscans consists of tombs and their contents, and it's difficult to reconstruct an entire culture simply by looking at its graveyards. Although we can read their language, what script we have goes into little beyond death, divination, and the divine.

What historians are surer of is that Etruscans became enamored of the Attic culture of Greece and adopted many of the Greek gods and myths in the 6th century B.C. This era coincided with the height of their considerable power. In fact, from the late 7th century until 510 B.C., Rome was ruled by Etruscan kings of the Tarquin dynasty. Although the Etruscan empire spread south almost to Naples, east to the Adriatic, and west onto Corsica, the heart and core called Etruria covered an area from the Arno east to the Apennines and south to the Tiber, encompassing most of Tuscany, half of Umbria, and northern Lazio. **Volterra** (p. 144) has a surviving Etruscan town gate, and a fine museum collection of Etruscan artifacts. **Cortona**'s civic museum (p. 193) also has several Etruscan finds, as does **Orvieto**'s (p. 225), and there are outstanding Etruscan bronzes in Florence's **Museo Archeologico** (p. 87).

In the 3rd century B.C. **Rome** began its expansion, and some of the first neighboring peoples to fall were the Etruscans. Some cities, such as Arezzo, allied themselves with

guelph OR GHIBELLINE?

Though it's admittedly not the perfect measure, you can sometimes tell a city's allegiances, at least at any given time, by looking at the battlements of the medieval town hall: The Guelphs favored squared-off crenellations and the Ghibellines swallowtail ones. There are (of course) exceptions to this: Siena's **Palazzo Pubblico** (p. 131) was built with blocky battlements during the briefly Guelph period of the Council of Nine. Florence's **Palazzo Vecchio** (p. 82) confusingly sports both kinds.

Rome and were merely absorbed, while others, including Volterra, were conquered outright. As the Romans gained power over the entire peninsula, the removal of political barriers and the construction of roads allowed trade to develop and flow relatively uninhibited. Many of the old cities flourished, and the general prosperity led to the founding of new cities throughout the region, especially as retirement camps for Roman soldiers. Roman remains in Tuscany are fairly paltry, however, though **Fiesole**'s Roman theater (p. 106) is still used for summer operatic and orchestral performances.

Goths, Lombards & Franks: The "Dark Ages" (6th C.–11th C.)

As the Roman Empire collapsed in the A.D. 5th century, Germanic tribes swept down from the north and wreaked mayhem on central Italian cities, as group after group fought their way down to Rome in a sacking free-for-all. The **Goths** swept down in the A.D. 6th century, and one of their leaders, **Totila,** conquered Florence in A.D. 552. Totila's historic meeting with St. Benedict, at Monte Cassino, covers key panels in the cloister frescoes at **Monte Oliveto Maggiore** (p. 175).

Perhaps the strongest force in the so-called "Dark Ages" was the **Lombards,** who established two major duchies in central Italy, one based at Lucca, which governed most of Tuscany, and the other at Spoleto, which took care of most of Umbria. When their ambitions threatened Rome (now a Church stronghold) in the 8th century, the pope invited the Frankish king Pepin the Short to come clear the Lombards out. Under Pepin, and more importantly, his son **Charlemagne,** the Lombards were ousted from Tuscany. The best example of the Lombard architectural style still standing in Tuscany is the abbey of **Sant'Antimo** (p. 174), outside Montalcino.

The Lombard duchy at Lucca was replaced by a Frankish margrave, with Tuscany ruled for almost 3 centuries as an outpost of the Holy Roman Empire. Among the Franks was one of the few women to have wielded real military power in medieval Europe, **Margrave Matilda of Tuscany** (1046–1115). Both pope and Holy Roman Emperors gradually lost control of the area, and central Italy was plunged into political chaos. Out of it emerged, for the first time, the independent city-state republic known as the *comune.*

The Medieval *Comune,* Guelphs & Ghibellines

In the late 11th century, merchants became wealthier, and more important to the daily economic life of small Italian cities. They organized themselves into **guilds** and gradually became the bourgeois oligarchic leaders of their cities. The self-governing *comuni* they established weren't the perfect democracies they're often made out to be. While many were ruled by popularly elected **councils,** usually only the guild members of the merchant class were enfranchised. The majority of city laborers, as well as rural farmers, remained powerless.

As the *comuni* stabilized their infrastructures—after dealing with blows like the 1348 Black Death, a plague that swept through Europe and left half of Tuscany's population dead—they also set about roughing up their neighbors and rivals. Battles were fought both to increase the city-states' trading power and to place more towns under their control (or at least to secure subservient allies). To this end, instead of raising militia armies, they hired *condottieri,* professional soldiers of fortune who controlled forces of armed mercenaries. Frances Stonor Saunders' "Hawkwood: Diabolical Englishman" (2005) tells the story of one of the most notorious mercenary commanders in Florentine history. (Sir John Hawkwood's portrait still graces the wall of the city's **cathedral**—locals called him "Giovanni Acuto"; see p. 74).

In the 12th century, the German throne of the Holy Roman Emperor sat empty. Otto IV's family, the Welf dynasty of Bavaria, fought for it against the lords of Waiblingen, where the house of Swabia ruled under the Hohenstaufen dynasty. The names were corrupted in Italian to **Guelph** and **Ghibelline,** respectively. When the Hohenstaufens came out winners with Frederick Barbarossa being crowned emperor, the Ghibellines stuck as the supporters of the emperor, and the Guelphs became the party that backed the pope. Across Italy, the old nobility, as Ghibellines, favored the imperial promise of a return to feudalism, and hence their own power. The Guelph merchant-and-banking class supported the pope and his free-trade attitudes. Although they all flip-flopped to some degree, Florence (plus Lucca, Arezzo, and Perugia) turned out Guelph, which made rivals Pisa, Pistoia, and Siena Ghibelline.

The Guelph–Ghibelline conflict not only spawned intercity warfare but also sparked intracity strife between rival factions. In the 13th century Florence split into Guelph and Ghibelline parties, under which names the parties waged a decades-long struggle over who'd control the city government. At the turn of the 14th century, when the Guelphs finally came out victorious, Florence began to enjoy a fairly stable republican rule—still of the old assembly system called now the **Signoria,** a ruling council elected from the major guilds. Florence slowly expanded its power, first allying with Prato, then conquering Pistoia, and by 1406 adding Volterra, Arezzo, and Pisa to the cities under its rule.

The Renaissance: Cue the Medici

The **Medici** came from the hills of the Mugello in the early Middle Ages, quite possibly charcoal burners (or perhaps pharmacists) looking for the good life of the city. The family found moderate success and even had a few members elected to public office in the *comune* government. At the turn of the 15th century, **Giovanni de' Bicci de' Medici** made the family fortune by establishing the Medici as bankers to the papal curia in Rome. His son, Cosimo de' Medici, later called **Cosimo il Vecchio,** orchestrated a number of important alliances and treaties for the Florentine Signoria, gaining him prestige and respect. He was a humanist leader who believed in the power of the emerging new art forms of the early Renaissance, and he commissioned works from the greatest painters, sculptors, and architects of the day. Like much of the dynasty, he is buried in the family church in Florence, **San Lorenzo** (p. 85).

Cosimo grew so attached to the sculptor Donatello that, as Cosimo lay dying, he made sure his son, **Piero the Gouty,** promised to care for the also aging artist and to see that he never lacked for work. Piero's rule was short and relatively undistinguished, quickly superseded by the brilliant career of his son, Lorenzo de' Medici, or **Lorenzo the Magnificent.** Under the late-15th-century rule of Lorenzo, Florence entered its golden era, during which time it became Europe's cultural and artistic focal point. It was Lorenzo who encouraged the young Michelangelo to sculpt (enrolling him in his own school), and he and Medici cousins commissioned paintings from Botticelli (now in the **Uffizi;** p. 76) and poetry from Poliziano (a native of **Montepulciano;** p. 164).

Although Lorenzo fought to maintain the precious balance of power between Italian city-states, in doing so he incurred the wrath of the pope and the Pazzi family, Florentine rivals of the Medici. The young Medici leader's troubles came to a head in the infamous 1478 **Pazzi Conspiracy,** in which Lorenzo and his brother were attacked during High Mass in the cathedral. The coup failed, and the Pazzi were expelled from the city. Lorenzo's son and successor, **Piero de' Medici,** was also forced to flee, this time from the invading armies of Charles VIII in 1494 (although Charles quickly withdrew from the Italian field). Into the power vacuum stepped puritanical preacher **Girolamo Savonarola.** This theocrat's apocalyptic visions and book-burning (the original Bonfire of the Vanities) held the public's fancy for about 4 years, until the pope excommunicated the entire city for following him, and Florentines put the torch to Savonarola as a heretic. A porphyry plaque marks the spot of his pyre, in **Piazza della Signoria** (p. 80), and his monastic cell in **San Marco** (p. 88) remains almost as he left it.

In 1512, however, papal armies set another of Lorenzo's sons, the boring young **Giuliano de' Medici,** duke of Nemours, on the vacant Medici throne. Giuliano, and later **Lorenzo de' Medici** (Lorenzo the Magnificent's grandson via the ousted Piero) were merely mouthpieces for the real brains of the family, Giuliano's brother, **Cardinal Giovanni de' Medici,** who in 1513 became **Pope Leo X** and uttered the immortal words, "God has given us the papacy, now let us enjoy it."

Pope Leo's successor as leader of the Medici was his natural cousin, **Giulio de' Medici,** illegitimate son of Lorenzo's brother Giuliano. Although blackguards such as Ippolito and **Alessandro de' Medici** held sway in Florence, they really took their orders from Giulio, who from 1523 to 1534 continued to run the family from Rome as **Pope Clement VII.** Emperor Charles V's armies sacked Rome in 1527, sending Clement VII scurrying to Orvieto for safety and giving the Florentines the excuse to boot Alessandro from town and set up a republican government. In 1530, however, the pope and Charles reconciled and sent a combined army to Florence, and eventually Alessandro was reinstated. This time he had an official title: **Duke of Florence.**

After decadently amusing himself as a tyrant in Florence for 7 years, Alessandro was murdered in bed by his distant cousin Lorenzaccio de' Medici, who plunged a dagger into the duke's belly and fled to Venice (where he was later assassinated). The man chosen to take Alessandro's place was a Medici of a different branch, young **Cosimo de' Medici.** Contrary to his immediate Medici predecessors, Cosimo I actually devoted himself to attending to matters of state. He built up a navy, created a seaport for Florence called **Livorno,** and even conquered age-old rival Siena after a brutal war from 1555 to 1557. A patron of Vasari, it was Cosimo who ordered the building of a "secret passage" from his home to his offices, now known as the **Corridoio Vasariano** (p. 82). His crowning moment came in 1569 when the pope declared him **Cosimo I, Grand Duke of Tuscany.** Except for the tiny Republic of Lucca, which happily trundled along independently until Napoleon gave it to his sister in 1806, the history of Tuscany was now firmly intertwined with that of Florence.

A TUSCAN wine label

It would take a book at least the size of this one to explain the byzantine Italian wine laws, and how they apply to Tuscany. Instead, here are some words to look out for:

Indicazione Geografica Tipica (IGT): A guarantee of grape variety and place of origin. Some of Tuscany's best wines are sold with IGT status.

Denominazione di Origine Controllata (DOC): The basic classification for a wine produced in a specific location, which has to conform to yield rules and quality checks.

Denominazione di Origine Controllata e Garantita (DOCG): Italy's best wines, which have to conform to the same checks as DOC wines and more.

Imbottigliato all'origine: A wine bottled where it was made—usually a good sign.

Riserva: A special, aged selection.

Brunello di Montalcino: Outstanding DOCG wine from the hills around Montalcino, made entirely from the Sangiovese grape. A good bottle will set you back around 40€. See p. 177.

Rosso di Montalcino: What people on modest budgets buy if they want a Montalcino wine: Fruitier than a Brunello, but without the structure to age nobly.

Vino Nobile di Montepulciano: First-rate DOCG wine from the hills around Montepulciano. See p. 171.

Chianti Classico: A red from the (classico) Chianti zone: a staple Tuscan wine the world over, and a perfect foil for meat or game. See p. 119.

Vin Santo: An almost yellow, sweet white dessert wine, traditionally aged under the tiles of Renaissance palaces.

"Super Tuscans": Words you won't see on a label, but a catchall term for innovative, modern, usually red wines that break the Tuscan mold. If someone offers you a Sassicaia, Tignanello or Ornellaia, say yes . . . as long as they are picking up the check.

Tuscany in a United Italy

In 1860 Florence and Tuscany became part of the newly declared Italian state. From 1865 to 1870, Florence was the capital of Italy, and it enjoyed a frenzied building boom—the medieval walls were torn down and the old market and Jewish ghetto demolished and replaced with the cafe-lined, somewhat grandiose **Piazza della Repubblica.** The army that was conquering recalcitrant states on the peninsula for **Vittorio Emanuele II,** first king of Italy, was commanded by **Gen. Giuseppe Garibaldi,** who spent much of the end of the war slowly subjugating the papal states—the pope was the last holdout against the new regime. This meant defeating the papal authorities in **Umbria.** Papal armies quickly retreated, leaving cities like Perugia to cheer on Garibaldi's troops as they freed the region from hundreds of years of papal oppression.

The demagogue **Benito Mussolini** came to power after World War I and did much to improve Italy's industrial and physical infrastructure, while simultaneously destroying much of its social fabric—or at least, trying to. Although the Tuscans certainly had their share of collaborators and die-hard Fascists, many Italians never bought into the war or the Axis alliance. The Tuscan partisan movement was always strong, with resistance fighters holed up particularly in the hills south of Siena. Tuscany became a battlefield as the occupying Nazi troops slowly withdrew across the landscape in the face of Allied advancement, but not without committing appalling massacres along the

RENAISSANCE reading

Whole libraries have been written on the Renaissance. The most accessible introductions include Peter and Linda Murray's "The Art of the Renaissance" (1963), Michael Levey's "Early Renaissance" (1967), and Evelyn Welch's "Art in Renaissance Italy 1350–1500" (2000)—it's certainly worth acquainting yourself with some of the themes and styles before you visit. Giorgio Vasari's "Lives of the Artists" was first published in 1550, and it remains the definitive work on the Renaissance artists—by one who knew some of them personally. It's also surprisingly readable. On the buildings, Peter Murray's "The Architecture of the Italian Renaissance" (1969) is a good read. In "The Stones of Florence" (1956), Mary McCarthy mixes brilliant architectural insight with no-holds-barred opinions.

way. In 2011, three former Nazi soldiers were found guilty in absentia of the murder of 184 civilians, in August 1944, in Padule di Fucecchio. In "War in Val d'Orcia" (1947), Iris Origo diarized her life during the hard, decisive months of German retreat through rural Tuscany.

Postwar Florence was hit with its greatest disaster when the **Great Arno Flood** of November 1966 covered much of the city with up to 6m (20 ft.) of sludge and water, destroying or severely damaging countless thousands of works of art and literature: 8,000 paintings in the Uffizi basement alone, and 1.5 million volumes in the National Library. Along with an army of experts and trained restorers, hundreds of volunteers nicknamed "Mud Angels" descended on the city, many of them foreign students, to pitch in and help dig out all the mud and salvage what they could of one of the greatest artistic heritages of any city on earth. You can still see signs of the inundation all over the city, including in the watermarked cloister at **Santa Maria Novella** (p. 86). Cimabue's Crucifix, now restored (as much as it ever will be) and returned to the small museum attached to **Santa Croce** (p. 89), became an international symbol for the destruction.

The political fortunes of Tuscany and Umbria have in the past decades have mainly followed those of Italy at large. However, even through the controversial right-wing governments of media magnate **Silvio Berlusconi,** both remained staunchly part of Italy's left-leaning "Red Quadrilateral."

TUSCAN ART & ARCHITECTURE
The Tuscan Romanesque: The 11th & 12th Centuries

When **Pisa** (p. 157) became a major medieval power, it did so as a huge shipping empire, and with this trade came contact with Eastern and Islamic cultures. Pisa poured its 11th-century prosperity into building a new religious core and cathedral, adapting many of the decorative elements from these Eastern contacts. The style that was developed in **Buscheto**'s Duomo (p. 161) and the associated baptistery and bell tower (yes, the one that leans) came to define the Romanesque and quickly spread across northern Tuscany.

The purest, earliest form that arose in Pisa and **Lucca** (p. 150)—known, sensibly, as the **Pisan–Luccan Romanesque**—was characterized by horizontal stripes of marbles

KNOW YOUR APSE FROM YOUR NAVE: A CRASH COURSE IN church terminology

Apse: The enclosed space behind the main altar

Basilica: Originally a Roman public hall, now often refers (interchangeably with *collegiata*) to an important church without a bishopric

Campanile: The bell-tower of a church

Cappella: A chapel, a dedicated religious space created off the aisles or transepts of a church

Chiostro: The cloisters—internal roofed walkways found in monasteries

Duomo: Another word for *cattedrale*—the cathedral (not to be confused with *cupola*, which refers to the dome itself)

Fresco: A picture that was painted onto wet plaster; thanks to this method, frescoes can survive for many centuries, if done properly

Lunette: The arched space between the walls and a vaulted ceiling

Nave: The central aisle of a church leading from the main door to the altar

Sacristy: The room—*sagrestia* in Italian—where the priest's garments and sacred bits and pieces are (or were) kept

Transept: The cross-arms of a church, running at 90° to the nave

on church facades, and eventually in some interiors as well. At first they used green and white; later, in **Siena's cathedral** (p. 130), it became black and white; and in neighboring Umbria the available local stone made it pink and white. Other key elements were curving semicircular arches; blind arcades of these arches often set with diamond-shaped decorative inlays called lozenges; open galleries supported by thin mismatched columns and often stacked three or four rows high on facades; lots of tiny detail in marble inlay; and often a nave flanked by two colonnaded aisles inside. **San Michele in Foro** (p. 156), in Lucca, is one perfect example.

The later form of the movement that was adapted in **Florence**—on the Baptistery and San Miniato al Monte in particular—and **Pistoia** (San Giovanni Fuoricivitas and, though later altered, the Duomo) was called the **Florentine Romanesque.** On the surface it was very similar to the Pisan–Lucchese school, but it was practiced along much stricter lines of a geometry gleaned from classical architecture, a predecessor to the mathematically proportional architecture of the Renaissance. Before "the big R," however, in the late 12th century a strong northern styling came into vogue called, after its supposed association with the historic conquerors from the north, the **Gothic.**

Tuscan Gothic: 13th & 14th Centuries

The **Gothic** first started infiltrating Italy as architecture. It was originally imported by French Cistercian monks, who in 1218 created the huge San Galgano abbey church, now roofless (and terribly romantic), off the road between Siena and **Massa Marittima** (p. 147). Although this French style of the Gothic never caught on, the church was still at the time revolutionary in introducing some of the new forms, which were adopted when **Giovanni Pisano** (ca. 1250–1315) overhauled Siena's cathedral and "Gothicized" it.

Thin-columned windows and lacelike stone tracery caught the Tuscan fancy and were incorporated into many palaces, especially in **Siena,** where the architectural forms otherwise pretty much stayed the same old, solid, medieval masonry. Out of this marriage were born the **Palazzo Pubblico** (p. 131) in Siena and, more influential, the town hall in **Volterra** (p. 144). The latter served as the model for Florence's famous **Palazzo Vecchio** and similar buildings across the region.

The Palazzo Vecchio's architect was **Arnolfo di Cambio,** the Gothic master of Florence's 1290s building boom. Arnolfo was also responsible for the Franciscan church of Santa Croce and the original plans for the Duomo. The kind of Frankish Gothic building most people associate the term "Gothic," with lots of spires and stony frills, really showed up only in the tiny carved stone jewel of Santa Maria della Spina along the banks of the Arno in Pisa. **Andrea Orcagna,** who was also a painter, gave us another bit of this sort of Gothic in miniature with his elaborate marble-inlaid tabernacle in Florence's Orsanmichele.

The Gothic style was at its most advanced in sculpture. **Nicola Pisano** probably emigrated from southern Apulia to work in Pisa, where he crowned that city's great Romanesque building project with a Gothic finale in 1260. He created for the **Baptistery** (p. 161) a great pulpit, the panels of which were carved in high relief with a new kind of figurative emotion displayed in the sway of the figures. By the time Nicola carved the panels on his second pulpit in **Siena Cathedral** (p. 130), along with his son **Giovanni Pisano,** the figures were moving into a radically new sort of interaction, with a multitude of squirming bodies and pronounced stylized curves to add a graceful rhythm and emotion to the characters. Giovanni went on to carve two more pulpits (in Pistoia, at **Sant'Andrea** [p. 114], perhaps the apogee of the genre, and back to Pisa for the Duomo). **Andrea Pisano** (no relation) picked up the thread in Florence when in 1330 he cast the first set of bronze baptistery doors in the now-established Gothic style.

In the 1290s, **Giotto di Bondone**—best known as a frescoist who left us masterpiece cycles in Assisi's **Basilica di San Francesco** (probably; see p. 212) and Florence's **Santa Croce** (p. 89) and Padua's Cappella degli Scrovegni (certainly)— completely broke away from the styling of his teacher, **Cimabue,** and invented his own method of painting, steeped in the ideas of humanism and grounded in realism. What he did was to give his characters real human faces displaying emotions; to use light and shadow to mold his figures, giving them bulk under their robes; to employ foreshortened architecture not only to provide a stage-set backdrop but also, and this was key, to give the paintings depth and real space. His "Ognissanti Madonna," now in Florence's **Uffizi** (p. 76), was another landmark achievement, and contains all of these elements.

Siena adapted some of the humanist content of realism and naturalism into its Gothic painting, but left by the wayside the philosophical hang-ups and quest for perfect perspective the Florentine Renaissance soon embarked upon (see below). The **Sienese School** ended up with a distinctive, highly decorative art form rich in colors, patterns, and gold leaf. It was often as expressive as Giotto's work, but this was achieved through the sinuous lines of its figures and subtle compositional interplay. **Duccio di Buoninsegna** gave the Sienese School a focus in the late 1200s, starting to adapt Gothic elements but still working in a Byzantine tradition—his 1311 "Maestà" (p. 132) defined a genre. **Jacopo della Quercia** became a towering figure in Sienese Gothic sculpture.

One of the next great Sienese painters came out of Duccio's workshop: **Simone Martini** developed a much more refined style of the Gothic flavor with his elegant lines, ethereal figures, and richly patterned fabrics—he's the star of Room 2 in Florence's **Uffizi.** Two more Duccio students were **Ambrogio** and **Pietro Lorenzetti,** both masters of color and composition who infused their art with the naturalness of common life. The former left the most important cycle of civic (that is, nonreligious) art ever painted, the "Allegories of Good and Bad Government" (1339) inside Siena's **Palazzo Pubblico** (p. 131).

The Black Death of 1348 nipped the emergent Sienese School in the bud. The Lorenzetti brothers perished, and the handful of citizens who lived through the plague were more intent on simple survival than on commissioning artworks, leaving Florence's version of the Renaissance to develop and eventually reign supreme. Renaissance painter **Domenico Beccafumi** was perhaps the only great Sienese artist of later generations.

Timothy Hyman's "Sienese Painting: The Art of a City Republic 1278–1477" (2003) is the best book on the subject, and accessible to nonspecialist readers.

The Early Renaissance: 15th Century

Tradition holds that the Renaissance "began" in 1401 when **Lorenzo Ghiberti** won a competition to cast Florence's new set of north doors for the **Baptistery** (p. 71). Although confined to Gothic frames, Ghiberti still managed to infuse his figures with an entirely new kind of naturalism that earned him accolades when the doors were finished 20 years later. Ghiberti was immediately commissioned to do another set, which became known as the "Gates of Paradise," one of the cornerstone pieces of the early Renaissance. These restored original doors are now displayed inside the **Museo Storico dell'Opera** (p. 76).

One of the men Ghiberti competed against for the first commission was **Filippo Brunelleschi,** who decided to study architecture after he lost the sculpture competition. When he came back from a learning trip to Rome, where he examined the classical construction of the ancients, he was full of groundbreaking ideas. These led to his ingenious red-tiled dome over Florence's **Duomo** as well as to a new kind of architecture based on the classical orders and mathematical proportions with which he filled Florentine church interiors—all done in smooth white plaster and soft gray *pietra serena* stone. **Santo Spirito** (p. 94) and the **Pazzi Chapel** at Santa Croce (p. 89) are prime examples of his adapted classicism.

One of his buddies was a sculptor named **Donatello,** who traveled with him to Rome and who on his return cast the first free-standing nude since antiquity (a "David," now in Florence's **Bargello;** p. 79) in an anatomically exacting style of naturalness. Donatello also developed the *schiacciato* technique of carving in very low relief, using the mathematical perspective trick his architect friend Brunelleschi taught him to achieve the illusion of great depth in shallow marble.

Brunelleschi also passed this concept of perspective along to a young painter named **Masaccio.** Masaccio added it to his experimental bag of tricks, which included using a harsh light to model his figures in light and shadow, bold brushstrokes and foreshortened limbs to imply movement and depth, and an unrelenting realism. He used all of these to create the frescoes in Florence's **Cappella Brancacci** (p. 93)—painters were still studying his technique a century later. Masaccio died in Rome, at age 27—which perhaps explains why he isn't much more famous.

Where Masaccio tried to achieve a new level of clarity and illusionistic reality with his perspective, **Paolo Uccello** became obsessed about experimenting with it, working out the math of perfect perspective and spatial geometry in some paintings and then warping it in others to see how far he could push the tenets for narrative and symbolic ends rather than making his work merely representative, at its best in the "Noah" fresco in Santa Maria Novella's **Chiostro Verde** (p. 86).

Outside Florence, Sansepolcro artist **Piero della Francesca** practiced a quiet, dramatic style, exploring of the geometry of perspective. He created crystalline-clear, spacious, haunting paintings with an unfathomable psychology in his figures' expressions, nowhere greater than in his "Legend of the True Cross" frescoes at San Francesco in **Arezzo** (p. 183).

The High Renaissance: Late 15th to Mid–16th Century

One of Piero della Francesca's students was **Luca Signorelli,** a Cortonan whose mastery of the male nude in such works as his **Cappella San Brizio** in Orvieto (p. 223) had a great effect on the painting of Michelangelo. His highly modeled figures of colorful and incisive geometry shared many similarities with the works of the nearby Umbrian school being developed by another of Piero's protégés, **Perugino.** Back in Florence, **Leonardo da Vinci** was developing a highly realistic style in the 1480s. His *sfumato* technique revolutionized perspective by softly blurring the lines of figures and creating different planes of distance basically by throwing far-off objects out of focus. Leonardo also studied anatomy with a frightening intensity, drawing models of bodies in various degrees of dissection to find out how to paint joints bending and muscles rippling in a realistic manner. In his spare time, he designed scientific inventions (usually on paper) such as parachutes, machine guns, water screws, and a few helicopters.

By age 23, following his first success in Rome with the "Pietà" now in St. Peter's, **Michelangelo Buonarroti** had established himself as the foremost sculptor of his age with the gargantuan "David" (1504), now in Florence's **Accademia** (p. 87). Michelangelo also revolutionized painting with his frescoes on the ceiling of Rome's Sistine Chapel (also evident in the Uffizi's "Doni Tondo"), where his twisting, muscularly modeled figures, limpid light, bold brush strokes, and revolutionary color palette of oranges, turquoises, yellows, and greens influenced a generation of artists. He died at the ripe old age of 89, in 1564, and is interred in **Santa Croce** (p. 89).

Eventually the High Renaissance began to feed off itself, producing vapid works of technical perfection but little substance, perhaps best exemplified by the painting of **Giorgio Vasari.** (Vasari was a much better architect and historian than he was a painter.) As Florentine art stagnated, several artists sought ways out of the downward spiral. Mannerism was the most interesting attempt, a movement that found its muse in the extreme torsion of Michelangelo's figures—in sculpture and painting—and his unusual use of oranges, greens, and other nontraditional colors. Other artists took these ideas and ran them to their logical limits. Florentines **Andrea del Sarto, Rosso Fiorentino,** and **Pontormo** led the way—all three painted panels in the cloister of **Santissima Annunziata** (p. 88). Waifish women with grotesquely long necks and pointy heads ran rampant as Mannerism developed. Color palettes became increasingly garish: Rosso's 1521 "Deposition" in Volterra's **Pinacoteca** (p. 145) is one unforgettable example.

The sculptors fared even better with the Mannerist idea, producing for the first time statues that needed to be looked at from multiple angles to be fully appreciated, such as **Giambologna's** "Rape of the Sabines" and **Benvenuto Cellini's** "Perseus with the Head of Medusa," both under Florence's **Loggia dei Lanzi** (p. 81).

The Baroque, the Neoclassical & the Present Day

The experiments of the Mannerists soon gave way to the excesses of the baroque. Architecturally, the baroque era rehashed and reinterpreted yet again the neoclassical forms of the Renaissance, introducing ellipses and more radically complicated geometric lines, curves, and mathematics to replace the right angles and simple arches of traditional buildings. **Bernardo Buontalenti** was the main Tuscan architect of note in the period, and he worked extensively for the Medici, building them villas and sumptuous gardens. His more accessible works in Florence include his **Tribuna** in the Uffizi, the facade of **Santa Trínita** (p. 83), and grottoes in the **Giardino di Boboli** (p. 91). His greatest achievement, however, was probably the seaport of **Livorno,** a beautiful bit of city planning he performed for the Medici in 1576.

The baroque artists achieved some success in the field of church facades and altar frames. At their most restrained, they produced facades like those on Florence's **Ognissanti.** But mainly they acted more like interior decorators with extremely bad taste—in the era of the Medici grand dukes and other over-rich princelings, the more different types of expensive marbles you could piece together to decorate a chapel, the better. The Medici-commissioned **Cappella dei Principi** (p. 84) in Florence is the perfect nauseating example. In truth, the art and architectural action had by now moved south, to Rome. Italy didn't have a major hand in developing many new styles after the baroque, although 19th-century works by Italy's master **neoclassical** sculptor Canova are scattered around Tuscany and Umbria, and Tuscany had one great neoclassical sculptor, **Giovanni Duprè,** born in Siena in 1817.

Tuscany had a brief moment in a very localized limelight again from the 1860s to around 1900 when the **Macchiaioli,** a group of artists in Florence and Livorno, junked the old styles and concentrated on exploring the structure of light and color in painting, concerned with the effect of the individual *macchie,* or marks of paint on the canvas. In effect, it was kind of a Tuscan Impressionism. Leading exponent Giovanni Fattori is the main draw at Florence's **Galleria d'Arte Moderna,** inside the Pitti Palace (p. 91).

Some 20th-century Tuscan talents are Livorno's **Modigliani,** who garnered fame in France for his innovative oblong portraits; the futurist **Gino Severini** from Cortona; and **Marino Marini,** a Pistoian sculptor known for his stylized bronze horses—his eponymous museum in Florence has an unrivaled collection (p. 85).

WHEN TO GO

The best months for traveling in Tuscany are from **April to June** and **mid-September to October,** when temperatures are usually comfortable and rural colors richer—wildflowers all spring, golden vineyards and woodland in autumn. The crowds aren't usually too intense. From **July through early September** the region's coastal hotspots teem with visitors, but **May and June** usually see the highest hotel prices in Florence.

August is the worst month in most places: Not only does it get uncomfortably hot, muggy, and crowded, but seemingly the entire country goes on vacation, at least from August 15 onward—and many Italians take off the entire month. In the cities, many family-run hotels, restaurants, and shops are closed: You will have many urban places almost to yourself, but hotels in Florence, Pisa, Prato, and other cities are heavily

devout TUSCANY

What with the mesmerizing scenery and rural idyll of a Tuscan holiday, there's a side that's easily missed. Every town and village, and even club and society, has its own patron **saint.** If you happen to be in town at the right time, you may chance upon Tuscans at prayer.

Cities such as Florence have several dates: The place goes nuts for St. John the Baptist on June 24, but lesser-known locals St. Zenobius (May 25) and St. Antoninus (May 10) are also marked. Pisa pulls out all the stops for St. Ranieri on June 17, whereas Catherine of Siena (Apr 29) is one of Italy's most revered saints.

San Gimignano shuts down for its namesake's feast on January 31, and again on March 12 for St. Fina (p. 140). Other fairytale hill towns celebrate their patrons in spring and summer: Agnes in Montepulciano on April 20, Volterra's St. Justus on June 5, and Arezzo's St. Donatus on August 7.

Interestingly, the most represented saint in Tuscan art isn't a local at all. St. Sebastian is depicted in San Gimignano's **Collegiata** (p. 139), Siena's **Palazzo Pubblico** (p. 131), and in art museums just about everywhere else. He's the patron saint of **plagues.**

discounted. Just be aware that fashionable restaurants and nightspots are usually closed for the whole month.

From **late October to Easter,** some attractions operate on shorter winter hours, and some hotels are closed for renovation or redecoration, though that is less likely if you are visiting the cities. Many family-run restaurants take a week or two off sometime between **November and February;** spa and beach destinations become padlocked ghost towns.

Weather

It's warm all over Italy in summer, and Tuscany can feel stifling during a July or August hot spell, especially in the cities. Higher summer temperatures (measured in Italy in degrees Celsius) usually begin everywhere in May, often lasting until sometime in October. Winters in the north of Tuscany are cold, with rain and snow over the Apennines. A biting wind whistles over the mountains into Florence, Lucca, and Pistoia. The region's rainiest months are usually October, November, and December.

Florence's Average Daily High Temperature & Monthly Rainfall

		JAN	FEB	MAR	APR	MAY	JUNE	JULY	AUG	SEPT	OCT	NOV	DEC
FLORENCE	Temp. (°F)	49	53	60	68	75	84	89	88	81	69	58	50
	Temp. (°C)	9	11	15	20	23	28	31	31	27	20	14	10
	Rainfall (in.)	1.9	2.1	2.7	2.9	3	2.7	1.5	1.9	3.3	4	3.9	2.8

Public Holidays

Offices, government buildings (though not usually tourist offices), and shops all over Italy are generally closed on: January 1 (*Capodanno,* or New Year); January 6 (*La Befana,* or Epiphany); Easter Sunday *(Pasqua);* Easter Monday *(Pasquetta);* April 25 (Liberation Day); May 1 (*Festa del Lavoro,* or Labor Day); June 2 (*Festa della Repubblica,* or Republic Day); August 15 (*Ferragosto,* or the Assumption of the Virgin); November 1 (All Saints' Day); December 8 (*L'Immacolata,* or the Immaculate

Conception); December 25 (*Natale,* Christmas Day); December 26 (*Santo Stefano,* or St. Stephen's Day). You'll also often find businesses closed for the annual daylong celebration dedicated to the local saint (for example, on Jan 31 in San Gimignano; on June 24 in Florence; see "Devout Tuscany," above).

Tuscany Calendar of Events

FEBRUARY

Carnevale, all over Tuscany. The most outstanding Tuscan Rite of Spring occurs in the coastal town of **Viareggio,** with a colorful and sophisticated parade of mechanized floats subtly lampooning political figures and celebrities. www.viareggio.ilcarnevale.com. Weekends throughout February.

MARCH/APRIL

Holy Week, regionwide. Processions and age-old ceremonies—some from pagan days, some from the Middle Ages—are staged. One of the most atmospheric of several solemn Good Friday processions ends at the Duomo in **Volterra.** Begins 4 days before Easter Sunday; sometimes at the end of March, but often in April.

Scoppio del Carro (Explosion of the Cart), Florence. At this ancient observance, a cart laden with flowers and fireworks is drawn by three white oxen to the Duomo, where at the noon Mass a mechanical dove detonates it from the altar. Easter Sunday.

MAY

Maggio Musicale Fiorentino (Florentine Musical May), Florence. Italy's oldest and most prestigious music festival emphasizes music from the 14th to the 20th centuries, but also presents ballet and opera. www.maggiofiorentino.it. Late April to end of June.

JUNE

Festa di San Ranieri, Pisa. The city honors its patron saint with candlelit parades, followed the next day by eight-rower teams competing in 16th-century costumes. June 16–17.

Calcio Storico (Historic Football), Florence. A revival of a raucous 15th-century form of football, pitting four teams in medieval costumes against one another. The matches usually culminate on June 24, the feast day of St. John the Baptist. Late June.

Gioco del Ponte, Pisa. Teams in Renaissance costume take part in a long-contested push-of-war on the Ponte di Mezzo, which spans the River Arno. Last Sunday in June.

JULY

Il Palio, Piazza del Campo, Siena. Palio fever grips this Tuscan hill town for a wild and exciting horse race from the Middle Ages. Pageantry, costumes, and the celebrations of the victorious *contrada* (sort of a neighborhood social club) mark the spectacle. It's a "no rules" event: Even a horse without a rider can win the race. July 2 and August 16.

Umbria Jazz, Perugia. One of Europe's best jazz festivals always attracts top-class artists. www.umbriajazz.com. Mid-July.

AUGUST

Bravio delle Botti (Barrel Race), Montepulciano. This is something akin to a medieval fraternity stunt. Teams of *poliziani* (the name for local residents) dress like their 14th-century ancestors in order to be the first to roll a 79kg (175-lb.) barrel uphill to the top of town. Come for the pageantry and feasting afterward. www.braviodellebotti.com. Late August.

SEPTEMBER

Giostra del Saracino (Saracen Joust), Arezzo. This jousting tournament is between mounted knights in 13th-century armor and the effigy of a "Saracen warrior." It's held on Arezzo's Piazza Grande, and is one of the few versions of this sport in which the target, which swivels and is armed with a whip, actually hits back. www.giostradelsaracino.arezzo.it. First Sunday in September.

Chianti Classico Expo (Rassegna del Chianti Classico), Greve in Chianti. Greve's annual wine fair showcases the newest vintages from both the top and the smaller vineyards in the Chianti Classico zone. www.expochianticlassico.com. Mid-September.

DECEMBER

Ostensione della Sacra Cintola (Display of the Virgin's Girdle), Prato. This is the final and most sumptuous of the five annual occasions on which the bishop releases Mary's Sacred Girdle—the belt she handed to Thomas upon her Assumption—from its jewel-encrusted treasure chest and shows it to the people massed inside the Duomo and crowding the piazza outside. Plenty of Renaissance-styled drummers and fifers are in attendance. The pomp is repeated at Easter, May 1, August 15, and September 8. Christmas Day.

SUGGESTED ITINERARIES

3

Tuscany and Umbria are densely populated with things to see, perhaps more so than any other region in Europe. It could take months to experience all of the area's art, architecture, food, and wine. Lovers of Renaissance art could spend a month in Florence and still discover new gems to admire. Wine buffs could sip and sniff their way through weeks in Chianti and Montalcino. Romantics could dream away days in Lucca alone. But most of us don't have that kind of time, so we've designed the 1-week and 2-week itineraries for first-time visitors to discover the best of Tuscany, with a little bit of Umbria, too. Then there is a tour for families, and one for food-and-wine enthusiasts, as well as an art tour that takes enthusiasts well beyond Florence's city limits.

A car will be indispensable in almost every case, because public transport connects the main towns efficiently—but no more. And the soul of central Italy is found in its countryside, through its sunflower fields and gently sloping vineyards, and its landscapes spotted with storied castles or lonely abbeys.

It is not a large place—you could drive from the top of Tuscany to the bottom on the highway in *about* 3 hours—but the roads of the hinterland are windy, narrow, and slow. Don't be daunted by the idea of spending much of your time in the car. Getting there, in this case, is half the fun.

The following itineraries all start in Florence—the lion's share of travelers arrive there via train, plane, or from airports in Milan or Rome, or even Pisa. See chapter 9 for trip-planning advice.

Timing is everything. Avoid peak season if at all possible. So many foreigners, especially Americans and northern Europeans, descend on Florence in June and July that they are sometimes literally corralled through the streets. Spring and early fall are the ideal times to visit. As anywhere else in the world, enotourists will get the most out of a vineyard visit just before harvest (early autumn), when the grapes are still on the vine. See "When to Go," p. 22.

THE REGIONS IN BRIEF

Tuscany and Umbria are, for now, divided into administrative provinces based around their major cities, Florence, Siena, Pisa, Perugia, and so on. This layer of government is due to be scrapped, perhaps as soon as 2015; see "Florence & Tuscany Today," in chapter 3. Anyway, these official designations were never designed for organizing a travel guide, so the following "regions" into which this book is divided group towns more logically.

Keep in mind that neither of the regions is very large in U.S. terms—Tuscany is, at 22,993 sq. km (8,877 sq. miles), a bit smaller than New Hampshire, and Umbria, at 8,456 sq. km (3,265 sq. miles), makes about two Rhode Islands.

Florence

The capital of Tuscany is **Florence,** one of Europe's most famous cities. It was once the home of the powerful Medici dynasty, which actively encouraged the development of the Renaissance by sponsoring sculptors and painters such as Donatello, Leonardo, and Michelangelo. Art treasures such as those found at the **Accademia** (Michelangelo's "David"), the **Uffizi** (Botticelli's "Birth of Venus"), and the **Pitti Palace** (Raphael's "La Velata") draw millions of visitors every year. Throw into the mix fabulous architecture (the Duomo with Brunelleschi's dome, Giotto's bell tower, churches like **Santa Maria Novella**), creative modern restaurants and earthy *trattorie,* and world-famous designer boutiques and bustling outdoor markets, and the city of the Renaissance becomes quite simply one of the world's must-see places.

Around Florence: Fiesole, the Chianti, Prato & Pistoia

Uphill, just beyond Florence's northern suburbs, the Etruscan town of **Fiesole** is actually older than its famous neighbor in the valley below. These days it's an ideal half-day escape from the crowds and stifling heat of Florence. The land of high hills stretching from Florence south to Siena is among the most vaunted countrysides on Earth, the vine-covered Arcadia of **Chianti.** Here you can drive along the Chiantigiana road, stopping to soak up the scenery and sample the *vino.* Northwest of Florence, the medieval textile center of **Prato** is one of Italy's fastest-growing cities and about the friendliest city in Tuscany. Its historic core is filled with Renaissance art treasures overlooked by many who don't realize a city just 16km (10 miles) from Florence can be so different and rewarding. Its neighbor **Pistoia,** a further 22km (14 miles), an old Roman town, is firmly stamped with the art stylings of the Romanesque Middle Ages.

Siena & Western Tuscany

Siena is Tuscany's medieval foil to the Renaissance of Florence. It's a city built of brick, with Gothic palaces, excellent pastries, and its own stylized school of Gothic painting. With steep back streets and a mammoth, art-packed cathedral, it's the region's second-most popular city. The hill towns west of it—medieval tangles of roads perched atop small mountains—are equally atmospheric: **San Gimignano,** with its medieval stone skyscrapers; and Etruscan **Volterra,** with its alabaster workshops. The elegant old republican city of **Lucca** is packed with Romanesque churches, livened by the music of native son Puccini, and always busy with grandmothers on bicycles going shopping. North of the city, the Apuan Alps kick off a series of mountain chains that rides across the northern edge of Tuscany, separating it from the neighboring region of Emilia-Romagna, to the north. South of Lucca, through the olive groves of the Monte Pisano, lies the ancient maritime republic of **Pisa,** with its tilting tower and "Field of Miracles."

Central & Eastern Tuscany

Arezzo was once an important Etruscan city, and today boasts the definitive Piero della Francesca frescoes and a world-class monthly antiques market. Thirty-eight kilometers (24 miles) northeast of Arezzo, near the Umbrian border, is Piero's hometown of

Florence, Tuscany & Umbria

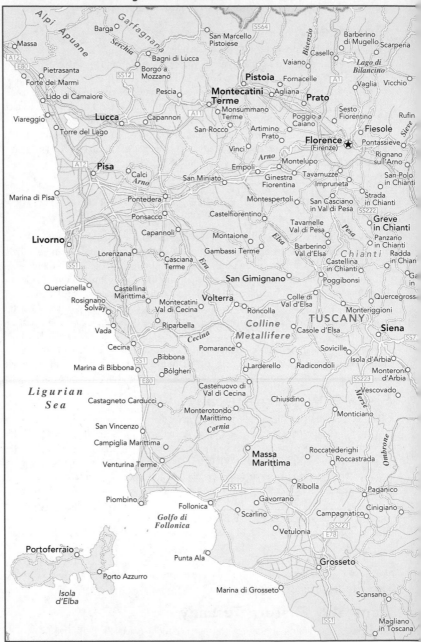

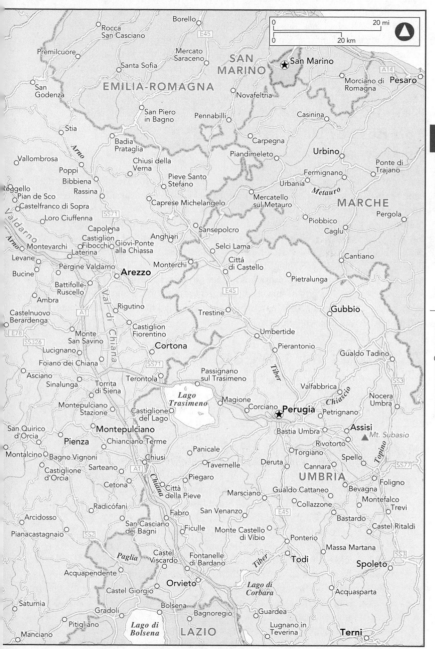

Sansepolcro, a modest city with an old core devoted to preserving Piero's great works. South of Arezzo stretches the **Chiana Valley,** where the cattle for Florence's famous steaks are raised, and the thriving art city of **Cortona,** which contains a couple of Tuscany's finest small museums. In the southeast the province of Siena stretches south to abut Umbria in a landscape of soft green hills, lonely farmhouses, stands of cypress, patches of cultivated fields, and the occasional weird erosion formations (known as the *Crete Senesi*). This area is kitchen-calendar Tuscany. The medieval hill towns of **Montalcino** and **Montepulciano** craft some of Italy's finest red wines, and **Pienza,** prodigious producer of pecorino sheep's cheese, sits like a balcony surveying the **Val d'Orcia** and is the only perfectly designed town center of the Renaissance.

The Best of Umbria

Perugia, the capital of Umbria, is a refined city of soft jazz, velvety chocolates, medieval alleys, and one of Italy's top painting galleries, featuring the works of Perugino, master of the modeled figure and teacher of Raphael. Just east is one of Italy's spiritual centers, the hill town of **Assisi,** birthplace of St. Francis. The basilica raised in his honor is the nerve center of the vast Franciscan monastic movement and home to some of the greatest frescos of the early Renaissance. Umbria gets wilder to the north, where the rocky border city of **Gubbio** is home to one of Italy's wildest festivals, the *Festa dei Ceri* or *Corsa dei Ceri* (Race of the Candles). **Spoleto** was once seat of the Lombard duchy that controlled most of Umbria in the Dark Ages, but it's most famous these days for its world-class music-and-dance Spoleto Festival. **Orvieto,** in the far south, is an implacable city of tufa rising above the valley on its volcanic outcropping, with a giant gem of a cathedral, a network of underground tunnels below-ground, and some of the best white wine in Italy.

TUSCANY IN 1 WEEK

This route brings you to some of Europe's must-see destinations, the very best of central Italy—Florence, Siena, Lucca, and Pisa among them—at a breakneck speed. Feel free to skip a stop or take a longer timeout: You could add days to any of the stops.

Days 1 & 2: Florence ★★★

You have 2 whole days to explore the city of Giotto, Leonardo, Botticelli, and Michelangelo. Start with their masterpieces at the **Uffizi** (p. 76), followed by the **Duomo** complex (p. 75): Scale Brunelleschi's ochre dome, and follow up with a visit to the adjoining **Battistero di San Giovanni, Museo Storico dell'Opera del Duomo,** and **Campanile di Giotto** (p. 74). Start the next day with "David" at the **Accademia** (p. 87). For the rest of your time, spend it getting to know the art at the **Palazzo Pitti** (p. 91), the intimate wall paintings of **San Marco** (p. 88), and Masaccio's revolutionary frescoes at the **Cappella Brancacci** (p. 93). In the evenings, head south of the Arno for lively wine bars and the best restaurants (p. 60) in the city. Be sure to check the opening hours of all museums before planning your itinerary and make reservations for the Uffizi and Accademia (p. 78). Some museums are closed on Monday, and a few churches are closed during the lunch break. Because the rest of the itinerary requires a **car,** you should book one well ahead of time since reservations fill up quickly (especially in summer).

Tuscany in 1 Week

1 & 2 Florence
3 Pistoia & Lucca
4 Pisa
5 Volterra & San Gimignano
6 Siena
7 The Chianti

Day 3: Pistoia ★ & Lucca ★★

Lucca (p. 150), 83 km (52 miles west of Florence) is the day's highlight, but art and architecture buffs would be remiss to skip a pause in **Pistoia** (p. 111) en route. You have plenty of time for the Romanesque monuments of Piazza del Duomo, and one of the great works of Gothic sculpture, Pisano's pulpit in **Sant'Andrea** (p. 114). Overnight in Lucca, stroll or cycle along its walls, enjoy the music of Puccini amid the unique acoustics of an ancient church, and savor a romantic dinner of *tortelli lucchesi* in its alleyways.

Day 4: Pisa ★★

If you haven't yet circumnavigated Lucca's **medieval walls,** rise early for a morning bicycle ride before making the short trip to **Pisa** (p. 157). Climb the **Leaning Tower,** snap all the de rigueur photos, visit the subtler art sights in the rest of the **Campo dei Miracoli,** then drink and dine in the "real" center of this lively student city. To make logistics easier, you needn't change your overnight base: It's under a half-hour by train between Lucca and Pisa. Alight at **Pisa San Rossore** station, rather than Pisa Centrale, for the fastest transfer to the monuments of the Campo.

Day 5: Volterra ★★ & San Gimignano ★★

Visit the Alabaster City of **Volterra** (p. 141), a medieval remnant and former center of the ancient Etruscan world. You'll find one of Tuscany's best Etruscan museum collections at the **Museo Etrusco Guarnacci** and an iconic work of Mannerist painting, Rosso Fiorentino's "Deposition," at the **Pinacoteca.** After lunch, continue a further 30 km (18 miles) to **San Gimignano.** The best time to approach San Gimignano is in the late afternoon, when the "medieval skyscrapers" of the hilltop city is bathed in the setting sun. Get to the **Collegiata** and **Sant'Agostino** before they close. Just wandering the medieval center at dusk, when the tour groups have left, is one of Tuscany's most memorable experiences. See p. 136.

Day 6: Siena ★★★

Unless you're there during the **Palio** (p. 122), the top sights in **Siena** can feasibly be visited in about 1 full day—if you move fast. The **Duomo** (p. 130) is one of Italy's most interesting, especially when its elaborate intarsia pavement is uncovered. The **Museo Civico** inside the town hall houses the most important secular frescoes in Tuscany, painted just before the Black Death of 1348 hit the town. Be sure to indulge in a feast in Siena, as its food is one of its greatest draws. See p. 128.

Day 7: The Chianti ★★

Spend the day on and around state road SS222, which takes you through the big-name towns in Chianti, and all the way back to Florence, 77km (48 miles) to the north. The three most worthy stops are **Greve, Panzano,** and **Castellina in Chianti,** all sitting at the heart of important winemaking areas. Although there are a number of great restaurants along the way, those on a tight budget might want instead to pick up picnic supplies in **Panzano,** and pay a visit to the "poet butcher," Dario Cecchini, who can recite Dante's "Inferno" in its entirety while chopping away at a rack of ribs. Be aware that many vineyards are family-run and require prebooking to tour. See "The Chianti," in chapter 5.

Tuscany & Umbria in 2 Weeks

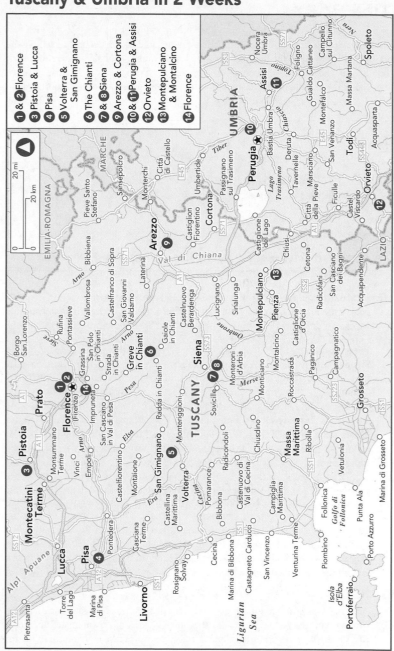

1 & 2 Florence
3 Pistoia & Lucca
4 Pisa
5 Volterra & San Gimignano
6 The Chianti
7 & 8 Siena
9 Arezzo & Cortona
10 & 11 Perugia & Assisi
12 Orvieto
13 Montepulciano & Montalcino
14 Florence

A 2-WEEK TUSCANY & UMBRIA ITINERARY

For a committed fly-driver who likes to keep moving, 2 weeks is ideal: It will give you enough time to see Tuscany's top destinations, with some additional time to sample the treasures of Umbria and the landscapes of the Val d'Orcia. The first 7 days follow, with a few tweaks, the itinerary suggested for "Tuscany in a Week," above. Thereafter, move on to the hills of southern and eastern Tuscany, as well as the best that Umbria has to offer: Perugia, Assisi, and Orvieto.

Days 1 & 2: Florence ★★★

Follow the itinerary suggested in "Tuscany in 1 Week," above.

Day 3: Pistoia ★ & Lucca ★★

Follow the itinerary suggested in "Tuscany in 1 Week," above.

Day 4: Pisa ★★

Follow the itinerary suggested in "Tuscany in 1 Week," above.

Day 5: Volterra ★★ & San Gimignano ★★

Follow the itinerary suggested in "Tuscany in 1 Week," above.

Day 6: The Chianti ★★

Follow the itinerary suggested in "Tuscany in 1 Week," above.

Days 7 & 8: Siena ★★★

With a little more room in your itinerary, you should spend an extra day in **Siena**—there's really nowhere quite like it in Italy. As well as the **Campo** and its crenellated Palazzo Pubblico, there's time to see the monuments of **Piazza del Duomo** at a leisurely pace: not just the **Duomo** and **Baptistery,** but the **Museo dell'Opera,** for Duccio's "Maestà" and the city's best view from the **Facciatone,** but one of Tuscany's best museums, the former medieval hospital of **Santa Maria della Scala** (p. 133). See chapter 6. Head off late afternoon to make the 66km (41-mile) drive to **Arezzo,** so you are up and ready for tomorrow's sightseeing.

Day 9: Arezzo ★ & Cortona ★★

Aside from the paintings of **Piero della Francesca** in **Arezzo** (p. 179) and the steep, cobblestone streets of **Cortona** (p. 188), the adopted home of "Under the Tuscan Sun" author Frances Mayes, one of the nicest parts of this day will be the 34km (21-mile) ride between the two. The SS71 is scattered with castles, vineyards, sunflower fields, and little towns clinging to the hills that line its eastern side all the way to Cortona.

Days 10 & 11: Perugia ★ & Assisi ★★

Perugia's **Galleria Nazionale** (p. 204) is a must-see on any visit to neighboring Umbria, but just hanging around the sidewalk cafes of this animated medieval city makes it worth the trip. Central Italy can be rather short on nightlife for young people, but Perugia's **university** scene makes the city a welcome exception—and don't forget to sample those Perugina **Baci** chocs. Nearby Assisi,

27km (17 miles) to the southeast, is one of the most revered places of pilgrimage in all of Italy, with the **Basilica di San Francesco** (p. 183) second in importance only to St. Peter's, in Rome. It will take the entire day to explore all the city's art, from Giotto's paintings to the recently restored **Rocca Maggiore** fortress. Make time for the tranquil **Eremo delle Carceri** (p. 210), St. Francis's old hermitage in the woods just outside town. See chapter 8.

Day 12: Orvieto ★

A former Etruscan stronghold, **Orvieto** now sits above a network of tunnels that honeycomb the volcanic rock beneath the town, and have been used for millennia as tombs, dovecotes, makeshift wine fridges, and more. A limited section is now open to the public as **Orvieto Underground** (p. 224). The medieval center is small, allowing you to move at a leisurely pace around the "Golden Lily of Cathedrals" with its Signorelli frescoes, and Umbria's best collection of Etruscan artifacts. Wandering Orvieto in the evening gives you a chance to see the city with a gorgeous hue, illuminated by the setting sun. Enjoy dinner in its medieval streets, along with some of its "liquid gold," of course. See p. 222.

Day 13: Montepulciano ★★ & Montalcino ★

Make your way into the Val d'Orcia via **Montepulciano** (p. 164) and from there to **Montalcino** (p. 173). These two wine-producing giants are worthy stops in their own right, especially the former for its handsome, *palazzo*-lined Corso. Between the two is the model Renaissance town, **Pienza** (p. 171), surrounded by the kind of captivating Tuscan landscape you see in promotional photos. (It's so small, you can roam the whole place in an hour, if you are pressed for time.) This is a busy day, but if you move fast you can glimpse them all. At dinner, tuck into hearty Montalcinese cooking—the *cinghiale* (wild boar) is king around here—accompanied with a bottle of mighty **Brunello di Montalcino.** The total journey, via the A1 *autostrada* and SS146 scenic state road, is 101km (63 miles). See chapter 7.

Day 14: From Southern Tuscany back to Florence

The drive from Montalcino north to Florence is 109km (68 miles). After you have dropped your car, you should have time for last-minute leather shopping in the **Scuola del Cuoio** (p. 99) and choosing Renaissance scents from the **Farmacia di Santa Maria Novella,** then perhaps to catch a couple sights you missed over the first 2 days. See chapter 7.

TUSCANY & UMBRIA FOR FAMILIES

Italy is probably the friendliest family vacation destination in all of Europe. Practically, it presents few challenges. But if you're traveling by rental car with young children, be sure to request safety car seats ahead of time. Let the rental company know the age of your child (up to 12) and they will arrange for a seat that complies with E.U. regulations.

As you tour, don't go hunting for "child-friendly" restaurants or special kids' menus. There's always plenty available for little ones—even dishes that aren't on offer to grown-up patrons. Never be afraid to ask if you have a fussy eater in the family: *Pasta al pomodoro* (pasta with fresh tomato sauce) or a plain breaded veal cutlet will almost always be available. In fact, pretty much any request is met with a smile.

Perhaps the main issue for travelers with children is spacing your museum visits so that you get a chance to see the masterpieces without having young kids suffer a meltdown after too many paintings of saints and *bambini.*

Remember to punctuate every day with a **gelato** stop—Tuscany has some of Italy's best ice cream. You will even find creative *soya* flavors for anyone with lactose intolerance. We also suggest planning fewer long, tiring daytrips out of town, especially by public transportation.

Days 1, 2 & 3: Florence: City of the Renaissance
★★★

Florence is usually thought of as more of an adult city, but there's enough here to fill 2 family days, plus a couple of daytrips. With 4 nights here, you should take an apartment rather than a hotel room, to give you all the more space to spread out. Among several apartment websites, **GoWithOh.com** and **HouseTrip.com** both have a good range of quality places. Close to the Duomo, **Residence Hilda** (p. 57) is a family-friendly place that rents large, apartment-style rooms from 1 night and more.

Begin with the city's monumental main square, **Piazza della Signoria,** now an open-air museum of statues. The **Palazzo Vecchio** (p. 82) dominates one side; you can all tour it with special family-friendly guides, including a docent dressed as a historical character. You won't want to miss the **Uffizi.** With young children, you could turn your visit into a treasure trail of the museum's collection by first visiting the shop to select some postcards of the key artworks. On the second morning, kids will delight in climbing to the top of Brunelleschi's dome on the **Duomo** for a classic panorama. Get there early—queues lengthen through the day. You'll still have time to climb the 414 steps up to the **Campanile di Giotto,** run around in the **Giardino di Boboli,** and stroll the **Ponte Vecchio** at dusk.

Day 4: Pisa & Its Leaning Tower ★★

If your kids are 7 or under, you should consider skipping **Pisa** (p. 157): 8 is the minimum age for the disorienting ascent up the bell tower of Pisa's cathedral, which more commonly goes by the name the **Leaning Tower.** Elsewhere in the city, kids will love the hyperrealist monuments of the **Campo dei Miracoli** and learning about the city's Galileo links: He was born here, and supposedly discovered his law of pendulum motion while watching a swinging lamp inside the **Duomo.** Before heading back to Florence, take them to taste a local specialty, *cecina* (or *farinata di ceci*)—a pizzalike garbanzo-bean flatbread served warm— at popular slice parlor **Il Montino.** Rail connections between Florence and Pisa are fairly fast (1 hr., 20 min.), frequent, and affordable (around 8€ each way).

Day 5: San Gimignano & Its Medieval "Skyscrapers" ★★

Rent a **car** (p. 227) for the remaining days of your family trip. First stop should be **San Gimignano** (p. 136), 52km (32 miles) to the southwest. Kids will see the tiny town and its cluster of towers as some kind of medieval Disneyland, especially when the crowds recede at the end of the afternoon and they can tear around the pedestrian piazzas. A climb up the 54m (177-ft.) **Torre Grossa** ends in one of Tuscany's great panoramas, of the rolling vine-clad hills that surround

Tuscany & Umbria for Families

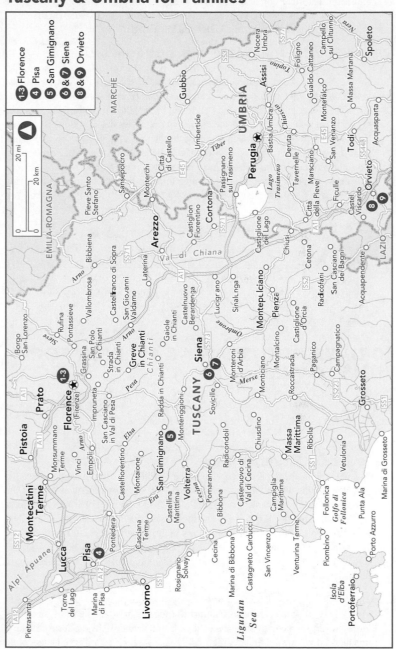

Legend:
- 1–3 Florence
- 4 Pisa
- 5 San Gimignano
- 6 & 7 Siena
- 8 & 9 Orvieto

the town. The **Museo della Tortura** is a Tuscan chamber of horrors, with an authentic historical collection of instruments of torture. (It may also be quite upsetting for little ones, so keep them away.) Everyone will love one of Tuscany's most famous gelato parlors, the **Gelateria "di Piazza."**

Days 6 & 7: Siena: Meet the Gothic ★★★

Count yourself lucky if you can visit **Siena** (p. 121) around July 2 or August 16 for the famous 4-day **Palio** celebrations, when horses race at breakneck speed around **Piazza del Campo.** Year-round, a couple of epic climbs will thrill the kids. The **Torre del Mangia,** the bell tower of the **Palazzo Pubblico,** ends in a dramatic view of the city and the enveloping countryside. Through the **Museo dell'Opera Metropolitana,** they can scale the "Facciatone" for an alternative view down into the Campo. At **Santa Maria della Scala,** they will find **Bambimus,** the art museum for kids, where paintings are hung at child-friendly heights. The zebra-striped **Duomo** is jazzy enough to pique their curiosity. Siena's many bakeries are famed for their sweet treats. Siena is 42km (26 miles) southeast of San Gimignano.

Days 8 & 9: Orvieto: Tunnels & Tombs ★

After 90 minutes or so in the car, kids will be ready to scramble down **Orvieto**'s (p. 220) ancient tunnels and its monumental Renaissance well, climb the **Torre del Moro,** and have a look through some of the puppets in toy stores along the *corso*. On the second day, you could make a daytrip to **Cortona** (p. 188), back in Tuscany, for a hike through the **Etruscan tombs** (p. 194) outside town. It's 167km (104 miles) straight up the A1 *autostrada* back to Florence.

10 DAYS IN TUSCANY & UMBRIA FOR WINE LOVERS

This loop includes some of Italy's best-known winegrowing regions, a few oenological surprises, and some major artistic sights, too, as neither man nor woman can live on wine alone. For a crash-course in how to read a Tuscan wine label, see p. 16.

Days 1 & 2: Florence ★★★

A good start for this tasting trip would be in Piazza Antinori, named after the vineyard barons who own some of Tuscany's finest red wine estates. One of the Chianti's finest estates has a favorite wine and food bar nearby, the **Cantinetta dei Verrazzano** (p. 100). For something more down-to-earth and local, hop round a couple of the excellent wine bars in the **Oltrarno** or **San Frediano;** see "Entertainment & Nightlife," p. 99. Note that most of the best bottles you will find at less expensive restaurants tend to be Chianti, while highbrow places have labels from farther afield.

Days 3, 4 & 5: Chianti ★★

Pick a base close to **Greve in Chianti** to lodge right at the heart of Tuscany's largest quality wine region It's also one of Europe's oldest: The rules for making this blended wine were first codified in 1716, and the wine has been made around here since at least the 7th century. (Wine theorists can learn more by visiting the excellent museum in **Castellina;** see p. 116.) Sangiovese-based Chianti is a

Tuscany & Umbria for Wine Lovers

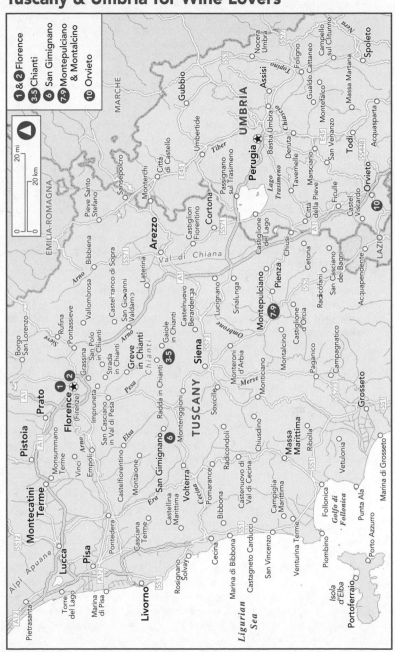

diverse wine: Chianti Classico denotes grapes from the original (and best) growing zone, and tasting opportunities abound at cellars such as **Villa Vignamaggio** and **Castello di Volpaia**—always book ahead if you require a tour (and you should do at least one). The Chianti is also famed for its butchers, selling everything from cuts of fresh beef (ideal if you're staying in a villa) to salami made from the local breed of pig, *Cinta Senese*. **Falorni,** in Greve, is outshone perhaps only by **Dario Cecchini,** in nearby Panzano. Also look out for extra virgin olive oil—the local elixir is among Italy's best. See "A Trip into the Chianti," in chapter 5.

Day 6: San Gimignano ★★

This can almost be considered a fourth day in Chianti because it is so close. But this is a day for white wine: **Vernaccia di San Gimignano,** the only DOCG dry white wine made in Tuscany. Partner this subtle, straw-colored wine with a bruschetta, at busy *enoteche* (wine caves) around the center, or visit the grandly titled **Museo del Vino Vernaccia** (it's actually a well-stocked enoteca) in the ruins of San Gimignano's former castle. Alternatively, San Gimignano's tourist office can advise on—and provide maps for—a scenic walk through the vineyards that come almost up to the town gate. If you feel the need to take a respite from cork sniffing instead, the lofty Etruscan town of **Volterra** is a pretty 30km (18-mile) drive to the west. You will, of course, pass vineyards en route. See chapter 6.

Days 7, 8 & 9: Montepulciano ★★ & Montalcino ★

Brunello di Montalcino and **Vino Nobile di Montepulciano** are two of Europe's most prized reds, and the countryside that yields them is spectacular. Begin with a walk up Montepulciano's handsome, steep Corso, from the town gate to **Piazza Grande,** monumental heart of the *comune.* Here you'll find the **Palazzo Comunale** (climb it for a panorama over the surrounding winelands) and **Cattedrale.** Oenophiles should make a beeline for the **Consorzio del Vino Nobile di Montepulciano** office, where you can taste vintages from small producers and seek advice for nearby wineries to visit. Our favorite cellar in the center itself is **Gattavecchi.** End the evening at **Acquacheta,** where the menu's all about beef— *"bistecca numero uno,"* is how Contucci winemaker Adamo describes it. The hills surrounding (mostly south of) nearby **Montalcino** are home to one of the world's great red wines, Brunello di Montalcino. You can taste several at the town's **Enoteca La Fortezza** (p. 178) or consult the tourist office for advice on visiting one of the many cellars in the surrounding countryside that welcome visitors.

Day 10: Orvieto ★

Vintners around this hilltop Umbrian city have been cultivating their famous whites since Roman times: They used to sail the barrels down the River Tiber to Rome, where Orvieto wine would stock the banquets of the emperors. Indeed, wine runs through the history of this Umbrian city. The key religions festival, **Corpus Domini** celebrates the 1263 "Miracle of Bolsena," when Eucharist wine supposedly turned to blood. Corpus Domini (also known as **Corpus Christi**) has seen a major medieval parade through central Orvieto ever since. Visitors at any time should explore the ancient **tunnels in the tufa rock,** which, among other uses, served as medieval wine fridges. While in town, hunt down a traditional type of Orvieto Classico known as *abboccato:* a type midway between dry and sweet that has become less fashionable as the modern palate has hardened in its love of bone-dry or ultrasweet wines. See p. 225.

AN ART LOVER'S WEEK IN TUSCANY— BEYOND FLORENCE

The devotee of Renaissance art will inevitably spend much of their time exploring the churches and *palazzi* of **Florence.** However, the smaller towns and cities of this exquisite Italian region are not short of masterpieces of their own. The city of Siena, Florence's traditional rival, contains ethereal art from the Sienese School of the Middle Ages. Pisa was home to the greatest Gothic sculptors in Italy. And smaller towns from Pienza to Arezzo have treasures that would be the pride of any city on Earth.

Day 1: Lucca: Elegant Walled City ★★

Leave Florence early and drive 72km (45 miles) west on the A11. (Ask your accommodation ahead of time about parking deals.) Inside its thick swath of Renaissance walls, bordered by gardens, the narrow streets of Lucca still follow a medieval plan. Lucca's main architectural attractions are its memorable facades, in the "Luccan–Romanesque" style. The **Duomo,** or **Cattedrale di San Martino,** has a green-and-white marble facade designed by Guidetto da Como. **San Michele in Foro** has one of the most elaborate church facades in all Tuscany, with its delicately twisted columns and arcades. Dating from slightly earlier, the facade of **San Frediano** sports a shimmering golden mosaic by Berlinghieri. You'll get the best view of the whole place when you circumnavigate the walls by **bicycle.** See p. 150.

Day 2: Pisa: City of the Romanesque ★★

Lucca lies only 21km (13 miles) northeast of Pisa. You could drive, but it's perhaps easier to visit as a day-trip by rail. (Alight at Pisa San Rossore, not Pisa Centrale.) Pisa's unmissable monuments center around its **Campo dei Miracoli (Field of Miracles),** so touring is easy. Start with the **Leaning Tower** (for which you should book tickets ahead of time), whose six floors of columned galleries wind around the spiral Next, prioritize the **Duomo** and **Battistero,** both stellar examples of the Pisan–Romanesque style, and housing two of the four great Pisano carved pulpits. If time remains, head across town to explore the haphazard but rewarding art collection at the **Museo Nazionale di San Matteo.** See p. 157.

Day 3: San Gimignano & Its Medieval Towers ★★

This city lies 92km (57 miles) southeast of Pisa. For the architectural enthusiast, wandering through the gates of San Gimignano is the start of a journey back to the Middle Ages. This is Italy's best-preserved medieval town, and some one dozen of the original 70-plus towers remain. At **San Gimignano 1300,** you'll see a faithful recreation of the town as it was 700 years ago. The town's art highlight is Domenico Ghirlandaio's Santa Fina frescoes in the **Collegiata.** There's more painting—and a great view across the vineyards surrounding the town—at the **Museo Civico & Torre Grossa.** See p. 136.

Day 4: Siena: Homage to the Middle Ages ★★★

Siena (42km/26 miles southeast of San Gimignano) caters to the lover of both art and architecture. With time pressed, base your visit around two key piazzas. The famous **Campo** is where you'll find the city's **Museo Civico,** home to monumental frescoes by Simone Martini and Ambrogio Lorenzetti. Uphill, around Piazza del Duomo, visit the **Duomo** itself (for Pinturicchio's Piccolomini Library and the Renaissance intarsia floor), the **Museo dell'Opera Metropolitana** (for Duccio's 1311 "Maestà"), and **Santa Maria della Scala,** the city's frescoed former hospital-turned-museum. If you still have time, dig deeper into the history of Sienese art at the **Pinacoteca Nazionale.** Although our breakneck tour calls for only 1 day here, 2 days is preferable if your schedule can accommodate it. See p. 121.

Day 5: Pienza: Ideal Renaissance City ★

The village of Pienza lies 55km (33 miles) southeast of Siena. It owes its overall look to its homegrown son, Pope Pius II, born here in 1405. He set out to transform Pienza into a model Renaissance town—and got as far as overseeing one elegant piazza. Bernardo Rossellino, a protégé of the great Renaissance theorist Leon Battista Alberti, carried out the mandate of the pope, creating a **Cattedrale** with a Renaissance facade and its original altarpieces still displayed in situ (a rarity in Tuscany), the **Palazzo Piccolomini** (Rossellino's masterpiece), and a main square, **Piazza Pio II,** which remains a miniature Renaissance jewel. See p. 171.

Day 6: Montepulciano & Its Noble Wine ★★

On the morning of the following day, drive a mere 13km (8 miles) east to Montepulciano. Begin your visit to Tuscany's highest hill town with the parade of handsome *palazzi* flanking its steep main street, the "Corso." The chief attractions for the devotee of Renaissance architecture are the **Palazzo Nobili-Tarugi** and **Tempio di San Biagio.** Everything centers around the monumental **Piazza Grande,** where you'll also find a rather plain **Duomo** with a huge Taddeo di Bartolo altarpiece inside. Leave some late afternoon and evening time for visiting a couple of tasting rooms and drinking the elegant local red wine, **Vino Nobile di Montepulciano,** at an enoteca. See p. 164.

Day 7: Arezzo: The Piero della Francesca Capital ★

Piero della Francesca was a visionary artist, one of the towering figures of the Italian Quattrocento (1400s). You'll find his masterpiece, the frescoes depicting "The Legend of the True Cross" (1452–66), on the walls of the apse chapel at the **Basilica di San Francesco,** in Arezzo. Piero also frescoed a "Mary Magdalene" inside the town's **Duomo**—also famed for its stained glass by Guillaume de Marcillat. Piero fans could also detour east along S73 for 39km (64 miles) to his birthplace, **Sansepolcro,** where the Museo Civico houses the master's "Resurrection" and his polyptych of the "Virgin of Mercy." Art lovers will also find much to admire in other paintings here, including works by Signorelli and Bassano. See p. 179.

Art Lovers' Tuscany

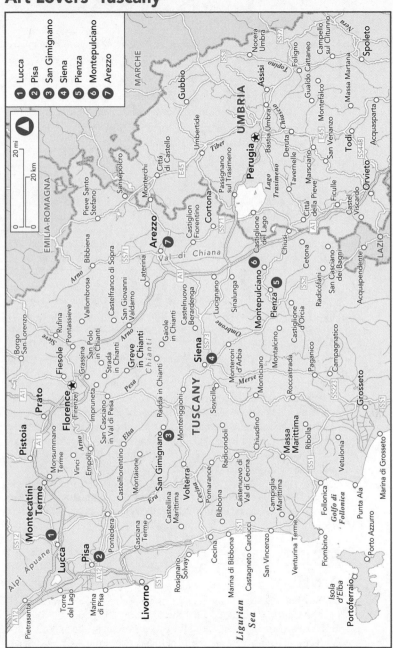

Legend:
1. Lucca
2. Pisa
3. San Gimignano
4. Siena
5. Pienza
6. Montepulciano
7. Arezzo

FLORENCE

4

t's the city of Botticelli, Michelangelo, and Leonardo da Vinci, and the cradle of Europe's Renaissance. Florence is a place where history still lives on the surface. With Brunelleschi's dome as a backdrop, follow the River Arno to the Uffizi Gallery (Florence's foremost museum) and soak in centuries of great painting. Wander across the Ponte Vecchio (Florence's iconic bridge), taking in the tangle of Oltrarno's medieval streets. Then sample seasonal Tuscan cooking in a Left Bank osteria. You've discovered the art of fine living in this masterpiece of a city.

Michelangelo's "David" stands tall (literally) behind the doors of the **Accademia,** and nearby are the delicate paintings of Fra' Angelico in the convent of **San Marco.** Works by Donatello, Masaccio, and Ghiberti fill the city's churches and museums. Once home to the Medici, the **Palazzo Pitti** is hung with Raphaels and Titians, and backed by the fountains of the regal **Boboli Garden.**

And it's not only about history, art, and architecture. Florentines love to shop: Italy's leather capital strains at the seams with handmade gloves, belts, bags, and shoes sold from workshops, family-run boutiques, and high-toned stores, as well as at tourist-oriented **San Lorenzo Market.** Splurge on designer wear from fashion houses along **Via de' Tornabuoni**—this is the city that Gucci, Pucci, and Ferragamo call home.

Florentine cuisine is increasingly cosmopolitan, but local flavors still have Tuscany at their core. Even in the best restaurants, meals might kick off with traditional concoctions like *ribollita* (seasonal vegetable stew) before moving onto the chargrilled delights of a *bistecca alla fiorentina* (Florentine beefsteak on the bone)—all washed down with a fine **Chianti Classico,** from the vine-clad hills just to the south. At lunchtime order a plate of cold cuts, or if you're feeling adventurous, *lampredotto alla fiorentina* (a sandwich of cow's stomach stewed in tomatoes and garlic).

When you've dined to your fill, retire to a wine bar in the **Oltrarno,** or to one of the edgier joints in **Sant'Ambrogio, Santo Spirito,** or **San Frediano.** If you're keen on opera, classical, theater, or jazz, you'll find it here, too.

ESSENTIALS

Arriving

BY PLANE   Several European airlines service Florence's **Amerigo Vespucci Airport** (© **055-306-1300** switchboard, 055-306-1700 for flight info; www.aeroporto.firenze.it), also called **Peretola,** just 5km (3 miles) northwest of town. There are no direct flights to or from the United States, but you can make connections through London, Paris, Amsterdam,

Frankfurt, and several other European cities. The half-hourly **SITA-ATAF "Vola in bus"** to and from downtown's bus station at Via Santa Caterina 15R (*℃* **800-424-500**), beside the train station, costs 6€ one-way or 10€ round-trip. Metered **taxis** line up outside the airport's arrival terminal and charge a flat rate of 20€ to city center hotels (22€ on Sun and holidays, 24€ after 10pm, additional 1€ per bag).

The closest major international airport with direct flights to North America (in high season only) is Pisa's **Galileo Galilei Airport** (*℃* **050-849-300**; www.pisa-airport. com), 97km (60 miles) west of Florence. Two to three **train services** per hour leave the airport for Florence. However, until the new **PisaMover** airport transit service opens in December 2015, these involve a short bus journey then a change to a rail service at Pisa Centrale (70–90 min.; 9.20€). For early-morning flights or anyone with lots of bags, one simpler solution is to take the regular train from Florence into Pisa Centrale, followed by a 10-minute taxi ride (around 10€) from the train station to Pisa Airport. Alternatively, 17 daily buses operated by **Terravision** (*℃* **06-9761-0632**; www.terravision.eu) connect downtown Florence directly with Pisa Airport in 1 hour. One-way ticket prices are 6€ adults, 4€ children ages 5 to 12; round-trip fares are 10€ and 8€, respectively.

BY TRAIN Florence is Tuscany's rail hub, with regular connections to all of Italy's major cities. To get here from Rome, take the high-speed Frecciarossa or Frecciargento trains (1½ hr.; www.trenitalia.com) or high-speed trains operated by private rail company **Italo** (www.italotreno.com; p. 230). Milan is under 100 minutes away by Frecciarossa or Italo high-speed trains. Florence also has regular rail connections with the rest of Tuscany, on slower, but affordable *Regionale* services: **Lucca** (7.10€), **Arezzo** (7.90€), and **Pisa** (7.90€) all lie within 80 minutes of Florence.

Most Florence-bound trains roll into **Stazione Santa Maria Novella,** Piazza della Stazione, which you'll see abbreviated as **S.M.N.** The station is an architectural masterpiece, albeit one dating to Italy's Fascist period, rather than the Renaissance, and lies on the northwestern edge of the city's compact historic center, a brisk 10-minute walk from the Duomo and a 15-minute walk from Piazza della Signoria and the Uffizi.

BY CAR The **A1 autostrada** runs north from Rome past Orvieto, Umbria, and Arezzo to Florence and continues northward over the Apennine mountains to Bologna. **Unnumbered superhighways** run to and from Siena (the *SI-FI raccordo*) and Pisa (the so-called *FI-PI-LI*). To reach Florence from Lucca and Pistoia (see chapter 6), take the A11 eastbound.

Driving to Florence is easy; the problems begin once you arrive. For most of the week, almost all cars are banned from the historic center—only residents or merchants with special permits are allowed into this camera-patrolled *zona a trafico limitato* (the "ZTL"). Have the name and address of you hotel ready and the traffic police wave you through. You can drop off baggage there (the hotel will give you a temporary ZTL permit); then you must relocate to a parking lot: Special rates are available through most hotels.

Your best bet for overnight or longer-term parking is one of the city-run garages. The best deal (better than many hotels' garage rates) is at the **Parterre parking lot** under Piazza Libertà (at Via Madonna delle Tosse 9; *℃* **055-5030-2209**). It's open round the clock, costs 2€ per hour, or 20€ for 24 hours; it's 70€ for up to a week's parking. There's more info on city car parks at **www.firenzeparcheggi.it**.

Don't park your car overnight on the streets in Florence without local knowledge; if you're towed and ticketed, it will set you back substantially—and the headaches to

4

FLORENCE | Essentials

retrieve your car are beyond description. If this does happen to you, start by calling the vehicle removal department (the *Recupero Veicoli Rimossi*) on 🕿 **055-422-4142.**

Visitor Information

TOURIST OFFICES   The most convenient tourist office is at Via Cavour 1R (🕿 **055-290-832;** www.firenzeturismo.it), 2 blocks north of the Duomo. The office is open Monday through Saturday from 8:30am to 6:30pm. Their free map is quite adequate for navigation purposes—there's no need to upgrade to a paid-for version.

The train station's nearest tourist office (🕿 **055-212-245**) is opposite the terminus at Piazza della Stazione 4. With your back to the tracks, take the left exit, cross onto the concrete median, and bear right; it's across the busy road junction about 30m (100 ft.) ahead. The office is usually open Monday through Saturday from 9am to 7pm (sometimes only to 2pm in winter) and Sunday 9am to 2pm. This office gets crowded; unless you're really lost, press on to the Via Cavour office.

Another helpful office is under the Loggia del Bigallo, at the corner of Piazza San Giovanni and Via dei Calzaiuoli (🕿 **055-288-496**), open Monday through Saturday from 9am to 7pm (often 5pm mid-Nov through Feb) and Sunday 9am to 2pm. There is also an information office at airport arrivals (🕿 **055-315-874**), open on the same timetable.

WEBSITES   The official Florence information website, **www.firenzeturismo.it,** contains a wealth of reasonably up-to-date information on Florence and its province. At **www.firenzeturismo.it/monumenti-musei-firenze** you'll find links to downloadable PDFs with the latest opening hours for all the major city sights. The best-informed city blogs are written in Italian by locals: **Io Amo Firenze** (www.ioamofirenze.it) is handy for reviews of the latest eating, drinking, and events in town. For one-off exhibitions and cultural events, **Art Trav** (www.arttrav.com) is an essential bookmark. For regularly updated Florence info, go to **www.frommers.com/destinations/florence**. Also see "Entertainment & Nightlife," p. 98.

City Layout

Florence is a smallish city, sitting on the River Arno and petering out to olive-planted hills rather quickly to the north and south, but extending farther west and east along the Arno valley with suburbs and light industry. It has a compact center, which is best negotiated on foot or by bike. No two major sights are more than a 25-minute walk apart, and most of the hotels and sights in this chapter are in the relatively small *centro storico* **(historic center),** a compact tangle of medieval streets and *piazze* (squares) where visitors spend most of their time. The bulk of Florence, including most of the tourist sites, lies north of the river, with the **Oltrarno,** an old working artisans' neighborhood, hemmed in between the Arno and the hills on the south side.

Neighborhoods in Florence

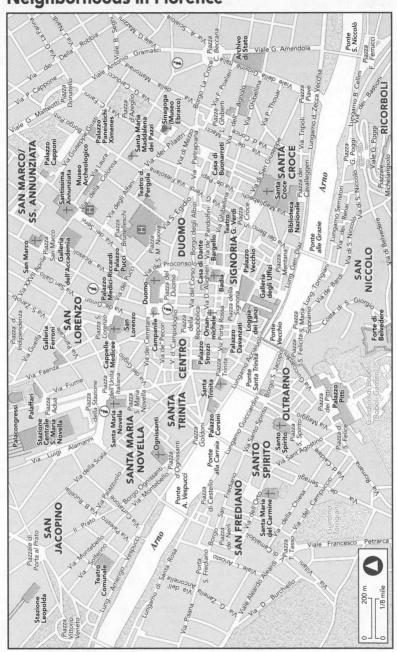

The Neighborhoods in Brief

The Duomo The area surrounding Florence's gargantuan cathedral is as central as you can get. The Duomo is halfway between the two monastic churches of Santa Maria Novella and Santa Croce, as well as at the midpoint between the Uffizi Gallery and the Ponte Vecchio to the south and San Marco and the Accademia with Michelangelo's "David" to the north. The streets south of the Duomo make up a medieval tangle of alleys and tiny squares heading toward Piazza della Signoria.

This is one of the oldest parts of town, and the streets still vaguely follow the grid laid down when the city was a Roman colony. The site of the Roman city's forum is today's **Piazza della Repubblica.**

The Duomo neighborhood is, understandably, one of the most hotel-heavy parts of town, offering a range from luxury inns to aging dives and everything in between. Several places around here rest on the laurels of their sublime location; you need to be choosy. The same goes—even more so—for dining in the area.

Piazza della Signoria This is the city's civic heart and perhaps the best base for museum hounds: The Uffizi Gallery, Bargello sculpture museum, and Ponte Vecchio leading toward the Pitti Palace are all nearby. It's a well-polished part of the tourist zone but still retains the narrow medieval streets where Dante grew up. The few blocks just north of the **Ponte Vecchio** have reasonable shopping, but unappealing modern buildings were planted here to replace those destroyed during World War II. The entire neighborhood can be stiflingly crowded in summer—**Via Por Santa Maria** is one to avoid—but in those moments when you catch it empty of tour groups, it remains the romantic heart of pre-Renaissance Florence. As with the Duomo neighborhood, you need to be *very* choosy when picking a restaurant or even an ice cream around here.

San Lorenzo & the Mercato Centrale This wedge of streets between the train station and the Duomo, centered on the Medici's old family church of San Lorenzo, is market territory. The vast indoor food market is here, and many of the streets are filled daily with stalls hawking leather and other tourist wares. It's a colorful neighborhood, blessed with a range of budget hotels and affordable eating and drinking, but not the quietest.

Piazza Santa Trínita This piazza sits just north of the river at the south end of Florence's shopping mecca, **Via de' Tornabuoni,** home to Gucci, Armani, and more. It's a pleasant, well-to-do (but still medieval) neighborhood in which to stay, even if you don't care about haute couture. If you're an upscale shopping fiend, there's no better place to be.

Santa Maria Novella This neighborhood, bounding the western edge of the *centro storico,* has two characters: an unpleasant zone around the train station, and a nicer area south of it between the church of Santa Maria Novella and the river.

In general, the train-station area is the least attractive part of town in which to base yourself. The streets are mostly heavily trafficked and noisy, and you're a little removed from the medieval atmosphere. This area does, however, have more good budget options than any other quarter, especially along **Via Faenza** and its tributaries. Try to avoid staying on busy **Via Nazionale.**

The situation improves dramatically as you move east into the San Lorenzo area (see above) or pass Santa Maria Novella church and head south toward the river. **Piazza Santa Maria Novella** and its tributary streets have quite a few top-priced, stylish boutique hotels.

San Marco & Santissima Annunziata These two churches are fronted by *piazze*—**Piazza San Marco,** a busy transport hub, and **Piazza Santissima Annunziata,** the most architecturally unified square in the city—that together define the northern limits of the *centro storico.* The neighborhood is home to Florence's university, the Accademia, the San Marco paintings of Fra' Angelico, and quiet streets with some hotel gems. The walk back from the heart of the action isn't as far as it looks on a map, and you'll likely welcome the escape from tourist crowds. But it's not (yet) a great dining or nightlife neighborhood.

Santa Croce The art-filled church at the eastern edge of the *centro storico* is the focal point of one of the most genuine neighborhoods left in the center. Few tourists roam too far east of **Piazza Santa Croce,** so if you want to feel like a Florentine, stay

here. The streets around the **Mercato di Sant'Ambrogio** and **Piazza de' Ciompi** have an especially appealing, local feel, and get lively after dark. The Santa Croce neighborhood boasts some of the best restaurants and bars in the city—*aperitivo* hour is vibrant along **Via de' Benci,** and there is always something going on along **Via Panisperna** and **Via de' Macci.**

The Oltrarno, San Niccolò & San Frediano "Across the Arno" is the artisans' neighborhood, still dotted with workshops. It began as a working-class neighborhood to catch the overflow from the expanding medieval city on the opposite bank, but became a chic area for aristocrats to build palaces on the edge of the countryside. The largest of these, the **Pitti Palace,** later became the home of the grand dukes and today houses a set of paintings second only to the Uffizi in scope.

The Oltrarno's lively tree-shaded center, **Piazza Santo Spirito,** is lined with bars and close to some great restaurants (and lively nightlife, too). West of here, the neighborhood of **San Frediano,** around the Porta Pisana, is becoming ever more fashionable, and **San Niccolò** at the foot of Florence's southern hills has buzzing cafe-bars. You may not choose to stay around here—the hotel range still isn't great—but when evening draws nigh, cross one of the bridges to drink and eat better food, at better prices, than you will generally find in the *centro storico.*

Getting Around

Florence is a **walking** city. You can leisurely stroll between the two top sights, Piazza del Duomo and the Uffizi, in 5 minutes. The hike from the most northerly major sights, San Marco with its Fra' Angelico frescoes and the Accademia with Michelangelo's "David," to the most southerly, the Pitti Palace across the Arno, should take no more than 30 minutes. From Santa Maria Novella eastward across town to Santa Croce is a flat 20- to 30-minute walk. But beware: Flagstones, some of them uneven, are everywhere—wear sensible shoes with some padding and foot support.

BY BUS You'll rarely need to use Florence's efficient **ATAF bus system** (✆ **800-424-500** in Italy; www.ataf.net) since the city is so compact. Bus tickets cost 1.20€ and are good for 90 minutes, irrespective of how many changes you make. A 24-hour pass costs 5€, a 3-day pass 12€, and a 7-day pass 18€. Tickets are sold at *tabacchi* (tobacconists), some bars, and most newsstands. If you cannot find a machine or vendor near your stop, pay 2€ to buy a ticket onboard, or if you have an Italian cellphone SIM

(p. 236), text the word "ATAF" to ✆ **488-0105** to buy a prevalidated ticket using your prepaid phone credit. *Note:* Once on board, validate your ticket in the box near the rear door to avoid a steep fine. Since traffic is limited in most of the historic center, buses make runs on principal streets only, except for four tiny electric buses (*bussini* services C1, C2, C3, and D) that trundle about the *centro storico*. The most useful lines to outlying areas are no. 7 (for Fiesole) and nos. 12 and 13 (for Piazzale Michelangiolo). Buses run from 7am until 8:30 or 9pm daily, with a limited night service on a few key routes (mostly local-focused).

BY TAXI   Taxis aren't cheap, and with the city so small and the one-way system forcing drivers to take convoluted routes, they aren't an economical way to get about. They're most useful to get you and your bags between the train station and your hotel. The standard rate is .91€ per kilometer, with a whopping minimum fare of 3.30€ to start the meter (which rises to 5.30€ on Sun or 6.60€ 10pm–6am), plus 1€ per bag. There's a taxi stand outside the train station and another in Piazza Santa Croce (by Via de' Benci); otherwise, call **Radio Taxi** at ✆ **055-4242** or 055-4798. For the latest taxi information, see **www.socota.it**.

BY BICYCLE & SCOOTER   Florence is largely flat and increasingly closed to cars, and so is ideal for seeing from the saddle. Many of the bike-rental shops in town are located just north of Piazza San Marco, such as **Alinari,** Via San Zanobi 38R (✆ **055-280-500;** www.alinarirental.com), which rents vintage-style city bikes (2.50€ per hour; 12€ per day) and mountain bikes (3€ per hour; 18€ per day). It also rents out 100cc scooters (15€ per hour; 55€ per day). Another renter with similar prices is **Florence by Bike,** Via San Zanobi 54R (✆ **055-488-992;** www.florencebybike.it). Make sure to carry a lock (one will be provided with your rental): Bike theft is common.

BY CAR   Trying to drive in the *centro storico* is a frustrating, useless exercise, and moreover, unauthorized traffic is not allowed past signs marked ZTL. On top of that, 2013 saw the introduction of a city charge even for residents to drive into the center to park. Florence is a maze of one-way streets and pedestrian zones, and it takes an old hand to know which laws to break in order to get where you need to go—plus you need a permit to do anything beyond dropping off and picking up bags at your hotel. Park your vehicle in one of the huge underground lots on the center's periphery and pound the pavement. (See "By Car" under "Getting There," p. 227.)

[FastFACTS] FLORENCE

Business Hours   Hours mainly follow the Italian norm (see chapter 9). In Florence, however, many of the larger and more central shops stay open through the midday *riposo* or nap (note the sign ORARIO NONSTOP).

Doctors   There's a walk-in **Tourist Medical Service,** Via Roma 4 (✆ **055-475-411;** www.medicalservice.firenze. it), open Monday to Friday

11am to noon, 1 to 3pm, and 5 to 6pm; Saturday 11am to noon and 1 to 3pm only. **Dr. Stephen Kerr** runs a surgery at Piazza Mercato Nuovo 1 (✆ **335-836-1682** or 055-288-055; www.dr-kerr. com), with office hours Monday through Friday from 3 to 5pm without an appointment (appointments are available 9am–3pm). The consultation fee is 50€ to

60€; it's slightly cheaper if you show student I.D.

Hospitals   The most central hospital is **Santa Maria Nuova,** a block northeast of the Duomo on Piazza Santa Maria Nuova (✆ **055-69-381;** www.asf.toscana.it), with an emergency room (*pronto soccorso*) open 24 hours. There is a comprehensive guide to medical services, including specialist care, on the official Florence city website. See www.firenzeturismo.it/en/other-useful-information/health-services-in-florence-and-surroundings.html.

Internet Access Every hotel we recommend offers wireless Internet, usually for free but occasionally for a small fee. Otherwise, head to the chain **Internet Train** (✆ **055-747-6540;** www.internettrain.it), with six locations in Florence, including their very first shop at Via dell'Oriuolo 40R, a few blocks from the Duomo; Via Guelfa 54R, near the train station; and Borgo San Jacopo 30R, in the Oltrarno. They also provide printing, and scanning, plus other services (bike rental, international shipping, and so forth) at some offices. Open hours vary, but generally run daily from 9am to 8:30pm, often later. Alternatively, if you have your own laptop or smartphone, several bars and cafes now offer free Wi-Fi to anyone buying a drink or snack.

Mail & Postage Florence's main post office (✆ 055-273-6481) is at Via Pellicceria 3, off the southwest corner of Piazza della Repubblica. It is open Monday through Friday from 8:20am to 7:05pm, Saturday 8:20am to 12:35pm.

Newspapers & Magazines Florence's national daily paper, "La Nazione," is on sale everywhere. "The Florentine" (www.theflorentine.net) is the city's bi-weekly English-language news and reviews publication, widely available at bars, cafes, and hotels. Overseas English-language newspapers are also widely available: The newsstands at the station are a safe bet, as is the booth under the arcade on the western side of Piazza della Repubblica, where you will find the "Financial Times," "Wall Street Journal," and London "Guardian," alongside the usual "International New York Times."

Pharmacies There is a 24-hour pharmacy (also open Sun and state holidays) in **Stazione Santa Maria Novella** (✆ **055-216-761;** ring the bell 1–4am). On holidays and at night, look for the sign in any pharmacy window telling you which ones are open locally.

Police To report lost property or passport problems, call the *questura* (police headquarters) at ✆ **055-49-771. *Note:*** It is illegal to knowingly buy fake goods anywhere in the city (and yes, a "Louis Vuitton" bag at 10€ counts as *knowingly*). You may be served a hefty on-the-spot fine if caught.

Safety As in any city, plenty of pickpockets are out to ruin your vacation, and in Florence you'll find light-fingered youngsters (especially around the train station), but otherwise you're generally safe. Do steer clear of the Cascine Park after dark, when it becomes somewhat seedy and you may run the risk of being mugged; likewise the area around Piazza Santo Spirito and in the backstreets behind Santa Croce after all the nightlife has gone off to bed. And you probably won't want to hang out with the late-night heroin addicts shooting up on the Arno mud flats below the Lungarno embankments on the edges of town. See chapter 9 for more safety tips.

WHERE TO STAY

In the past few years, thanks to growing competition, recent global and local financial crises, and unfavorable euro–dollar exchange rates, the forces of supply and demand have brought hotel prices in Florence down . . . a little. But it is still difficult to find a high-season double you'd want to stay in for much less than 100€. In addition, some of the price drops have been added back in taxes: Since 2012, Florence's city government has levied an extra 1€ per person per night per government-rated hotel star, for the first 5 nights of any stay. The tax is payable on departure, and is not usually included in quoted rates.

Peak hotel season is mid-March through early July, September through early November, and December 23 through January 6. May, June, and September are

Florence Hotels

Via Guelfa

Palaffari

2

Via Jacopo
da Diacceto

**Stazione
Centrale
S. Maria
Novella**

Piazza
Adua

Via Faenza

1

Via Nazionale

Via Panicale

Via

Via della Scala

Via Luigi
Alamanni

Via Fiume

Piazza
della Stazione

Piazza del
Mercato
Centrale

Via d. Orti

Piazza
dell'Unità
Italiana

Via S. Antonino

Piazza S.
Lorenzo

**Cappelle
Medicee**

Via della Scala

**S. Maria
Novella**

Via de' Panzani

Via del Giglio

**San
Lorenzo**

Borgo S. Lorenzo

Via Palazzuolo

Piazza
S. Maria
Novella

3

Via
dei Banchi

Via de' Belle Donne

Via dei Cerretani

Piazza
S. Giovanni

Ognissanti

Piazza
d'Ognissanti

Lungarno Amerigo Vespucci

Borgo
Ognissanti

Via de' Fossi

Via del Moro

V. della Spada

Via del Sole

Via de' Tornabuoni

CENTRO

Via Roma

8

7

Lung. Santa Rosa

Piazza
Goldoni

Via della Vigna Nuova

V. d. Parioze

Via d. Strozzi

Piazza
della
Repubblica

Arno

**Palazzo
Strozzi**

Via Calimala

Porta
S. Frediano

Piazza
di Cestello

Lungarno Soderini

Ponte
alla Carraia

**Palazzo
Corsini**

Lung. Corsini

**Santa
Trinita**

Piazza
Trinita

Via Porta Rossa

Orsan-
michele

Borgo
San

Via San
Giovanni

Borgo

Frediano

Ponte
S. Trinita

SAN FREDIANO

Lungarno Guicciardini

Ponte

S. Trinita

**Palazzo
Davanzati**

12

Lung. Acciaiuoli

Borgo SS. Apostoli

13

15

V. Por S. Maria

V. dell'Orto

Piazza del
Carmine

Via Santo Spirito

**SANTO
SPIRITO**

Ponte
Vecchio

**Loggia
dei Lanzi**

V. di Camaldoli

Via del Leone

Via Santa
Monaca

Borgo San Jacopo

**Santa Maria
del Carmine**

Via dell'
Ardiglione

Via Sant'
Agostino

**Santo
Spirito**

V. Vellutini

OLTRARNO

Via Guicciardini

Piazza
S. Felicita

Piazza
S. Maria
Soprarno

Piazza
S. Tasso

Piazza
S. Spirito

Via della Chiesa

Via de' Serragli

Via
Mazzetta

Via
Maggio

Via Tegolaio

Piazza
dei Pitti

Viale Francesco Petrarca

*Giardino
Torrigiani*

Via del Campuccio

Borgo

Via Romana

**Palazzo
Pitti**

**Forte di
Belvedere**

0 _____ 1/8 mile

0 _____ 200 meters

*Giardino di Boboli
(Boboli Garden)*

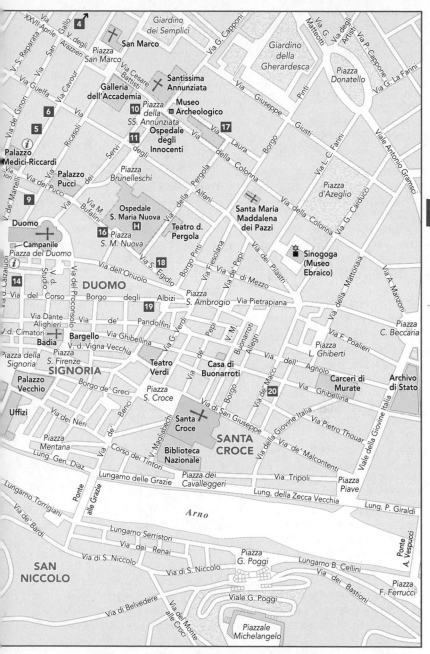

particularly popular. January, February, and August are the time to grab a bargain—never be shy to haggle if you're coming in these months.

To help you decide which area you'd like to base yourself in, consult "The Neighborhoods in Brief," p. 48. Note that we have included parking information only for those places that offer it. As indicated below, many hotels offer babysitting services; note, however, these are generally "on request." At least a couple of days' notice is advisable.

Hotels by Price

EXPENSIVE

Brunelleschi ★★, p. 54
Continentale ★★★, p. 55
Residence Hilda ★★, p. 57

MODERATE

Alessandra ★, p. 56
Antica Dimora Johlea ★★, p. 57
Davanzati ★★, p. 56
Il Guelfo Bianco ★★, p. 55
La Casa di Morfeo ★, p. 58
La Dimora degli Angeli ★★★, p. 54
Loggiato dei Serviti ★★, p. 58

Morandi alla Crocetta ★★, p. 58
Palazzo Galletti ★★, p. 59
Riva Lofts ★★, p. 59
Rosso 23 ★, p. 56
Tourist House Ghiberti ★, p. 58

INEXPENSIVE

Academy Hostel ★, p. 55
Azzi ★, p. 56
Casci ★, p. 55
Locanda Orchidea ★, p. 59
Plus Florence ★★, p. 57

Near the Duomo

EXPENSIVE

Brunelleschi ★★　The Brunelleschi manages to pull off a couple of neat tricks. It exceeds the usual standards of a 21st-century "design hotel" without losing track of where it's from: Rooms and public areas are framed with *pietra serena,* the gray stone used liberally by Florentine architect Brunelleschi. It's big, but feels small, thanks to its entrance on a quiet little piazza and a labyrinthine layout, ranged around the oldest standing building in Florence. Rooms are midsized with parquet floors and contemporary-classic styling. Although many look onto busy Via Calzaiuoli, impressive soundproofing means you won't hear any noise. Apparently a favorite of author Dan Brown, the hotel appears in both "The Da Vinci Code" and "Inferno."

Piazza Santa Elisabetta 3 (just off Corso). ✆ **055-27-370.** www.hotelbrunelleschi.it. 96 units. 159€–800€ double. Rates include breakfast. Parking 35€–39€. Bus: C2. **Amenities:** 2 restaurants; bar; concierge; gym; room service; Wi-Fi (free).

MODERATE

La Dimora degli Angeli ★★★　In 2012, this B&B added a whole new floor, and now occupies two levels of a grand apartment building in one of the city's busiest shopping areas. Rooms on the original floor are for romantics; bright, modern wallpaper clashes pleasingly with iron-framed beds and traditional furniture. (Corner room Beatrice is the largest, with a view of Brunelleschi's dome—only just.) The new floor, below, is totally different, with the kind of decor you find in an interiors magazine, all sharp lines and bespoke leather or wooden headboards. Breakfast is served at a local cafe, but if you prefer, you can grab a morning coffee in the B&B and use your token for a light lunch instead.

Via Brunelleschi 4. ✆ **055-288-478.** www.ladimoradegliangeli.com. 12 units. 88€–190€ double. Rates include breakfast (at nearby cafe). Parking 26€. Bus: C2. **Amenities:** Wi-Fi (free).

INEXPENSIVE

Academy Hostel ★ If a gated courtyard right in the center appears rather a grand address for a hostel, that is because this is no ordinary student traveler dive. The two private rooms (one with an en-suite bathroom) come plainly decorated, certainly, with whitewashed walls and functional furniture. But they are also bright and spacious, and include linen and towels in the (bargain) price. Communal areas are comfy, staff is full of advice, and the place is small, spotless, and within a minute's walk of both the Duomo and "David." You will need to book well ahead to bag a room here: They go fast, especially in high season.

Via Ricasoli 9. ℭ **055-239-8665.** www.academyhostel.it. 10 units. 79€–94€ double. Bus: C1. **Amenities:** Wi-Fi (free).

Near Piazza della Signoria
EXPENSIVE

Continentale ★★★ Everything about the Continentale is cool, and the effect is achieved without a hint of frostiness. Rooms are uncompromisingly modern, decorated in bright-white and bathed in natural light—even the deluxe units built into a medieval riverside tower, which have mighty walls and medieval-sized windows (small, in plain English). Standard rooms are large, for Florence, and there's a 1950s feel to the overall styling. Communal areas are a major hit, too: The second-floor relaxation room has a glass wall with a front-row view of the Ponte Vecchio. The top-floor **La Terrazza** (p. 101) has Florence's best rooftop cocktails.

Vicolo dell'Oro 6R. ℭ **055-27-262.** www.lungarnocollection.com. 43 units. 220€–730€ double. Parking 35€–37€. Bus: C3 or D. **Amenities:** Bar; concierge; gym; spa; Wi-Fi (free).

Near San Lorenzo & the Mercato Centrale
MODERATE

Il Guelfo Bianco ★★ Decor in this former noble Florentine family home retains its authentic *palazzo* feel, though carpets have been added for comfort and warmth. No two rooms are the same—stone walls this thick cannot just be knocked through— and several have antiques integrated into their individual schemes. Grand rooms at the front (especially 101, 118, and 228) have spectacular Renaissance-coffered ceilings and masses of space. Bathrooms are plainer by comparison. Sleep at the back or looking onto the internal courtyard and you'll wake to an unusual sound in Florence: birdsong. The adjacent bistro, **Il Desco,** is under the same ownership and serves seasonal Mediterranean dishes made with organic ingredients; its open to guests and nonguests alike (lunch only Oct–Easter).

Via Cavour 29 (near corner of Via Guelfa). ℭ **055-288-330.** www.ilguelfobianco.it. 40 units. 99€– 250€ double. Rates include breakfast. Valet parking 27€–33€. Bus: C1. **Amenities:** Restaurant; bar; babysitting; concierge; room service; Wi-Fi (free).

INEXPENSIVE

Casci ★ The front part of the palace now occupied by the Casci was once composer Rossini's Florence digs. This affordable, central hotel has been a Frommer's favorite for 2 decades, and the recent partial pedestrianization of Via Cavour makes it an even more attractive base. Rooms follow a labyrinthine layout, split between Rossini's old *piano nobile* and a now-joined former convent to the rear, where the bigger rooms are located, including a couple of spacious family units. Rooms are simply decorated and some can get a little dark, though a rolling program of modernization has installed new, light-toned furniture to counteract that—now in 16 rooms and counting. The welcome from some of Florence's friendliest family hoteliers is a permanent fixture.

Via Cavour 13 (btw. Via dei Ginori and Via Guelfa). ℂ **055-211-686.** www.hotelcasci.com. 25 units. 80€–150€ double; 100€–190€ triple; 120€–230€ quad. Rates include breakfast. Valet parking 21€–25€. Bus: C1. Closed 2 weeks in Dec. **Amenities:** Bar; babysitting (10€ per hour); concierge; Wi-Fi (free).

Near Piazza Santa Trínita

MODERATE

Alessandra ★   This typical Florentine *pensione* immediately transports you back to the age of the gentleman and lady traveler. Decor has grown organically since the place opened as a hotel in 1950—Alessandra is a place for evolution, not revolution. A pleasing mix of styles is the end result: some rooms with hefty armoires, terracotta tiling, carved headboards, gilt frames, and gold damask around the place, others with herringbone parquet and eclectic postwar furniture, like something from a period movie set. A couple have views beyond a medieval bell tower to the Arno . . . but then again, Borgo SS. Apostoli, on the front side, is one of the center's most atmospheric streets. There's a small river-view terrace for everyone to share; grab a glass of wine from the honesty bar and kick back.

Borgo SS. Apostoli 17. ℂ **055-283-438.** www.hotelalessandra.com. 27 units. 150€–180€ double. Rates include breakfast. Garage parking 25€. Bus: C3 or D. Closed Christmas and a few days around Aug 15. **Amenities:** Concierge; Wi-Fi (free).

Davanzati ★★   Although installed inside a historic building, the Davanzati never rests on its medieval laurels: There is still a laptop in every room for guest use and HD movies streamed to your TV, and lobby newspapers now come on an iPad. Rooms are simply decorated in the Tuscan style, with color-washed walls; half-canopies over the beds add a little flourish. Room 100 is probably the best family hotel room in Florence, full of nooks, crannies, and split levels that give the adults and the kids a sense of private space. The complimentary evening drink for all guests remains part of the Davanzati's family welcome.

Via Porta Rossa 5 (at Piazza Davanzati). ℂ **055-286-666.** www.hoteldavanzati.it. 25 units. 122€–199€ double; 152€–229€ superior (sleeping up to 4). Rates include breakfast. Valet parking 26€. Bus: C2. **Amenities:** Bar; babysitting; concierge; Wi-Fi (free).

Near Santa Maria Novella

MODERATE

Rosso 23 ★   The design hotels of Piazza Santa Maria Novella are frequented by fashion models, rock stars, and blue-chip businessfolk. You can get a taste of that, for a fraction of the price, at this boutique hotel with attitude. Most rooms are not large, but each is immaculate, and reflects the hotel's scarlet and *pietra serena* gray palette. It is well worth paying the 20€ to 30€ extra for a Superior room at the front. These are larger and overlook one of Florence's liveliest and most fashionable squares—not to mention its prettiest church facade, on Santa Maria Novella itself.

Piazza Santa Maria Novella 23. ℂ **055-277-300.** www.hotelrosso23.com. 42 units. 74€–180€ double. Rates include breakfast. Garage parking 35€. Bus: C2, 6, 11, or 22. **Amenities:** Concierge; Wi-Fi (free).

Between Santa Maria Novella & the Mercato Centrale

INEXPENSIVE

Azzi ★   This quirky, somewhat bohemian joint is also known as the Locanda degli Artisti. Each of its rooms is brightly decorated, and most in the more characterful, original area of the hotel feature an antique piece or colorfully painted wall to add ambience. Occasional floorboards are artfully distressed (by both time and design), and pictures or wall mirrors have wistfully weathered frames. In short, each is exactly the kind of room you could imagine for a struggling artist to lay his head at night. Refitted in 2013, 8 newer rooms have a totally different feel, with laminate flooring, white furniture, and shiny, new travertine bathrooms.

Via Faenza 88R. ✆ **055-213-806.** www.hotelazzi.com. 24 units. 54€–130€ double; 95€–140€ triple. Rates include breakfast. Garage parking 22€. Bus: 1, 2, 12, 13, 28, 36, 37, or 57. **Amenities:** Bar; Wi-Fi (free).

Plus Florence ★★ There's quite simply nowhere in Florence with as many services for your buck, including seasonal indoor and outdoor swimming pools, all in a price bracket where you are usually fortunate to get an en-suite bathroom (and Plus has those, too). The best rooms in this large, well-equipped hostel are in the new wing, opened in 2013 and housing private rooms only. Units here are dressed in taupe and brown, with subtle uplighting and enough space (in some) for up to four beds. Room 657 is the only one with a terrace—it looks right at the center's spires and domes. The only minuses: an unpicturesque building; and the location, between two busy roads (request a room facing the internal courtyard if you are a light sleeper).

Via Santa Caterina d'Alessandria 15. ✆ **055-462-8934.** www.plusflorence.com. 187 units. 40€–100€ double; 50€–130€ triple. Bus: 8, 12, or 20. **Amenities:** Restaurant; bar; concierge; gym; 2 swimming pools; sauna (winter only); Wi-Fi (free).

Near San Marco & Santissima Annunziata
EXPENSIVE
Residence Hilda ★★ There's not a hint of the Renaissance here: These luxurious mini-apartments are all bright-white decor and designer soft furnishings, with stripped-wood flooring and modern gadgetry to keep everything working. Each is spacious, cool in summer, and totally cocooned from Florence's permanent background noise. Each apartment also has a mini-kitchen, kitted out just fine for preparing a simple meal—ideal if you have kids in tow, especially if you make use of the grocery delivery service. Unusually for apartments, they are bookable by the single night and upward. Staff is some of the friendliest in the city.

Via dei Servi 40 (2 blocks north of the Duomo). ✆ **055-288-021.** www.residencehilda.com. 12 units. 150€–450€ per night for apartments sleeping 2–4. Valet garage parking 31€. Bus: C1, 6, 19, 31, or 32. **Amenities:** Airport transfer; babysitting; concierge; room service; Wi-Fi (free).

MODERATE
Antica Dimora Johlea ★★ There is a real neighborhood feel to the streets around this *dimora* (traditional Florentine home) guesthouse—which means evenings are lively and Sundays are silent (although it's under a 10-min. walk from the buzz of San Lorenzo). Standard-sized rooms are snug; upgrade to an Executive if you need more space, but there is no difference in the standard of the decor, a mix of Florentine and earthy, boho styling, with parquet floor, silk drapes, and Persian rugs. Help yourself to coffee, soft drinks, or a glass of wine from the honesty bar and head up to a knockout roof terrace for views over the terra-cotta rooftops to the center and hills beyond. It is pure magic at dusk. No credit cards.

Via San Gallo 80. ✆ **055-463-3292.** www.johanna.it. 6 units. 90€–180€ double. Rates include breakfast. Parking 12€. Bus: C1, 1, 7, 11, 17, 19, 20, or 25. **Amenities:** Honesty bar; Wi-Fi (free).

Loggiato dei Serviti ★★   Stay here to experience Florence as the travelers of the Grand Tour did. For starters, the building is a genuine Renaissance landmark, having been built by Sangallo the Elder in the 1520s. There is a sense of faded grandeur and unconventional luxury throughout—no gadgetry or chromotherapy showers here, but you will find rooms with writing desks and occasional tables dressed with lamps. No unit is small, but most of the standard rooms lack a view of either Brunelleschi's dome or the perfect piazza outside: An upgrade to Superior represents good value. Air conditioning is pretty much the only concession to the 21st century—and you will love it that way.

Piazza Santissima Annunziata 3. ✆ **055-289-592.** www.loggiatodeiservitihotel.it. 38 units. 130€–330€ double. Rates include breakfast. Valet parking 21€. Bus: C1, 6, 19, 31, or 32. **Amenities:** Babysitting; concierge; Wi-Fi (free).

Morandi alla Crocetta ★★   Like many in Florence, this hotel is built into the shell of a former convent. Morandi alla Crocetta has retained the original layout, meaning some rooms are snug—though that does not apply to the 2 rooms added in 2014, ranged around the old cloister downstairs. Anyway, what you lose in size, you more than gain in character: Every single one oozes *tipico fiorentino*. Rooms have parquet flooring thrown with rugs and dressed with antique wooden furniture. Original Zocchi prints of Florence, made in 1744, are scattered around the place. It's definitely worth upgrading to a Superior if you can: These have more space and either a private courtyard terrace or, in one, original frescoes decorating the entrance to the former convent chapel, now blocked-up into the wall. The hotel is on a quiet street.

Via Laura 50 (1 block east of Piazza Santissima Annunziata). ✆ **055-234-4747.** www.hotelmorandi. it. 12 units. 100€–167€ double. Rates include breakfast. Garage parking 24€. Bus: C1, 6, 19, 31, or 32. **Amenities:** Bar; babysitting; concierge; Wi-Fi (free).

Tourist House Ghiberti ★   There is a pleasing mix of the traditional and the modern at this backstreet guesthouse named after a famous former resident—the creator of the Baptistery's "Gates of Paradise" had workshops on the top floor of the *palazzo*. Rooms have plenty of space, with high ceilings, herringbone terra-cotta floors, whitewashed walls, and painted wood ceilings in a vaguely Renaissance style. There is a sauna and Jacuzzi for communal use, if you need to soak away the aches and pains after a day's sightseeing; new memory-foam mattresses added in 2014 should help, too. Email direct if you want to bag the best room rate.

Via M. Bufalini 1. ✆ **055-284-858.** www.touristhouseghiberti.com. 5 units. 69€–179€ double. Rates include breakfast. Garage parking 20€. Bus: C1. **Amenities:** Jacuzzi; sauna; Wi-Fi (free).

Near Santa Croce
MODERATE

La Casa di Morfeo ★   For a cheery, affordable room in the increasingly lively eastern part of the center, look no further than this small hotel that opened in 2012 on the second floor of a grand, shuttered palace. There is no huge difference in quality of the rooms. Each is midsized, with modern gadgetry, and painted in bright contemporary colors, the individual scheme corresponding to the flower after which the room is named. Our favorite is Mimosa, painted in light mustard, with a ceiling fresco and a frontside view over Via Ghibellina. Colored lighting adds a bit of fun to the units.

Via Ghibellina 51. ✆ **055-241-193.** www.lacasadimorfeo.it. 9 units. 79€–189€ double. Rates include breakfast. Valet parking 25€. Bus: C2 or C3. **Amenities:** Wi-Fi (free).

A Soothing Central Spa

If you can't splurge for one of Florence's upscale spa hotels, book a session at **Soulspace,** Via Sant'Egidio 12 (℃ **055-200-1794;** www.soulspace.it). This calming spot has a heated pool and hammam (Turkish bath), and a range of modern spa treatments for women and men including aromatherapy massages. Day spa packages cost from 50€ upward.

Palazzo Galletti ★★   Not many hotels give you the chance to live like a Florentine noble on a sensible budget. Rooms here have towering ceilings and an uncluttered arrangement of antique furniture—each piece carefully chosen—and most have frescoed or painted-wood showpiece ceilings. Bathrooms, in contrast, are modern and decked out in travertine and marble. Aside from two street-facing suites, every room has a small balcony, ideal for a pre-dinner glass of wine. If you're here for a once-in-a-lifetime trip, spring a little extra for "Giove" or (especially) "Cerere"; both are large suites, and the latter has walls covered in original frescoes from the 1800s.

Via Sant'Egidio 12. ℃ **055-390-5750.** www.palazzogalletti.it. 12 units. 100€–160€ double; 160€–240€ suite. Rates include breakfast. Garage parking 30€. Bus: C1 or C2. **Amenities:** Wi-Fi (5€ per day).

INEXPENSIVE

Locanda Orchidea ★   Over several visits to Florence, this has been a go-to inn for stays on a tight budget. Rooms spread over two floors of a historic *palazzo*—spot the original "wine hole" by the front door, once used by noble owners to sell direct to thirsty Florentines. The best rooms upstairs face a quiet, leafy rear courtyard. Furniture is a fun mix of mismatched flea-market finds and secondhand pieces; tiled floors and bold print wallpaper and fabrics keep up the charmingly outdated feel. Note that bathrooms are shared (although they have good water pressure), and there is no air conditioning or onsite breakfast. But the price, value, character, and welcome are hard to beat in this price bracket.

Borgo degli Albizi 11 (close to Piazza San Pier Maggiore). ℃ **055-248-0346.** www.hotelorchidea florence.it. 7 units. 45€–75€ double. Garage parking 18€–22€. Bus: C1 or C2. **Amenities:** Wi-Fi (free).

West of the Center

MODERATE

Riva Lofts ★★   The traditional Florentine alarm call—a morning mix of traffic and tourism—is replaced by birdsong when you awake in one of the stylish rooms here, on the banks of the River Arno. A former stone-built artisan workshop, Riva has had a refit to match its "loft" label: There's a taupe-and-white color scheme with laminate flooring, marble bathrooms with rainfall showers, and clever integration of natural materials in such features as original wooden workshop ceilings. Breakfast is served until 11:45am and noon checkouts as a standard are a seriously traveler-friendly touch. The center is a half-hour walk, or jump on one of Riva's vintage-style bikes and cycle to the Uffizi along the Arno banks. Yet another standout feature in this price bracket: a shaded garden with outdoor plunge pool.

Via Baccio Bandinelli 98. ℃ **055-713-0272.** www.rivalofts.com. 9 units. 165€–255€ double. Rates include breakfast. Garage parking 20€ (or park out front for free). Bus: 6/Tram: T1 (3 stops from central station). **Amenities:** Bike rental (free); honesty bar; outdoor pool; Wi-Fi (free).

New York has the hot dog. London has pie and mash. Florence has . . . cow's intestine in a sandwich. The city's traditional street food, *lampredotto* (the cow's fourth stomach) stewed with tomatoes and onions, has made a big comeback over the last decade, including on the menus of some fine-dining establishments. However, the best places to sample it are still the city's *trippai*, tripe vendors who sell it from takeaway vans around the center—alongside "regular" sandwiches for the less adventurous. The most convenient are in **Piazza de' Cimatori** and on **Via de' Macci** at the corner of Piazza Sant'Ambrogio. A hearty, nutritious lunch should come to around 4€. Most are open Monday through Saturday, but close in August, when Florentines flee the city.

Apartment Rentals & Alternative Accommodations

One of the best city specialists is **Florence and Abroad** (© 055-487-004; www.florenceandabroad.com), which matches different tastes and budgets to a wide range of apartments. Another reputable agency for top-end, short-term rentals is **Windows on Tuscany** (© 055-268-510; www.windowsontuscany.com). Online agencies **Cross Pollinate** (© 800-270-1190 in U.S., or 06-99369799; www.cross-pollinate.com) and **RentXpress** (© 646-568-5446 in the U.S.; www.rentxpress.com) also have good apartment portfolios covering Florence. **GoWithOh.com** has a user-friendly website that incorporates verified guest feedback into its portfolio of city apartments.

An alternative budget option is to stay in a religious house. A few monasteries and convents in the center receive guests for a modest fee, including the **Suore di Santa Elisabetta,** Viale Michelangiolo 46 (close to Piazza Ferrucci; © 055-681-1884; www.csse-roma.eu), in a colonial villa just south of the Ponte San Niccolò. The **Istituto Oblate dell'Assunzione,** Borgo Pinti 15 (© 055-2480-582), has simple, peaceful rooms in a Medici-era building ranged around a leafy courtyard garden in the lively eastern part of the city. The easiest way to book a monastery and convent itinerary in Florence and Tuscany is via U.S.–based agent **Monastery Stays** ★ (www.monasterystays.com). Most religious houses have a curfew, generally 11pm or midnight; the welcome is always friendly, as you would expect.

Tip: For basic grocery shopping in the center, try **Conad,** Via dei Servi 56R (© 055-280-110), or any central branch of **Supermercato il Centro.** Both the **Mercato Centrale** and **Mercato di Sant'Ambrogio** are well stocked with fresh produce (see "Florence's Best Markets," p. 97).

WHERE TO EAT

Florence is awash with restaurants, though many in the most touristy areas (around the Duomo, Piazza della Signoria, Piazza della Repubblica, and Ponte Vecchio) are of low quality, charge high prices, or both. We point out a few below that are worth a visit. The highest concentrations of excellent *ristoranti* and *trattorie* are around Santa Croce and Sant'Ambrogio, and across the river in the Oltrarno and San Frediano. Bear in mind that menus at restaurants in Tuscany can change weekly or even (at the very best places) daily.

Reservations are strongly recommended if you have your heart set on eating anywhere, especially at dinner on weekends.

Restaurants by Cuisine

CAFES
Caffetteria delle Oblate ★★, p. 100
Le Murate ★★, p. 101
Le Terrazze ★, p. 100
Rivoire ★, p. 100

CONTEMPORARY ITALIAN
Il Santo Bevitore ★, p. 68
Olio e Convivium ★★, p. 68

CONTEMPORARY TUSCAN
iO: Osteria Personale ★★, p. 68
Ora d'Aria ★★★, p. 61

FLORENTINE
Bondi ★, p. 64
Da Tito ★, p. 66
Il Magazzino ★, p. 68
Mario ★, p. 64
Nerbone ★, p. 65

FRENCH
La Brasserie ★★, p. 67

GELATO
Carapina ★★, p. 69
Gelateria della Passera ★★, p. 69
Gelateria de' Neri ★, p. 69
Il Procopio ★, p. 69
La Carraia ★★, p. 69
Le Parigine ★, p. 70
Vivaldi ★, p. 70

GRILL
Cipolla Rossa ★, p. 64

JAPANESE
Kome ★, p. 66

KOSHER
Ruth's ★, p. 67

LIGHT FARE
Antica Macelleria Falorni ★, p. 66
Bondi ★★, p. 64
I Fratellini ★, p. 64

MODERN ITALIAN
La Brasserie ★★, p. 67
Vagalume ★★, p. 67
Vivanda ★, p. 68

PIZZA
GustaPizza ★★, p. 69

SUSHI
Kome ★, p. 66

SEAFOOD
Pescheria San Pietro ★★, p. 65

TUSCAN
Antica Macelleria Falorni ★, p. 66
Cibrèo ★, p. 66
Cipolla Rossa ★, p. 64
Coquinarius ★, p. 64
Da Tito ★★, p. 66
Il Latini ★, p. 65
Osteria Pastella ★★, p. 65

VEGETARIAN
Brac ★★, p. 67
Ruth's ★, p. 67
Vivanda ★, p. 68

Near the Duomo & Piazza della Signoria

EXPENSIVE

Ora d'Aria ★★★ CONTEMPORARY TUSCAN If you want to see what the latest generation of Tuscan chefs can do in a kitchen, this place should top your list. The mood is modern and elegant, and never stuffy. Dishes are subtle and creative, and use traditional Tuscan ingredients in an original way. The menu changes daily, but expect the likes of spaghetti with extract of peppers, capers, and smoked ricotta or beef tartare marinated in beer with black truffle and roasted melon. If you can't stretch the budget for a dinner here, book a table at lunch to taste simpler, cheaper (12€–18€) dishes such

Florence Restaurants

Antica Macelleria
  Falorni **22**
Bondi **4**
Brac **23**
Carapina **18**
Cibrèo **29**
Cipolla Rossa **7**
Coquinarius **20**
Da Tito **10**
Gelateria
  della Passera **17**
Gelateria de' Neri **24**
GustaPizza **15**
I Fratellini **21**
Il Latini **8**
Il Magazzino **16**
Il Procopio **26**
Il Santo Bevitore **11**
iO: Osteria
  Personale **2**
Kome **25**
La Brasserie **30**

La Carraia **9**
Le Parigine **14**
Mario **6**
Nerbone **5**
Olio e Convivium **13**
Ora d'Aria **19**

Osteria Pastella **3**
Pescheria San Pietro **1**
Ruth's **27**
Vagalume **28**
Vivaldi **31**
Vivanda **12**

Where to Eat

FLORENCE

Via Guelfa
Via Faenza
Via Nazionale
Via Panicale
Piazza del Mercato Centrale
Piazza della Stazione
Via Luigi Alamanni
Via della Scala
Via Palazzuolo
Piazza dell'Unità Italiana
Piazza Via S. Antonino
Via S. Antonino
Cappelle Medicee
Piazza S. Lorenzo
S. Maria Novella
Piazza S. Maria Novella
Via de' Panzani
Via dei Banchi
Via del Giglio
San Lorenzo
Borgo S. Lorenzo
Via dei Cerretani
CENTRO
Piazza S. Giovanni
Ognissanti
Piazza d'Ognissanti
Lungarno Amerigo Vespucci
Borgo Ognissanti
Via de' Fossi
Via del Moro
V. della Spada
Via dei Sole
Via delle Belle Donne
Via dei Tornabuoni
Via Roma
Via d. Strozzi
Piazza della Repubblica
Piazza d. Pariene
Palazzo Strozzi
Arno
Piazza di Cestello
Lungarno Soderini
Piazza Goldoni
V. d. Parione
Via della Vigna Nuova
Palazzo Corsini
Santa Trinita
Piazza Trinita
Via Porta Rossa
Palazzo Davanzati
Borgo SS. Apostoli
Orsanmichele
V. Calimala
Ponte alla Carraia
San Borgo
Via San Giovanni
Via dell'Orto
Via del Leone
SAN FREDIANO
Frediano
Lungarno Guicciardini
Via Santo Spirito
Lung. Corsini
Lung. Acciaiuoli
S. Trinita
V. Por S. Maria
Ponte Vecchio
Loggia dei Lanzi
Piazza del Carmine
Via Santa Monaca
SANTO SPIRITO
Santo Spirito
Borgo San Jacopo
Ponte
Via di Camaldoli
Via del Leone
Santa Maria del Carmine
Via dell'Ardiglione
Via Sant'Agostino
Piazza S. Spirito
Via Maggio
V. Vellutini
Via Guicciardini
Piazza S. Felicita
Piazza S. Maria Soprarno
OLTRARNO
Piazza S. Tasso
Via de' Serragli
Via della Chiesa
Via del Campuccio
Borgo
Via Mazzetta
Via Tegolaio
Piazza dei Pitti
Palazzo Pitti
Viale Francesco Petrarca
Giardino Torrigiani
Via Romana
Forte di Belvedere
Giardino di Boboli
(Boboli Garden)

0 1/8 mile
0 200 meters

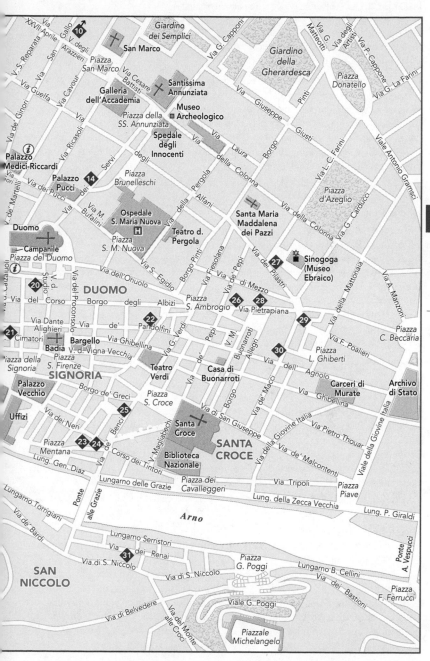

as cold salad of salt cod with Pratese vermouth and sweet potato, served in full-size or half-price "tapas" portions. Reservations are essential.

Via dei Georgofili 11–13R (off Via Lambertesca). ☎ **055-200-1699.** www.oradariaristorante.com. Main courses 32€–45€ (at dinner); tasting menu 70€–75€. Tues–Sat 12:30–2:30pm; Mon–Sat 7:30–10pm. Closed 3 weeks in Aug. Bus: C3 or D.

MODERATE

Coquinarius ★ TUSCAN   There is a regular menu here—pasta; mains such as pork filet with peaches, rosemary, and balsamic vinegar; traditional desserts. But the real pleasure is tucking into a couple of sharing plates and quaffing from an excellent wine list. Go for something from an extensive carpaccio list (beef, boar, octopus, salmon, and more) or pair a *misto di salumi e formaggi* (mixed Tuscan salami and cheeses) with a full-bodied red wine, to cut through the strong flavors of the deliciously fatty and salty pork and Tuscan sheep's milk cheese, *pecorino.*

Via delle Oche 11R. ☎ **055-230-2153.** www.coquinarius.com. Main courses 14€–18€. Daily 12:30–3:30pm and 6:30–10:30pm. Bus: C1 or C2.

INEXPENSIVE

I Fratellini ★ LIGHT FARE   This hole-in-the-wall has been serving food to go since 1875. The drill is simple: Choose your sandwich filling, pick a drink, then eat your fast-filled roll on the curb opposite or find a perch in a nearby piazza. There are around 30 fillings to choose from, including the usual Tuscan meats and cheeses—salami, *pecorino* cheese, cured ham—and more flamboyant combos such as goat cheese and Calabrian spicy salami or *bresaola* (air-dried beef) and wild rocket salad. A glass of wine to wash it down costs from 2€. No credit cards accepted.

Via dei Cimatori 38R (at corner of Via Calzaiuoli). ☎ **055-239-6096.** Sandwiches 3€. Daily 9:30am–dusk (July–Aug often closed Sun). Closed 2 weeks in mid-Aug. Bus: C2.

Near San Lorenzo & the Mercato Centrale

MODERATE

Cipolla Rossa ★ TUSCAN/GRILL   Carnivores, stop here. This modern trattoria near the Medici Chapels is tricked out in a half-butcher shop, half-enoteca way for a reason: This is a place for enjoying *ciccia e vino* (meat and wine). The setting, under a high ceiling vault on the ground floor of a *palazzo,* is ideal for devouring the likes of a *lombatina di vitella* (veal chop) expertly cooked on the grill. Cuts of *maiale* (pork) are equally good, as is the *bistecca alla fiorentina*—a large T-bone-like cut grilled on the bone and sold by weight (find out the price before ordering one).

Via dei Conti 53R. ☎ **055-214-210.** www.osteriacipollarossa.com. Main courses 14€–22€. Daily noon–3pm and 7–11pm. Bus: C2 or 22.

INEXPENSIVE

Bondi ★★ FLORENTINE/LIGHT FARE   To label this place behind the Mercato Centrale a mere sandwich joint is like describing the Super Bowl as "a football game." Bondi specializes in *piadine* in the Florentine style, prepped to order from a long list of traditional and unusual combinations. Order at the bar and take a seat on rustic wooden benches to wait the arrival of your flatbread (toasted or cold) filled with any number of combos, including radicchio and mozzarella, herrings and baby tomatoes, or eggplant *parmigiana.* Wash the *piadina* down with a glass of Chianti at 2€ a shot. No credit cards.

Via dell'Ariento 85. ☎ **055-287-390.** Sandwiches 2.50€–4€. Daily 11am–11pm. Bus: C1.

Mario ★ FLORENTINE   There is no doubt that this traditional market workers' trattoria is now firmly on the tourist trail. But Mario's clings to the traditions and ethos it adopted when it first fired up the kitchen burners 60 years ago. Food is simple and hearty and served at communal benches—["]check in" on arrival and you will be offered seats together wherever they come free. Think *zuppa di fagioli* (bean soup) followed by traditional Tuscan piquant beef stew, *peposo*. No reservations accepted.

Via Rosina 2R (north corner of Piazza Mercato Centrale). *C* **055-218-550.** www.trattoriamario.com. Main courses 7.50€–14€. Mon–Sat noon–3:30pm. Closed Aug. Bus: C1.

Nerbone ★ FLORENTINE Since 1872, this place has been serving simple Florentine food to go from a stall inside the covered market. It is famous for its *panino con bollito,* sliced beef boiled in its own juices and served warm in a roll. Nerbone is also strong on classic Florentine workers' food like *lampredotto* (stewed intestines) and *stracotto* (slow-cooked beef stew; usually Wed and Sat only). Get here early if you want to avoid the inevitable line—and even earlier if you want to sit at one of a handful of tables. No credit cards or reservations.

Inside the Mercato Centrale, Via dell'Ariento, stand no. 292 (ground floor). *C* **055-219-949.** Dishes 3.50€–8.50€. Mon–Sat 9am–2pm. Closed 3 weeks in Aug. Bus: C1.

Near Piazza Santa Trínita
MODERATE

Il Latini ★ TUSCAN This place is the closest you'll come in downtown Florence to the experience of digging into a hearty, gut-busting meal at a typical Tuscan countryside *osteria.* It's a place where everyone jams together under a canopy of hanging hams and makes like they're dining at a tavern on some saint's feast day. It sounds hokey, but it's a chaotic, spirited experience that truly does feel Italian—even if all the diners are tourists. But the food is first rate. Meats are all tasty, so if you are having trouble deciding between them, go for the *arrosto misto,* a mixed plate of juicy roast meats.

Via dei Palchetti 6R (off Via della Vigna Nuova). *C* **055-210-916.** www.illatini.com. Main courses 14€–22€. Tues–Sun 12:30–2:30pm and 7:30–10:30pm. Closed 2 weeks in Aug and Dec 24–Jan 6. Bus: C3, 6, or 11.

Near Santa Maria Novella
MODERATE

Osteria Pastella ★★ TUSCAN There is an air of sophistication about this place that opened near Piazza Santa Maria Novella in 2014. Pasta is handmade in the window, and the offering includes ribbons in classic boar or seafood sauces, as well as sublime *tortelloni* filled with 3 types of ricotta and served with a light seasonal sauce, perhaps butter and sage or artichokes. The *bistecca alla fiorentina* (grilled T-bonelike steak) is up there with the best in the city. Grand, upcycled dining room furniture, a complimentary glass of prosecco while you browse the menu, and a *chanteuse* background soundtrack set just the right mood for the classic Tuscan food. Live music most Fridays—piano, sax, and the like—hits just the right, classy note.

Via della Scala 17R. *C* **055-267-0240.** www.osteriapastella.it. Main courses 15€–23€. Daily 11:45am–3pm and 6:30–10:30pm. Closed 2 weeks in Nov. Bus: C2.

Pescheria San Pietro ★★ SEAFOOD It takes a big serving of confidence to open a seafood restaurant, on two floors, in one of Florence's less-fashionable quarters. This place, opened in 2014, has the chops (and the chefs) to pull it off. The fishy focus is unwavering: A route through the menu might take in tuna carpaccio, followed by *tagliatelle* with baby sardines and cherry tomatoes, then a *gran fritto* (mixed fry) of seafood and seasonal vegetables in light tempura batter—though you'd do well to manage that, because portions here are generous. With open kitchens, clanking cutlery, brisk service, and a great value "business lunch" (15€ all-in, including a glass of wine), San Pietro is classic seafood bistro all over.

Via Alamanni 7R. © **055-238-2749**. www.pescheriasanpietro.it. Main courses 14€–18€. Daily 11am–11pm. Bus: C2, D, 2, 13, 28, 29, 30, 35, 36, or 37/Tram: T1.

Near San Marco & Santissima Annunziata

San Marco is the place to head for *schiacciata alla fiorentina*, sweetish olive-oil flatbread loaded with savory toppings. You will find some of the best in the city at **Pugi,** Piazza San Marco 9b (© **055-280-981**; www.focacceria-pugi.it), open 7:45am (8:30am Sat) to 8pm Monday to Saturday, but closed most of August.

MODERATE

Da Tito ★ TUSCAN/FLORENTINE   Sure, they ham it up a little for the tourists, but every night feels like party night at one of central Florence's rare genuine trattorias. (And for that reason, it's usually packed—book ahead.) Both the welcome and the dishes are authentically Florentine, with a few modern Italian curveballs thrown in for variety: Start, perhaps, with the *risotto con piselli e guanciale* (rice with fresh peas and cured pork cheek) before going on to a traditional grill such as *lombatina di vitella* (veal chop steak). The neighborhood location, a 10-minute walk north of San Lorenzo, and mixed clientele keeps quality at Da Tito very consistent.

Via San Gallo 112R. © **055-472-475**. www.trattoriadatito.it. Main courses 12€–18€. Mon–Sat 12:30–2pm and 7:30–10:30pm. Bus: C1, 1, 7, or 25.

Near Santa Croce
EXPENSIVE

Cibrèo ★ TUSCAN   This restaurant blazed a trail when it opened in 1979, and it is still a place to discover reliable, high-end Florentine cooking overseen by head chef Fabio Picchi. Traditional Tuscan ingredients are prepared simply, combined creatively, and presented with a touch of style. Oh, and there is no pasta. But you won't miss it as you dig into the likes of *passata di pesce piccante* (spicy fish thick soup) followed by *piccione arrosto farcito di mostarda di frutta* (roast pigeon stuffed with fruit confit). Reservations are essential.

Via Andrea del Verrocchio 8R (next to Sant'Ambrogio Market). © **055-234-1100**. www.edizioniteatrodelsalecibreofirenze.it. Main courses 40€. Tues–Sun 12:50–2:30pm and 7–11:15pm. Closed last week in July to early Sept. Bus: C3.

Kome ★ JAPANESE/SUSHI   Perch at the downstairs counter to get the best out of this fashionable Japanese joint. The vibe and decor are more 21st century than Medici, with a contoured wooden ceiling sculpture and lots of glass. Grab the dishes as they spin around the bar on a conveyor belt; the sashimi, tempura, and *nigiri* are authentically flavored and prepped right in front of you. The set lunch of six sushi plates for 15€, including green tea, is a steal. No reservations at the sushi bar, but Kome's Japanese BBQ dining room does accept reservations.

Via de' Benci 41R. © **055-200-8009**. www.komefirenze.it. Sushi 3.50€–8€. Mon–Sat noon–3pm; daily 7–11pm. Bus: C3 or 23.

MODERATE

Antica Macelleria Falorni ★ TUSCAN/LIGHT FARE   "Eat at the butcher's"— it's a carnivore's dream. One of the Chianti's most famous butchers has set up in central Florence. As you might expect, it's all about the meat. The drill is informal: Order at the counter, cutlery is plastic, crockery is made from cardboard, and your

Where to Eat

FLORENCE

"dining table" is a marble mock-butchery counter. There is nothing synthetic about the food, however. Veal tartare is the star, and comes six ways, including topped with diced fennel salami and figs. Traditional Tuscan dishes include wild boar stew, *ribollita* (winter vegetable soup-stew), and *pappa al pomodoro* (thick tomato and bread soup). Portions are not large: This place is perfect for a light lunch.

Via Matteo Palmieri 35. ✆ **055-245-430.** www.falorni.it. Dishes 8€–14€. Tues–Sun 11am–10pm. Bus: C1 or C3.

Brac ★★ VEGETARIAN   An artsy cafe-bookshop for most of the day, at lunch and dinner this place turns into one of Florence's best spots for vegetarian or vegan food. There are plenty of seasonal salads and creative pasta dishes, but a *piatto unico* works out best value for hungry diners: one combo plate loaded with three dishes from the main menu, perhaps a tomato, onion, and oregano salad; potato and broccoli lasagne with ginger and parsley sauce; plus an eggplant and mozzarella *pane carasau* (Sardinian flatbread). The atmosphere, with tables ranged around an internal courtyard, is intimate and romantic—yet singletons won't feel at all out of place eating at the bar out front. Booking at dinner is a must in high season and on weekends.

Via dei Vagellai 18R. ✆ **055-094-4877.** www.libreriabrac.net. Main courses 10€–14€. Mon–Sat 10am–midnight, Sun noon–midnight. Bus: C1, C3, or 23.

La Brasserie ★★ FRENCH/MODERN ITALIAN   This peculiar, and successful, fusion of Paris and Florence opened in the increasingly buzzy streets around the Mercato di Sant'Ambrogio in 2013. There's a Parisian feel to the decor, with whitewashed walls, olive-green banquettes, French dressers, and wooden bistro furniture. The menu marries France and Florence, too: Begin, say, with a seasonal risotto, then follow it with kidneys in a mustard sauce. The drinks list takes its beers as seriously as its wines; ask for advice on pairing Tuscan microbrew labels like Monte Amiata and Piccolo Birrificio Clandestino with your *primo* and *secondo*.

Via de' Macci 77. ✆ **055-247-8326.** www.labrasseriefirenze.it. Main courses 16€–18€. Tues–Sun 12:30–2:30pm and 7:30–10:30pm. Bus: C2 or C3.

Ruth's ★ KOSHER/VEGETARIAN   Ruth's bills itself as a "kosher vegetarian" joint, but you will also find fish on the menu. It's small (around 12 tables), so book ahead if you want to be certain of a table. The interior is cafelike and informal, the menu likewise. Skip the Italian *primi* and go right for Eastern Mediterranean *secondi* such as vegetarian couscous with harissa or fish moussaka, a layered bake of eggplant, tomato, salmon, and spiced rice served with salad and *caponata* (a cold vegetable preserve). A rabbi from the adjacent synagogue oversees the kosher credentials.

Via Farini 2a. ✆ **055-248-0888.** www.kosheruth.com. Main courses 10€–18€. Sun–Fri 12:30–2:30pm; Sat–Thurs 7:30–10pm. Bus: C2 or C3.

Vagalume ★★ MODERN ITALIAN   The style at this place is *"tapas fiorentine"*—there are no "courses" and no pasta, and you compile a dinner from a range of good-sized dishes in any order you please. Dishes are seasonal and change daily, but could include a soufflé of gorgonzola, hazelnuts, and zucchini; stewed cuttlefish; or a marinated mackerel salad with fennel and orange. To go with the modern menu, there's modern, stripped-back decor, jazz and funk played in the background on an old record player, and an emphasis on beers—three on tap, plus a bottle list, which is strong on European styles. The wine list is short, but expertly chosen.

Via Pietrapiana 40R. ✆ **055-246-6740.** Dishes 8€–13€. Daily 6:30–11pm. Bus: C2 or C3.

In the Oltrarno, San Niccolò & San Frediano

EXPENSIVE

iO: Osteria Personale ★★ CONTEMPORARY TUSCAN There's a definite hipster atmosphere here, with the stripped brick walls and young staff, but the food ethos is unshakable. Ingredients are staunchly Tuscan and traditional, but combined in a way you may not have seen before, on a menu that rejects pasta. The menu is modular, and diners are free to combine seafood, meat, and vegetarian dishes in any order they choose. Perhaps tempura zucchini flowers stuffed with tomato sorbet followed by guinea-hen "Caesar salad" carbonara. Reservations are advisable.

Borgo San Frediano 167R (at Piazza di Verzaia). ✆ **055-933-1341.** www.io-osteriapersonale.it. Main courses 13€–21€; tasting menus 40€ 4 dishes, 55€ 6 dishes. Mon–Sat 7:30–10:30pm. Closed 10 days in Jan and all Aug. Bus: D or 6.

Olio e Convivium ★★ CONTEMPORARY ITALIAN You can assemble a gourmet picnic at this deli-diner, from a range of wines and counter ingredients, but the refined restaurant in the back is the star turn. Soft jazz provides the background as you navigate a menu that gives familiar ingredients a creative twist. Main courses might include pork filet cooked at low temperature and served in an orange sauce with beans wrapped in *guanciale* (cured pork cheek) or a *flan di stracchino con salsiccia croccante* (cheese soufflé with crisp-fried salami sausage). There's a short, well-chosen range of red and white wines by the glass, plus a long list of dessert wines.

Via Santo Spirito 6. ✆ **055-265-8198.** www.conviviumfirenze.it. Main courses 15€–24€. Tues–Sun noon–2:30pm and 7–10:30pm. Closed 2 weeks in mid-Aug. Bus: C3, D, 11, 36, or 37.

MODERATE

Il Magazzino ★ FLORENTINE A traditional osteria that specializes in the flavors of old Florence. It looks the part, too, with its terracotta tiled floor and barrel vault, chunky wooden furniture, and hanging lamps. If you dare, this is a place to try tripe or *lampredotto* (intestines), the traditional food of working Florentines, prepared expertly here in *polpettine* (little meatballs), boiled, or *alla fiorentina* (stewed with tomatoes and garlic). The rest of the menu is fairly carnivore-friendly, too: Follow *tagliatelle al ragù bianco* (pasta ribbons with a "white" meat sauce made with a little milk instead of tomatoes) with *guancia di vitello in agrodolce* (veal tongue stewed with baby onions in a sticky-sweet sauce).

Piazza della Passera 3. ✆ **055-215-969.** Main courses 9€–16€. Daily noon–3pm and 7:30–11pm. Bus: C3 or D.

Il Santo Bevitore ★ CONTEMPORARY ITALIAN There's no doubt this place has lost some of its in-the-know, local buzz. But the commitment to top produce served simply, and the trademark take on Tuscan ingredients, is unwavering: Reservations are still a must. Carefully sourced cold cuts make an ideal sharing *antipasto—prosciutto crudo* from Umbria, *pecorino* cheese from Pienza, southern Tuscany. Mains are eclectic and come in all appetite sizes, from a whole *burrata* (fresh cheese) served with spinach to pan-fried cockerel. There is a long, expertly compiled wine list, with about ten offered by the glass (a little pricey), plus craft beers.

Via Santo Spirito 66R (corner of Piazza N. Sauro). ✆ **055-211-264.** www.ilsantobevitore.com. Main courses 10€–24€. Mon–Sat 12:30–2:30pm; daily 7:30–11:30pm. Closed 10 days in mid-Aug. Bus: C3, D, 6, 11, 36, or 37.

Vivanda ★ MODERN ITALIAN/VEGETARIAN This small, modern deli-diner is ideal for a light, healthy lunch, or for a light dinner if you have eaten heartily in the middle of the day. Wines and vegetables are organic, pasta is made on the premises, and there's a good proportion of the menu that caters to vegetarians, vegans, and anyone on a gluten-free or celiac diet. Dishes aimed at the latter include a range of salads and couscous with seasonal vegetables. They also do delivery, and in high season run daily organic food and wine tastings.

Via Santa Monaca 7R. ✆ **055-238-1208.** www.vivandafirenze.it. Main courses 12€. Daily 11am–3pm and 6pm–midnight. Closed 2 weeks in Aug. Bus: D.

INEXPENSIVE

GustaPizza ★★ PIZZA   Florentines aren't known for their pizza-making skills, so I guess it's just as well that this place is run by Calabrians. Pizzas are in the Naples style, with fluffy crusts, doughy bases, and just the classic toppings on a menu that you could write on the back of a napkin: The likes of Margherita (mozzarella cheese, tomato, basil) and Napoli (cheese, tomatoes, anchovies, oregano, capers) are joined by a couple of simple specials, such as mozzarella and basil pesto. It is self-service, but there are a few tables if you want to eat with a knife and fork (no reservations). On hot evenings, take the pizza out to the steps of Santo Spirito, round the corner.

Via Maggio 46R. ✆ **055-285-068.** Pizzas 4.50€–8€. Tues–Sun 11:30am–3pm and 7–11pm. Closed 3 weeks in Aug. Bus: D, 11, 36, or 37.

Gelato

Florence has a fair claim to being the birthplace of gelato, and has some of Italy's best *gelaterie*—but many, many poor imitations, too. Steer clear of spots around the major attractions with air-fluffed mountains of ice cream and flavors so full of artificial colors that they glow in the dark. If you can see the Ponte Vecchio or Piazza della Signoria from the front door of the *gelateria,* you may want to move on. You may only have to walk a block, or down a side street, to find a genuine artisan in the gelato kitchen.

Carapina ★★   Militant seasonality ensures the fruit gelato here is the best in the *centro storico. Note:* This branch usually closes at 7pm.

Via Lambertesca 18R. ✆ **055-291-128.** www.carapina.it. Cone from 2.50€. Bus: C3 or D. Also at: Piazza Oberdan 2R (✆ 055-676-930).

Gelateria della Passera ★★   Milk-free water ices here are some of the most intensely flavored in the city, and relatively low in sugary sweetness. Try pink grapefruit or jasmine tea.

Via Toscanella 15R (at Piazza della Passera). ✆ **055-291-882.** www.gelaterialapassera.wordpress.com. Cone from 2€. Bus: C3, D, 11, 36, or 37.

Gelateria de' Neri ★   There's a large range of fruit, white, and chocolate flavors here, but nothing overelaborate. If the ricotta and fig flavor is on, you are in luck.

Via dei Neri 9R. ✆ **055-210-034.** Cone from 1.80€. Bus: C1, C3, or 23.

Il Procopio ★   Rich, elaborate concoctions are the thing here, including signature flavor "La Follia," a *crema* (cream) gelato with toasted almonds and caramelized figs, and Sachertorte, based on the sweet, spiced Austrian cake.

Via Pietrapiana 60R. ✆ **055-234-6014.** Cone from 2.20€. Bus: C1.

La Carraia ★★   Packed with locals late into the evening on summer weekends—for a good reason. The range is vast and quality is consistently high.

Piazza N. Sauro 25R. ✆ **055-280-695.** www.lacarraiagroup.info. Cone from 2.30€. Bus: C3, D, 6, 11, 36, or 37. Also at: Via de' Benci 24R (✆ 329-363-0069).

Le Parigine ★ Nothing overelaborate here, just fresh, flavorful gelato made with seasonal ingredients such as hazelnut, strawberry, and lemon. Closes at 8pm.

Via dei Servi 41R. ℂ **055-239-8470.** www.leparigine.it. Cone from 1.80€. Bus: C1.

Vivaldi ★ Relative newcomer in a handy spot for a burst of sustenance before or after a walk up to Piazzale Michelangiolo. The flavor range is not vast, but includes creative combos such as *latte e menta* (milk and mint).

Via dei Renai 15R. ℂ **338-472-1211.** Cone from 1.50€. Bus: D or 23.

EXPLORING FLORENCE

Most museums accept cash only at the door. Staff is usually happy to direct you to the nearest ATM *(un bancomat)*. Note, too, that the last admission to the museums and monuments listed is usually between 30 and 45 minutes before the final closing time.

Index of Attractions & Sites

Piazza del Duomo

The cathedral square is filled with tourists and caricature artists during the day, strolling crowds in the early evening, and knots of students strumming guitars on the Duomo's steps at night. It's always crowded and the piazza's vivacity and the glittering facades of the cathedral and Baptistery doors keep it an eternal Florentine sight. The square's closure to traffic in 2009 has made it a more welcoming space than ever.

Battistero (Baptistery) ★★★ RELIGIOUS SITE In choosing a date to mark the beginning of the Renaissance, art historians often seize on 1401, the year

DISCOUNT tickets FOR THE CITY

Visitors to Florence in mid-2013 got a shock when they went to purchase the discount **Firenze Card** (www.firenzecard.it). Launched in 2011 at 50€ per person, the card was suddenly priced at 72€, a hefty rise. So is it still a good buy? If you are plotting a busy, culture-packed break here, the Firenze Card works out to good value. If you only plan to see a few museums, don't purchase it.

But for culture vultures, the "new" card (still valid for 72 hr.), now allows entrance to around 60 sites; the list includes a handful that are free anyway, but also the Uffizi, Accademia, Cappella Brancacci, Palazzo Pitti, Brunelleschi's dome, San Marco, and many more paid-admission places around Florence. In fact, *everything* we recommend in this chapter except San Lorenzo and the Museo Gucci is included in the price of the card, as well as some sites in Fiesole (p. 95). It also gets you into much shorter lines, taking ticket prebooking hassles out of the equation—another saving of 3€ to 4€ for busy museums, above all the Uffizi and Accademia. It also includes 3 days' free bus travel (which you probably won't use) and free Wi-Fi (which you might).

Amici degli Uffizi membership (www.amicidegliuffizi.it) is the ticket to choose if you want to delve deeper into a smaller range of Florence museums, especially if you want to make multiple visits to the vast collections at the Uffizi and Palazzo Pitti, or if you plan on visiting Florence more than once in a calendar year. It costs 60€ for adults, 40€ anyone 26 and under, 100€ for a family, and is valid for a calendar year (Jan 1–Dec 31). It secures admission (without major queuing) into 15 or so state museums, including the Uffizi, Accademia, San Marco, Palazzo Davanzati, Bargello, Cappelle Medicee, and everything at the Palazzo Pitti. Two children go free with a family ticket, and membership permits multiple visits. Join Tuesday through Saturday inside Uffizi entrance no. 2; take photo I.D., plus a little patience because the membership desk is not always manned.

The Opera del Duomo has also dispensed with single entry tickets to its sites in favor of a value *biglietto cumulativo*, the **Grande Museo del Duomo** ticket. It covers Brunelleschi's dome, the Baptistery, Campanile di Giotto, Museo Storico, and archaeological excavations of Santa Reparata (inside the cathedral) for 10€, free for accompanied children up to age 14. You have 24 hours from first use to enter them all. Buy it at the ticket office almost opposite the Baptistery, on the north side of Piazza San Giovanni. See **www.ilgrandemuseodel duomo.it** for more details.

Florence's powerful wool merchants' guild held a contest to decide who would receive the commission to design the **North Doors ★★** of the Baptistery to match its Gothic **South Doors,** cast 65 years earlier by Andrea Pisano. The era's foremost Tuscan sculptors each cast a bas-relief bronze panel depicting his own vision of "The Sacrifice of Isaac." Twenty-two-year-old Lorenzo Ghiberti, competing against the likes of Donatello, Jacopo della Quercia, and Filippo Brunelleschi, won. He spent the next 21 years casting 28 bronze panels and building his doors.

The result so impressed the merchants' guild—not to mention the public and Ghiberti's fellow artists—they asked him in 1425 to do the **East Doors ★★★,** facing the Duomo, this time giving him the artistic freedom to realize his Renaissance ambitions. Twenty-seven years later, just before his death, Ghiberti finished 10 dramatic lifelike Old Testament scenes in gilded bronze, each a masterpiece of

Florence Attractions

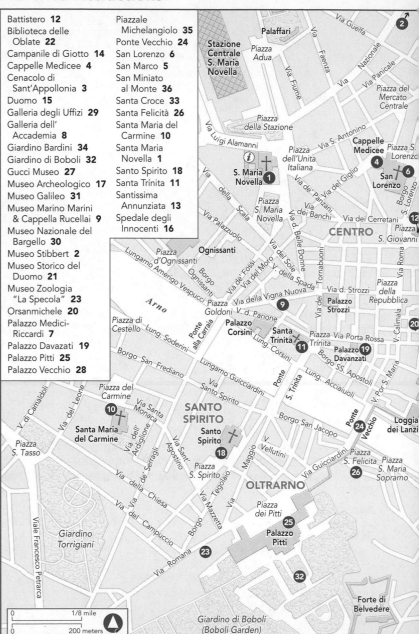

4

FLORENCE | Exploring Florence

72

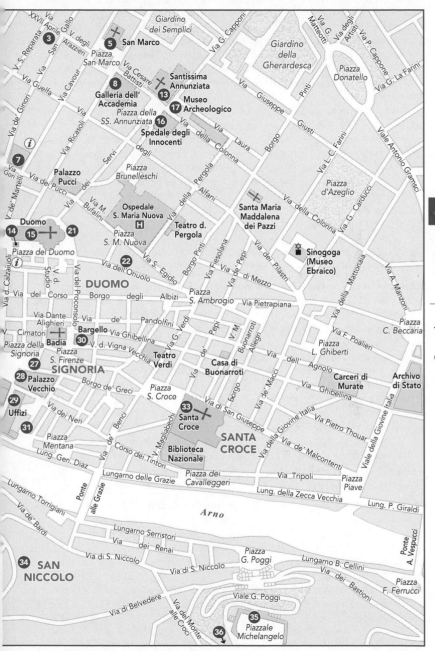

Renaissance sculpture and some of the finest examples of low-relief perspective in Italian art. Each illustrates episodes in the stories of Noah (second down on left), Moses (second up on left), Solomon and the Queen of Sheba (bottom right), and others. The panels mounted here are excellent copies; the originals are in the **Museo Storico dell'Opera del Duomo** (see below). Years later, Michelangelo was standing before these doors and someone asked his opinion. His response sums up Ghiberti's accomplishment as no art historian could: "They are so beautiful that they would grace the entrance to Paradise." They've been nicknamed the Gates of Paradise ever since.

The building itself is ancient. It is first mentioned in city records in the 9th century, and was probably already 300 years old by then. Its interior is ringed with columns pilfered from ruined Roman buildings and is a spectacle of mosaics above and below. The floor was inlaid in 1209, and the ceiling was covered between 1225 and the early 1300s with glittering **mosaics ★★**. Most were crafted by Venetian or Byzantine-style workshops, which worked off designs drawn by the era's best artists. Coppo di Marcovaldo drew sketches for the over 7.8m-high (26-ft.) "Christ in Judgment" and the "Last Judgment" that fills over a third of the ceiling. Bring binoculars (and a good neck masseuse) if you want a closer look.

Piazza San Giovanni. ✆ **055-230-2885.** www.ilgrandemuseodelduomo.it. Admission included with 10€ Grande Museo del Duomo ticket; see above. Mon–Sat 11:15am–6:30pm (June–Sept Thurs–Sat until 10:30pm); Sun and 1st Sat of month 8:30am–2pm. Bus: C2, 14, or 23.

Campanile di Giotto (Giotto's Bell Tower) ★★ HISTORIC SITE

In 1334, Giotto started the cathedral bell tower but completed only the first two levels before his death in 1337. He was out of his league with the engineering aspects of architecture, and the tower was saved from falling by Andrea Pisano, who doubled the thickness of the walls. Andrea, a master sculptor of the Pisan Gothic school, also changed the design to add statue niches—he even carved a few of the statues himself—before quitting the project in 1348. Francesco Talenti finished the job between 1350 and 1359.

The **reliefs** and **statues** in the lower levels—by Andrea Pisano, Donatello, Luca della Robbia, and others—are all copies; the weatherworn originals are housed in the Museo Storico dell'Opera (see below). We recommend climbing the 414 steps to the top of the tower; the **view ★★** is memorable as you ascend, and offers the best close-up shot in the entire city of Brunelleschi's dome. Queues are also much shorter than the often epic lines to climb Brunelleschi's dome itself (see below).

Piazza del Duomo. ✆ **055-230-2885.** www.ilgrandemuseodelduomo.it. Admission included with 10€ Grande Museo del Duomo ticket; see above. Daily 8:30am–6:50pm. Bus: C2.

Duomo (Cattedrale di Santa Maria del Fiore) ★★ CATHEDRAL

By the late 13th century, Florence was feeling peevish: Its archrivals Siena and Pisa sported huge, flamboyant new cathedrals while it was saddled with the tiny 5th- or 6th-century Santa Reparata. So, in 1296, the city hired Arnolfo di Cambio to design a new Duomo, and he raised the facade and the first few bays before his death (probably around 1310). Work continued under the auspices of the Wool Guild and architects Giotto di Bondone (who concentrated on the bell tower) and Francesco Talenti (who expanded the planned size and finished up to the drum of the dome). The facade we see today is a neo-Gothic composite designed by Emilio de Fabris and built from 1871 to 1887.

The Duomo's most distinctive feature is its enormous **dome ★★★** (or *cupola*), which dominates the skyline and is a symbol of Florence itself. The raising of this dome, the largest in the world in its time, was no mean architectural feat, tackled by

ONE MAN & HIS dome

Filippo Brunelleschi, a diminutive man whose ego was as big as his talent, managed in his arrogant, quixotic, and brilliant way to reinvent Renaissance architecture. Having been beaten by Lorenzo Ghiberti in the contest to cast the Baptistery doors (see above), Brunelleschi resolved he would rather be Florence's top architect than its second-best sculptor and took off for Rome to study the buildings of the ancients. On returning to Florence, he combined subdued gray *pietra serena* stone with smooth white plaster to create airy arches, vaults, and arcades of perfect classical proportions in his own variant on the ancient Roman orders of architecture. He designed Santo Spirito, the elegant geometry of the Ospedale degli Innocenti, and a new sacristy for San Lorenzo. But his greatest achievement was erecting the dome over Florence's cathedral.

The Duomo, then the world's largest church, had already been built, but nobody had been able to figure out how to cover the daunting space over its center without spending a fortune—plus no one was sure whether they could create a dome that would hold up under its own weight. Brunelleschi insisted he knew how, and once granted the commission, revealed his ingenious plan—which may have been inspired by close study of Rome's Pantheon.

He built the dome in two shells, the inner one thicker than the outer, both shells thinning as they neared the top, thus leaving the center hollow and removing a good deal of the weight. He also planned to construct the dome of giant vaults with ribs crossing them, with each of the stones making up the actual fabric of the dome being dovetailed. In this way, the walls of the dome would support themselves as they were erected. In the process of building, Brunelleschi found himself as much an engineer as architect, constantly designing winches, cranes, and hoists to carry the materials (plus food and drink) faster and more efficiently up to the level of the workmen.

His finished work speaks for itself, 45m (148 ft.) wide at the base and 90m (295 ft.) high from drum to lantern. For his achievement, Brunelleschi was accorded a singular honor: He is the only person ever buried in Florence's cathedral.

Filippo Brunelleschi between 1420 and 1436 (see "One Man & His Dome," above). You can climb up between its twin shells for one of the classic panoramas across the city—something that is not recommended for claustrophobes or anyone lacking a head for heights. At the base of the dome, just above the drum, Baccio d'Agnolo began adding a balcony in 1507. One of the eight sides was finished by 1515, when someone asked Michelangelo—whose artistic opinion was by this time taken as cardinal law—what he thought of it. The master reportedly scoffed, "It looks like a cricket cage." Work was halted, and to this day the other seven sides remain rough brick.

The cathedral is rather Spartan inside, though check out the fake equestrian "statue" of English mercenary soldier Sir John Hawkwood painted on the north wall in 1436, by Paolo Uccello.

Piazza del Duomo. © **055-230-2885.** www.ilgrandemuseodelduomo.it. Admission to church free; Santa Reparata excavations and cupola included with 10€ Grande Museo del Duomo ticket (see above). Church Mon–Wed and Fri 10am–5pm; Thurs 10am–4:30pm (July–Sept until 5pm, May and Oct until 4pm); Sat 10am–4:45pm; Sun 1:30–4:45pm. Cupola Mon–Fri 8:30am–6:20pm; Sat 8:30am–5pm; closed during religious festivals. Bus: C1, C2, 14, or 23.

Museo Storico dell'Opera del Duomo (Cathedral Works Museum) ★
ART MUSEUM For now, the excellent Cathedral Museum displays a somewhat emasculated version of its collection. The site (where Michelangelo worked on "David") is undergoing major redevelopment, in time to reopen with twice as much floor space during 2015. However, the museum's prize exhibit is on show, after a restoration completed in 2012: the original **Gates of Paradise** ★★★ cast by Lorenzo Ghiberti in the early 1400s (see "Baptistery," above). These doors will form the centerpiece of a reconstruction of the part of the piazza they were designed to adorn when the new museum is complete. You can stand and gaze, and read from interpretation panels that explain the Old Testament scenes.

Until later in 2015, the only other major work on display, halfway up the staircase, is a (mostly) Michelangelo **"Pietà"** ★★ that nearly wasn't—the artist's final work. Early on in the process he had told students that he wanted this "Pietà" to stand at his tomb, but when he found an imperfection in the marble, he began attacking it with a hammer (look at Christ's left arm). The master never returned to the work, but his students later repaired the damage. The figure of Nicodemus was untouched, legend has it, because this was a self-portrait of the artist—a Michelangelo legend that, for once, is probably true.

Piazza del Duomo 9 (behind back of the cathedral). (C) **055-230-2885.** www.ilgrandemuseodel duomo.it. Admission included with 10€ Grande Museo del Duomo ticket; see above. Mon–Sat 9am–6:50pm; Sun 9am–1pm. Bus: C1, C2, 14, or 23.

Around Piazza della Signoria & Santa Trínita

Galleria degli Uffizi (Uffizi Gallery) ★★★ ART MUSEUM There is no collection of Renaissance art on the planet that can match the Uffizi. Period. For all its crowds and other inconveniences, the Uffizi remains a must-see.

And what will you see? Some 60-plus rooms and marble corridors—built in the 16th century as the Medici's private office complex, or *uffici*—all jam-packed with famous paintings, among them Giotto's "Ognissanti Madonna," Botticelli's "Birth of Venus," Leonardo da Vinci's "Annunciation," Michelangelo's "Holy Family," and many, many more.

Start with **Room 2** for a look at the pre-Renaissance, Gothic style of painting. First, compare teacher and student as you examine Cimabue's "Santa Trínita Maestà" painted around 1280, and Giotto's **"Ognissanti Madonna"** ★★★ done in 1310. The similar subject and setting for both paintings allows the viewer to see how Giotto transformed Cimabue's iconlike Byzantine style into something more real and human. Giotto's Madonna actually looks like she's sitting on a throne, her clothes emphasizing the curves of her body, whereas Cimabue's Madonna and angels float in space, looking like portraits on coins, with flattened positioning and stiff angles. Also worth a looksee: Duccio's **"Rucellai Madonna"** ★ (1285), one of the founding works of the ethereal Sienese School of painting.

Room 3 showcases the Sienese School at its peak, with Simone Martini's dazzling **"Annunciation"** ★★ (1333) and Ambrogio Lorenzetti's "Presentation at the Temple" (1342). The Black Death of 1348 wiped out this entire generation of Sienese painters, and most of that city's population along with them. **Room 6** shows Florentine painting at its most decorative, in the style known as "International Gothic." The iconic work is Gentile da Fabriano's **"Procession of the Magi"** ★★★ (1423). The line to see the newborn Jesus is full of decorative and comic elements, and is even longer than the one outside the Uffizi.

Exploring Florence

FLORENCE

Room 8 contains the unflattering profiles of Duke Federico da Montefeltro of Urbino and his duchess, done by **Piero della Francesca** in 1472. The subjects are portrayed in an unflinchingly realistic way. The duke, in particular, exposes his warts and his crooked nose, broken in a tournament. This focus on the earthly, rather than on the Christian, elements harkens back to the teachings of classical Greek and Roman times, and is made all the more vivid by depiction (on the back) of the couple riding chariots driven by the humanistic virtues of faith, charity, hope, and modesty for her; prudence, temperance, fortitude, and justice for him.

Also here are works by **Filippo Lippi** from the mid–15th century. His most celebrated panel, **"Madonna and Child with Two Angels"** ★★, dates from around 1465. The background, with distant mountains on one side and water on the other, framing the portrait of a woman's face, was shamelessly stolen by Leonardo da Vinci 40 years later for his "Mona Lisa." Lippi's work was also a celebrity scandal. The woman who modeled for Mary was said to be Filippo's lover—a would-be nun called Lucrezia Buti whom he had spirited away from her convent before she could take vows—and the child looking toward the viewer the product of their union. That son, Filippino Lippi, became a painter in his own right, and some of his works hang in the same room. However, it was Filippo's student (who would, in turn, become Filippino's teacher) who would go on to become one of the most famous artists of the 15th century. His name was Botticelli.

Rooms 10 to 14—still collectively numbered as such, even though the walls were knocked down in 1978 to make one large room—are devoted to the works of Sandro Filipepi, better known by his nickname "Little Barrels," or Botticelli. His 1485 **"Birth of Venus"** ★★ hangs like a highway billboard you have seen a thousand times. Venus's pose is taken from classical statues, while the winds Zephyr and Aura blowing her to shore, and the muse welcoming her, are from Ovid's "Metamorphosis." Botticelli's 1478 **"Primavera"** ★★★, its dark, bold colors a stark contrast to the filmy, pastel "Venus," defies definitive interpretation (many have tried). But again it features Venus (center), alongside Mercury, with the winged boots, the Three Graces, and the goddess Flora. Next to it Botticelli's "Adoration of the Magi" contains a self-portrait of the artist—he's the one in yellow on the far right.

Leonardo da Vinci's **"Annunciation"** ★★★ anchors **Room 15.** In this painting, though completed in the early 1470s while Leonardo was still a student in Verrocchio's workshop, Da Vinci's ability to orchestrate the viewer's focus is masterful: The line down the middle of the brick corner of the house draws your glance to Mary's delicate fingers, which themselves point along the top of a stone wall to the angel's two raised fingers. Those, in turn, draw attention to the mountain in the center of the two parallel trees dividing Mary from the angel, representing the gulf between the worldly and the spiritual. Its perspective was painted to be viewed from the lower right.

Reopened after restoration in 2012, the **Tribuna** ★ is an octagonal room added to the Uffizi floor plan by Francesco I in the 1580s. Although visitors can no longer walk through it, you can view the mother-of-pearl ceiling and the **"Medici Venus"** ★, a Roman statue dating from the 1st century B.C., from outside.

As soon as you cross to the Uffizi's west wing—past picture windows with views of the Arno River to one side and the perfect, Renaissance perspective of the Uffizi's little piazza to the other—you're walloped with another line of masterpieces. However, it is impossible to be certain of the precise layout: The museum is undergoing a major facelift, to create the "New Uffizi." Among the highlights of this "second half" is Michelangelo's 1505–08 **"Holy Family"** ★. The twisting shapes of Mary, Joseph, and Jesus recall those in the Sistine Chapel in Rome for their sculpted nature and the bright

4

FLORENCE | Exploring Florence

If you're not buying a cumulative ticket (see "Discount Tickets for the City," above), you should bypass the hours-long line at the Uffizi by reserving a ticket and an entry time in advance by calling **Firenze Musei** at ℰ **055-294-883** (Mon–Fri 8:30am–6:30pm; Sat until 12:30pm) or visiting www.firenzemusei.it (you may need to have patience with its website, however). You can also reserve for the Accademia Gallery (another interminable line, to see "David"), as well as the Galleria Palatina in the Pitti Palace, the Bargello, and several others—but usually only the Uffizi and Accademia are *essential*. There's a 3€ fee (4€ for the Uffizi or Accademia); you can pay by credit card. You can also reserve in person, in Florence, at a kiosk in the facade of Orsanmichele, on Via dei Calzaiuoli (closed Sun), or a desk inside bookshop **Libreria My Accademia,** Via Ricasoli 105R (closed Mon; ℰ **055-288-310;** www.myaccademia. com), almost opposite the Accademia. You can also reserve, for the Uffizi only, at the Uffizi itself; do so at the teller window inside entrance number 2. Ticket collection point at the Uffizi is across the piazza, at entrance number 3.

colors. The torsion and tensions of the painting (and other Michelangelo works) inspired the next generation of Florentine painters, known as the **Mannerists.** Andrea Del Sarto, Rosso Fiorentino, and Pontormo are all represented in the revamped **Sale Rosse (Red Rooms),** opened downstairs in 2012. Here too, the Uffizi has a number of Raphaels, including his recently restored and often-copied **"Madonna of the Goldfinch"** ★★, with a background landscape lifted from Leonardo and Botticelli.

Titian's reclining nude **"Venus of Urbino"** ★★ is another highlight of the Uffizi's later works. It's no coincidence that the edge of the curtain, the angle of her hand and leg, and the line splitting floor and bed all intersect in the forbidden part of her body. The Uffizi also owns a trio of paintings by Caravaggio, notably his enigmatic **"Bacchus"** ★, and many by the 17th- to 18th-century *caravaggieschi* artists who copied his *chiaroscuro* (bright light and dark shadows) style of painting. Greatest among them was Artemisia Gentileschi, a rare female baroque painter. Her brilliant **"Judith Slaying Holofernes"** ★ (ca. 1612), is one of the more brutal, bloody paintings in the gallery.

Rooms 46 to 55 also opened in 2012 to showcase the works of foreign painters in the Uffizi—the museum owns a vast and varied collection, much of which lay in storage until the opening of these new galleries. The best among these so-called *Sale Blu,* or "Blue Rooms," is the Spanish gallery, with works by Goya, El Greco's "St. John the Evangelist" (1600), and Velázquez's **"Self-Portrait"** ★. **Room 49** displays two of Rembrandt's most familiar self-portraits.

If you find yourself flagging at any point (it happens to us all), there is a **coffee shop** at the far end of the west wing. Prices are in line with the piazza below, plus you get a great close-up of the Palazzo Vecchio's facade from the terrace. Fully refreshed, you can return to discover works by the many great artists we didn't have space to cover here: Cranach and Dürer; Giorgione, Bellini, and Mantegna; Uccello, Masaccio, Bronzino, and Veronese. The collection goes on and on (there are countless original Roman statues, too). There is nowhere like it in Italy, or the world.

Piazzale degli Uffizi 6 (off Piazza della Signoria). ℰ **055-238-8651.** www.uffizi.firenze.it. (To reserve tickets, see below.) Admission 6.50€ (11€ during compulsory temporary exhibition). Tues–Sun 8:15am–6:50pm. Bus: C1, C2, C3, or D.

Gucci Museo ★ MUSEUM This private museum tells the story of the Gucci empire, from humble beginning to worldwide megabrand. Guccio Gucci got his flash of inspiration while working as a lift boy at London's Savoy Hotel: His first product designs were for travel luggage to suit the lives and lifestyles of the kinds of people he would meet in the lift every day.

Of course, as well as the history, the museum's 3 floors are packed with swag that carries the famous "double-G" logo, including a limited edition 1979 Cadillac Seville—only 200 were ever made. You'll see day bags and duffle bags—and photos of Audrey Hepburn, David Niven, Sophia Loren, and Princess Grace in Gucci gear—plus there's a room devoted to revering the dresses that have graced the reddest of red carpets.

The museum places Gucci right at the heart of Florence's artisan traditions—which of course, is where it belongs.

Piazza della Signoria. ✆ **055-7592-3302.** www.guccimuseo.com. Admission 6€. Daily 10am–8pm. Bus: C1 or C2.

Museo Nazionale del Bargello (Bargello Museum) ★★ MUSEUM This is the most important museum anywhere for Renaissance **sculpture**—and often inexplicably quieter than other museums in the city. In a far cry from its original use as the city's prison, torture chamber, and execution site, the Bargello now stands as a three-story art museum containing some of the best works of Michelangelo, Donatello, and Ghiberti, as well as of their most successful Mannerist successor, Giambologna.

In the ground-floor Michelangelo room, you'll witness the variety of his craft, from the whimsical 1497 **"Bacchus"** ★★ to the severe, unfinished "Brutus" of 1540. "Bacchus," created when Michelangelo was just 22, really looks like he's drunk, leaning back a little too far, with his head off kilter, with a cupid about to bump him over. Nearby is Giambologna's twisting **"Mercury"** ★, who looks like he's about to take off from the ground, propelled by the breath of Zephyr.

Upstairs an enormous vaulted hall is filled, among other beauties, with some of Donatello's most accomplished sculptures, including his original "Marzocco" (from outside the Palazzo Vecchio; p. 82), and **"St. George"** ★ from a niche on the outside of Orsanmichele. Notable among them is his **"David"** ★★ (which might correctly be named "Mercury"), done in 1440, the first freestanding nude sculpture since Roman times. The classical detail of these sculptures, as well as their naturalistic poses and reflective mood, is the essence of the Renaissance style.

On the back wall are the contest entries submitted by Ghiberti and Brunelleschi for the commission to do the Baptistery doors in 1401. Both had the "Sacrifice of Isaac" as their biblical theme, and both displayed an innovative use of perspective. Ghiberti won the contest, perhaps because his scene was more thematically unified. Brunelleschi could have ended up a footnote in the art history books, but instead he gave up the chisel and turned his attentions to architecture instead, which turned out to be a wise move (see "One Man & His Dome," p. 75).

Via del Proconsolo 4. ✆ **055-238-8606.** www.polomuseale.firenze.it. Admission 4€ (7€ during compulsory temporary exhibition). Daily 8:15am–1:50pm (until 5pm during exhibition). Closed 1st, 3rd, and 5th Sun, and 2nd and 4th Mon of each month. Bus: C1 or C2.

Orsanmichele ★★ RELIGIOUS SITE/ARCHITECTURE This bulky structure halfway down Via dei Calzaiuoli looks more like a Gothic warehouse than a church—which is exactly what it was, built as a granary and grain market in 1337. After a miraculous image of the Madonna supposedly appeared on a column inside, however,

PIAZZA DELLA signoria

When the medieval Guelph party finally came out on top after their political struggle with the Ghibellines, they razed part of the old city center to build a new palace for civic government. It's said the Guelphs ordered architect Arnolfo di Cambio to build what we now call the **Palazzo Vecchio** (see below) in the corner of this space, but to be careful that not 1 inch of the building sat on the cursed former Ghibelline land. This odd legend was probably fabricated to explain Arnolfo's quirky off-center architecture.

The space around the *palazzo* became the new civic center of town, L-shaped **Piazza della Signoria ★★**, named after the oligarchic ruling body of the medieval city (the "Signoria"). Today, it's an outdoor sculpture gallery, teeming with tourists, postcard stands, horses and buggies, and expensive outdoor cafes.

The statuary on the piazza is particularly beautiful, starting on the far left (as you're facing the Palazzo Vecchio) with Giambologna's equestrian statue of "Grand Duke Cosimo I" (1594). To its right is one of Florence's favorite sculptures to hate, the **"Fontana del Nettuno"** ("Neptune Fountain"; 1560–75), created by Bartolomeo Ammannati as a tribute to Cosimo I's naval ambitions but nicknamed by the Florentines "Il Biancone," or "Big Whitey." The **porphyry plaque** set in the ground in front of the fountain marks the site where puritanical monk Savonarola held the Bonfire of the Vanities: With his fiery apocalyptic preaching, he whipped the Florentines into a reformist frenzy, and hundreds filed into this piazza, arms loaded with paintings, clothing, and other effects that represented their "decadence." They consigned it all to the flames. However, after a few years the pope (not amused by Savonarola's criticisms) excommunicated first the monk and then the entire city for supporting him. On May 23, 1498, Florentines decided they'd had enough of the rabid-dog monk, dragged him and two followers to the torture chamber, pronounced them heretics, and led them into the piazza for one last day of fire and brimstone. In the very spot

the lower level was turned into a shrine and chapel. The city's merchant guilds each undertook the task of decorating one of the outside Gothic tabernacles around the lower level with a statue of their guild's patron saint. Masters such as Ghiberti, Donatello, Verrocchio, and Giambologna all cast or carved masterpieces to set here (those remaining are mostly copies, including Donatello's "St. George").

In the dark interior, the elaborate Gothic **Tabernacle ★** (1349–59) by Andrea Orcagna protects a luminous 1348 "Madonna and Child" painted by Giotto's student Bernardo Daddi, to which miracles were ascribed during the Black Death of 1348–50.

Every Monday (9am–5pm) you can access the upper floors, which house many of the original sculptures that once lived in Orsanmichele's exterior niches. Among the treasures of the so-called **Museo di Orsanmichele ★** are a trio of bronzes: Ghiberti's "St. John the Baptist" (1412–16), the first life-size bronze of the Renaissance; Verrocchio's "Incredulity of St. Thomas" (1483); and Giambologna's "St. Luke" (1602). Climb up one floor farther, to the top, for an unforgettable 360° **panorama ★★** of the city. The Museo is staffed by volunteers, so donate if you are able.

Via Arte della Lana 1. *©* **055-210-305.** Free admission. Daily 10am–5pm. Bus: C2.

where they once burned their luxurious belongings, they put the torch to Savonarola himself. The event is marked by an anonymous painting kept in Savonarola's old cell in San Marco (p. 88) and by the plaque here.

To the right of Neptune is a long, raised platform fronting the Palazzo Vecchio known as the *arringheria*, from which soapbox speakers would lecture to crowds before them (we get our word "harangue" from this). On its far left corner is a copy (original in the Bargello; see above) of Donatello's **"Marzocco,"** symbol of the city, with a Florentine lion resting his raised paw on a shield emblazoned with the city's emblem, the *giglio* (lily). To its right is another Donatello replica, **"Judith Beheading Holofernes."** Farther down is a man who needs little introduction, Michelangelo's **"David,"** a 19th-century copy of the original now in the Accademia. Near enough to David to look truly ugly in comparison is Baccio Bandinelli's **"Heracles"** (1534). Poor Bandinelli was trying to copy Michelangelo's muscular male

form but ended up making his Heracles merely lumpy.

At the piazza's south end is one of the square's earliest and prettiest embellishments, the **Loggia dei Lanzi ★★** (1376–82), named after the Swiss guard of lancers (*lanzi*) whom Cosimo de' Medici stationed here. The airy loggia was probably built on a design by Andrea Orcagna—spawning another of its many names, the Loggia di Orcagna (yet another is the Loggia della Signoria). At the front left stands Benvenuto Cellini's masterpiece in bronze, **"Perseus" ★★★** (1545), holding aloft the severed head of Medusa. On the far right is Giambologna's **"Rape of the Sabines" ★★**, one of the most successful Mannerist sculptures in existence, and a piece you must walk all the way around to appreciate, catching the action and artistry of its spiral design from different angles. Talk about moving it indoors, away from the elements, continues . . . but for now, it's still here.

Palazzo Davanzati ★★ PALACE/MUSEUM   One of the best-preserved 14th-century palaces in the city is open as a museum dedicated to domestic life in the medieval and Renaissance period—for nobles and the wealthy, at least. It was originally built for the Davizzi family in the mid-1300s, then bought by the Davanzati clan; check out the latter's family tree, dating back to the 1100s, on the wall of the ground-floor courtyard.

The palace's painted wooden ceilings and murals have aged well (even surviving damage during World War II), but the emphasis remains not on the decor but on providing visitors with an insight into medieval life for a noble Florentine family: feasts and festivities in the Sala Madornale; the private, internal well for secure water supply when things got sticky for the family or city; and magnificent bedchamber frescoes dating to the 1350s, which recount, comic-strip style, "The Chatelaine of Vergy," a 13th-century morality tale.

An interesting footnote: It was a New York auction of furnishings from this palace, in 1916, that helped spread the "Florentine style" in U.S. interior design circles.

Via Porta Rossa 13. ☏ **055-238-8610.** www.polomuseale.firenze.it. Admission 2€. Daily 8:15am–1:50pm. Closed 2nd and 4th Sun, and 1st, 3rd, and 5th Mon of each month. Bus: C2.

Vasari's Corridor

The enclosed passageway that runs along the top of the Ponte Vecchio is part of the **Corridoio Vasariano (Vasari Corridor)** ★★, a private elevated link between the Palazzo Vecchio and Palazzo Pitti, and now hung with the world's best collection of artists' self-portraits. Duke Cosimo I found the idea of mixing with the hoi polloi on the way to work rather distressing—and there was a credible threat of assassination—and so commissioned Vasari to design his V.I.P. route in 1565. He built it in less than a year. It's often possible to walk the corridor, although closures for restoration work are common. **Context Travel** (p. 94) operates an excellent guided walk through the corridor, costing 100€ per person. **CAF Tours** (p. 94) runs a regular half-day tour of the corridor and Uffizi for 130€, or a short walk along the corridor for 55€. Booking in advance for any corridor tour is essential.

Palazzo Vecchio ★ PALACE/MUSEUM Florence's fortresslike town hall was built from 1299 to 1302 on the designs of Arnolfo di Cambio, Gothic master builder of the city. The palace was home to the various Florentine republican governments (and is today to the municipal government). Cosimo I and his ducal Medici family moved to the *palazzo* in 1540 and engaged in massive redecoration. Michelozzo's 1453 **courtyard** ★ was left architecturally intact but frescoed by Vasari with scenes of Austrian cities to celebrate the 1565 marriage of Francesco de' Medici and Joanna of Austria.

The grand staircase leads up to the **Sala dei Cinquecento,** named for the 500-man assembly that met here in the pre-Medici days of the Florentine Republic, and site of the greatest fresco cycle that ever wasn't. Leonardo da Vinci was commissioned in 1503–05 to paint one long wall with a battle scene celebrating a Florentine victory at the 1440 Battle of Anghiari. He was always trying new methods and materials and decided to mix wax into his pigments. Leonardo had finished painting part of the wall, but it wasn't drying fast enough, so he brought in braziers stoked with hot coals to try to hurry the process. As others watched in horror, the wax in the fresco melted under the intense heat and the colors ran down the walls to puddle on the floor. The search for whatever remains of his work continues, and some hope was provided in 2012 with the discovery of pigments used by Leonardo, in a cavity behind the current wall.

Michelangelo never even got past making the preparatory drawings for the fresco he was supposed to paint on the opposite wall—Pope Julius II called him to Rome to paint the Sistine Chapel. Eventually, the bare walls were covered by Vasari and assistants from 1563 to 1565 with subservient frescoes exalting Cosimo I and the military victories of his regime, against Pisa (on the near wall) and Siena (far wall). Opposite the door you enter, is Michelangelo's statue of **"Victory"** ★, carved from 1533 to 1534 for Julius II's tomb but later donated to the Medici.

The first series of rooms on the second floor is the **Quartiere degli Elementi,** frescoed with allegories and mythological characters, again by Vasari. Crossing the balcony overlooking the Sala dei Cinquecento, you enter the **Apartments of Eleonora di Toledo** ★, decorated for Cosimo's Spanish wife. Her small private chapel is a masterpiece of mid-16th-century painting by Bronzino. Farther on, under the coffered ceiling of the **Sala dei Gigli,** are Domenico Ghirlandaio's fresco of "St. Zenobius Enthroned" with figures from Republican and Imperial Rome; and Donatello's original **"Judith and Holofernes"** ★ bronze (1455), one of his last works.

The Renaissance **Palazzo Strozzi** ★★ (📞 **055-264-5155;** www.palazzostrozzi. org), Piazza Strozzi, and basement **Strozzina** are Florence's major spaces for temporary and contemporary art shows, and have been experiencing a 21st-century renaissance of their own under energetic directorship. Big hits of recent years have included 2011's "Picasso, Miró, Dalí" and "Pontormo and Rosso" in 2014. There's always lots going on including talks, late-night events, and openings (usually Thurs), discounted admission (again, usually Thurs), and even discovery trails aimed at 5- to 9-year-olds. Check **www.palazzostrozzi. org** for the latest exhibition news.

Since 2012 visitors have been admitted to the **Torre di Arnolfo** ★, the palace's crenellated tower. If you can bear the small spaces and 418 steps, the views are grand. The 95m (312-ft.) Torre is accessed on a separate ticket, and is closed during high winds or rain; the minimum age to climb it is 6, and children ages 17 and under must be accompanied by an adult.

Piazza della Signoria. 📞 **055-276-8325.** http://museicivicifiorentini.comune.fi.it. Admission to Palazzo or Torre 10€; admisson to both 14€. Palazzo Fri–Wed 9am–7pm (Apr–Sept until midnight); Thurs 9am–2pm. Torre Fri–Wed 10am–5pm (Apr–Sept 9am–9pm); Thurs 9am–2pm. Bus: C1 or C2.

Ponte Vecchio ★ ARCHITECTURE The oldest and most famous bridge across the Arno, the Ponte Vecchio was built in 1345 by Taddeo Gaddi to replace an earlier version. The characteristic overhanging shops have lined the bridge since at least the 12th century. In the 16th century, it was home to butchers until Cosimo I moved into the Palazzo Pitti across the river. He couldn't stand the stench, so he evicted the meat cutters and moved in the classier gold- and silversmiths, and jewelers occupy it to this day.

The Ponte Vecchio's fame saved it in 1944 from the Nazis, who had orders to blow up all the bridges before retreating out of Florence as Allied forces advanced. They couldn't bring themselves to reduce this span to rubble—so they blew up the ancient buildings on either end instead to block it off. The Great Arno Flood of 1966 wasn't so discriminating, however, and severely damaged the shops. Apparently, a private night watchman saw the waters rising alarmingly and called many of the goldsmiths at home, who rushed to remove their valuable stock before it was washed away.

Via Por Santa Maria/Via Guicciardini. Bus: C3 or D.

Santa Trínita ★★ CHURCH Beyond Bernardo Buontalenti's late-16th-century **facade** lies a dark church, rebuilt in the 14th century but founded by the Vallombrosans before 1177. The third chapel on the right has what remains of the detached frescoes by Spinello Aretino, which were found under Lorenzo Monaco's 1424 "Scenes from the Life of the Virgin" frescoes covering the next chapel along.

In the right transept, Domenico Ghirlandaio frescoed the **Cappella Sassetti** ★ in 1483 with a cycle on the "Life of St. Francis," but true to form he set all the scenes against Florentine backdrops and peopled them with portraits of contemporary notables. His "Francis Receiving the Order from Pope Honorius" (in the lunette) takes place under an arcade on the north side of Piazza della Signoria—the Loggia dei Lanzi is featured in the middle, and on the left is the Palazzo Vecchio. (The Uffizi between them hadn't been built yet.) In the little group on the far right, the man with the red cloak is Lorenzo the Magnificent, who ruled Florence until his death in 1492. The church was the original home to two of the Uffizi's greatest treasures, Cimabue's "Santa Trínita Maestà" and Gentile da Fabriano's "Procession of the Magi" (p. 76).

The south end of the piazza leads to the **Ponte Santa Trínita ★★**, Florence's most graceful bridge. In 1567, Ammannati built a span here that was set with four 16th-century statues of the seasons in honor of the marriage of Cosimo II. After the Nazis blew up the bridge in 1944, it was rebuilt, and all was set into place—save the head on the statue of Spring, which remained lost until a team dredging the river in 1961 found it by accident. If you want to photograph the Ponte Vecchio, head here at dusk.

Piazza Santa Trínita. 𝄐 **055-216-912.** Free admission. Mon–Sat 8am–noon and 4–5:45pm; Sun 8–10:45am and 4–5:45pm. Bus: C3 or D.

Around San Lorenzo & the Mercato Centrale

Until a controversial—and *perhaps* temporary—move in 2014, the church of San Lorenzo was practically lost behind the leather stalls and souvenir carts of Florence's vast **San Lorenzo street market** (see "Shopping," later in this chapter). In fact, the hawking of wares and bustle of commerce characterize all the streets of this neighborhood, centered on both the church and the nearby **Mercato Centrale** food hall. It's a colorful scene, but one of the most pickpocket-happy in the city, so be wary.

Cappelle Medicee (Medici Chapels) ★ MONUMENT/MEMORIAL When Michelangelo built the New Sacristy between 1520 and 1533 (finished by Vasari in 1556), it was to be a tasteful monument to Lorenzo the Magnificent and his generation of relatively pleasant Medici. When work got underway on the adjacent **Cappella dei Principi (Chapel of the Princes)** in 1604, it was to become one of the world's most god-awful and arrogant memorials, dedicated to the grand dukes, some of Florence's most decrepit tyrants. The Cappella dei Principi is an exercise in bad taste, a mountain of cut marbles and semiprecious stones—jasper, alabaster, mother-of-pearl, agate, and the like—slathered onto the walls and ceiling with no regard for composition and still less for chromatic unity. The pouring of ducal funds into this monstrosity began in 1604 and lasted until the rarely conscious Gian Gastone de' Medici drank himself to death in 1737, without an heir—but teams kept doggedly at the thing, and they were still finishing the floor in 1962.

Michelangelo's **Sagrestia Nuova (New Sacristy) ★★**, built to jibe with Brunelleschi's Old Sacristy in San Lorenzo proper (see below), is much calmer. (An architectural tidbit: The windows in the dome taper as they get near the top to fool you into thinking the dome is higher.) Michelangelo was supposed to produce three tombs here (perhaps four) but ironically got only the two less important ones done. So Lorenzo de' Medici ("the Magnificent")—wise ruler of his city, poet of note, grand patron of the arts, and moneybags behind much of the Renaissance—ended up with a mere inscription of his name next to his brother Giuliano's on a plain marble slab against the entrance wall. Admittedly, they did get one genuine Michelangelo sculpture to decorate their slab, a not-quite-finished **"Madonna and Child" ★**.

On the left wall of the sacristy is Michelangelo's **"Tomb of Lorenzo" ★**, duke of Urbino (and Lorenzo the Magnificent's grandson), whose seated statue symbolizes the contemplative life. Below him on the elongated curves of the tomb stretch "Dawn" (female) and "Dusk" (male), a pair of Michelangelo's most famous sculptures. This pair mirrors the similarly fashioned "Day" (male) and "Night" (female) across the way. One additional point "Dawn" and "Night" brings out is that Michelangelo perhaps hadn't seen too many naked women.

Piazza Madonna degli Aldobrandini (behind San Lorenzo, where Via Faenza and Via del Giglio meet). 𝄐 **055-238-8602.** www.polomuseale.firenze.it. Admission 6€ (8€ during compulsory temporary exhibition). Daily 8:15am–1:50pm (until 4:50pm during exhibition). Closed 1st, 3rd, and 5th Mon, and 2nd and 4th Sun of each month. Bus: C1, C2, 6, 11, or 22.

Palazzo Medici-Riccardi ★ PALACE The Palazzo Medici-Riccardi was built by Michelozzo in 1444 for Cosimo de' Medici il Vecchio; it's the prototype Florentine *palazzo,* on which the more overbearing Strozzi and Pitti palaces were later modeled. It remained the Medici private home until Cosimo I officially declared his power as duke by moving to the city's traditional civic brain center, the Palazzo Vecchio. A door off the courtyard leads up a staircase to the **Cappella dei Magi,** the oldest chapel to survive from a private Florentine palace; its walls are covered with dense and colorful Benozzo Gozzoli **frescoes ★★** (1459–63) in the International Gothic style. Rich as tapestries, the walls depict an extended "Journey of the Magi" to see the Christ child, who's being adored by Mary in the altarpiece.

Via Cavour 3. ℭ **055-276-0340.** www.palazzo-medici.it. Admission 7€ adults, 4€ ages 6–12. Thurs– Tues 9am–6:30pm. Bus: C1.

San Lorenzo ★ CHURCH A rough brick anti-facade and undistinguished stony bulk hide what is most likely the oldest church in Florence, founded in A.D. 393. It was later the Medici family's parish church, and Cosimo il Vecchio, whose wise behind-the-scenes rule made him popular with the Florentines, is buried in front of the high altar. The plaque marking the spot is inscribed PATER PATRIE—"Father of His Homeland."

Off the left transept is the **Sagrestia Vecchia (Old Sacristy) ★**, one of Brunelleschi's purest pieces of early Renaissance architecture. The focal sarcophagus contains Cosimo il Vecchio's parents, Giovanni di Bicci de' Medici and his wife, Piccarda Bueri, and a side chapel is decorated with an early star map that shows the night sky above the city in the 1440s (a scene that also features, curiously, in Brunelleschi's Pazzi Chapel, in Santa Croce; see p. 89).

On the wall of the left aisle is Bronzino's huge fresco of the **"Martyrdom of San Lorenzo" ★**; the poor soul was roasted on a grill in Rome.

Left of the church's main door is an entrance to the cloister and inside it a stairwell leading up to the **Biblioteca Laurenziana (Laurentian Library) ★★**. Michelangelo designed this library in 1524 to house the Medici's manuscript collection, and it stands as one of the most brilliant works of Mannerist architecture.

Piazza San Lorenzo. ℭ **055-214-042.** Admission to church 4.50€; admission to library 3€; combined admission 7€. Church Mon–Sat 10am–5:30pm (Mar–Oct also Sun 1:30–5:30pm). Laurentian Library Mon–Sat 9:30am–1:30pm. Bus: C1.

Near Piazza Santa Maria Novella

Piazza Santa Maria Novella ★ has patches of grass, seating, and a central fountain, but no shade. The two squat obelisks, resting on the backs of Giambologna tortoises, once served as the turning posts for the "chariot" races held here from the 16th to the mid–19th century. Once a depressed and down-at-heel part of the center, the area now hosts some of Florence's priciest hotels.

Museo Marino Marini & Cappella Rucellai ★ MUSEUM/RELIGIOUS SITE One of Florence's most unusual museums features the work of sculptor Marino Marini (1901–80). A native of nearby Pistoia, Marini worked mostly in bronze, with "horse and rider" a recurring theme in his semi-abstract work. The wide open spaces, thin crowds, monumental sculptures, and fun themes in Marini's work make this museum a good bet with any kids who are becoming weary of the Renaissance.

But they won't escape it entirely . . . because tagged onto the side of the museum is the **Cappella Rucellai,** a Renaissance chapel housing the **Tempietto ★★**. Returned to public view in 2013 after an exquisite restoration, this polychrome marble tomb was completed by L. B. Alberti for Giovanni de' Rucellai in 1467. Decorated with symbols of both the Rucellai and Medici families, and frescoed on the inside, the tomb was supposedly based on drawings of the Holy Sepulcher in Jerusalem.

Piazza San Pancrazio. ℭ **055-219-432.** www.museomarinomarini.it. Mon and Wed–Sat 10am–5pm. Admission 6€. Bus: C3, 6, or 11.

Santa Maria Novella ★★ CHURCH The Santa Maria Novella complex is reunited again, with the church and frescoed cloisters all visitable on one admission ticket. (Although, confusingly, there are two separate entrances, through the church's garden and via the tourist office at the rear, on Piazza della Stazione.)

Of all Florence's major churches, the home of the Dominicans is the only one with an original **facade** ★★ that matches its era of greatest importance. The lower Romanesque half was started in the 14th century by architect Fra' Jacopo Talenti, who had just finished building the church itself (begun in 1246). Renaissance architect and theorist Leon Battista Alberti finished the facade, adding a classically inspired Renaissance top that not only went seamlessly with the lower half but also created a Cartesian plane of perfect geometry.

Inside, on the left wall, is **Masaccio's "Trinità"** ★★★ (ca. 1425), the first painting ever to use perfect linear mathematical perspective. Florentine citizens and artists flooded in to see the fresco when it was unveiled, many remarking in awe that it seemed to punch a hole back into space, creating a chapel out of a flat wall. The **transept** is filled with frescoed chapels by Filippino Lippi and others. The **Sanctuary** ★ behind the main altar was frescoed after 1485 by Domenico Ghirlandaio with the help of his assistants and apprentices, probably including a young Michelangelo. The left wall is covered with a cycle on the "Life of the Virgin" and the right wall with a "Life of St. John the Baptist." (Read from the bottom upward; there are boards that explain the scenes.) The works are not just biblical stories but also snapshots of the era's fashions and personages, full of portraits of the Tornabuoni family who commissioned them. The **Cappella Gondi** to the left of the high altar contains a Crucifix carved by Brunelleschi around 1415.

The **Chiostro Verde (Green Cloister)** ★★ was partly frescoed between 1431 and 1446 by Paolo Uccello, a Florentine painter who became increasingly obsessed with the mathematics behind perspective. His Old Testament scenes include an "Inundation," which ironically was badly damaged by the Great Arno Flood of 1966. Off the cloister, the **Spanish Chapel** ★ is a complex piece of Dominican propaganda, frescoed in the 1360s by Andrea di Bonaiuto. The reopened **Chiostro dei Morti (Cloister of the Dead)** ★★ is one of the oldest parts of the convent, dating to the 1200s, and was another area badly damaged in 1966. Its low-slung vaults and chapels were decorated by Andrea Orcagna, Nardo di Cione, and others. It is especially atmospheric early in the morning, with the cloister empty and birdsong at full volume.

Piazza Santa Maria Novella/Piazza della Stazione 4. ℭ **055-219-257.** www.chiesasantamariano vella.it. Admission 5€. Mon–Thurs 9am–5:30pm; Fri 11am–5:30pm; Sat 9am–5pm; Sun 1–5pm (July–Sept opens noon). Bus: C2, D, 6, 11, or 22.

Near San Marco & Santissima Annunziata

Cenacolo di Sant'Apollonia ★ ART MUSEUM/CONVENT Painter Andrea del Castagno (1421–57) learned his trade painting the portraits of condemned men in the city's prisons, and it's clear to see the influence of his apprenticeship on the faces of the Disciples in his version of **"The Last Supper,"** the first of several painted in Florence during the Renaissance. The giant fresco, completed around 1447, covers an entire wall at one end of this former convent refectory. It is easy to spot Judas, banished to the other side of the communal table and painted as a satyr with a faux-marble panel in turmoil above his head.

Above Castagno's "Last Supper," his "Crucifixion," "Deposition," and "Entombment" complete the story of the final days of the Christian story.

Via XXVII Aprile 1. ✆ **055-238-8607.** Free admission. Daily 8:15am–1:50pm. Closed 1st, 3rd, and 5th Sun and 2nd and 4th Mon of each month. Bus: 1, 6, 11, 14, 17, or 23.

Galleria dell'Accademia ★★ ART MUSEUM   **"David"** ★★★—"Il Gigante"— is much larger than most people imagine, looming 4.8m (16 ft.) on top of a 1.8m (6-ft.) pedestal. He hasn't faded with time, either, and a 2004 cleaning makes the marble gleam as if it were opening day, 1504. Viewing the statue is a pleasure in the bright and spacious room custom-designed for him after the icon was moved to the Accademia in 1873, following 300 years of pigeons perched on his head in Piazza della Signoria. Replicas now take the abuse there, and at Piazzale Michangiolo. The spot high on one flank of the Duomo, for which he was originally commissioned, stands empty.

But the Accademia is not only about "David"; you will be delighted to discover he is surrounded by an entire museum stuffed with other notable Renaissance works. Michelangelo's unfinished **"Prisoners"** ★★ statues are a contrast to "David," with the rough forms struggling to free themselves from the raw stone. They also provide a unique glimpse into how Michelangelo worked a piece of stone; he famously said that he tried to free the sculpture within from the block, and you can see this quite clearly here. Rooms showcase paintings by Perugino, Filippino Lippi, Giotto, Giovanna da Milano, Andrea Orcagna, and others.

Be sure also to visit the back room leading to the Academy part of the Accademia, where you'll see a warehouse of old replica **plaster casts** ★, the work of years of students. It's almost as if a Roman assembly line has just stopped for lunch. The best of them were made by Lorenzo Bartolini in the 1800s.

Via Ricasoli 60. ✆ **055-238-8609.** www.polomuseale.firenze.it. Admission 6.50€ (11€ with compulsory temporary exhibition; to reserve tickets, see p. 78). Tues–Sun 8:15am–6:50pm. Bus: C1, 14, or 23.

Museo Archeologico (Archaeological Museum) ★ MUSEUM   If you can force yourselves away from the Renaissance, rewind a millennium or two at one of the most important archaeological collections in central Italy, which has a particular emphasis on the **Etruscan** period. You will need a little patience, however: The collection is in a seemingly endless state of reorganization, and displays are somewhat user-unfriendly. Exhibits have a habit of moving around, but you will quickly find the **"Arezzo Chimera"** ★★, a bronze figure of a mythical lion–goat–serpent dating to the 4th century B.C. It is perhaps the most important bronze sculpture to survive from the Etruscan era, and usually shares a room with the "Arringatore," a lifesize bronze of an orator dating to the 1st century, just as Etruscan culture was being subsumed by Ancient Rome. The top floor is not always open, but if it is hunt down the **"Idolino"** ★, an exquisite and slightly mysterious, lithe bronze. The collection is also strong on Etruscan-era *bucchero* pottery and funerary urns from digs around Tuscany, and Egyptian relics that include several sarcophagi displayed in a series of eerie galleries.

One bonus: Such is the dominance of medieval and Renaissance sites in the city that you may have the place to yourself.

Piazza Santissma Annunziata 9b. ℂ **055-23-575.** Admission 4€. Tues–Fri 8:30am–7pm; Sat–Mon 8:30am–2pm (Aug closed Sun). Bus: C1, 6, 19, 31, or 32.

San Marco ★★★ ART MUSEUM   We have never quite understood why this place is not mobbed; perhaps because it showcases, almost exclusively, the work of Fra' Angelico, Dominican monk and Florentine painter in the style known as "International Gothic." His decorative impulses and the sinuous lines of his figures mark his work as standing right on the cusp of the Renaissance. This is the most important collection in the world of the master's altarpieces and painted panels, residing in this former 13th-century convent the artist-monk once called home.

The most moving and unusual work is his **"Annunciation"** ★★★ and frescoed scenes from the life of Jesus painted not on one giant wall, but scene by scene, on the individual walls of small monks' cells that honeycomb the upper floor. The idea was that these scenes, painted by Fra' Angelico and his assistants, would aid in the monks' prayer and contemplation; and the paintings are intimate and entrancing. The final cell on the left corridor belonged to the fundamentalist firebrand preacher Savonarola, who briefly incited the populace of the most art-filled city in the world to burn their paintings, illuminated manuscripts, and anything else he felt was a worldly betrayal of Jesus' ideals. Ultimately, he ran afoul of the pope and was burned at the stake. You'll see his notebooks, rosary, and what's left of the clothes he wore that day in his cell, as well as an anonymous panel painted to show the day in 1498 when he was burned at the stake in Piazza della Signoria.

There is much more Fra' Angelico secreted around the cloistered complex, including a **"Crucifixion"** ★ in the Chapter House. The former Hospice is now a gallery dedicated to Fra' Angelico and his contemporaries; look out especially for his **"Tabernacolo dei Linaioli"** ★★, glowing after a 2011 restoration, and a seemingly weightless **"Deposition"** ★★.

If you are planning a visit here, beware the unusual opening hours.

Piazza San Marco 1. ℂ **055-238-8608.** www.polomuseale.firenze.it. Admission 4€ (7€ with compulsory temporary exhibition). Mon–Fri 8:30am–1:50pm; Sat–Sun 8:15am–4:50pm. Closed 1st, 3rd, and 5th Sun and 2nd and 4th Mon of each month. Bus: C1, 1, 6, 7, 11, 14, 17, 19, 20, 23, or 25.

Santissima Annunziata ★ CHURCH   In 1233, seven Florentine nobles had a spiritual crisis, gave away all their possessions, and retired to the forests to contemplate divinity. In 1250, they returned to what were then fields outside the city walls and founded a small oratory, proclaiming they were Servants of Mary, or the Servite Order. The oratory was enlarged by Michelozzo (1444–81) and later redesigned in the baroque style. The main art interest is in the **Chiostro dei Voti (Votive Cloister),** designed by Michelozzo with Corinthian-capitaled columns and decorated with some of the city's finest Mannerist **frescoes** ★★ (1465–1515). Rosso Fiorentino provided an "Assumption" (1513) and Pontormo a "Visitation" (1515) just to the right of the door. Their master, Andrea del Sarto, contributed a "Birth of the Virgin" (1513), in the far right corner, one of his finest works. To the right of the door into the church is a damaged but still fascinating "Coming of the Magi" (1514) by del Sarto, who included a self-portrait at the far right, looking out at us from under his blue hat.

The **interior** is excessively baroque. Just to the left as you enter is a huge tabernacle hidden under a mountain of *ex votos* (votive offerings). It was designed by Michelozzo to house a small painting of the "Annunciation." Legend holds that it was started by a friar who, vexed that he couldn't paint the Madonna's face as beautifully as it should be, gave it up and took a nap. When he awoke, he found an angel had filled in the face for him—and the painting became one of a rare group of images known as *"acheiropoieta,"* miraculous objects reputedly made "without hands." Newlywed brides in Florence don't toss their bouquets: They head here after the ceremony to leave their flowers at the shrine for good luck. This is very much a working church, hence the restricted opening hours for the interior. The cloister is open all day, however.

On **Piazza Santissima Annunziata** ★★ outside, flanked by elegant Brunelleschi porticos, is an equestrian statue of "Grand Duke Ferdinand I," Giambologna's last work; it was cast in 1608 after his death by his student Pietro Tacca, who also did the two fountains of fantastic mermonkey-monsters. You can stay right on this spectacular piazza, at one of our favorite Florence hotels, the Loggiato dei Serviti (p. 58).

Piazza Santissima Annunziata. ℂ **055-266-181.** Free admission. Daily 4–5:15pm. Bus: C1, 6, 19, 31, or 32.

Spedale degli Innocenti ★ ARCHITECTURE   Europe's oldest foundling hospital, opened in 1445, is still going strong as a convent orphanage, though times have changed a bit. The Lazy Susan set into the wall on the left end of the arcade—where once people left unwanted babies, swiveled it around, rang the bell, and ran—was blocked up in 1875. The colonnaded **portico** ★ (built 1419–26) was designed by Filippo Brunelleschi when he was still a goldsmith. It was his first great achievement as an architect and helped define the new Renaissance style he was developing. Its repetition by later artists in front of other buildings on the piazza makes it one of the most exquisite squares in Italy. The spandrels between the arches of Brunelleschi's portico are set with glazed **terra-cotta reliefs** of swaddled babes against rounded blue backgrounds—hands-down the masterpieces of Andrea della Robbia.

The museum inside is undergoing extensive restoration through 2015.

Piazza Santissima Annunziata 12. ℂ **055-203-7308.** Admission (to courtyard only during restoration) 3€. Mon–Sat 10am–4pm. Bus: C1, 6, 19, 31, or 32.

Around Piazza Santa Croce

Piazza Santa Croce is pretty much like any grand Florentine square—a nice bit of open space ringed with souvenir and leather shops and thronged with tourists. But once a year (during late June) it's covered with dirt and violent, Renaissance-style soccer is played on it in the tournament known as **Calcio Storico Fiorentino.**

Santa Croce ★★ CHURCH   The center of the Florentine Franciscan universe was begun in 1294 by Gothic master Arnolfo di Cambio in order to rival the church of Santa Maria Novella being raised by the Dominicans across the city. The church wasn't consecrated until 1442, and even then it remained faceless until the neo-Gothic **facade** was added in 1857. It's an art-stuffed complex that demands 2 hours of your time to see properly.

The Gothic **interior** is vast, and populated with the tombs of rich and famous Florentines. Starting from the main door, immediately on the right is the first tomb of note containing the bones of the most venerated Renaissance master, **Michelangelo Buonarroti,** who died in Rome in 1564 at the ripe age of 89. The pope wanted him buried in the Eternal City, but Florentines managed to sneak his body back to Florence. Two berths along from Michelangelo's monument is a pompous 19th-century cenotaph to

Dante Alighieri, one of history's great poets, whose "Divine Comedy" codified the Italian language. Elsewhere, seek out monuments to philosopher **Niccolò Machiavelli, Gioacchino Rossini** (1792–1868), composer of "The Barber of Seville," sculptor **Lorenzo Ghiberti,** and scientist **Galileo Galilei** (1564–1642).

The right transept is richly decorated with frescoes. The **Cappella Castellani** was frescoed with stories of saints' lives by Agnolo Gaddi, with a tabernacle by Mino da Fiesole and a Crucifix by Niccolò Gerini. Agnolo's father, Taddeo Gaddi, was one of Giotto's closest followers, and the senior Gaddi is the one who undertook painting the **Cappella Baroncelli ★** (1328–38) at the transept's end. The frescoes depict scenes from the "Life of the Virgin," and include an "Annunciation to the Shepherds" that constitutes the first night scene in Italian fresco painting.

Giotto himself frescoed the two chapels to the right of the high altar. The frescoes were whitewashed over during the 17th century but uncovered from 1841 to 1852 and inexpertly restored. The **Cappella Peruzzi ★**, on the right, is a late work and not in the best shape. The many references to antiquity in the styling and architecture of the frescoes reflect Giotto's trip to Rome and its ruins. Even more famous, including its setting for a scene in "A Room with a View," is the **Cappella Bardi ★★**. Key panels here include the "Trial by Fire Before the Sultan of Egypt" on the right wall, full of telling subtlety in the expressions and poses of the figures. In one of Giotto's most well-known works, the "Death of St. Francis," monks weep and wail with convincing pathos. Realistic scene-setting was one of Giotto's great innovations, and it set painting on course for the Renaissance a century after him. Before you head outside into the cloister, pause by Donatello's **"Cavalcanti Annunciation Tabernacle" ★** (1435), an intricate relief.

Outside in the cloister is the **Cappella Pazzi ★**, one of Filippo Brunelleschi's architectural masterpieces (faithfully finished after his death in 1446). Giuliano da Maiano probably designed the porch that now precedes the chapel, set with glazed terra cottas by Luca della Robbia. The rectangular chapel is one of Brunelleschi's signature pieces, decorated with his trademark *pietra serena* gray stone. It is the defining example of (and model for) early Renaissance architecture. Curiously, the ceiling of the smaller dome depicts the night sky at the same moment as the Old Sacristy in San Lorenzo (p. 85).

From the cloister enter the **Museo dell'Opera.** Displayed here is the Cimabue **"Crucifix" ★** that was almost destroyed by the Arno Flood of 1966, and became an international symbol of the ruination wreaked by the river that November day. Taddeo Gaddi also frescoed a whole wall with a "Tree of Life" and a "Last Supper."

Piazza Santa Croce. www.santacroceopera.it. ℭ **055-246-6105.** Admission 6€ adults, 4€ ages 11–17. Mon–Sat 9:30am–5pm; Sun 2–5pm. Bus: C1, C2, or C3.

The Oltrarno, San Niccolò & San Frediano

Museo Zoologia "La Specola" ★ MUSEUM   The wax anatomical models are one reason the Zoology Museum might be the only one in Florence where kids eagerly pull their parents from room to room. Vast, impressive, but creepy collections of pickled creepy-crawlies and stuffed specimens from every branch of the animal kingdom kick things off. These exhibits transition into rooms filled with lifelike human bodies suffering from horrible dismemberments, flayings, and eviscerations—all in the name of science. These wax models served as anatomical illustrations for medical students studying at this scientific institute from the 1770s. The grisly wax plague dioramas in the final room were created in the early 1700s to satisfy the lurid tastes of Cosimo III.

Via Romana 17. ℭ **055-275-5100.** www.msn.unifi.it. Admission 6€ adults, 3€ children 6–14 and seniors 65 and over. Jun–Sept Tues–Sun 10:30am–5:30pm; Oct–May Tues–Sun 9:30am–4:30pm. Bus: D, 11, 36, or 37.

Giardino Bardini (Bardini Garden) ★ PARK/GARDEN   Hemmed in to the north by the city's medieval wall, the handsome Bardini Garden is less famous—and so less hectic—than its neighbor down the hill, the Boboli Garden (see below). From its loftier perch over the Oltrarno, it beats the Boboli hands down for views and new angles on the city. Check out the side view of Santa Croce, with the copper dome of the Synagogue in the background; see how the church's 19th-century facade was bolted on to a building dating to the 1200s.

Costa San Giorgio 2. © **055-2006-6206.** www.bardinipeyron.it. Admission on combined ticket with Giardino di Boboli; see below. Same hours as Boboli Garden; see below. Bus: C3 or D.

Palazzo Pitti (Pitti Palace) ★★ MUSEUM/PALACE   Although built by and named after a rival of the Medici—merchant Luca Pitti—in the 1450s, this gigantic *palazzo* soon fell into Medici hands. It was the Medici family's principal home from the 1540s, and continued to house Florence's rulers until 1919. The Pitti contains five museums, including one of the best collections of canvases by Raphael in the world. Out back are elegant Renaissance gardens, the **Boboli** (see below).

GALLERIA PALATINA ★★: No gallery comes closer to Mark Twain's description of "weary miles" in "Innocents Abroad" than the art-crammed rooms of the Pitti's Galleria Palatina. Paintings are displayed like cars in a parking garage, stacked on walls above each other in the "Enlightenment" method of exhibition. Rooms are alternately dimly lit, or garishly bright; this is how many of the world's great art treasures were seen and enjoyed by their original commissioners and collectors.

You will find important historical treasures amid the Palatina's vast and haphazard collection. Some of the best efforts of Titian, Raphael, and Rubens line the walls. Botticelli and Filippo Lippi's "**Madonna and Child**" ★ (1452) provide the key works in the **Sala di Prometeo (Prometheus Room).** Two giant versions of the "Assumption of the Virgin," both by Mannerist painter Andrea del Sarto, dominate the **Sala dell'Iliade (Iliad Room).** Here you will also find another Biblical woman painted by Artemisia Gentileschi, "Judith." The **Sala di Saturno (Saturn Room)** ★ is stuffed with Raphaels and a giant panel by his teacher, Perugino; next door in the **Sala di Giove (Jupiter Room)** you'll find his sublime, naturalistic portrait of **"La Velata" ★★**, as well as **"The Ages of Man"** ★. The current attribution of the painting is awarded to Venetian Giorgione, though that has been disputed.

APPARTAMENTI REALI: At the "Royal Apartments," you get an excellent feeling for the conspicuous consumption of the Medici Grand Dukes and their Austrian and Belgian Lorraine successors—and see some notable paintings in their original, ostentatious setting. The rooms earned their "Royal" label because Italy's first king lived here for several years during Italy's 19th-century unification process—when Florence was Italy's second capital, after Turin—until Rome was finally conquered and the court moved there. Much of the stucco, fabrics, furnishings, and general decoration is in thunderously poor taste, but you should look out for Caravaggio's subtle **"Knight of Malta"** ★ canvas.

GALLERIA D'ARTE MODERNA ★: The Pitti's "modern" gallery has a fairly good collection, this time of 19th-century Italian paintings with a focus on Romanticism, Neoclassical works, and the **Macchiaioli**—a school of Italian painters who worked in an "impressionistic style" before the French Impressionists. If you have limited time, make right for the major works of the latter, in Sala 18 through 20, which displays the Maremma landscapes of **Giovanni Fattori** ★ (1825–1908).

GALLERIA DEL COSTUME & MUSEO DEGLI ARGENTI: The Pitti's pair of lesser museums—the Costume Gallery and Museum of Silverware—combine to show that wealth and taste do not always go hand in hand. Unless you're a scholar or true aficionado of such things, they are in no way worth the admission price, but if you already have the cumulative ticket, pop in to spend some time among the Medici's over-the-top gold and jewel-encrusted household items. One thing you will notice in the Costume Gallery is how much smaller Florentines were just a few centuries ago.

Piazza de' Pitti 1. Galleria Palatina, Appartamenti Reali, and Galleria d'Arte Moderna: ℰ **055-238-8614;** to reserve tickets, see p. 78. Admission 8.50€ (13€ during compulsory temporary exhibition). Tues–Sun 8:15am–6:50pm. Museo degli Argenti and Galleria del Costume: ℰ **055-238-8709.** Admission (includes Giardino di Boboli and Giardino Bardini) 7€ (10€ during compulsory temporary exhibition). Same hours as Giardino di Boboli; see below. Cumulative ticket for everything, including Giardino di Boboli (see below), valid 3 days, 12€ (18€ during compulsory temporary exhibition). Visitors ages 17 and under or 65 and over enter free. Bus: D, 11, 36, or 37.

Giardino di Boboli (Boboli Garden) ★★ PARK/GARDEN   The statue-filled park behind the Pitti Palace is one of the earliest and finest Renaissance gardens, laid out mostly between 1549 and 1656 with box hedges in geometric patterns, groves of ilex (holm oak), dozens of statues, and rows of cypress. Just above the entrance through the courtyard of the Palazzo Pitti is an oblong **amphitheater** modeled on Roman circuses, with a **granite basin** from Rome's Baths of Caracalla and an **Egyptian obelisk** of Ramses II. In 1589 this was the setting for the wedding reception of Ferdinando de' Medici's marriage to Christine of Lorraine. For the occasion, the Medici commissioned entertainment from Jacopo Peri and Ottavio Rinuccini, who decided to set a classical story entirely to music and called it "Dafne"—the world's first opera. (Later, they wrote a follow-up hit "Erudice," performed here in 1600; it's the first opera whose score has survived.)

Toward the south end of the park is the **Isolotto** ★, a dreamy island marooned in a pond full of huge goldfish, with Giambologna's "L'Oceano" sculptural composition at its center. At the north end, down around the end of the Pitti Palace, are some fake caverns filled with statuary, attempting to invoke a classical sacred grotto. The most famous, the **Grotta Grande,** was designed by Giorgio Vasari, Bartolomeo Ammannati, and Bernardo Buontalenti between 1557 and 1593, dripping with phony stalactites and set with replicas of Michelangelo's unfinished "Prisoners" statues. You can usually get inside on the hour (but not every hour, and not at all on Mon) for 15 minutes.

Entrance via Palazzo Pitti, Piazza de' Pitti. ℰ **055-238-8791.** www.polomuseale.firenze.it. Admission (includes Giardino Bardini, Museo degli Argenti, and Museo del Costume) 7€ (10€ during compulsory temporary exhibition). Nov–Feb daily 8:15am–4:30pm; Mar daily 8:15am–5:30pm; Apr–May and Sept–Oct daily 8:15am–6:30pm; June–Aug daily 8:15am–7:30pm. Closed 1st and last Mon of month. Cumulative ticket for everything in Palazzo Pitti and Giardino di Boboli, valid 3 days, 12€ (18€ during compulsory temporary exhibition). Visitors age 17 and under or 65 and over enter free. Bus: D, 11, 36, or 37.

Piazzale Michelangiolo ★ SQUARE   This panoramic piazza is a required stop for every tour bus. The balustraded terrace was laid out in 1869 to give a sweeping **vista** ★★ of the entire city, spread out in the valley below and backed by the green hills of Fiesole beyond. The bronze replica of "David" here points right at his original home, outside the Palazzo Vecchio.

Viale Michelangelo. Bus: 12 or 13.

San Miniato al Monte ★★ CHURCH   High atop a hill, its gleaming white-and-green facade visible from the city below, San Miniato is one of the few ancient churches of Florence to survive the centuries virtually intact. The current building began to take shape in 1013, under the auspices of the powerful Arte di Calimala guild, whose symbol, a bronze eagle clutching a bale of wool, perches on the **facade ★★**. This Romanesque facade is a particularly gorgeous bit of white Carrara and green Prato marble inlay. Above the central window is a 13th-century mosaic of "Christ Between the Madonna and St. Miniato" (a theme repeated in the apse).

The **interior** has a few Renaissance additions, but they blend in well with the overall medieval aspect—an airy, stony space with a raised choir at one end, painted wooden trusses on the ceiling, and tombs interspersed with inlaid marble symbols of the zodiac paving the floor.

Below the choir is an 11th-century **crypt** with remains of frescoes by Taddeo Gaddi. Off to the right of the raised choir is the **sacristy,** which Spinello Aretino covered in 1387 with cartoonish yet elegant frescoes depicting the **"Life of St. Benedict" ★**. Off the left aisle of the nave is 15th-century **Cappella del Cardinale del Portogallo ★★**, a collaborative effort by Renaissance artists built to honor young Portuguese human- ist Cardinal Jacopo di Lusitania, who was sent to study in Perugia but died an untimely death at age 25 in Florence.

The Benedictine monks usually celebrate mass here in Gregorian Chant at 5:30pm.

Around the back of the church is San Miniato's **monumental cemetery ★**, one enormous "city of the dead," whose streets are lined with tombs and mausoleums built in elaborate pastiches of every generation of Florentine architecture (with a marked preference for the Gothic and the Romanesque). It's a peaceful spot, soundtracked only by birdsong and the occasional tolling of the church bells.

Via Monte alle Croci/Viale Galileo Galilei (behind Piazzale Michelangiolo). 🕿 **055-234-2731.** Free admission. Daily 8am–1pm and 3:30–dusk (closed some Sun afternoons and often open through *riposo* in summer). Bus: 12 or 13.

Santa Felicità ★ CHURCH   The 2nd-century Greek sailors who lived in this neighborhood brought Christianity to Florence with them, and this little church was probably the second to be established in the city, the first edition of it rising in the late 4th century. The current version was built in the 1730s. The star works are in the first chapel on the right, the Brunelleschi-designed **Cappella Barbadori–Cap- poni:** paintings by Mannerist master Pontormo (1525–27). His **"Deposition" ★★** and frescoed "Annunciation" are rife with his garish color palette of oranges, pinks, golds, lime greens, and sky blues, and exhibit his trademark surreal sense of figure.

Piazza Santa Felicità (on left off Via Guicciardini across Ponte Vecchio). 🕿 **055-213-018.** Free admission (take 1€ for lights). Daily 9:30am–12:30pm and 3:30–5:30pm. Bus: C3 or D.

Santa Maria del Carmine ★★★ CHURCH   Following a 1771 fire that destroyed everything but the transept chapels and sacristy, this Carmelite church was almost entirely reconstructed in high baroque style. To see the famous **Cappella Bran- cacci ★★★** in the right transept, you have to enter through the cloisters (doorway to the right of the church facade) and pay admission. The frescoes here were commis- sioned by an enemy of the Medici, Felice Brancacci, who in 1424 hired Masolino and his student Masaccio to decorate it with a cycle on the "Life of St. Peter." Masolino probably worked out the cycle's scheme and painted a few scenes along with his pupil before taking off for 3 years to serve as court painter in Budapest, Hungary, during which time Masaccio kept painting, quietly creating the early Renaissance's greatest frescoes. Masaccio left for Rome in 1428, where he died at age 27. The cycle was completed between 1480 and 1485 by Filippino Lippi.

Masolino was responsible for the "St. Peter Preaching," the upper panel to the left of the altar, and the two top scenes on the right wall, which shows his fastidiously decorative style in a long panel of "St. Peter Healing the Cripple" and "Raising Tabitha," and his "Adam and Eve." Contrast this first man and woman, about to take the bait offered by the snake, with the **"Expulsion from the Garden"** ★★, opposite it, painted by Masaccio. Masolino's figures are highly posed, expressionless models. Masaccio's Adam and Eve, on the other hand, burst with intense emotion. The top scene on the left wall, the **"Tribute Money"** ★★, is also by Masaccio, and it showcases another of his innovations, linear perspective. The two scenes to the right of the altar are Masaccio's as well, with the **"Baptism of the Neophytes"** ★★ taking its place among his masterpieces.

Piazza del Carmine 14. ℂ **055-238-2195.** www.museicivicifiorentini.comune.fi.it/brancacci. Free admission to church; Cappella Brancacci 6€. Mon and Wed–Sat 10am–5pm; Sun 1–5pm. Bus: D.

Santo Spirito ★ CHURCH   One of Filippo Brunelleschi's masterpieces of architecture, this 15th-century church doesn't look like much from the outside (no true facade was ever built). But the **interior** ★ is a marvelous High Renaissance space—an expansive landscape of proportion and mathematics worked out in classic Brunelleschi style, with coffered ceiling, tall columns, and the stacked perspective of arched arcading. Good late-Renaissance and baroque paintings are scattered throughout, but the best stuff lies up in the transepts, especially the **Cappella Nerli** ★, with a panel by Filippino Lippi. The church's extravagant **baroque altar** has a ciborium inlaid in *pietre dure* around 1607—and frankly, looks a bit silly against the restrained elegance of Brunelleschi's architecture. A room off the left aisle displays a wooden Crucifix that has, somewhat controversially, been attributed to Michelangelo. See (and judge) for yourself.

Piazza Santo Spirito ★ outside is one of the focal points of the Oltrarno, shaded by trees and lined with trendy cafes that see some bar action in the evenings. There are often a few farmers selling their fruit and vegetables on the piazza.

Piazza Santo Spirito. ℂ **055-210-030.** Free admission. Mon–Tues and Thurs–Sat 10am–12:30pm and 4–5:30pm; Sun 4–5:30pm. Bus: C3, D, 11, 36, or 37.

Organized Tours

If you want to get under the surface of the city, **Context Travel** ★★ (www.context-travel.com; ℂ **800/691-6036** in the U.S. or 06-9672-7371 in Italy) offers insightful culture tours led by academics and other experts in their field in a variety of specialties, from the gastronomic to the archaeological and artistic. Group tours are limited to a maximum of 6 people and cost around 70€ per person. Context also conducts a guided walk through the Vasari Corridor (subject to corridor closures; see p. 82). The quality of Context's walks are unmatched, and well worth the outlay.

CAF Tours (www.caftours.com; ℂ **055-283-200**) offers two half-day bus tours of town (48€), including visits to the Uffizi, Accademia, and Piazzale Michelangiolo, as well as several walking tours, museum visits, and cooking classes costing from 27€ to 130€. **ArtViva** (www.italy.artviva.com; ℂ **055-264-5033**) has a select array of Florence walks and food- and drink-themed activities for every budget, starting at 25€. Their offering includes a unique, distinctly dark "Sex, Drugs, and the Renaissance" walking tour launched in 2013 (2½ hr.; 39€). **I Just Drive** (www.ijustdrive.us; ℂ **055-093-5928**) offers fully equipped cars (Wi-Fi, complimentary bottle of prosecco) plus English-speaking driver for various themed visits, or just rentable by the hour. Their full-day "Chianti's Best" (110€) minivan tour is ideal if you want to go wine tasting in the hills but can't agree on a designated driver; or ride in a Bentley Limousine up to

FIESOLE escape

Although it's only a short city bus ride away in the hills north of Florence, **Fiesole** ★ is very proud of its status as an independent municipality. In fact, a hilltop village was probably founded in the 6th century B.C. on the site of a Bronze Age settlement. "Faesulae" later became the most important Etruscan center in the region. Although it eventually became a Roman town—it was first conquered in 90 B.C.—building a theater and adopting Roman customs, it always retained a bit of the Etruscan otherness. Even with the big city so close by, Fiesole endures as a Tuscan small town to this day, mostly removed from Florence at its feet and hence a perfect escape from summertime crowds. It stays relatively cool all summer long, and while you sit at a cafe on Piazza Mino, sipping an iced cappuccino, it might seem as

though the lines at the Uffizi and pedestrian traffic around the Duomo are very distant indeed.

To get to Fiesole, take bus no. 7 from Florence. It departs from Via La Pira, down the right flank of San Marco. A scenic 25-minute ride through the greenery above Florence, takes you to Fiesole's main square, Piazza Mino.

Fiesole also hosts an eclectic annual summer arts festival, the **Estate Fiesolana** ★. Venues including the Teatro Romano showcase what can only be described as "a bit of everything": One recent edition included a Terry Gilliam movie retrospective, orchestral music, and a live reinterpretation of The Beatles' "White Album." You will find the program posted at www.estatefiesolana.it.

For more on Fiesole, see chapter 5.

San Miniato al Monte, on the dusk "Gregorian Chant Tour" (1½ hr.; 18€), to hear the monks' evening prayers.

Websites such as **Viator.com** and **GetYourGuide.com** have a vast selection of locally organized tours and activities, reviewed and rated by users. Both have good apps for the major smartphone platforms. *Note:* Don't be tempted to book airport or rail station transfers via the tour companies—it is *much* cheaper to call a cab and pay the very reasonable fixed local rates; see "Taxis" (p. 50).

Call **I Bike Italy** (℃ 342-935-2395; www.ibikeitaly.com) to sign up for 1-day rides into the Chianti wine country for 84€, including shuttle service to the start point, English-speaking guide, wine and olive oil tastings, and lunch. A half-day cycle (morning or early evening) costs 74€, including a visit to a Tuscan villa. No churches, no museums, no crowds, guaranteed.

Especially for Kids

You have to put in a bit of work to reach some of Florence's best views—and the climbs, up claustrophobic, medieval staircases, are a favorite with many kids. The massive ochre dome of **Santa Maria del Fiore** (p. 74), the **Palazzo Vecchio**'s (p. 82) Torre di Arnolfo, and the **Campanile di Giotto** (p. 74) are perfect for any youngster with a head for heights.

You can also help them to dig a little deeper into the city's history: Probably the best kids' activities with an educational component are run by the **Museo dei Ragazzi** ★★ (℃ 055-276-8224; www.museoragazzi.it), not a standalone museum but a program that offers daily child's-eye tours around the Palazzo Vecchio's Quartieri Monumentali, led by guides in period costumes and offered in English. Check the program online, email to enquire on **info.museoragazzi@comune.fi.it**, or make for the desk next to the Palazzo Vecchio ticket booth.

A couple of museums not listed in the sections above have a particular interest for younger visitors. For all their faults, the later Medici and Lorraine grand dukes did take an avid interest in science, and the **Museo Galileo** ★, Piazza dei Giudici 1 (*©* **055-265-311;** www.museogalileo.it) showcases scientific instruments from their collections. There is an emphasis on astronomy and telescopes—Galileo worked under Medici patronage, and the museum preserves the middle finger of his right hand in a jar. Admission costs 9€, 5.50€ for children ages 6 to 18 and seniors 65 and over. The museum is open daily 9:30am to 6pm, but closes at 1pm on Tuesdays.

You'll need a bus (no. 4) or a taxi to get to the site, but any swords, sorcery, or Harry Potter fans will thank you for a visit to **Museo Stibbert** ★, Via Stibbert 26 (*©* **055-475-520;** www.museostibbert.it). It's essentially the giant toy box of an eccentric British–Italian arms-and-armor collector, which was made into a private museum in 1906. Among the medieval mayhem, with every variety of historic weapon, armor, and shield from Europe and the Islamic world, the museum boasts the biggest collection of Japanese armor outside of Tokyo. The museum is open Monday to Wednesday 10am to 2pm, Friday to Sunday 10am to 6pm. Admission costs 8€, 6€ for children ages 4 to 12.

If you have very young children who just need a crowd-free timeout space, head for the top floor of the **Biblioteca delle Oblate,** Via dell'Oriuolo 26 (*©* **055-2616-512;** http://bibliotecadelleoblate.comune.fi.it). There's a library with books for little ones, as well as space to spread out, color, draw, and generally goof around. It's free and open all day, except for Monday morning and all day Sunday. The Oblate's **cafe** (p. 100) is an excellent place to kick back anyway. The complex is closed for 2 weeks in mid-August.

There's only one game in town when it comes to spectator sports: *calcio.* To Italians, soccer/football is something akin to a second religion, and an afternoon at the stadium can offer you more insight into local culture than a lifetime in the Uffizi. The Florence team, **Fiorentina** (nicknamed *i viola,* "the purples"), plays in Italy's top league, *Serie A.* You can usually catch them alternate Sundays from September through May at the Stadio Comunale Artemio Franchi, Via Manfredo Fanti 4 (www.violachannel.tv). Tickets are best arranged ahead of time by emailing the club box office on **tickets@ acffiorentina.it**. The official ticket office at Via dei Sette Santi 28R (directly on the corner of Via Giovanni Dupré) is also open from 9:30am on matchdays, if you have made a spontaneous decision to go to a game (take photo I.D.). To reach the stadium from the center, take bus no. 10 or 20 from San Marco (10–15 min.). To get kitted out in the home colors, visit **Alè Viola,** Via del Corso 58R (*©* **055-295-306**), before the match.

And remember: You are in the **gelato** capital of Italy, perhaps even the world (p. 69). At least one gelato per day is the minimum recommended dose.

SHOPPING

After Milan, Florence is **Italy's top shopping city**—beating even the capital, Rome. Here's what to buy: leather, fashion, shoes, marbleized paper, hand-embroidered linens, artisan and craft items, handmade jewelry, *pietre dure* (known also as "Florentine mosaic," inlaid semiprecious stones), and antiques.

General Florentine **shopping hours** are Monday through Saturday from 9:30am to noon or 1pm and 3 or 3:30 to 7:30pm, although increasingly, many shops are staying open on Sunday and through that midafternoon *riposo* or nap, especially the larger stores and those around tourist sites.

The Top Shopping Streets & Areas

AROUND SANTA TRÍNITA The cream of the crop of Florentine shopping lines both sides of elegant **Via de' Tornabuoni,** with an extension along **Via della Vigna Nuova** and other surrounding streets. Here you'll find the big Florentine fashion names like **Gucci ★** (at no. 73R, and for kids at no. 81R; ℂ **055-264-011;** www.gucci. com), **Pucci ★** (at no. 22R; ℂ **055-265-8082;** www.emiliopucci.com), and **Ferragamo ★** (at no. 4R; ℂ **055-292-123;** www.ferragamo.com) ensconced in old palaces or modern minimalist boutiques. Stricter traffic controls have made shopping Via de' Tornabuoni a more sedate experience, though somewhat at the expense of its surrounding streets.

AROUND VIA ROMA & VIA DEI CALZAIUOLI These are some of Florence's busiest streets, packed with storefronts offering mainstream shopping. It is here you will find the city's major department stores, **Coin,** Via dei Calzaiuoli 56R (ℂ **055-280-531;** www.coin.it), and **La Rinascente,** Piazza della Repubblica (ℂ **055-219-113;** www.rinascente.it), alongside quality chains such as Geox and Zara.

VIA DEI SERVI Leading from the Duomo to Piazza Santissima Annunziata, this street is a genuine oddity in the old center. While others around it cater to the tourist dollar, here you will find small indie booksellers, shops selling work uniforms, and traditional picture framers. Check out the displays at stamp collector's store **Filatelia Brioschi** (at no. 31R; ℂ **055-214-082**) or buy a hand-bound journal at **Scriptorium ★** (at no. 7R; ℂ **055-211-804;** www.scriptoriumfirenze.com).

AROUND SANTA CROCE The eastern part of the center has seen a flourishing of one-off stores, with an emphasis on young, independent fashions. **Borgo degli Albizi** and its tributary streets repay a roam. This is also where you will find the daily flea market, the **Mercato delle Pulci** (see below).

Florence's Best Markets

Mercato Centrale ★ The center's main food market stocks the usual fruit, vegetables, and fresh meat. But you can also browse for (and taste) cheeses, salamis and cured hams, Tuscan wines, takeout food, and more. It is picnic-packing heaven. Here you will also find one of Florence's best value lunches, at **Nerbone** (p. 65). It runs Monday to Saturday until 2pm (until 5pm Sat for most of the year). Btw. Piazza del Mercato Centrale and Via dell'Ariento. No phone. Bus: C1.

Mercato delle Pulci ★★ The little piazza behind the Loggia del Pesce—originally built under Cosimo I for the city's fishmongers—hosts a daily flea market. Rifle through the stalls and little shops in search of costume jewelry, Tiffany lamps, secondhand dolls, vintage postcards, weird objects, mismatched crockery, and other one-off ephemera. The market runs daily, although not every unit is open every day. Piazza de' Ciompi. No phone. Bus: C1, C2, or C3.

Mercato di San Lorenzo ★ The city's busiest tourist street market is a fun place to pick up T-shirts, marbleized paper, or a city souvenir. Leather wallets, purses, bags, and jackets are another popular purchase—but be sure to assess the quality of the workmanship, and haggle for your life. The market runs daily; watch out for pickpockets. In 2014 it was controversially ejected from part of its traditional home, in Piazza

San Lorenzo, and now spreads around Piazza del Mercato Centrale; whether it will ever move back is as yet undecided. Via dell'Ariento and Via Rosina. No phone. Bus: C1.

Mercato di Sant'Ambrogio ★ A proper slice of Florentine life, 6 mornings a week. The piazza outside has fruit, vegetables, costume jewelry, preserves, and end-of-line clothing. Go inside the market building for meat, olive oil, a cafe, or a budget bite to eat at "Da Rocco." Piazza Ghiberti. No phone. Bus: C2 or C3.

Mercato Nuovo/Mercato della Paglia ★ Alternatively known as the "New" Market or the Straw Market, this handsome little loggia now shelters stalls stuffed with affordable souvenirs and trinkets, and aimed exclusively at tourists. Pay a visit if only to see the "Porcellino," a small bronze boar cast in the 1600s by Pietro Tacca. Rub his nose and the legend says you will return to Florence. It runs daily. Piazza del Mercato Nuovo. No phone. Bus: C2.

Bookshops

Babele ★★ Small but spectacular shop selling fine graphic art books and limited edition prints. Via delle Belle Donne 41R (at Via del Moro). ℰ **055-283-312.** www.babelefirenze. com. Bus: 6 or 11.

Feltrinelli International ★ The best Florence branch of this national chain for anyone seeking English-language books. Via dei Cerretani 32R. ℰ **055-238-2652.** www. lafeltrinelli.it. Bus: C2 or 22.

Paperback Exchange ★ New and secondhand titles, all in English. Includes guidebooks and children's titles. Closed Sundays. Via delle Oche 4R. ℰ **055-293-460.** www. papex.it. Bus: C2.

Crafts & Artisans

Florence has a longstanding reputation for its craftsmanship. And although the storefront display windows along heavily touristed streets are often stuffed with cheap foreign imports and mass-produced goods, you can still find genuine handmade, top-quality items if you search around.

To get a better understanding of Florence's artisans, including a visit to a workshop, **Context Travel** (p. 94) runs a guided walk around the Oltrarno, the city's traditional craft area. The "Made in Florence" walk costs 75€ and lasts 3 hours.

Madova ★ For almost a century, this has been the best city retailer for handmade leather gloves, lined with silk, cashmere, or lambs' wool. Expect to pay between 40€ and 60€ for a pair. You perhaps wouldn't expect it a few paces from the Ponte Vecchio, but this place is the real deal. And it's not only about tradition: They also do a line of touchscreen gloves for gadget addicts. Via Guicciardini 1R. ℰ **055-239-6526.** www.madova. com. Bus: C3 or D.

Masks of Agostino Dessi ★ This little shop is stuffed floor to ceiling with handmade masks. Each is made by hand from papier-mâché, leather, and ceramics, then hand finished expertly. Items cover both Venetian Carnevale and *commedia dell'arte* styles. Via Faenza 72R. ℰ **055-287-370.** www.alicemasks.com. Bus: C1 or 4.

Officina Profumo-Farmaceutica di Santa Maria Novella ★★★ A shrine to scents and skincare, and also Florence's most historic herbal pharmacy with roots in the 17th century, when it was founded by Dominicans based in the adjacent convent of Santa Maria Novella. Nothing is cheap, but the perfumes, cosmetics, moisturizers, and other products are made from the finest natural ingredients and packaged exquisitely. Via della Scala 16. ✆ **055-216-276.** www.smnovella.it. Bus: C2.

Scuola del Cuoio ★★   Florence's leading leather school is also open house for visitors. You can watch trainee artisans at work (Mon–Fri only) then visit the small shop to buy items made from the best soft leather. Portable items like wallets and bags are a good buy. Closed Sundays in off-season. Via San Giuseppe 5R (or enter through Santa Croce, via right transept). ✆ **055-244-534.** www.scuoladelcuoio.com. Bus: C3.

ENTERTAINMENT & NIGHTLIFE

Florence has bundles of excellent, mostly free, listings publications, both in print and online At the tourist offices, pick up the free monthly **"Informacittà"** (www.informacitta.net), which is strong on theater and other arts events, as well as markets. Younger and hipper, **"Zero"** (http://firenze.zero.eu) is hot on the latest eating, drinking, and nightlife. **"Firenze Spettacolo,"** a 2€ Italian-language monthly sold at most newsstands, is the most detailed and up-to-date listing of nightlife, arts, and entertainment. **"iOVO"** (www.iovo.it) is good on contemporary arts and cultural goings-on in the city.

If you just want to wander and see what grabs you, you will find plenty of tourist-oriented action in bars around the city's main squares. For something a little livelier—with a slightly younger and more local focus—walk **Borgo San Frediano, Piazza Santo Spirito,** or the northern end of **Via de' Macci,** close to where it meets Via Pietrapiana. **Via de' Benci** is usually buzzing around *aperitivo* time, and is popular with an expat crowd. **Via de' Renai** and the bars of San Niccolò around the **Porta San Miniato** are often lively too, with a mixed crowd of tourists and locals.

Performing Arts & Live Music

Florence does not have the musical cachet or historic opera houses of Milan or Venice, but there are two symphony orchestras and a fine music school in Fiesole. The city's public theaters are respectable, and most major touring companies stop in town on their way through Italy. Get tickets to all cultural and musical events online; they will send an e-mail with collection instructions—or buy in person at **Box Office,** Via delle Carceri 1 (✆ **055-210-804;** www.boxofficetoscana.it).

Many concerts and recitals staged in private halls and other spaces are sponsored by the **Amici della Musica** (✆ **055-607-440;** www.amicimusica.fi.it), so check their website to see what "hidden" concert might be on while you are here.

St. Mark's ★   Operatic duets and full-scale opera performances in costume are the lure here. The program sticks to the classics like "Carmen," "La Traviata," and "La Bohème," and runs most nights of the week all year. Via Maggio 18. ✆ **340-811-9192.** www.concertoclassico.info. Tickets 20€–40€. Bus: D, 11, 36, or 37.

Teatro Comunale ★   Alongside the new Teatro dell'Opera, this is Florence's main opera, ballet, and orchestral music stage. It also co-hosts the Maggio Musicale Fiorentino, one of Italy's major classical music festivals, staged each May. Corso Italia. ✆ **055-277-9350.** www.maggiofiorentino.it. Tickets 15€–80€. Bus: C3/Tram: T1.

Teatro dell'Opera ★★   Vast new concert hall and arts complex that seats up to 1,800 in daring modernist surrounds. Much delayed, the venue co-hosted its first Maggio Musicale Fiorentino in 2014. Viale Fratelli Rosselli 7R. ✆ **055-277-9350.** www.operadifirenze.it. Tickets 10€–85€. Tram: T1.

Teatro Verdi ★   Touring shows, "serious" popular music, one-off revues, classical music and dance, as well as the Orchestra della Toscana, occupy the stage at Florence's leading all-round theater. Via Ghibellina 97. ✆ **055-212-320.** www.teatroverdifirenze.it. Closed 2nd half of July and all Aug. Bus: C1, C2, or C3.

Volume ★   By day, it's a laid-back cafe selling coffee, books, and crepes. By night, a buzzing bar with acoustic sets at least a couple of nights of the week. Piazza Santo Spirito 5R. ✆ **055-238-1460.** www.volumefirenze.com. No cover. Bus: D, 11, 36, or 37.

Cafes

Florence no longer has a glitterati or intellectuals' cafe scene, and when it did—from the late-19th-century Italian Risorgimento era through *la dolce vita* of the 1950s—it was basically copying the idea from Paris. Although they're often overpriced tourist spots today—especially around **Piazza della Repubblica**—Florence's high-toned cafes are fine if you want pastries served to you while you sit and people-watch.

Caffetteria delle Oblate ★★   Relaxing terrace popular with local families and students, and well away from the tourist crush (and prices) on the streets below. As a bonus, it has unique perspective on Brunelleschi's dome. Also serves light lunch and *aperitivo.* Closed all-day Sunday and Monday mornings. Top floor of Biblioteca dell'Oblate, Via del Oriuolo 26. ✆ **055-263-9685.** www.lospaziochesperavi.it. Bus: C1 or C2.

Le Terrazze ★   The prices, like the perch, are a little elevated (3€–5€ for a coffee). But you get to enjoy your drink on a hidden terrace in the sky, with just the rooftops, towers, and Brunelleschi's dome for company Top floor of La Rinascente, Piazza della Repubblica. ✆ **055-219-113.** www.larinascente.it. Bus: C3 or D.

Rivoire ★   If you are going to choose one overpriced pavement cafe in Florence, make it this one. The steep prices (6€ for a cappuccino, 4.50€ for a small mineral water) help pay for the loan of one of the prettiest slices of real estate on the planet. Piazza della Signoria (corner of Via Vaccherreccia). ✆ **055-214-412.** www.rivoire.it. Bus: C2.

Wine Bars, Cocktail Bars & Craft Beer Bars

If you want to keep it going into the small hours, you will likely find Italian **nightclubs** to be rather cliquey—people usually go in groups to hang out and dance only with one another. There's plenty of flesh showing, but no meat market. Singles hoping to find random dance partners will often be disappointed.

Beer House Club ★★   Come here for the best artisan beers from Tuscany, Italy, and further afield. Their own line, brewed for the bar in nearby Prato, includes IPA, Imperial Stout, and Saison styles. From 5 to 8pm, house beers are 4.50€ a pint instead of 6€. Corso Tintori 34R. ✆ **055-247-6763.** www.beerhouseclub.it. Bus: C1, C3, or 23.

Caffè Sant'Ambrogio ★   Wine and cocktail bar in a lively part of the center, northeast of Santa Croce. It is popular with young locals without being too achingly hip. In summer, the action spills out onto the little piazza and church steps outside. Piazza Sant'Ambrogio 7R. No phone. www.caffesantambrogio.it. Bus: C2 or C3.

Cantinetta dei Verrazzano ★★   One of the coziest little wine and food bars in the center is decked out with antique wooden wine cabinets, in genuine *enoteca* style. The wines come from the first-rate Verrazzano estate, in Chianti. Via dei Tavolini 18R. ✆ **055-268-590.** www.verrazzano.com. Bus: C2.

Fuori Porta ★   Friendly San Niccolò wine bar with a terrace at the foot of the climb to Piazzale Michelangiolo. There are plenty of cold cuts to accompany the wine, plus the kitchen knocks out excellent pasta and larger dishes. Wines by the glass from 3.50€ and a handful of Tuscan craft beers in bottle. It is often open all day in high season (Apr–Oct), without an afternoon closure; otherwise, every lunchtime and evening. Via Monte alle Croci 10R. © 055-234-2483. www.fuoriporta.it. Bus: D or 23.

Golden View Open Bar ★   All modernist bright-white formica and marble, this is one of the city's most elegant *aperitivo* spots. Pay 10€ to 15€ for a cocktail or glass of bubbly and help yourself to the buffet between 7 and 9:30pm every night. There is also live jazz 4 nights a week from 9:15pm. Via dei Bardi 58R. © 055-214-502. www.golden viewopenbar.com. Bus: C3 or D.

King Grizzly ★   Grungy but friendly beer bar smack in the center of the *centro storico*. There is a well-chosen selection on 8 or so taps, from all over the world, sold at fair prices considering the location (5€ large, 3€ small). The bottle fridge also chills worldwide craft labels. Piazza de' Cimatori 5R. No phone. Bus: C2.

La Divina Enoteca ★   Relaxed wine bar behind Florence's Mercato Centrale. The wine list has 10 or 12 labels by the glass, and they also stock beers from Italian microbreweries like Birrificio del Ducato, Bruton, and Lilium. It closes at 8:30pm, and all day Monday. Via Panicale 19R. © 055-292-723. www.ladivinaenoteca.it. Bus: C1.

La Terrazza at the Continentale ★★   There are few surprises on the list here—a well-made Negroni, Cosmopolitan, and the like—and prices are a little steep at around 15€ a cocktail. But the setting, on a rooftop right by the Ponte Vecchio, makes them cheap at the price. The atmosphere is fashionable but casual (wear what you like) and staff is supremely welcoming. La Terrazza opens from 4pm; arrive at sundown to see the city below start to twinkle. Inside the Continentale Hotel, Vicolo dell'Oro 6R. © 055-27-262. Bus: C3 or D.

Le Murate ★★   It bills itself as a "literary cafe," so the stripped-brick decor and hipster clientele are taken as read. As well as coffee by day—in the courtyard of the city's former prison—there are themed food evenings, *aperitivo,* and a cocktail list as long as your arm. Piazza delle Murate. © 055-234-6872. www.lemurate.it. Bus: C2 or C3.

Mostodolce ★   Burgers, pizza, Wi-Fi, and sports on the screen—so far, so good. And Mostodolce also has its own artisan beer on tap, brewed just outside Florence (some are very strong). Happy hour is 3:30 to 7:30pm, when it is .50€ off a beer. Via Nazionale 114R. © 055-230-2928. www.mostodolce.it/firenze. Bus: C1.

Pitti Gola e Cantina ★   A quietly upscale, but not ostentatious, wine bar right opposite the Pitti Palace that specializes in niche labels from Tuscany and beyond. Wines by the glass from 6.50€. They also sell plates of food (around 10€) to complement their wines, and run a mail-order wine club. Piazza Pitti 16. © 055-212-704. www. pittigolaecantina.com. Bus: D, 11, 36, or 37.

Volpi e L'Uva ★   The wines by the glass list is 30-strong, the atmosphere is relaxed, and the terrace on a little piazza beside Santa Felicità is a delight. It's the kind of place you just sink into. Glasses from 4€. Closed Sundays. Piazza dei Rossi 1. © 055-239-8132. www.levolpieluva.com. Bus: C3 or D.

YAG Bar ★   A gay, lesbian, bi, and trans crowd gathers for lively, relaxed drinks before a night on the town. Via de' Macci 8R. © 055-246-9022. www.yagbar.com. Bus: C2 or C3.

AROUND FLORENCE

As if Florence wasn't endowed with enough attractions to keep you interested for months, within a very small radius of the city is a wealth of other attractions. Some, like Prato and Pistoia, are art cities filled with sculpture and painting that can easily contribute to your sensory overload. The Chianti wine county is a good antidote, providing a tonic of rolling green hillsides and a taste of some of Italy's best wines. Fiesole is the easiest break from city life, topping a hilltop that's a bus ride of a mere half hour or so away from Florence. You will lengthen the list of possibilities almost inordinately if you consider that just about anywhere in Tuscany, and many places in Umbria, are an easy train journey away from Florence—Lucca, Pisa, Siena, San Gimignano, and Volterra are short trips away (see chapter 6), as are Arezzo, Cortona, and Montepulciano (see chapter 7). Umbria's Perugia and Assisi are also relatively short journeys away (see chapter 8). In the meantime, though, here are some worthy choices well under an hour away from the Tuscan capital.

FIESOLE

9km (6 miles) NW of Florence

You can enjoy half a day in Fiesole without poking your head into a church or scrutinizing a fresco. You can also do those things if you wish, and even see some Roman ruins, but the real reasons to make the trip into the hills above Florence are to take in the views, catch a breeze, and get a taste of the Tuscan countryside without really leaving Florence. While Fiesole is a place apart, and was once a formidable foe to Florence (Dante refers to "the beasts of Fiesole"), the Florentines have been using the airy hillside as a summer retreat since the 14th century and often come up here for a breath of fresh air and a quick break from the city below.

Essentials

GETTING THERE   Take bus no. 7 from Florence, from the station or along stops on Via La Pira for the scenic, 25-minute ride through well-tended hillside gardens up to Fiesole's main square, Piazza Mino.

VISITOR INFORMATION   The tourist office is at Via Portigiani 3 (© **055-596-1323;** www.comune.fiesole.fi.it) and is open daily from 10:30am to 1pm and 1:30 to 5pm. You can buy tickets here for the Estate Fiesolana (www.estatefiesolana.it), 2 months of music, ballet, film, and

Around Florence

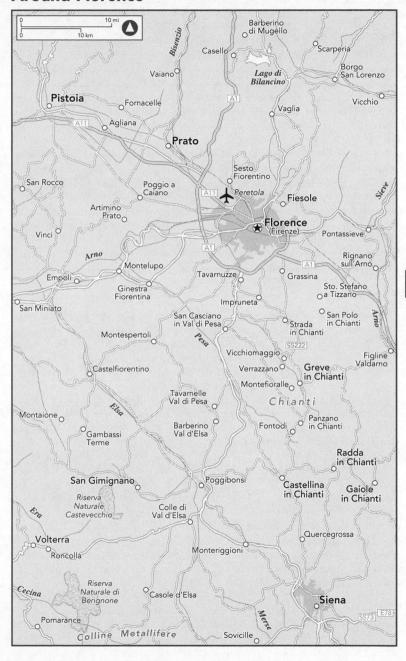

theater from late June to August in the restored A.D.-1st-century Roman theater. Listening to Mozart and Verdi under the stars in a 2,000-year-old theater is an experience to savor.

Exploring Fiesole

A stroll through Fiesole, much if it an uphill climb, begins in Piazza Mino, where the Duomo looms to one side. This landmark is remarkably forbidding and unattractive, in part because it's been destroyed twice, once by invading Florentines and again by ham-handed 19th-century restorers. St. Romulus, Fiesole's 1st-century patron saint, has been left undisturbed in his crypt beneath the altar and is pictured in a series of 15th-century panels near the altar. Legend (probably more colorful than actual truth) has it that the saint's mother, a girl of noble birth, bore him after a liaison with one of her father's slaves then abandoned him to be raised, like the same-named hero of Roman legend, by wolves. He was captured and baptized by St. Peter, and before the Romans caught up to him, spread Christianity around Central Italy. A walk up hill from here takes you past the town's Roman ruins (see below) and two lovely churches. Beyond the plain facade of the church of Sant'Alessandro is a wonderful parade of marble columns and arches (summer Mon–Sat 9am–6pm, Sun 10am–1pm and 2–6pm; winter Mon–Sat 9am–5pm and Sun 10am–1pm). Off to one side of the Gothic church of San Francesco are some peaceful little cloisters

Via San Francesco. © **055-59175.** free admission; daily 9am–noon and 3–5pm (until 7pm in summer). Just beyond are the Giardini Pubblici (Public Gardens), where the terraces are a spectacular balcony above Florence.

Convent of San Domenico ★ RELIGIOUS SITE   The large Dominican monastery in the hamlet of San Domenico just below Fiesole is the place to see frescos. A young man, Guido di Pietro (later known as Fra Angelico), entered this convent around 1407 and soon became famous in the Renaissance world for his religious paintings. Fra Angelico's career took him throughout Tuscany and Umbria and to Rome, sometimes fleeing the plague and papal disputes and more often to work on commissions, and he painted some his best known work in the convent of San Marco in Florence (p. 88) and in Cortona (p. 193); many of his other works are in museums around the world. On display here are some one of this earlier pieces. The best of them is in the church and known as the Fiesole Altarpiece, with the very popular 15th-century theme of the Maestà, or Madonna Enthroned. The Virgin is on a throne holding the Christ Child, who clutches two roses, one white, for purity, and one red, for the passion with which he would redeem humankind. Flanking them are angels, saints of the Dominican order, and St. Barnabus, namesake of the wealthy Florentine who had just footed the bill to restore the monastery. Two qualities stand out: Fra Angelico's training as an illuminator, a discipline that taught him the art of minute detail (notice the finally embroidered robes) and a deep spirituality and religious conviction—the friar believed that it was essential to portray Christ with absolute perfection and spent long hours at prayer before paining sessions. He also did a Crucifixion and a Madonna and Child for the Convent, in the Chapter House (ask a custodian to let you in).

It's a pleasant walk of about 1km (½ mile) from Fiesole down to San Domenico on the shady Via Vecchia Fiesolana, and you'll pass villas that Florentines once used as summer retreats (you can also take the number 7 bus back down the hill). Among them is the Villa Medici, built for Cosimo il Vecchio in the mid–15th century as gathering places for artists and men of letters, with beautiful gardens cut into the hillside. For

Fiesole

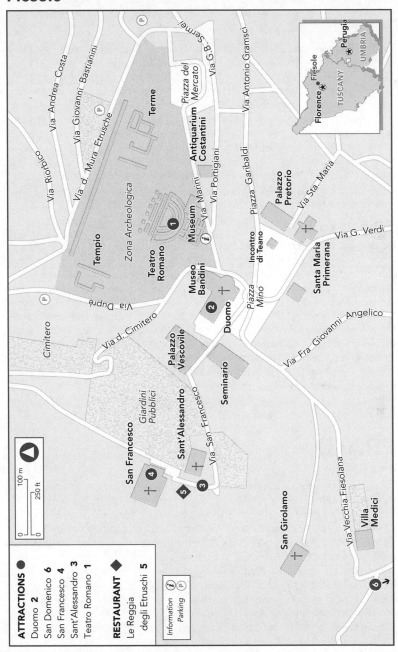

Via Andrea Costa
Via Giovanni Bastianini
Via Riohbco
Via d. Mura Etrusche
Via G.B. Sermei
Via Antonio Gramsci
Piazza del Mercato
Terme
Antiquarium Costantini
Via Marini
Via Portigiani
Piazza Garibaldi
Palazzo Pretorio
Via Sta. Maria
Tempio
Zona Archeologica
Teatro Romano
Museum
Incontro di Teano
Via G. Verdi
Santa Maria Primerana
Museo Bandini
Piazza Mino
Duomo
Via Fra Giovanni Angelico
Via Dupré
Cimitero
Via d. Cimitero
Palazzo Vescovile
Seminario
Giardini Pubblici
San Francesco
Sant'Alessandro
Via San Francesco
San Girolamo
Via Vecchia Fiesolana
Villa Medici

Perugia
UMBRIA
Fiesole
TUSCANY
Florence

100 m
250 ft

5

AROUND FLORENCE | Fiesole

105

much of the 19th and 20th centuries the villa was home to wealthy English and American ex-patriots (it can only be visited by prior arrangement; call © **055-2398994**).

Via San Domenico. sandomenicodifiesole.op.org. © **055-59230.** Free admission. Mon–Sat 8am–noon and 4–6pm; Sun 8–10:30am.

Teatro Romano ★ The ancients prized Fiesole's hilltop location and the Etruscans settled here long before the Romans established a colony in what is now Florence in the valley below. Remains of these past residents are fairly scant, with the exception of a 1st-century-B.C. Roman theater, uncovered in the 19th century and in such good shape that the *cavea* can still seat 3,000 for summertime Estate Fiesolana music concerts under the stars (see above). Other ruins scattered across the hillside are romantically overgrown with grasses and include A.D.-1st-century baths and a 1st-century-B.C. Roman temple, built atop an Etruscan one. From the far edge of the archaeological zone you can look over a stretch of 4th-century-B.C. Etruscan city walls. A small museum shows off the fragments of statuary and other finds from the ruins.

Via Portigiani 1. © **055-59118.** 10€ adults, 6€ students and age 6–17, free for children 6 and under; family ticket (up to 2 adults and 2 children) 20€.

Where to Eat

Le Reggia degli Etruschi ★ Your climb up the steep hill to this former monastery just below the church of San Francesco is rewarded with an eyeful of views from the terrace and the dining rooms of this former monastery. The Tuscan classics "updated with a touch of modernity" are exhilarating, too, as you'll discover as soon as you begin with some homemade *gnocchetti* (small potato dumplings), served with a non-Tuscan but decidedly successful sauce of Roquefort cheese and white pepper. Or, you might want to begin with the carpaccio (thin slices of raw beef) with arugula, Parmesan shavings, and thin strips of mango. Some dishes are strictly old school, better not to tamper with, such as *tagliate di petto d'anatra con riduzione d'aceto balsamico riserva* (duck breast with a Balsamic vinegar reduction). The wine list is traditional, too, sticking to excellent Tuscans.

Via San Francesco 18. www.lareggiadeglietruschi.com. © **055-59385.** Main courses 15€–20€. Daily 12:30–3pm and 7:30–10:30pm.

PRATO ★

20km (12 miles) W of Florence

Though Prato is a busy workaday place, set not amidst olive groves and vineyards but industrial suburbs, you have at least two, if not more, compelling reasons to visit. One is to see the exuberantly colorful frescoes with which the Renaissance painter Fra Filippo Lippi decorated the cathedral of Santo Stefano; another is to sample at the source the city's almond biscotti that just about everyone in Italy agrees are better than those baked anywhere else. You can also throw in the whiff of scandal, for it was here in Prato that the monk-artist Fra Lippo Lippi first set eyes on the young nun Lucrezia Buti, who became his lover and set tongues wagging throughout Renaissance Italy. Adding another element to the scene is the presence of many Chinese residents, who comprise the second largest Asian community in Italy, after Milan, and for the most part are the workforce behind the city's centuries-old textile industry.

Prato

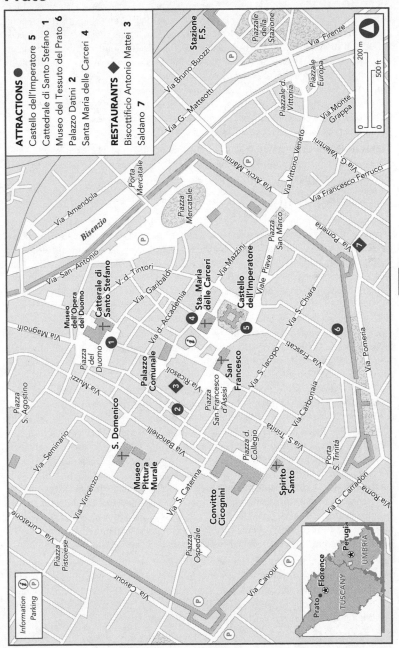

ATTRACTIONS ●
Castello dell'Imperatore **5**
Cattedrale di Santo Stefano **1**
Museo del Tessuto del Prato **6**
Palazzo Datini **2**
Santa Maria delle Carceri **4**

RESTAURANTS ◆
Biscottificio Antonio Mattei **3**
Saldano **7**

Stazione F.S.

Via Firenze

Piazzale della Stazione

Via Bruno Buozzi

Piazzale Europa

Via G. Matteotti

Piazzale d. Vittoria

Via Monte Grappa

Via G. Valentini

Via Arciv. Martini

Via Vittorio Veneto

Via Francesco Ferrucci

Porta Mercatale

Piazza Mercatale

Via Amendola

Bisenzio

Via San Antonio

Piazza San Marco

Via Pomeria

Via Magnolfi

Museo dell'Opera del Duomo

V. d. Tintori

Catterale di Santo Stefano

Via Garibaldi

Via d. Accademia

Sta. Maria delle Carceri

Via Mazzini

Viale Piave

Castello dell'Imperatore

Via S. Chiara

Via Muzzi

Piazza del Duomo

Palazzo Comunale

Via Ricasoli

San Francesco

Via S. Iacopo

Via Frascati

Via Pomeria

Piazza S. Agostino

Via Bandelli

Piazza San Francesco d'Assisi

Via Carbonaia

S. Domenico

Via Seminario

Museo Pittura Murale

Via S. Caterina

Piazza d. Collegio

Via S. Trinità

Porta S. Trinità

Via Vincenzo

Convitto Cicognini

Spirito Santo

Via G. Carradori

Via Roma

Via Curtatone

Piazza Pistoiese

Piazza Ospedale

Via Cavour

Via Cavour

Information ℹ
Parking Ⓟ

200 m
500 ft

Prato ★ Florence ★
TUSCANY
Perugia ★
UMBRIA

Essentials

GETTING THERE   Prato is on the Florence-Pistoia-Lucca-Viareggio and the Florence-Bologna **train** lines, with more than 50 trains daily from Florence (trip length: 20-40 min. depending on interim stops). From Pisa, change at Lucca or Florence Rifredi. All trains stop at Prato Centrale, a 10-minute walk southeast from the center, and some at Prato Porta al Serraglio, outside the gate a couple of blocks north of the Duomo (head straight down Via Magnolfi and you're there).

If you're traveling by **car,** take the A11 from Florence or Pistoia, exit at either Prato Est or Prato Ovest and follow signs. The best place to park is on Piazza Mercatale, where there are a small number of free spaces (indicated by white markings) along the southeastern edge, and payment by the hour in the rest of the lot.

VISITOR INFORMATION   The **tourist office** (✆ **0574-24-112**) is at Piazza Santa Maria delle Carceri 15, and is open Monday to Saturday 9am to 1pm and 3 to 6pm, Sunday 10am to 1pm.

Exploring Prato

Tuscany's second-largest city is quite a sprawl, but tucked away behind what remains of medieval walls is an elegant old town, with airy piazzas and lovely churches. These fortifications didn't do much to prevent the city from being sacked by papal forces in 1512, when thousands of citizens were slaughtered in the streets and the city came under the rule of the Florentine Medici family. A couple of centuries before then, Holy Roman Emperor Frederick II established a beachhead of his powerful and far-reaching dynasty in Prato, erecting the still-formidable though never-finished Castello dell'Imperatore on Piazza Santa Maria della Carceri. On the same square is a Renaissance attempt to restore classical ideals of order and symmetry, the templelike church of Santa Maria delle Carceri, designed on the plan of a Greek cross by Giuliano da Sangallo, a military engineer who branched out into churches and palaces under the patronage of the Medicis.

Prato's textile trade has flourished here since the Middle Ages, and Palazzo Datini was the home of Prato's kingpin of the medieval rag trade, Francesco di Marco Datini (1330–1410); you can still make out some of the frescoes on the proud facade at the corner of Via Mazzei and Via Rinaldesca (✆ **0574-21391;** the palace is open Mon–Fri 9am–12:30pm and 3–6pm [mornings only July–Aug], Sat 9am–12:30pm; free admission). The scrupulously tightfisted magnate, who invented the promissory note, inscribed each of the 500 ledgers he left behind in wooden crates with his motto, "For God and Profit." He did his meticulous recordkeeping in rooms frescoed with charmingly soothing scenes of plants and animals. The Anglo-American biographer Iris Origia, who was raised in the Villa Medici in Fiesole and spent most of her life on a vast estate in Tuscany's Val d'Orcia (p. 176), provides a fascinating account of Datini's 14th-century world in her wonderful book "The Merchant of Prato."

Cattedrale di Santo Stefano ★★ CATHEDRAL   In 1456, the Medicis sent their troublesome but favored artist Fra Lippo Lippi to Prato to paint frescoes behind the main altar of the cathedral. Chronically broke, the friar had just been imprisoned in Florence on swindling charges (allegedly trumped up) and he spent the next 12 years working on what is widely considered his finest work.

THE MAIN CHAPEL   Lippi's luminous and wonderfully evocative masterpieces depict events in the lives of St. Stephen, the first Christian martyr and the town's patron, on the right as you face the paintings, and John the Baptist, on the left. The panels are arranged so episodes from similar periods of the saints' lives face each other across the chapel—birth and youth at top, famous saintly moments in the middle, and death at the bottom. Looking at the panels it's important to remember that Lippi often merged several episodes from the saints' lives into a single scene. Handsome young Stephen lies on his funeral pyre in a medieval church, enjoying peaceful eternal rest, while intruding onto the edge of the scene is a rocky outcropping in which the saint is being stoned. In Lippi's emotional and colorful scenes of John's demise, the artist portrays a medieval banquet; as the famous story goes, the ruler Antipas tells his stepdaughter, Salome, that he will grant her any wish, and at the prompting of her mother, Herodias, the girl requests the head of St. John on the platter (the saint had proclaimed that the marriage of Herodias and her current husband, a descendant of King Herod, was incestuous, and she was out for revenge). It's all here—John being decapitated; Salome presenting the head to her mother (who looks vaguely bemused, while the revelers around her seem quite unconcerned by the presence of a severed head intruding upon their revelries); and, of course, the famous dance of Salome, portrayed as a radiant beauty in medieval garb modeled on the nun Lucrezia (who bore two of Lippi's children, including the likewise-talented painter Filippino Lippi). An especially touching scene in the top panel depicts young John taking leave of his aged parents, Elizabeth and Zecharaiah, as he sets off to live in the wilderness and preach the word of God.

CAPELLA DI SACRA CINTURA (CHAPEL OF THE GIRDLE) The cathedral is the repository of one of Christendom's most important relics, the girdle of the Virgin Mary. As the story goes, colorfully told in luminous frescoes by Angolo Gaddi, the girdle was found in the tomb of St. Thomas (see the box, "Doubting Thomas") and became part of a dowry of a young woman in Jerusalem who married Michele Dagomari, a merchant from Prato who fought in the First Crusade at the end of the 11th century. Returning to Prato (quite recognizably depicted in one of the panels). Michele gave the girdle to the church, which, as word spread, became an important site of pilgrimage for pregnant women—as it still is. The chapel was built soon after to house the relic, which is brought out for display five times a year, from a pulpit projecting from a corner of the exterior of the cathedral—on the Feast of the Assumption (Aug 15); the birthday of the Virgin (Sept 8); Christmas Day; Easter; and May 1, the beginning of the month of the Virgin. At other times of the year the girdle resides in a white-gold casket beneath a statue of the Madonna and Child by Giovanni Pisano, best known for his sculpted pulpit in Pisa's cathedral (p. 161). The pulpit is a reproduction; the original is in the adjacent Museo dell'Opera del Duomo, allowing you to see close-up the graceful dancing figures that Donatello, who left so many sculptures behind in Florence, carved between 1428 and 1438.

CAPPELLA DELL'ASSUNZIONE (CHAPEL OF THE ASSUMPTION) Frescoes in this tall, vaulted chapel near the altar are by Paolo Uccello and the less gifted Andrea Manzini, who in 1435 were commissioned by a wealthy weaver and merchant to paint scenes from the lives of St. Stephen and the Virgin Mary. When you look at the paintings, pay close attention to those by Uccello, and especially his depiction of architecture and use of perspective. The artist was an ardent student of both, and was allegedly so obsessed with perspective that he spent his sleepless nights trying to determine vanishing points in the spaces around him. In the "Disputation of St. Stephen," the saint stands in front of a dome, a reference to Brunelleschi's just-completed dome for Santa Maria del Fiore Duomo in Florence, a hot topic in 1436, when the dome was topped off and the frescoes were painted. The saint is arguing his case with

Doubting Thomas

As legend has it, the apostle Thomas was preaching in India when he was drawn up in a cloud of dust into the sky, where he witnessed the Virgin Mary rise from her tomb and ascend toward heaven. As she passed, she removed her belt and threw it to Thomas, saying, "Receive this, my friend." (The gesture suggests the sacred equivalent of a femme fatale throwing a garment to a paramour as a keepsake to remember her by.) The recipient was the infamously Doubting Thomas, the apostle who was not present at the resurrection of Christ and, in one of Christianity's most famous piques of skepticism, com-plained that until "I shall see in his hands the print of the nails, and put my finger into the print of the nails, and thrust my hand into his side, I will not believe." In a scene that was a favorite with Renaissance masters, Christ reappears, instructing Thomas, "Reach hither thy finger, and behold my hands; and reach hither thy hand, and thrust it into my side: and be not faithless, but believing," then added the admonishment, "blessed are they that have not seen, and yet have believed." Taking pity on Thomas' lack of faith, the Virgin threw him the girdle as proof positive that the she had ascended.

authorities who bear uncomfortable resemblance to 14th-century merchants of Prato, finely turned out in luxurious capes and fur-trimmed hats. A keen-eyed architectural historian can pick out more works by Brunelleschi in "The Stoning of Stephen," where thuggish rock-throwers (by Uccello's co-artist) stand in front of Uccello's fascinating group of towers, loggias, spires, and a Brunelleschi-like dome. The "Birth of the Virgin" and "Presentation of the Virgin at the Temple" are also crowded with architectural elements and executed with complex perspective that lend the scenes of color-rich, almost whimsical characters their dramatic intensity.

Piazza del Duomo. (℃) **0574 24112.** Admission to church free; 3€ to chapel with Filippo Lippi frescoes. Church: Mon–Sat 7:30–7, Sun 7:30–noon and 1–7pm. Filippo Lippi frescoes: Mon–Sat 10am–5pm, Sun 1–5pm.

Museo del Tessuto del Prato ★ MUSEUM A 19th-century mill within the medieval walls is the evocative setting for displays that trace Prato's 800 years as a center of the textile trade. Centuries-old Renaissance garb and other pieces from Prato and around the world, along with exhibitions that often focus on contemporary fashion, are set amid looms and huge weaving machines that were powered by water supplied by underground channels and once kept most of Prato employed.

Via Puccetti 3. www.museodeltessuto.it. (℃) **0574-611503.** 8€. Tues–Thurs 10am–3pm, Fri–Sat 10am–7pm, Sun 3–7pm; winter daily 9am–noon and 3–5pm.

Where to Eat

Even if you have Chinese food in Prato (and you have a lot of choices around Porta Pratese) you will want to top off a meal with *cantuccini,* the city's famous twice-baked biscuits. Made with almonds and pine nuts, *cantuccini* are a staple throughout Italy, but Prato has the edge with a centuries-old recipe that yields an especially delicious product, which here in Tuscany is often dipped in Vin Santo, a sweet dessert wine, or in coffee, depending on the time of day. The time-honored place to try them is **Biscottificio Antonio Mattei** at Via Ricasoli 20 ((℃) **0574-25756**).

Another Prato legend concerns the events of 1312, when an unfortunate fellow from nearby Pistoia named Giovanni di Ser Landetto, aka Musciattino, stole the city's cherished relic, the girdle of the Virgin Mary. Rushing home in a thick fog, he became disoriented and wandered right back into the center of Prato, where he was apprehended, tied to a donkey's tail, dragged through town, and burned at the stake. But not before his right hand was cut off—this the mob threw against the side of the cathedral, where its bloody imprint is said to be visible to this day.

Saldano ★ TUSCAN An old Prato institution that's been serving almost a century specializes in no-nonsense food at affordable prices and has two locations, one near the Duomo and one on a small lane on the south edge of the old town. Both are homey and as unfussy as the food, hung with black-and-white photos,. Nothing on the menu at either is going to surprise, and that's the point: *tortellini in brodo* (filled pasta in clear broth), *osso buco* (braised veal shank), *salsicce alla griglia* (grilled sausage), and all the other classics are here, served to an appreciative crowd of locals at extremely good-value prices.

Via Pomeria 23. www.trattoriasoldano.it. ℂ **0574-34665.** Via della Sirena 12: ℂ 0574-830913. Hours for both locations: Mon–Sat noon–2:30pm and 7:30–10pm. Main courses 6–8€.

PISTOIA ★

38km (23 miles) W of Florence

For much of their history, the Pistoiesi have been considered a fearsome lot. Even the well-reasoned Michelangelo complained that the Pistoiesi were "proud, envious [and] enemies of heaven," people who find "the simplest charity a labor." Dante made a 13th-century nobleman named Vanni Fucci from Pistoia into one of his most thuggish, Hell-doomed reprobates who does the unthinkable and makes an obscene gesture to God in Heaven. The bad reputation may have originated as early as 200 B.C., when Pistoium was a rough-and-tumble garrison town that supplied legionnaires defending the frontiers. The Roman conspirator Catiline was slaughtered outside town in 62 B.C., and by the Middle Ages Pistoiesi were stabbing each other with highly effective results using daggers the city's metal smiths were adept at crafting; soon assassins all across Europe were clamoring for the Pistoia weapons, and later for the small guns the city produced (whether Pistoia lent its name to "pistol" is up for debate). The Pistoiese were reportedly the instigators of the schism between Black and White Guelphs that turned 13th-century Florence into a war zone. As the story goes, two Pistoiese children of Neri (Black) and Bianchi (White) factions were playing with wooden swords and one was hurt, so the father of the injured boy cut off the hand of the other youth with the admonishment, "Iron, not words, is the remedy for sword wounds" (the local interpretation of "spare the rod and you'll spoil the boy").

This tumultuous past aside, Pistoia has retained its pretty churches, some nice art, and well-preserved dark medieval alleyways and stony piazzas.

Essentials

GETTING THERE Pistoia is on the Florence-Lucca-Viareggio **train** line, with more than 35 trains daily from Florence (45–55 min.). The train station is on Piazza Dante Alighieri. To reach the center from there, walk right ahead on Via XX Settembre for about 5 blocks as far as Via Cavour in the city center.

By **car,** from east or west, take the A11: from Florence, past Prato, and from Pisa or Lucca past Montecatini. From the south, a slower but panoramic drive heads north from Empoli through olive groves and past Vinci. The most convenient free parking is signposted "Cellini," and lies just southeast of the city walls.

VISITOR INFORMATION The **tourist information** office (⏴ **0573-21-622;** www.turismo.pistoia.it; also visit www.comune.pistoia.it) is at Via Roma 1/Piazza del Duomo 4 (inside the Antico Palazzo dei Vescovi). It's open daily 9am (10am on Sun) to 1pm and 3 to 6pm.

Exploring Pistoia

Pistoia's civil and religious landmarks are clustered around the lovely Piazza del Duomo. The squat, octagonal Battisero (Baptistery) of green and white striped marble anchors one corner of the stage-set-like space. A curious presence off to one side is the Catiline tower, named for the conspirator who almost brought down the Roman empire and in the minds of many made the good-natured and righteous consul Cicero into a tyrant. In A.D. 63 Cicero began a campaign to suppress a coup that Catiline and other young aristocrats were fomenting. He had Catiline tracked down in Pistoia and executed without trial, a transgression against Roman law for which the consul was exiled to Greece.

A walk up the narrow lane on the north end of the square reveals the spectacular facade of the Ospedale del Ceppo (Hospital of the Tree Trunk), named for the "poor man's stump," a hollowed-out log that in the middle ages was placed in front of the door to collect alms. Giovanni della Robbia, of the well-known clan of Florentine sculptors who worked in ceramics, decorated the Renaissance portico with images of the Seven Works of Mercy (feeding the hungry, clothing the naked, and so forth) and the Cardinal Virtues (prudence, justice, fortitude, and temperance)—practices that all Christians are expected to perform, and should you need a refresher course, these beautiful and colorful panels provide an artful brush-up.

The side facade of San Giovanni Fuorcivitas, just south of Piazza Grande on Via Crispi, is an orderly and utterly delightful festival of blind arcades, inlaid diamond lozenges, and enough stripes to put a zebra to shame. West of the Duomo, on Via degli Orafi, is a show of early-20th-century exuberance, the Art Nouveau Galleria Vittorio Emanuele. The steel-and-glass structure with shops surrounded by elaborate metal scrollwork is a little tattered looking, but nonetheless reminiscent of grand shopping arcades in Milan and other European cities.

Cappella de Tau ★ MUSEUM The monks of the order of St. Anthony who built this hospice complex in 1360 wore the Greek letter "T" (tau) on their cloaks as a symbol of a crutch, in keeping with their dedication to caring for the sick and crippled. They hired Florentine Niccolò di Tommaso to cover every inch of their chapel with frescoes of Stories from the Old Testament (upper register and vaults; a scene of a terribly dejected Adam and Eve being banished from the Garden of Eden is especially moving); Stories from the New Testament (middle register); and Life of St. Anthony Abbot (lower register); and facing the door, a huge Last Judgment. The chapel came

Pistoia

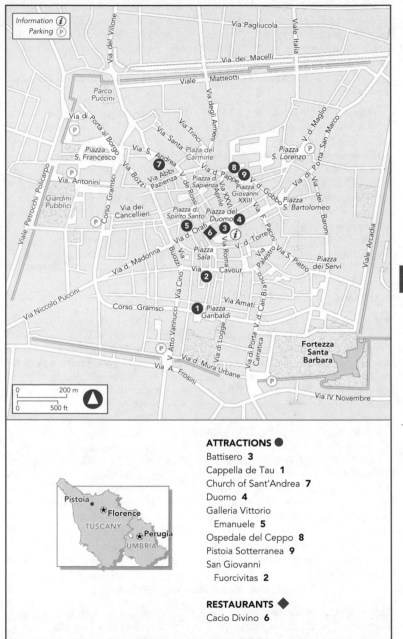

Information ⓘ
Parking Ⓟ

ATTRACTIONS ●
Battisero **3**
Cappella de Tau **1**
Church of Sant'Andrea **7**
Duomo **4**
Galleria Vittorio
  Emanuele **5**
Ospedale del Ceppo **8**
Pistoia Sotterranea **9**
San Giovanni
  Fuorcivitas **2**

RESTAURANTS ◆
Cacio Divino **6**

into private hands centuries ago and the frescoes were covered with whitewash and somewhat clumsily restored. What remains hints at their one-time color and vibrancy. Scenes from the life of St. Anthony—who though of noble birth lived as a hermit in the deserts of Egypt and is considered to be the founder on monasticism—include revealing vignettes of the works of his hospital's monks in the Middle Ages. The frescoes now surround giant bronze equestrian statues and nudes by Pistoia-born sculptor Marino Marini (1901–80).

Piazza San Michele. (ℂ) **0583-48-459.** Free admission. Summer daily 7:40am–noon and 3–6pm; winter daily 9am–noon and 3–5pm.

Church of Sant'Andrea ★ CHURCH   One of Pistoia's great masterpieces is the pulpit in this church, completed by Giovanni Pisano in 1301. If you've been to Pisa, you've seen the pulpit that Giovanni's father, Nicola, created in the baptistery there, and the similarities are obvious, though Giovanni's work may well be superior. At least that's what the inscription immodestly says, proclaiming "Giovanni carved it, who performed no empty work. The son of Nicola, and blessed with higher skill, Pisa gave him birth, endowed with mastery greater than any seen before." Nicola does indeed capture emotion in a way no one previously had, setting the stage for the naturalism that would come to the fore in the Renaissance. Especially emotional is a panel of the Slaughter of the Innocents, depicting Roman soldiers carrying out Harod's decree, upon hearing that a Messiah had been born, to kill all newborn male children in Bethlehem. Pisano's gut-wrenching scene shows knife-wielding Romans executing infants as their mothers try to protect their children and wail in grief.

Via Sant'Andrea, 35. (ℂ) **0573-442291.** Free admission. Mon–Sat 8am–1pm and 3:30–7:30pm.

Duomo ★★ CATHEDRAL   Pistoia's 12th-century cathedral is topped by the city's two patrons, St. Zeno and St. Jacopo. The presence of both show Pistoia, despites its reputation, to be a good-natured place, as Zeno was known for his devotion to charity and helping children and Jacopo (James), the fisherman who became one of the apostles, is the patron of pilgrims, who often found hospitality in Pistoia on the well-trod path to and from Rome. In fact, pilgrims throughout Europe often wore his emblem, a cockle shell on their travel attire. An eclectic yet pleasing mix of striped marble and arched loggias rise below a clumsy old defensive tower that was heightened with a slender, arched top for use as a campanile.

James is honored inside with the Dossale di San Jacopo (the altar of St. James), a masterful piece of silversmithing begun in 1287 and almost 2 centuries in the making, fashioned from more than a ton of silver. The spectacle was Pistoia's big attraction for medieval pilgrims on the Via Francigena, the road between Rome and Canterbury, England, and, quite lucratively for local tradesfolk, put the town on the map. No fewer than 628 figures populate the biblical scenes and episodes from the life of James, and with a close look you can pick out lively and intricate reenactments of such well-known stories as the angel announcing the birth of Jesus to shepherds in the fields and the demise of James, the first martyr, at the hands of sword-wielding Roman soldiers.

Piazza del Duomo. (ℂ) **0573-25095.** Free admission. Daily 10:30am–6pm.

Pistoia Sotterranea ★   Short of falling ill, the way into the Ospedale del Ceppo (Hospital of the Tree Trunk, see above) is to burrow beneath it. You'll learn about the hospital, founded in 1277 and the city's main hospital through the days of the Black Death (and still operating), as you follow the bed of a now-dry stream that once coursed beneath the complex and powered an olive press and simultaneously served as a laundry and source of drinking water. Tours, sometimes available in English, end at the tiny, frescoed teaching and autopsy theater built in the 1700s.

Piazza Giovanni XXIII 13. www.irsapt.it. ℂ **0573-368023.** Tour 9€. Daily at 10:30, 11:30am, 12:30, 2, 3, 4, 5pm (Apr–Sept also 6pm).

Where to Eat

A snack or light meal at **Caffe Duomo** (Piazza del Duomo 7; ℂ **0573-21283**) comes with a view of Pistoia's magnificent main square, and in good weather you can take a seat at one of few tables out front to enjoy simple and inexpensive snack food that includes delicious little squares of pizzalike bread.

Cacio Divino ★★ CONTEMPORARY TUSCAN   The attractive, contemporary-styled, bottle-lined room in a narrow lane near Pistoia's produce market is small but the ambitions of the kitchen are large and focus on delicious and innovative takes on traditional standards. *Pici Toscani al formaggio Shropshire* tops thick pici noodles with a cheddar cheese sauce; and *secondi* include several variations of beef tartare. Don't worry if you'd rather stick with the basics, because *fegatello di S. Miniato con cipolla brasata al balsamico* (that's liver and onions) and even simple *fagioli* (beans) are done to perfection, and the wine list is soundly grounded in many excellent local choices.

Via del Lastrone. www.cacio-divino.it. ℂ **0573-1941058.** Main courses 9€–13€.

A TRIP INTO THE CHIANTI

For many visitors to Italy, heaven on earth is the 167 sq. km (64 sq. miles) of land between Florence and Siena, known as the Chianti. Traversing the gentle hillsides south of Florence on the SS222, the Chiantigiana, only about 60km (36 miles) in length, is one of Italy's classic drives, especially the 20km (12-mile) stretch between between Greve and Castellina in Chianti. Landscapes are smothered in vineyards—some 4,000 hectares (9,884 acres) are blanketed with vines—and dark green and dusty silver olive groves, punctuated by woodland and peppered with *case coloniche,* stone farmsteads with trademark square dovecotes protruding from the roofs.

Essentials

VISITOR INFORMATION   You can pick up some information on the Chianti at the **Florence tourist office** (p. 46) or the **Siena tourist office** (p. 124). The unofficial capital of the area is Greve in Chianti, and its **tourist office** (ℂ **055-854-6299**), on the main square at Piazza Matteotti 11, makes an effort to provide some Chianti-wide info. From Easter to October, it's open daily from 10am to 1pm and 2 to 7pm, although out of season you may find that the place is closed. Online, you can also try the excellent **www.chianti.it** (with an especially helpful section on itineraries) for more information on the region.

How to See Chianti Country

The choices come down to renting a car or taking an organized tour; traveling by public bus you can get to towns along the route and see the countryside but you won't be able to reach most of the wineries and many of the sights. **SITA** (ℂ **055-214-721;** www.sitabus.it) from Florence services most of the town in the region but service is infrequent and geared to the schedules of residents not sightseers. Whichever option you choose, don't overdo it. You should limit visits to two or three wineries, so you can get the full experience of each. Three especially worthy stops are **Villa Vignamaggio, Badia a Coltibuono,** and **Castello di Brolio,** where wine tasting comes with a big dose of weighty history. See below for details on all of them.

If you rent a car (p. 227), you'll find it easy to find and follow the SS222, which is well marked and signposted along the way. You can easily see the sights and visit some wineries on a day's excursion and be back in Florence in time for dinner. Among organized tours, the most enjoyable are those geared to small groups that visit small wineries, so you don't find yourself part of a mob overrunning a huge operation. Some of the most respectable and consistently reliable are the van tours operated by **Tuscan Wine Tours** (© 331-3583823; www.tuscan-wine-tours.com), which take in two or three family-run wineries, with a stop for lunch. Super Chianti is an 8-hour tour and includes lunch with Panzano butcher Dario Cecchini, a stop in Greve, and the company of a wine expert (150€). The 6-hour Chianti Wine Time also includes lunch (but not with Dario) but does not include the stop in Greve or the company of a wine expert (you'll encounter those at the properties, and the tour begins with an intro talk at the Tuscan Wine School in Florence); 95€.

Biking through the Chianti can be one of Tuscany's most rewarding and scenic workouts. Use a reliable tour company (p. 230) or go on your own by renting a bike in central Greve at Ramuzzi, Via Italo Stecchi 23 (© **055-853-037;** www.ramuzzi.com); the cost is 20€ per day for a road bike or mountain bike, and 55€ a day for a scooter (discounts are available for multiple days). The company also organizes tours of a few days with local guides. The region's low mountains and stands of ancient forest are also excellent for hiking. For exploring by any means, you'll need an appropriate map, available in book and souvenir stores in the Chianti, Siena, and Florence. The free maps distributed by tourist offices aren't sufficient for veering far off the beaten path.

Exploring Chianti

First stop for wine lovers is the **Castello di Verrazzano** (© **055-854-243** or 055-290-684; www.verrazzano.com), the 12th-century seat of the Verrazzano family; it's only about 20km (12 miles) south of Florence, just outside the village of Gretti (well signposted). Young Giovanni Verrazzano, born here in 1485, left Chianti for adventure and discovered New York. The estate has been making wine at least since 1170, and you can sample it daily at the roadside shop; tasting is free. Their "jewel" is a 100 percent sangiovese called Sasello, while the Bottiglia Particolare (Particular [Special] Bottle) is in the Super Tuscan style, at 70 percent sangiovese and 30 percent cabernet. Tours of the gardens and cellars run Monday through Friday; book ahead at least 1 day in advance, a week or more in high season.

Greve in Chianti, about 30km (18 miles) south of Florence, is the center of the wine trade and the unofficial capital of Chianti. The central **Piazza Matteotti** is a rough triangle furnished with a statue of Verrazzano and surrounded by a mismatched patchwork arcade—each merchant had to build the stretch in front of his own shop. Greve is the host of Chianti's annual September wine fair, and there are, naturally, dozens of wine shops in town. The best is the **Enoteca del Chianti Classico,** Piazzetta Santa Croce 8 (© **055-853-297**). At Piazza Matteotti 69–71 is one of Italy's most famous butchers, **Macelleria Falorni** (© **055-854-363;** www.falorni.it), established in 1700 and still containing a cornucopia of hanging *prosciutti* and dozens of other cured meats, along with a decent wine selection. It's open daily.

Greve was the birthplace of another explorer, Amerigo Vespucci (1452–1512), whose family seat is in tiny Montefioralle, on a hillside about 2km (1 mile) west of

The Chianti

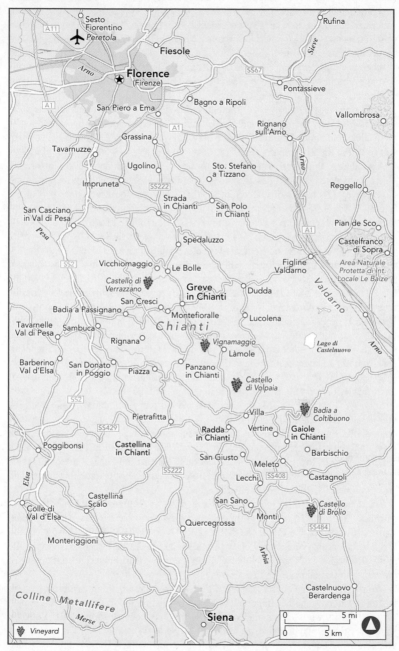

Vineyard

town. Educated in Florence, Vespucci went to work for the Medicis, who sent him to Spain to investigate their shipping interests. Vespucci was drawn into the world of navigation and was on the voyage in which navigators defined the coast of the South American continent, to which Vespucci lent his first name. Another famous Vespucci was Simonetta, wife of Amerigo's brother Mario and considered to be the greatest beauty of her age. It's often been said that the artist Botticelli used Simonetta, who died of tuberculosis at the young age of 21, as his model for Venus and his other great beauties; at his request, the artist is buried at her feet in the Vespucci church of Ognissanti in Florence.

One kilometer (⅔ mile) west of (and almost as high above) Greve perches the solid stone 14th-century medieval hamlet of Castello di Montefioralle, where the circular main street and enticing alleyways have only a few electric cables to remind you that you're still in the 21st century.

A winding, often rough road continues for several miles then drops into a lush valley where the isolated **Badia a Passignano** is set amid a cypress grove atop vineyards and olive groves. (As bad as this stretch of road is, 800 years ago it was once part of the "strada senese del Sambuco," the main route between Florence and Siena.) The fortified monastery, with corner defensive towers, was established by St. Giovanni Gualberto, a Florentine who became a Benedictine monk early in the 11th century after witnessing a miracle: Setting out to avenge the murder of a relative, he took mercy when his victim laid himself before him with arms outstretched in the form of a cross. Gualberto stopped afterward to pray before a crucifix, and the Christ figure bowed his head. He soon became a Benedictine monk, but yearning for a more perfect life, he founded the Vallombrosan order here in 1049 (the name is Latin for Vallis Umbrosa or Umbrosa Valley). Gualberto died at the monastery in 1073 and is buried in the small Romanesque church of San Michele. From here you can tour a few other parts of the monastery, including the refectory where Domenico Ghirlandaio, teacher of Michelangelo, and his younger brother Davide painted a fresco of the Last Supper in 1476. A shop selling the monastery's wine is open most days but usually it's possible to visit the refectory only on Sunday afternoon at 3pm (© **055-8071622**).

South of Greve, the SS222 takes you past the left turn for Lamole. Along that road you'll find **Villa Vignamaggio** (© **055-854-661;** www.vignamaggio.com), a russet-orange villa surrounded by cypress and elegant gardens where Lisa Gherardini, who grew up to pose for Leonardo da Vinci's "Mona Lisa," was born in 1479. The estate's wine was famous in the past and in 1404 became the first red wine of these hills to be referred to as "chianti" in written record. Book ahead at least a week in advance and you can tour the cellar and ornate gardens and sample the wines.

The Chiantigiana next cuts through the town of **Panzano in Chianti,** 10km (6 miles) south of Greve, known for its embroidery and for another famed butcher, **Antica Macelleria Cecchini,** Via XX Luglio 11 (© **055-852-020**). Dario Cecchini loves to entertain visitors with classical music and tastes of his products, while he recites the entirety of Dante's "Inferno" from memory. (Dario is fast becoming one of the most famous butchers in the world.)

From Castellina in Chianti, just a few mile down the road, a turn east brings you to Radda in Chianti, another important wine center that retains its medieval street plan and a bit of its walls. The center of town is the 15th-century **Palazzo del Podestà,** studded with the mayoral coats of arms of past *podestà;* among the 51 coats of arms you can make out that of the Medici, with its telltale balls. (These emblems, which might be no more poetic than representations of the cupping balls the family used in

A WINE TO crow ABOUT

This is the world's definitive wine region, in both history and spirit; these hills have been an oenological center for several thousand years. Indeed, one local grape, the *canaiolo nero*—one of the varietals that traditionally goes into Chianti Classico—was known to the ancients as the "Etruscan grape." The name Chianti, probably derived from that of the local noble Etruscan family Clantes, has been used to describe the hills between Florence and Siena for centuries, but it wasn't until the mid–13th century that Florence created the Lega del Chianti to unite the region's three most important centers, Castellina, Radda, and Gaiole, and the new confederation chose the black rooster as their symbol. By 1404, the red wine long produced here was being called chianti as well, and in 1716 a grand ducal decree defined the boundaries of the Chianti and laid down general rules for its wine production, making it the world's first officially designated wine-producing area.

In the 19th century, one vintner, the "Iron Baron" Ricasoli, experimented with varietals using the Sangiovese grape as his base. Working off centuries of refinement, he eventually came up with the perfect balance of grapes that became the unofficial standard for all chianti.

Soon the title "chianti" was being used by hundreds of poor-quality, vino-producing hacks, both within the region and from far-flung areas, diminishing the reputation of the wine. To fight against this, Greve and Castelnuovo Berardenga joined the original Lega cities and formed the Consorzio del Gallo Nero in 1924, reviving the black rooster as their seal. The *consorzio* (still active—their members produce about 80 percent of the Chianti Classico that's bottled) pressed for laws regulating the quality of chianti wines and restricting the Chianti Classico name to their production zone. When Italy devised its DOC and DOCG laws in the 1960s, chianti was one of the first to be defined as DOCG, guaranteeing its quality as one of the top wines in Italy. Today, of the 100 sq. km (39 sq. miles) of vineyards in the hills between Florence and Siena, some 6,972 hectares (17,228 acres) are devoted to the grapes that will eventually become Chianti Classico and carry the seal of the black rooster.

their humble origins as mere doctors, have been the brunt of jokesd since the clan's heyday; one contemporary of Cosimo II quipped that the Medicis were determined to show off their balls even in monks' privies.) The local butcher here is a true artisan; **Porciatti** will give you a taste of traditional salami and cheeses at their *alimentari* on Piazza IV Novembre 1 at the gate into town (© **0577-738-055;** www.casaporciatti.it).

Seven kilometers (4⅓ miles) north of Radda on a secondary road is the **Castello di Volpaia** ★★ (© **0577-738-066;** www.volpaia.com), a Florentine holding buffeted by Sienese attacks and sieges from the 10th to 16th centuries. The still-impressive central keep is all that remains, but it's surrounded by an evocative 13th-century *borgo* (village) containing the Renaissance La Commenda church. You can tour the winery daily; the tour includes a tasting of the wines and their fantastic olive oil. The central tower has an enoteca for drop-in tastings and sales, plus award-winning (and scrumptious) olive oils and farm-produced white and red vinegars.

Some of the most beautiful scenery in Chianti surrounds the little village of **Gaiole in Chianti,** just to the east of Radda, where vineyard-carpeted hillsides are crowned with castles and churches. The **Castello di Brolio,** just north of Gaiole, is one of the most important and scenic strongholds in Chianti. For a time in the 12th century the castle was Florence's southernmost holding, a show of might menacingly close to rival Siena; it was said that, "When Brolio growls, all of Siena trembles." From the lovely Renaissance gardens, Siena appears like a mirage in the distance across a broad sweep of undulating southern Chianti countryside. The castle is best known these days as the domain of the Ricasoli family, who've been in residence for the past 10 centuries. An especially formidable member was Baron Bettino Ricasoli (1809–80), an astute states-man who served as Italy's second prime minister and became known as the Iron Baron for his adept maneuvers in helping piece together the modern nation. Another of the baron's long-lasting accomplishments is said to have been the invention of the recipe for Chianti, and the family continues to produce some of the region's most esteemed labels at its **Baroni Ricasoli** winery (© **0577–730220;** www.baronericasoli.com). The family's illustrious history and the history of the wine they introduced come to light on tours Monday, Tuesday, Wednesday, Friday, and Saturday at 10:30am and also at 3:30pm Tuesday and Friday, for 10€, and the gardens and small museum can be visited independently for 8€; the cellars and an extensive wine shop are open January to mid-March, Monday to Friday 9am to 1pm and 2 to 5:45pm; mid- to late March Monday to Friday 9am to 7pm and Saturday and Sunday 11am to 7pm; and April to mid-October Monday to Friday 9am to 7:30pm and Saturday to Sunday 11am to 7pm.

Top prize for most romantic spot in Chianti might go to the lovely **Badia a Coltibu-ono** (© **0577-746110;** www.coltibuono.com), or Abbey of the Good Harvest, about 6km (4 miles) north of Gaiole and well sign-posted. Founded in 1051, the abbey and surrounding gardens, farm fields, and vineyards were the holding of Benedictine monks until the 19th century. The gardens are a romantic concoction of hedges, beds of lavender, pools, and pergolas dripping with vines, all surrounded with magnificent cypresses and fir trees. The abbey is now the home of the Stucchi-Prinetti family, who sell their wine in their atmospheric old cellars. The estate is open to the public by guided tour (5€), mid-April to October, daily at 2, 3, 4, and 5pm.

SIENA & WESTERN TUSCANY

Outside Florence, Tuscany's role as the cradle of the Renaissance and an ancient center of power and culture comes most to the fore in lovely Siena and the lands, towns, and city to the west. Surrounded by golden landscapes where walled towns cap hilltops and are surrounded by fertile plains are the narrow medieval lanes and stony piazzas of Lucca, the sublime art and architecture of Gothic Siena, the remarkable architectural assemblage of the Campo Santo in Pisa, the Etruscan tombs in Volterra, and the tall towers of San Gimignano. These are near the top of the list of the region's many attractions, but so are *so* many other sights and experiences. Just for starters, consider also:

PIAZZAS Piazza del Campo, the scallop-shaped setting for Siena's famous Palio race, is the heart of the city and an icon of medieval town planning.

CHURCHES The icing-white, four-tiered facade of the church of San Michele in Foro makes you understand why local son Giacomo Puccini was inspired to compose his world's favorite operas.

PAINTINGS Siena's Museo Civico is a showcase for Ambrogio Lorenzetti's civic "Allegories."

ARCHITECTURE No building in the world is more instantly recognizable than Pisa's 12th-century Leaning Tower.

SIENA ★★★

70km (43 miles) S of Florence, 232km (144 miles) N of Rome

Siena was Florence's longtime rival, and this medieval city of brick seems to have come out on top in terms of grace and elegance. With steep, twisting stone alleys and proud churches, palaces, and crenellated public buildings draped across its gentle hillsides, Siena is for many admirers the most beautiful town in Italy. At its heart is a ravishing piazza and from its heights rises a magnificent duomo of striped marble.

The city trumpets the she-wolf as its emblem, a holdover from its days as Saena Julia, the Roman colony founded by Augustus about 2,000 years ago (though the official Sienese myth has the town founded by the sons of Remus, younger brother of Rome's legendary forefather). Civic projects and artistic prowess reached their greatest heights in the 13th and 14th

A DAY AT THE races

Siena lets its guard down every year, on July 2 and again on August 16, when the Palio delle Contrade transforms the Piazza del Campo into a racetrack and hordes of spectators squeeze through the city's narrow alleyways to watch. This aggressive bareback horserace around the Campo involves 10 of Siena's 17 *contrade* (districts), chosen by lot to participate, and is preceded by a showy flag-waving ceremony and parade. The race itself is over in just 2 minutes. Frenzied celebrations greet the winning rider, and the day is rounded off with communal feasts in each district.

To witness the event, you'll end up standing for hours in the sun and waging battle to get to a toilet. An easier way to enjoy the experience is to settle for the trial races, also held in the Campo (starting June 2 and Aug 13). There's a crowd, but it's smaller and tamer, and while trial races are not as fast and furious as the real thing, they are just as photogenic and fun to watch; there are usually six: mornings (9am) and late evenings (7:45pm June, 7:15pm Aug).

Another way to view the Palio in comfort is to reserve a spot in the temporary stands, on one of the surrounding terraces, or even at a window overlooking the campo. You should reserve a year in advance and expect to pay at least 350€ and as much as 700€ each. Among the travel agents handling arrangements is 2Be Travel Designers (www.paliotickets.com).

centuries, when artists invented a distinctive Sienese style while banking and a booming wool industry made Siena one of the richest Italian republics. Then, in 1348, the Black Death killed perhaps three-quarters of the population, decimating the social fabric and devastating the economy. Siena never recovered, and much of this city of rose-colored brick has barely changed since, inviting you to slip into the rhythms and atmosphere of the Middle Ages.

Essentials

GETTING THERE   Some 19 **trains** daily connect Siena with Florence (usually 90 min.), via Empoli. Siena's train station is at Piazza Roselli, about 3km (1¾ miles) north of town. Take the no. 9 or 10 bus to Piazza Gramsci (buy your ticket at the newsstand in the station). Bus stops are poorly marked, but you do not want the one right out front; instead, cross the street, go into the big brick shopping center, and take the escalator down to the underground bus stop—be sure to say "Gramsci" when you board, or you can end up in a far-flung outlying district. You can also take a series of escalators up to town from the shopping center—these too are poorly marked, but as long as you're going up you're moving in the right direction.

Buses are faster and let you off right in town: TRAIN (www.trainspa.it) and SITA (www.sitabus.it) codeshare express (*corse rapide;* around 25 daily; 75 min.) and slower buses (*corse ordinarie;* 14 daily; 95 min.) from **Florence**'s main bus station to Siena's Piazza Gramsci. Siena is also connected with **San Gimignano** (at least hourly Mon–Sat; 10 direct, rest change in Poggibonsi; 65–80 min. not including layover), **Perugia** (2–4 daily; 90 min.), and **Rome**'s Tiburtina station (5–9 daily; 3 hr.).

There's a fast **road** direct from **Florence** (it has no route number; follow the green signs toward Siena), or take the more scenic route, down the Chiantigiana SS222. From **Rome** get off the A1 north at the Val di Chiana exit and follow the SS326 west

Siena & Western Tuscany

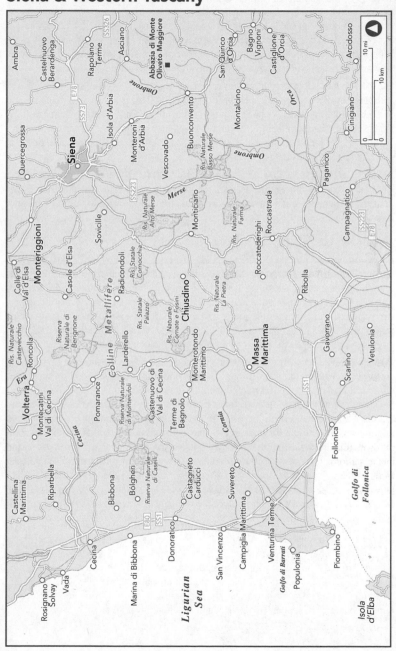

Ambra

Castelnuovo
Berardenga

Rapolano
Terme

Asciano

SS326

Abbazia di Monte
Oliveto Maggiore

San Quirico
d'Orcia

Bagno
Vignoni

Castiglione
d'Orcia

Arcidosso

Quercegrossa

E78

SS73

Isola d'Arbia

Ombrone

Buonconvento

Montalcino

Orcia

Cinigiano

Siena

Monteroni
d'Arbia

Vescovado

Ris. Naturale
Basso Merse

Ombrone

Paganico

Monteriggioni

SS223

Merse

Monticiano

Ris. Naturale
Alto Merse

Ris. Naturale
Farma

Roccastrada

Campagnatico

SS223

E78

Colle di
Val d'Elsa

Sovicille

Ris. Naturale
Castevecchio

Roncolla

Ero

Casole d'Elsa

Radicondoli

Ris. Statale
Cornocchia

Roccatederighi

Ribolla

Riserva
Naturale di
Berignone

Colline Metallifere

Larderello

Ris. Statale
Palazzo

Chiusdino

Ris. Naturale
La Pietra

Gavorrano

Volterra

Montecatini
Val di Cecina

Pomarance

Ris. Naturale
Cornate e Fosini

Monterotondo
Marittimo

Massa
Marittima

Scarlino

Vetulonia

Cecina

Riserva Naturale
di Monterufoli

Castelnuovo di
Val di Cecina

Terme di
Bagnolo

Cornia

SS1

Castellina
Marittima

Riparbella

Bibbona

Bólgheri

Riserva Naturale
di Caselli

Castagneto
Carducci

Suvereto

Follonica

Golfo di
Follonica

Rosignano
Solvay

Vada

Marina di Bibbona

E80

SS1

Donoratico

San Vincenzo

Campiglia Marittima

Venturina Terme

Piombino

Ligurian
Sea

Golfo di Baratti

Populonia

Isola
d'Elba

123

for 50km (31 miles). From **Pisa** take the highway toward Florence and exit onto the SS429 south just before Empoli (100km/62 miles total). The easiest way into the center is from the Siena Ovest highway exit.

Siena **parking** (✆ **0577-228-711**; www.sienaparcheggi.com) is in well-signposted lots outside the city gates. An especially handy lot is Santa Caterina, from which escalators whisk you up to town. Most charge between .50€ and 1.60€ per hour and many hotels have discount arrangements with lots (around 15€ per day).

GETTING AROUND   You can get anywhere you want to go on foot, with a bit of climbing. **Minibuses,** called *pollicini* (✆ **0577-204-246**; www.sienamobilita.it), run quarter-hourly (every half-hour Sat afternoon and all day Sun) from the main gates into the city center from 6:30am to 8:30pm.

You can call for a radio **taxi** at ✆ **0577-49-222** (7am–9pm only); they also queue at the train station and in town at Piazza Matteotti.

VISITOR INFORMATION   The **tourist office** (✆ **0577-280-551**; www.terresiena. it), where you can get a fairly useless free map or pay .50€ for a detailed one, is at Piazza del Campo 56; it's open Monday through Saturday 9am to 7pm (10am–5pm Nov–Mar) and Sunday 10am to 1pm.

Where to Stay

It's best to come to this popular town with a reservation. If you don't have one, stop by the Siena Hotels Promotion booth on Piazza San Domenico (✆ **0577-288-084;** www.hotelsiena.com), where for 1.50€ to 4€ per booking, depending on the category of hotel, they'll find you a room and reserve it—but remember, this is a private agency that works on commission with hotels, so their selection is limited to hotels with which they have a deal. The booth is open Monday through Saturday from 9am to 7pm (until 8pm in summer). The city tourist office also books accommodations for a fee.

Antica Torre ★   This 16th-century tower house dishes up no-end of medieval atmosphere, with eight smallish rooms tucked onto four floors. If you don't mind the climb, the two on the top floor come with the advantage of views across the tile rooftops, and just treading on the old stones on the staircase is a pleasure. All rooms have marble floors, brick and timbered ceilings, handsome iron bedsteads, and enough additional character that for some guests may compensate for the fairly cramped quarters, small bathrooms, and lack of many hotel services. Continental breakfast (extra) can get the day off to a rocky start, literally, as it's served downstairs in a rough-hewn stone vault.

Via di Fiera Vecchia 7. ✆ **0577-222-255.** www.anticatorresiena.it. [8 units. 110€ double. **Amenities:** Smoke-free rooms; Wi-Fi (free).

Campo Regio Relais ★★   A "Room with a View" ambience pervades this stylish old house a 10-minutes' walk from the Campo, where two of the rooms do have spectacular views up a hillside crowned with the Duomo—and all guests enjoy the same outlook from the breakfast room/lounge and terrace. The old-fashioned pension vibe is enhanced with a sophisticated take on modern updates that includes rich fabrics and traditionally elegant furnishings that are chic rather than staid. Amenities include an honesty bar, a library, attentive service, and excellent breakfast.

Via della Sapienza 25. ✆ **0577-222073.** www.camporegio.com. 6 units. Doubles 150€–450€. Rates include buffet breakfast. Usually closed Jan to mid-Mar.

Central Siena

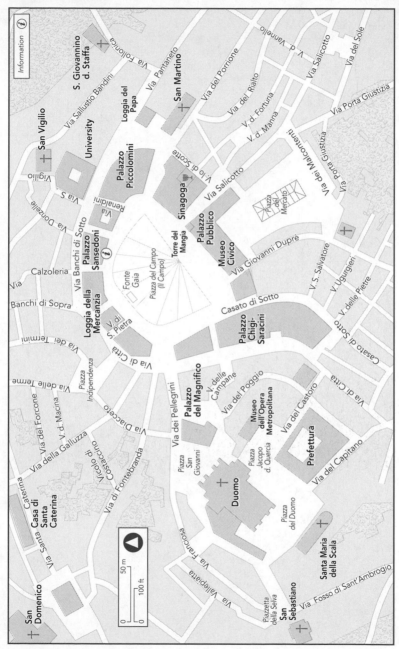

Information

S. Giovannino
d. Staffa

San Vigilio

University

Via Follonica

Via Pantaneto

Via Sallustio Bandini

Loggia del
Papa

Via del Porrione

San Martino

Via del Rialto

V. d. Vannello

Via Salicotto

Via del Sole

Via S. Vigilio

Palazzo
Piccolomini

Via Renaldini

Sinagoga

V.lo di Scotte

V. del Fortuna

V. d. Manna

Via Porta Giustizia

Via S. Vigilio

Via Donzelle

Calzoleria

Via Banchi di Sotto

Palazzo
Sansedoni

Torre del
Mangia

Palazzo
Pubblico

Via Salicotto

Piazza
del
Mercato

Via del Malcontenti

Via Porta Giustizia

Banchi di Sopra

Via

Loggia della
Mercanzia

Fonte
Gaia

Piazza del Campo
(Il Campo)

Museo
Civico

Via Giovanni Duprè

V. S. Salvatore

Via delle Pietre

V. Ugurgieri

Via dei Termini

Via di Città

V. di
S. Pietra

Casato di Sotto

Palazzo
Chigi-
Saracini

Casato di Sotto

Piazza
Indipendenza

Via delle Terme

Via del Forcone

Via della Galluzza

V. d. Macina

Vicolo di
Costaccino

Via Diaceto

Via dei Pellegrini

Palazzo
del Magnifico

V. delle
Campane

Via del Poggio

Museo
dell'Opera
Metropolitana

Via del Castoro

Via di Città

Prefettura

Via del Capitano

Santa Santa Caterina

Casa di
Santa
Caterina

Via di Fontebranda

Piazza
San
Giovanni

Piazza
Jacopo
d. Quercia

Duomo

Piazza
del Duomo

Santa Maria
della Scala

Via Fosso di Sant'Ambrogio

San
Domenico

Via Franciosa

Via Vallepiatta

San
Sebastiano

Piazzetta
della Selva

50 m

100 ft

0

0

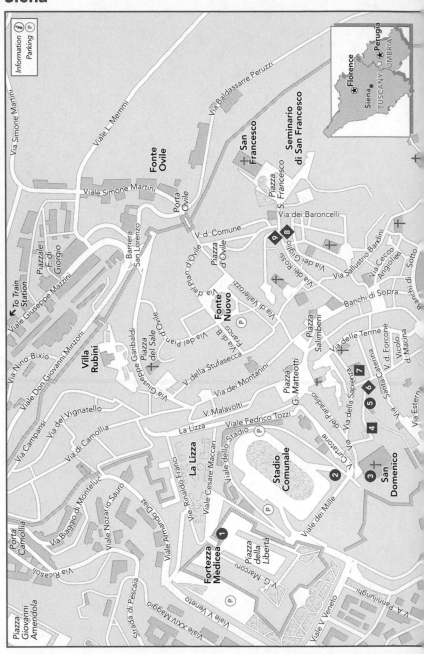

Information ⓘ
Parking ℗

6 | **Siena**

Via Simone Martini

Via L. Memmi

Viale L. Memmi

Viale Simone Martini

Viale Simone Martini

Via Baldassarre Peruzzi

**Fonte
Ovile**

Porta
Ovile

**San
Francesco**

Piazza
S. Francesco

**Seminario
di San Francesco**

Via dei Baroncelli

V. d. Comune

Piazza
d'Ovile

❾ ❽

Via dei Rossi

Via del Giglio

Via Sallustio Bandini

Via di Cecco
Angiolieri

Banchi di Sopra

Banchi di

Sotto

Piazzale
F. di
Giorgio

Barriera
San Lorenzo

To Train
Station

Viale Giuseppe Mazzini

Via d. di Pian d'Ovile

**Fonte
Nuovo**

Via d'Vallerozzi

Piazza
Salimbeni

Via delle Terme

V. d. Forcone

Vicolo
d'Macina

Viale Don Giovanni Minzoni

Via Nino Bixio

**Villa
Rubini**

Via Giuseppe Garibaldi

Piazza
del Sale

Via di B.
Franco

V. della Stufasecca

Via dei Montanini

Santa Caterina

❼

❻

Via della Sapienza

Via Esterna

Via Campansi

Via del Vignatello

Via di Camollia

V. Malavolti

La Lizza

Viale Fedrico Tozzi

Piazza
G. Matteotti

Via del Paradiso

❺

❹

Porta
Camollia

Via Biaggio di Monteluc

Viale Nozario Sauro

Via Rinaldo Franci

La Lizza

Viale Cesare Maccari

Viale dello Stadio

℗

**Stadio
Comunale**

V. Curtatone

❷

❸

**San
Domenico**

Via Ricasoli

Viale Armando Diaz

℗

Viale dei Mille

❶

Piazza
della
Libertà

V. G. Marconi

**Fortezza
Medicea**

Piazza
Giovanni
Amendola

Strada di Pescaia

Viale XXIV Maggio

Viale V. Veneto

Viale V. Veneto

V. A. Pannilunghi

Florence

Siena

Perugia

TUSCANY UMBRIA

UMBRIA

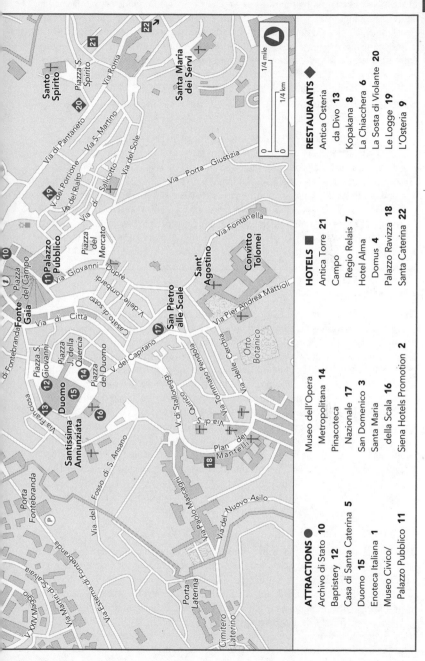

ATTRACTIONS ●

Archivo di Stato **10**

Baptistery **12**

Casa di Santa Caterina **5**

Duomo **15**

Enoteca Italiana **1**

Museo Cívico/
Palazzo Pubblico **11**

Museo dell'Opera
Metropolitana **14**

Pinacoteca
Nazionale **17**

San Domenico **3**

Santa Maria
della Scala **16**

Siena Hotels Promotion **2**

HOTELS ■

Antica Torre **21**

Campo
Regio Relais **7**

Hotel Alma
Domus **4**

Palazzo Ravizza **18**

Santa Caterina **22**

RESTAURANTS ◆

Antica Osteria
da Divo **13**

Kopakana **8**

La Chiacchera **6**

La Sosta di Violante **20**

Le Logge **19**

L'Osteria **9**

Hotel Alma Domus ★ The modern redo of the former drying rooms of a medieval wool works is run by the nuns of St. Catherine, who provide crisply homey and spotless lodgings with a slightly contemporary flair. Terraced into the hillside below San Domenico church, near the Fontebranda, the oldest and most picturesque of the city's fountains, the place has a quiet, retreat like air—even a meditative, monastic calm, if you choose to see it that way—along with a great perk, city-view balconies in many rooms. Breakfast is included, but it's a bit monastic and you may want to walk up the hill and enjoy a cappuccino in the Campo.

Via Camporegio 37. ✆ **0577-44-177.** www.hotelalmadomus.it. 28 units. 54€–61€ double. Rates include breakfast. Bus: A (red). **Amenities:** Smoke-free rooms, Wi-Fi (fee).

Palazzo Ravizza ★★★ Generations of travelers have fallen under the spell of this 17th-century Renaissance *palazzo,* where high ceilings, oil paintings, highly polished antiques, and the gentle patina of age all seem to suggest an age of grand travel. High-ceilinged salons are set up for lounging, with deep couches and card tables, even a grand piano, and a large garden in the rear stretches towards green hills. All the rooms are different, though most have wood beams and a surfeit of period detail, including frescoes and coffered ceilings in some; furnishings throughout are comfortable and traditionally stylish. While this wonderful old place has the aura of a country hideaway, it's right in the city center, just a few streets below the Piazza del Campo.

Pian dei Mantellini 34 (near Piazza San Marco). ✆ **0577-280-462.** www.palazzoravizza.it. 35 units. 90€–150€ double. Rates include breakfast. Free parking. Closed early Jan to early Feb. Bus: A (green, yellow). **Amenities:** Bar; babysitting; concierge; room service; smoke-free rooms; Wi-Fi (free).

Santa Caterina ★★ You'll forgo a center of town location to stay here, but being just outside the walls—literally so, as this is the first house after Porta Roma, about a 10-minute walk from Piazza del Campo—comes with the advantage of making you feel like you are in the countryside. A large, shady garden enhances the feeling, and you can breakfast and enjoy a drink under the trees in good weather; for indoor lounging, there's a snug little bar, a well-upholstered, book-lined lounge, and a glass-enclosed breakfast room. Most of the cozy and atmospheric rooms, with wood-beamed ceilings, simple wood furnishings, and nice old prints on the walls, face the back, where wide-sweeping views of the rolling greenery of the Val d'Orcia seem to go on forever. One choice room has a little balcony overlooking this scene, and a few others are two-level, with bedrooms tucked beneath the eaves. Just make sure to get a room at the back of the house, because facing the street out front would mean missing the wonderful view out back.

Via Enea Silvio Piccolomini 7. ✆ **0577-221-105.** www.hscsiena.it. 22 units. 85€–195€ double. Rates include buffet breakfast. Bus: A (pink) or 2. **Amenities:** Babysitting; bikes; concierge; parking (fee); smoke-free rooms; Wi-Fi (free).

Where to Eat

The **Enoteca Italiana** in the 16th-century Fortezza Medicea di Santa Barbara is the only state-sponsored wine bar in Italy, in vaults that were built for Cosimo de' Medici in 1560 (✆ **0577-228-843;** www.enoteca-italiana.it; Mon noon–8pm; Tues–Sat noon–1am). You can sample a choice selection of Italian wines by the glass and accompany your choices with small plates of meats and cheeses. Every Italian city has a favorite *gelateria,* and Siena's is **Kopakabana,** at Via de' Rossi 52–54 (✆ **0577-223-744;** www.gelateriakopakabana.it; mid-Feb to mid-Nov noon–8pm, later in warm weather), with flavors that include *panpepato,* based on the peppery Sienese cake.

Antica Osteria da Divo ★★ CONTEMPORARY SIENESE   It's hard to know what the appropriate cuisine for this almost-eerie setting of brick vaulting, exposed timbers, walls of bare rock, and even some Etruscan tombs might be—either some sort of medieval gruel or maybe something innovatively refined, which is where the menu goes. Many of the offerings are uniquely Sienese, as in *pici alla lepre* (thick spaghetti in hare sauce), *sella di cinghiale* (saddle of wild boar braised in Chianti), or a breast of guinea fowl *(faraona)* roasted with balsamic vinegar. All of the entrees are well paired with vegetables, often caramelized onions or crisp roasted potatoes with herbs, service is outstanding, and as befits one of the most romantic meals in town, the intimate spaces are beautifully candlelit at night.

Via Franciosa 25–29 (2 streets down from the left flank of the Duomo). © **0577-284-381.** www. osteriadadivo.it. Main courses 20€–24€. Wed–Mon noon–2:30pm and 7–10:30pm. Closed 2 weeks Jan–Feb. Bus: A (green, yellow).

La Chiacchera ★★ SIENESE   A hole in the wall is an apt description for one tiny, rustically decorated room tucked about halfway along a steep alleyway—the climb can help work up an appetite or work off the large portions of *ribollita,* a hearty bread and vegetable soup; *salsicce e fagioli* (sausage and white beans); or *tegamata di maiale,* a Sienese pork casserole. Good weather provides a unique dining experience on the street out in front, where the legs of the tables and chairs have been especially cut to accommodate the steep slope.

Costa di Sant'Antonio 4 (near San Domenico). © **0577-280-631.** www.osterialachiacchera.it. Main courses 7€–8€. Daily noon–3pm and 7pm–midnight. Bus: A (red).

La Sosta di Violante ★★ SIENESE   This warm, friendly, rose-hued dining room is only a 5-minute walk from Piazza del Campo but just far enough off the beaten track to seem like a getaway (*sosta* means rest or break, as in "take a break"). The surroundings and menu attract a mostly neighborhood crowd that has come to count on the kitchen for excellent preparations of *parpadelle, pici,* and other classic Tuscan pastas in rich sauces. Grilled Florentine steaks are another specialty, but so are many unusual vegetarian menu choices, including delicious *fritelle di pecorino,* pecorino cheese fritters, and a cauliflower *(cavolfiore)* soufflé. Any civic-minded Sienese would get this reference to Violante, the Bavarian born 18th-century duchess who, after the death of her Medici husband from syphilis, became a beneficent governor of Siena and divided the city into its famous present-day *contrade.*

Via di Pantaneta 115. © **0577-43774.** www.lasostadiviolante.it. Main courses 7€–15€. Mon–Sat 12:30–2:30pm and 7:30–10:30pm. Bus: A (pink).

Le Logge ★★ TUSCAN   This former pharmacy, where the shelves are now filled with wine bottles, provides refined and old-fashioned ambience close to the Campo, a suitable setting for the serious cooking that many Sienese come to enjoy on a night out—sometimes just to fulfill a craving for a famous house specialty, *malfatti all'osteria,* ricotta and spinach dumplings in a cream sauce. The veal is the tastiest in town, and the delicate black truffle is used liberally in season, most notably in *taglierini al tartufo,* in a light butter sauce that doesn't mask the delicate flavor of the black truffles. Service at the fresh-flower-graced tables is polished and personable. It's a good idea to reserve, especially for weekend dinners.

Via del Porrione 33. © **0577-48013.** Main courses 16€–26€. Mon–Sat noon–2:45pm and 7–10:45pm.

Siena should offer a free bottle of wine to visitors who manage to figure out the bewildering range of reduced-price cumulative ticket combos on offer. The two you should care about and purchase (at participating sights) are the **Musei Comunali** pass, 11€, valid for 2 days, for admission to Museo Civico and Santa Maria della Scala, both of which

are must-sees, and the **OPA** pass, for entry to the Duomo, Museo dell'Opera Metropolitana, Baptistery, Cripta, and Oratorio di San Bernardino, 12€ from March through October and 8€ the rest of the year—the savings on entrance to the first three alone, not to be missed, make the pass a good investment.

L'Osteria ★★ TUSCAN/GRILL   One of Siena's great culinary treasures is this simple, tile-floored, wood-beamed room where straightforward local cuisine is expertly prepared and served at extremely reasonable prices. Truffles occasionally appear in some special preparations, but for most of the year the short menu sticks to the classics—*pici al cinghale* (with wild boar sauce), tripe *(trippa)* stew, and thick steaks, accompanied by *fagioli bianchi* (white beans) and *patate fritte* (fried potatoes). Service can be brusque, but that's just because nightly crowds keep the waiters hopping.

Via de' Rossi 79–81. ℭ **0577-287-592.** Main courses 8€–21€. Mon–Sat 12:30–2:30pm and 7:30–10:30pm. Bus: A (red).

Exploring Siena

At the heart of Siena is the most beautiful square in Italy (a highly debatable claim), the sloping, scallop-shell–shaped Piazza del Campo (Il Campo). Laid out in the 1100s on the site of the Roman forum, the welcoming expanse is a testament to the city's civic achievements; it's dominated by a crenellated town hall, the **Palazzo Pubblico** (1297–1310), and the herringbone brick pavement is divided by white marble lines into nine sections representing the city's medieval ruling body, the Council of Nine. A poor 19th-century replica of Jacopo della Quercia's 14th-century fountain, the Fonte Gaia, is on one side of the square (some of the restored, but badly eroded, original panels are in Santa Maria della Scala; see below). The dominant public monument is the slender 100m-tall (328-ft.) brick **Torre del Mangia** (1338–48), named for a slothful bell ringer nicknamed Mangiaguadagni, or "profit eater." (There's an armless statue of him in the courtyard.) From the platform at top of the 503 steps the undulating Tuscan hills seem to rise and fall to the ends of the earth (8€; mid-Oct to Feb 10am–4pm, Mar to mid-Oct 10am–7pm).

Duomo ★★★ CATHEDRAL   Much of the artistic greatness of Siena comes together in the black-and-white-marble cathedral, begun in the 12th century and completed in the 13th century, a magnificent example of Italian Gothic architecture. You should come away from a visit with a greater appreciation for the Pisanos, father and son. Nicola was the principal architect of the church, until he fell out of favor with the group overseeing construction and left Siena, while young Giovanni did much of the carving on the facade, where a vast army of prophets and apostles appears around the three portals (most of the originals are now in the Museo dell'Opera Metropolitana; see below). They both worked on the pulpit, where the faithful may have taken great comfort in the sumptuously sculpted scenes of the life of Christ and the prophets and evangelists announcing salvation.

Siena's "newest" work of art is a cycle of frescoes painted between 1270 and 1275, discovered during excavation work in 1999. The colorful works are on view in the subterranean room called the Cripta, though it was never used for burials. Most likely the room was a lower porch for the duomo (staircases lead to the nave) but became a store-room when the choir above was expanded. What remains are fascinating fragments of scenes from the New Testament, full of emotion and done in vibrant colors. Scholars are still trying to determine who painted what in the room. Entry is included on the OPA pass, which includes the Duomo upstairs and other sights, or is 6€).

Beneath the pulpit spreads a flooring mosaic of 59 etched and inlaid **marble panels** (1372–1547), a showpiece for 40 of Siena's medieval and Renaissance artistic luminaries. Most prolific among them was Domenico Beccafumi, born into a local peasant family and adopted by his lord, who saw the boy's talent for drawing. Beccafumi studied in Rome but returned to Siena and spent much of his career designing 35 scenes for the flooring (from 1517–47); his richly patterned images are a repository of Old Testament figures. Matteo di Giovanni, another Sienese, did a gruesome Slaughter of the Innocents—a favorite theme of the artist, whose fresco of the same scene is in Santa Maria della Scala (see below). Many of the panels are protected by cardboard overlays and uncovered only from mid–August to early October in honor of the Palio.

Umbrian Renaissance master Bernardino di Betto (better known as Pinturicchio, or Little Painter, because of his stature) is the star in the Libreria Piccolomini, entered off the left aisle. Cardinal Francesco Piccolomini (later Pope Pius III—for all of 18 days before he died in office) built the library in 1487 to house the illuminated manuscripts of his famous uncle, a popular Sienese bishop who later became Pope Pius II. Pinturicchio's frescoes depict 10 scenes from the pope's life, including an especially dramatic departure for the Council of Basel as a storm rages in the background.

In the Baptistery (not a separate building but beneath the choir), the great trio of Sienese and Florentine sculptors of the early Renaissance, Jacopo della Quercia, Lorenzo Ghiberti, and Donatello, crafted the gilded bronze panels of the baptismal font. Donatello wrought the dancing figure of Salome in the "Feast of Herod," and della Quercia did the statue of St. John that stands high above the marble basin.

Piazza del Duomo. ✆ **0577-283-048.** Admission on cumulative ticket, or 3€, except when floor uncovered 6€. Mar–May and Sept–Oct Mon–Sat 10:30am–7:30pm, Sun 1:30–5:30pm; Nov–Feb Mon–Sat 10:30am–6:30pm, Sun 1:30–5:30pm; June–Aug Mon–Sat 10:30am–8pm, Sun 1:30–6pm. Baptistery: Piazza San Giovanni (down the stairs around the rear right flank of the Duomo). ✆ **0577-283-048.** Admission on cumulative ticket, or 3€. Mid-June to mid-Sept daily 9:30am–8pm; mid-Sept to Oct and Mar to mid-June daily 9:30am–7pm; Nov–Feb daily 10am–5pm.

Museo Civico/Palazzo Pubblico ★★★ ART MUSEUM   Siena's medieval governors, the Council of Nine, met in the Sala della Pace, and to help ensure they bore their duties responsibly, in 1338 Ambrogio Lorenzetti frescoed the walls with what has become the most important piece of secular art to survive from medieval Europe. His "Allegory of Good and Bad Government and Their Effects on the Town and Country-side" provides not only a moral lesson but also a remarkable visual record of the Siena and the surrounding countryside as it appeared in the 14th century. Probably not by accident, the good government frescoes are nicely illuminated by natural light, while scenes of bad government are cast in shadow and have also deteriorated over the years. In an uplifting panorama on the good side of the room, the towers, domes, and rooftops of Siena appear much as they do today, with horseman, workers, and townsfolk going about their daily affairs; in the countryside, genteel lords on horseback overlook bountiful fields. On the bad government side, streets are full of rubble, houses are collapsing in frame, and soldiers are killing and pillaging; in the countryside, fields are barren and villages are ablaze.

Among other frescoes in these rooms is Sienese painter Simone Martini's greatest work, and his first, a "Maestà" (or Majesty), finished in 1315 (he went over it again in 1321), in the Sala del Mappamondo. He shows the Virgin Mary as a medieval queen beneath a royal canopy, surrounded by a retinue of saints, apostles, and angels. The work introduces not only a secular element to a holy scene but also a sense of three-dimensional depth and perspective that later came to the fore in Renaissance painting. Mary's presence here in the halls of civil power reinforces the idea of good government, with the Virgin presiding as a protector of the city. Just opposite is another great Martini work (though the attribution has been called into question), the "Equestrian Portrait of Guidoriccio da Fogliano." The depiction of a proud mercenary riding past a castle he has just conquered was part of a long lost *"castelli,"* or "castles," fresco cycle that showed off Sienese conquests.

The Archivio di Stato, a near neighbor off the southeast corner of the Campo at Via Banchi di Sotto 52, preserves Boccaccio's will and Jacopo della Quercia's contract for the Fonte Gaia (✆ **0577-241-745;** free admission; Mon–Sat hourly viewings at 9:30, 10:30, and 11:30am) Most riveting is a remarkable set of wooden covers dating back to 1258 and made for the city's account books, the "Tavolette di Biccherna." They're painted with religious scenes, daily working life in the civic offices, and important events in Siena's history.

Palazzo Pubblico, Piazza del Campo. ✆ **0577-292-226.** Admission on cumulative ticket with Torre del Mangia 13€; or 7.50€ adults with reservation, 8€ adults without reservation; 4€ students and seniors 65 and over with reservation, 3.50€ students and seniors without reservation; free for ages 11 and under. Nov–Mar 15 daily 10am–6pm; Mar 16–Oct daily 10am–7pm. Bus: A (pink), B.

Museo dell'Opera Metropolitana ★★ MUSEUM In 1339, Siena decided to show off its political, artistic, and spiritual prominence by expanding the Duomo. Work had just begun when the Black Death killed more than half the city's inhabitants in 1348, and the project ground to a halt, never to be resumed—partly because it was discovered the foundations could not support the massive structure. The abortive new nave, part of the so-called "New Duomo," now houses many of the church's treasures, including the glorious-if-worse-for-wear statues by Giovanni Pisano that once adorned the facade and the 30 sq. m (323 sq. ft.) stained glass window made for the apse in the late 1280s; the nine colorful panels, beautifully illuminated to full effect in these new surroundings, depict the Virgin Mary, Siena's four patron saints, and the four Biblical Evangelists.

Upstairs is the "Maestà" by Duccio di Buoninsenga, considered a masterpiece from the day the altarpiece was unveiled in 1311 and carried in a solemn procession from the painter's workshop on Via Stalloreggi to the Duomo's altar. As a contemporary wrote, "all honorable citizens of Siena surrounded said panel with candles held in their hands, and women and children followed humbly behind." The front depicts the Madonna and Child surrounded by saints and angels while the back once displayed 46 scenes from the lives of Mary and Christ. In 1711 the altarpiece was dismantled and pieces are now in collections around the world, though what remains here shows the genius of Duccio, who slowly broke away from a one-dimensional Byzantine style to imbue his characters with nuance, roundness, and emotion.

The Facciatone, a walkway atop the would-be facade of the "New Duomo," is the city's second most popular viewpoint, with a stunning perspective of the black-and-white-striped cathedral across the piazza and sweeping views over the city's rooftops to Siena's favorite height, the Torre del Mangia towering over the Campo.

Piazza del Duomo 8. ℰ **0577-283-048.** www.operaduomo.siena.it. Admission on cumulative ticket, or 6€. Mid-June to mid-Sept daily 9:30am–8pm; mid-Sept to Oct and Mar to mid-June daily 9:30am–7pm; Nov–Feb daily 10am–5pm.

Pinacoteca Nazionale ★ ART MUSEUM The greatest works of Sienese art have long since been dispersed to museums around the world, but here you'll have the chance to get an overview of the works of the city's major artists, especially those working in the 12th through the 16th centuries, nicely displayed in the Brigidi and Buonsignori palaces. What you'll soon notice is that while the Renaissance was flourishing in Florence, Siena held to its old ways, and works are rich in Byzantine gold and an almost Eastern influence in the styling. The collection tends to shift around a bit, but a walk through the second floor galleries will show you what you want to see.

Among the works of Duccio (of the famous "Maestà" in the Museo dell'Opera) is an enchanting "Madonna and Child with Saints," in which a placid, otherworldly looking Mary holds a very wise-looking Jesus. Simone Martini (painter of Siena's other great "Maestà," in the Museo Civico) did the wonderful "Agostino Novello" altarpiece, in which the saint is shown performing all sorts of heroic deeds, such as flying over boulders to save a monk trapped in a ravine; in many of the panels you'll notice Sienese street scenes. Works by the Lorenzetti brothers include some charming landscapes by Ambrogio (artist of "Allegory of Good and Bad Government and Their Effects on the Town and Countryside" in the Palazzo Pubblico); his "Castle on the Lake" is almost surrealistic, an architectural fantasy reminiscent of the 20th-century works of Giorgio di Chirico. Pietro's "Madonna of the Carmelites," an altarpiece the artist executed for the Carmelite church in Siena, shows the Virgin and Child in a distinctly medieval setting, surrounded by members of the order in 14th-century garb, along with a typically Sienese landscape, complete with horsemen and planted hillsides. Domenico Beccafumi's cartoons, or sketches, for his floor panels in the Duomo are on the first floor.

Via San Pietro 29. ℰ **0577-286-143.** Admission 4€. Sun–Mon 9am–1pm; Tues–Sat 8:15am–7:15pm.

Santa Maria della Scala ★★ MUSEUM One of Europe's first hospitals, probably founded around 1090, raised abandoned children, took care of the infirm, fed the poor, and lodged pilgrims who stopped in Siena as they made their way to and from Rome. These activities are recorded in scenes in the Sala del Pellegrinaio (Pilgrims' Hall), where colorful depictions of patients and healers from the Middle Ages looked down upon rows of hospital beds as recently as the 1990s. Along with the "Allegory of Good and Bad Government and Their Effects on the Town and Countryside," these are some of the finest secular works of the period. The color-rich 15th-century frescoes by Domenico di Bartolo and others show surgeons dressing a leg wound or holding a flask of urine to the light and caregivers offering fresh clothing to an indigent young man. One of Bartolo's panels encapsulates an orphan's lifetime experience at the hospital, as he pictures infants being weaned, youngsters being instructed by a stern-looking mistress, and a young couple being wed (young women raised in the hospital

6 | SIENA'S saintly SCHOLAR

Catherine Benincasa (1347–80), 1 of 25 children of a wealthy Sienese cloth dyer, had her first vision of Christ when she was 5 or 6 and vowed to devote her entire life to God. She took a nun's veil but not the vows when a teenager, was wed "mystically" to Christ when she was 21, and became known for helping the poor and infirm. She and her followers traveled throughout central Italy promoting "the total love for God" and a stronger church. Aside from founding a woman's monastery outside Siena, she served as Siena's ambassador to Pope Gregory XI in Avignon, encouraging his return to Rome, and continued to write him and other Italian leaders and to travel extensively, begging for peace and the reform of the clergy and the papal states. She fasted almost continually, and the toll this took on her health is attributed to her death at age 33.

The cavernous, stark church of San Domenico in Piazza San Domenico (free admission; 9am–6:30pm daily) houses Catherine's venerated head, preserved in a gold reliquary, and her thumb. Her family home, the Casa di Santa Caterina, Costa di Sant'Antonio (℃ **0577-44177;** free admission; 9am–6pm daily), has been preserved as a religious sanctuary; the former kitchen is now an oratory with a spectacular 16th-century majolica-tiled floor.

were given dowries). As these activities transpire, a dog and cat scuffle, foundlings climb up ladders toward the Virgin Mary, and wealthy benefactors stand on Oriental carpets.

Elsewhere in the hospital complex are other frescoes and altarpieces commissioned by the hospital as it acquired huge landholdings and considerable wealth over the centuries. One gallery houses some original panels from Jacopo della Quercia's 14th-century fountain in the Piazza del Campo, the Fonte Gaia. In the cellars is the dark and eerie **Oratorio di Santa Caterina della Notte,** where St. Catherine allegedly passed her nights in prayer.

Piazza del Duomo 2. ℃ **0577-534-571.** www.santamariadellascala.com. Admission on cumulative ticket, or 10€, free for ages 11 and under. Mar 17–Oct 15 daily 10:30am–6:30pm; Oct 16–Mar 16 daily 10:30am–4:30pm.

Shopping

Siena is famous for its *panforte,* a sweet, dense cake city bakers created in the Middle Ages and is still sold in shops all over town. Made from candied fruit and nuts, glued together with honey, it resembles a gloopy fruitcake. Each shop has its own recipe, with the most popular varieties being sweet Panforte Margherita and bitter Panforte Nero. Try a slice at **Drogheria Manganelli,** Via di Città 71–73 (℃ **0577-280-002**), which has made its own *panforte* and soft *ricciarelli* almond cookies since the 19th century.

Authentic Sienese ceramics feature only black, white, and the reddish-brown "burnt sienna," or terra di Siena. **Ceramiche Artistiche Santa Caterina,** with showrooms at Via di Città 74–76 (℃ **0577-283-098**) sells high-quality pieces, courtesy of Maestro Marcello Neri, who trained at Siena's premier art and ceramics institutions, and his son, Fabio. **Martini Marisa** (Via del Capitano 5–11; ℃ **0577-288177;** www.anti casiena.it), another fine purveyor of hand-painted Sienese majolica (ceramics), uses designs based on the traditional black, white, and burnt sienna motif, based on floor panels in the Duomo. **Vitra** (Via dei Termini 2, at Piazza Independenza; $©$ **0577-51208**) offers a modern take on local crafts with glassware in all shapes and sizes (glasses, bowls, vases, and objets d'art); everything is handmade in Siena.

Via Stalloreggi, a little street where Duccio di Buoninsegna once had his studio, still houses some of the last remaining artisan workshops within the city's walls. **Sator Print,** Via Stalloreggi 70 ($©$ **0577-247478;** www.satorprint.com), sells hand-decorated prints and calligraphy based on historic Sienese designs. Nothing inside is cheap, but you'll find an affordable, authentic gift or souvenir with little trouble—or just stop by to see the maestro at work. At the **Bottega d'Arte,** Via Stalloreggi 47 ($©$ **339-2700280;** www.arteinsiena.it), you can buy original art in the style (and using the techniques) of the old Sienese masters.

Side Trips from Siena

If the Disney empire were to set up shop in Tuscany, it would have some ready-made stage sets near Siena.

Monteriggioni, 14km (8½ miles) northwest of Siena along the SS2, is one of the most perfectly preserved fortified villages in all of Italy. The town was once a Sienese outpost, begun in 1213, where soldiers patrolled the walls and kept an eye out for Florentine troops from the towers. All 14 of these vantage points have survived more or less intact since the day Dante likened them to the circle of Titans guarding the lowest level of Hell. Between April and September, you can climb up to a couple to admire the view; the ticket booth is open daily 9:30am to 1:30pm and 2 to 7:30pm, and access costs 3.50€, and includes admission to a small museum on the town's history. The other thing to do in Monteriggioni is to walk from one end of town to the other, and the trip takes about 5 minutes, passing stone houses and garden plots that are tucked against the walls and once kept townsfolk nourished during times of siege. The **tourist office** ($©$ **0577-304-810;** www.monteriggioniturismo.it) is at Piazza Roma 23; it's open daily, 9:30am to 1:30pm and 2 to 7:30pm (until 4pm Nov–Mar). Siena city buses 130A and 130R depart for Monteriggioni every hour.

Outside the village of **Chiusdino,** about 40km (25 miles) southwest of Siena via S73, lies the **Abbey of San Galgano** ($©$ **055-756700;** www.prolocochiusdino.it) in a grassy meadow on the banks of the River Merse. This may be the most enchanting place in Tuscany, with two magical ingredients: the mossy ruins of a once great church and a saintly hermitage that is the setting for Italy's own Sword in the Stone legend. Galgano, born in Siena in 1148, was pursuing his career as a knight when the archangel Michael appeared to him in a vision and led him up a steep path to a circular-shaped temple outside the village of Montesiepi, where he was met by the Twelve Apostles. So Galgano went off to Montesiepi, drove his sword into a stone to renounce his knighthood and prove his devotion, and built a round stone hermitage. Upon the saint's death in 1182 his simple dwelling was expanded into a rather spectacular rotunda, with a dome built of 24 alternating rows of brick and stone. The Hermitage became the center of a community of Cistercian monks until the brothers outgrew their quarters and built a Gothic abbey down the hill. From here they traveled throughout Tuscany constructing churches, including the cathedral in Siena. Decimated by the Black Death of 1348, the community never rebounded. The remaining monks sold off part of the lead roof of the abbey in the 16th century, and the bell tower collapsed in 1786. What remains is an evocative ruin, where you can make out high arches, carved capitals, stone settings for the long-vanished stained-glass windows, and cloister walls. The saint's tomb is up the hill in the Hermitage, where his sword remains in place in a stone, with only the cross-shaped handle protruding. St. Galgano's body long ago went missing and his tomb is empty, though his head is preserved in Siena's cathedral. The abbey is open daily (June–Aug 9am–8pm, Mar–May and Sept–Oct 9am–7pm, Nov–Feb 10am–5pm); admission is 2€.

At **Rapolano,** 38km (23 miles) southeast of Siena, the magic bubbles forth in the form of thermal waters, enjoyed since Roman times. Today they feed huge pools at the town's thermal establishments. While the waters provide treatment for respiratory and vascular problems and other ailments, they are also ideal for soothing soaks at bathing establishments where the 39°C (102°F) waters are channeled into large indoor and outdoor swimming pools equipped with fountains, whirlpools, and other features (the waters are cooled slightly in some pools). Pools at **Terme Antica Querciolaia** (Via Trieste 22; ℰ **0577-724091;** www.termeaq.it) and **Terme San Giovanni** (Via Terme San Giovanni; ℰ **0577-724030;** www.termesangiovanni.it) are open daily from 9am to 7pm (until midnight some weekend evenings) and day tickets costs 14€, with special family rates. You can drive to Rapolano along the E78; Siena Mobilita buses (ℰ **0577-204111;** www.sienamobilita.it) makes the trip Monday through Saturday about every 40 minutes.

SAN GIMIGNANO ★★

42km (26 miles) NW of Siena, 52km (32 miles) SW of Florence

Let's just get the clichés out of the way, shall we?—"Manhattan of the Middle Ages" and "City of Beautiful Towers." There, it's said. As every brochure will tell you, in the 12th and 13th centuries more than 70 towers rose above the tile roofs of San Gimignano, built partly to defend against outside invaders but mostly as command centers and status symbols for San Gimignano's powerful families. A dozen towers remain, and from the distance, as you approach across the rolling countryside, they do indeed appear like skyscrapers and give the town the look of a fantasy kingdom. Once inside the gates, you'll also better understand the reference to Manhattan, because visitors throng the narrow lanes shoulder to shoulder, laying asunder the medieval aura you've come to savor. Bus tours pour in from Siena and Florence, almost anyone on the hill town circuit makes a stop here, and Italians come on weekend outings. If you want to be swept back to the Middle Ages, you're best off visiting during the week in off season, or late on weekday afternoons after the buses have loaded up for the return journey.

Essentials

GETTING THERE Approximately 30 daily **trains** run between **Siena** and **Poggibonsi** (one about every half-hour, trip time: 25–40 min.), from where more than 30 buses make the 25-minute run to San Gimignano Monday through Saturday (only buses on Sun). Buses stop at Porta San Giovanni; you can easily walk into town from here, but shuttle buses make the run up to Piazza della Cisterna (.75€, buy a ticket from a newsstand or on the bus).

SITA (ℰ **055-47-821;** www.sitabus.it) and TRAIN (ℰ **0577-204-111;** www.train spa.it) codeshare hourly (at least, but fewer on Sun) **buses** for most of the day from both **Florence** (50 min.) and **Siena** (45 min.) to Poggibonsi, many of which meet right up with the connection to San Gimignano (a further 20–25 min.). From **Siena** there are also 10 direct buses (1¼ hr.) Monday through Saturday.

Arriving by **car,** take the Poggibonsi Nord exit off the **Florence-Siena** highway or the SS2. San Gimignano is 12km (7½ miles) from Poggibonsi.

San Gimignano

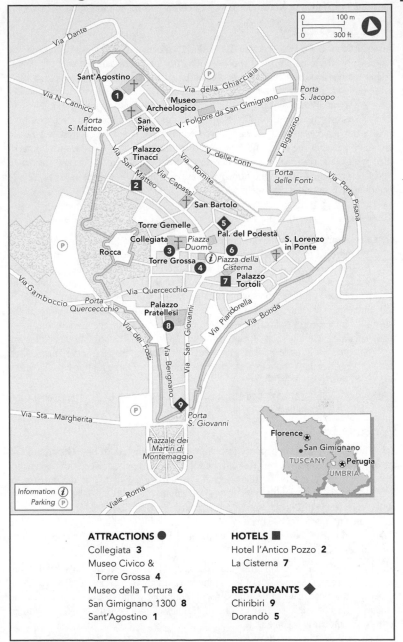

0   100 m
0   300 ft

Via Dante

Sant'Agostino ①

Via N. Cannicci

Porta
S. Matteo

Museo
Archeologico

San
Pietro

Via della Ghiacciaia

Via Folgore da San Gimignano

Porta
S. Jacopo

V. Bigazzino

Palazzo
Tinacci

Via San Matteo

Via Capassi

Via Romite

V. delle Fonti

Porta
delle Fonti

Via Porta Pisana

② San Bartolo

Torre Gemelle

Collegiata

Rocca

Piazza
Duomo

Pal. del Podestà ⑤

S. Lorenzo
in Ponte

③

Torre Grossa

ⓘ ④

⑥ Piazza della
Cisterna

⑦ Palazzo
Tortoli

Via Gamboccio

Porta
Quercecchio

Via Quercecchio

Palazzo
Pratellesi

⑧

Via dei Fossi

Via San Giovanni

Via Berignano

Via Piandorella

Via Bonda

Via Sta. Margherita

Ⓟ

⑨

Porta
S. Giovanni

Piazzale dei
Martiri di
Montemaggio

Florence ✪
San Gimignano

TUSCANY ✪ Perugia

UMBRIA

Information ⓘ
Parking Ⓟ

Viale Roma

ATTRACTIONS ●

Collegiata **3**
Museo Civico &
  Torre Grossa **4**
Museo della Tortura **6**
San Gimignano 1300 **8**
Sant'Agostino **1**

HOTELS ■

Hotel l'Antico Pozzo **2**
La Cisterna **7**

RESTAURANTS ◆

Chiribiri **9**
Dorandò **5**

VISITOR INFORMATION   The **tourist office** (© 0577-940-008; www.sangimignano.com) is at Piazza Duomo 1; it's open daily March through October from 9am to 1pm and 3 to 7pm, and November through February from 9am to 1pm and 2 to 6pm.

Where to Stay

Hotel l'Antico Pozzo ★★★   When this 15th-century *palazzo* was a convent, the namesake well served a grim purpose—young novices were dangled over the depths when they resisted droit de seigneur, the feudal rights of noblemen to have their way with young women living on their lands. That might not be the most inviting inducement to stay at a hotel, and the best in town at that, but the present incarnation is all about taste, elegance, and comfort. Some of the character-filled rooms reached by a broad stone staircase (or an elevator if you choose) are beamed and frescoed, others have nice views of the town and Rocca, and all are good sized and beautifully decorated with classic furnishings that sometimes include canopied beds and decorated with fine prints and other appointments. A grassy garden in the rear is an especially welcome treat from the daytime crowds.

Via San Matteo 87. © **0577-942014.** www.anticopozzo.com. 18 units. 120€–170€ double. Rates include breakfast. **Amenities:** Bar, Wi-Fi (free).

La Cisterna ★   Even if you haven't worked a night in San Gimignano into the Tuscan itinerary, the ivy-clad entrance right on the town square might tempt you to stay. Rooms vary considerably in size and outlook, and some of the smaller ones overlook a quaint but viewless courtyard; some of the larger rooms and suites come with balconies and views that extend for miles. Furnishings throughout are simply and unobtrusively traditional Tuscan, with wrought-iron bedsteads and some flourishes like arches, tile floors, and stone walls to impart a bit of character to surroundings that, along with the service, can seem a bit impersonal. The restaurant and terrace out front, along with a view filled, glassed-in dining room upstairs, serve Tuscan food that is a lot better than you'd expect, given the presence of large tour groups that often pile in for lunch.

Piazza della Cisterna 24. © **0577-940-328.** www.hotelcisterna.it. 48 units. 85€–145€ double. Rates include breakfast. **Amenities:** Restaurant, bar, Wi-Fi (free).

Where to Eat

San Gimignano's slightly peppery dry white wine, **Vernaccia di San Gimignano,** is the only DOCG white wine in Tuscany, and it has quite a provenance, too: It's cited in Dante's "Divine Comedy." A relaxing place to sip a glass or two is **diVinorum,** in former stables with a small terrace at Via degli Innocenti 5 (© 0577-907-192). At the famous **Gelateria di Piazza,** Piazza della Cisterna 4 (© 0577-942-244; www.gelateria dipiazza.com), master gelato maker Sergio offers creative combinations like refreshing Champeigmo, with sparkling wine and pink grapefruit, and *crema di Santa Fina,* made with saffron and pine nuts.

Chiribiri ★ ITALIAN   This tiny vaulted cellar almost next to the walls seems more serious about what it sends out of the kitchen than many of the more expensive places closer to the center of town do. Ravioli with pumpkin, white beans and sage, beef in Chianti, wild boar stew, and other Tuscan classics are done well and served without fuss. No credit cards accepted.

Piazzetta della Madonna 1. © **0577-941-948.** Main courses 8€–12€. Daily 11am–11pm.

Dorandò ★★ TUSCAN   Three stone-walled rooms with brick-vaulted ceilings are the setting for San Gimignano's most elegant and best dining option, though there's nothing fussy about the cooking. Ingredients are locally sourced and recipes are decidedly local—beef is done in a sauce of Chianti classic, local pork comes with an apple puree, and *cibrèo,* a rich ragout, comes with chicken livers and giblets scented with ginger and lemon. If you want to include a dinner here on an overnight in San Gimignano, you'll need a reservation.

Vicolo dell'Oro 2. ✆ **0577-941-862.** www.ristorantedorando.it. Main courses 20€–24€. Tues–Sun noon–2:30pm and 7–9:30pm (daily Easter–Sept). Closed Dec 10–Jan 31.

Exploring San Gimignano

You'll see the town at its lively best if you come on a Thursday or Saturday morning, when the interlocking **Piazza della Cisterna** and **Piazza del Duomo** fill with market stalls. When the Florentines took over San Gimignano in 1353 they built a hilltop Rocca, fortress, to protect against attack from Siena and to quell any interstrife that might arise in the town. The grassy expanses surrounding the tattered walls and mostly ruined turrets are a welcome spot to escape the crowds.

Collegiata ★★ CHURCH   San Gimignano's main church is awash in frescoes, including a gruesome "Last Judgment" by Sienese artist Taddeo di Bartolo (1410) around the main door in which mean-looking little devils taunt tortured souls. Bartolo allegedly modeled some of the characters after townsfolk who rubbed him the wrong way. Much of the nave is also covered in the flat, two-dimensional frescoes of the Sienese school that are in effect a comic-strip–like Poor Man's Bible, illustrating familiar stories for the illiterate faithful in simple and straightforward fashion. The left wall is frescoed with 26 scenes from the Old Testament (look for an especially satisfying panel showing the Pharaoh and his army being swallowed by the Red Sea) and the right wall with 22 scenes from the New Testament (a very shifty looking Judas receives his 30 pieces of silver for betraying Christ).

The best **frescoes** in the church are the two in the tiny Cappella di Santa Fina off the right aisle, where Renaissance master Domenico Ghirlandaio decorated the walls with airy scenes of the life of Fina, a local girl who, though never officially canonized, is one of San Gimignano's patron saints. Little Fina was very devout and when she fell ill with paralysis refused a bed and lay instead on a board, never complaining even when worms and rats fed off her decaying flesh. As you'll see in one of the panels, St. Gregory appeared and foretold the exact day (his feast day, Mar 12) on which Fina would die. She expired right on schedule and began working miracles immediately—all the bells in town rang spontaneously at the moment of her death. The second panel shows her funeral and another miracle, in which one of her nurses regained the use of her hand (paralyzed from long hours cradling the sick girl's head) when she laid it in Fina's lifeless hand.

Piazza del Duomo. ✆ **0577-940-316.** Admission 3.50€ adults, 1.50€ ages 6–18. Nov–Mar Mon–Sat 10am–4:40pm, Sun 12:30–4:40pm; Apr–Oct Mon–Fri 10am–7:10pm, Sat 10am–5:10pm, Sun 12:30–7:10pm. Closed 1st Sun in Aug, Mar 12, Nov 16–30, and Jan 16–31.

Museo Civico & Torre Grossa ★★ ART MUSEUM   The late-13th-century home of the city government, Palazzo del Commune, is topped with San Gimignano's tallest tower, the aptly named Torre Grossa (Big Tower), finished in 1311. Your reward for a climb to the top will be views of the cityscape and rolling countryside of the Val d'Elsa, but save your 5€ and enjoy the same outlook for free by making the 5-minute climb uphill from Piazza del Duomo to the ruined Rocca.

Inside the Camera del Podestà (Room of the Mayor) are San Gimignano's most famous frescoes, Memmo di Filippuccio's "Scenes of Married Life." In one scene, a couple takes a bath together, and in the other, the scantily clad fellow climbs into bed beside his naked wife. The great treasure in the adjoining painting gallery is the "Coppo di Marcovaldo Crucifix," an astonishingly touching work in which Christ appears vulnerably human and is surrounded by six intricate little scenes of the Crucifixion. Copo, a Florentine soldier, was captured by the Sienese, who realized what a treasure they had in the artist and persuaded him to do this and other master-pieces that show a slight transition away from flat Byzantine style to more varied texture and three-dimensionality.

St. Fina's head (see the Collegiata, above) is in a room to the right, in the "Taber-nacle of Santa Fina" (1402), painted with scenes of four of the teenager saint's mira-cles. Taddeo di Bartolo, who did the terrifying "Last Judgment" in the Collegiata, painted the "Life of St. Gimignano" (or "Geminianus") for the room. The saint was a 5th-century bishop of Modena in the Emilia-Romagna region who allegedly saved his flock by attack from Attila the Hun by conjuring up a dense fog. Hearing the news, the little town then known as Silvia changed its name to San Gimignano to buy a bit of insurance. Gimignano cradles his namesake in his lap, towers and all, figuratively offering the protection he was so often called upon to provide.

Piazza del Duomo. © **0577-990-312.** Admission 5€ adults, 4€ ages 6–18 and 65 and over. Apr–Sept daily 9:30am–7pm; Oct–Mar daily 10am–5:30pm.

Museo della Tortura ★ MUSEUM

If you're feeling a bit sunny about human nature, just step into these arched medieval galleries to be convinced anew of the depths of depravity to which we are capable of descending. Many medieval European towns and cities show off the racks and breast-rippers medieval residents left behind, but this homage to sadism is one of the most thorough. The entire repertoire is here, more than 100 devices in all: the Virgin, a sarcophagus in which spikes penetrated the flesh but not vital organs, inflicting maximum pain not relieved by death; two little forks mounted to the neck to penetrate the chin and the chest; all sorts of chairs fitted with pain-inflicting spikes; and on and on they go, with the plain old guillotine seem-ing rather humdrum and humane in comparison. Detailed text and graphic drawings illustrate the devices' terrifying uses and placards high-mindedly remind us that many cultures continue to inflict torture today, but don't fall for any attempt at altruism—this show of grisly might is meant to be a gruesome crowd pleaser and will be especially popular with the young companions you've been dragging through art museums (but it's definitely not for very young children).

Via del Castello 1–3 (at Piazza della Cisterna). © **0577-940526.** 12€. Apr–Oct daily 10am–7pm (sometimes until midnight in midsummer); Nov–Feb Mon–Fri 10:30am–4:30pm, Sat–Sun 10am–6pm; Mar daily 10am–5pm.

Sant'Agostino ★ CHURCH

An especially appropriate presence in this 13th-century church at the north end of town is St. Sebastian, the "saint who was mar-tyred twice." In 1464, a plague swept through San Gimignano and, when it finally passed, the town hired Benozzo Gozzoli to paint a thankful scene. The Florentine shows St. Sebastian getting some divine help to fend off the harmful effects of the arrows soldiers are shooting into his torso. In real life, the 3rd-century early Chris-tian could not stay out of harm's way. When Sebastian proclaimed his faith, the

Towers and medieval ambience aside, you'll also be delighted to discover that San Gimignano is awash in frescoes—in churches, public buildings, and even outdoors. In Piazza Pecori, reached through the archway to the left of the Collegiata's facade, is a fresco of the "Annunciation," possibly painted in 1482 by the Florentine Domenico Ghirlandaio. The door to the right of the tourist office leads into a courtyard of the Palazzo del Commune, where Taddeo di Bartolo's 14th-century "Madonna and Child" is flanked by two works on the theme of justice by Sodoma, including his near-monochrome "St. Ivo"—an appropriate presence, given Ivo's role as patron saint of lawyers.

emperor Diocletian ordered that he be taken to a field and shot full of arrows (for which he has rather cynically been named the patron saint of archers). Sebastian miraculously survived and was nursed back to health. Once back on his feet, he stood on a step and harangued Diocletian as he passed in royal procession, and the emperor had him bludgeoned to death on the spot. San Gimignano, too, saw hard times again, despite its protective fresco. As a stop on trade and pilgrimage routes, the town was especially susceptible to the plague, which continued to decimate the population time and again. Gozzoli also frescoed the choir behind the main altar floor-to-ceiling with 17 scenes from the life of St. Augustine, a worldly well-traveled scholar who, upon having to make the decision to give up his concubine, famously prayed, "Grant me continence and chastity but not yet." The scenes are straightforward (without a great deal of religious symbolism) and rich in landscape and architectural detail.

Piazza Sant'Agostino. ℰ **0577-907-012.** Free admission. Daily 7am–noon and 3–7pm (Nov–Apr closes at 6pm, and Jan to mid-Apr closed Mon mornings).

San Gimignano 1300 ★ MUSEUM The year 1300 was San Gimignano's heyday, when more than 13,000 townsfolk prospered from their lucrative location along trade routes. The plague of 1348 reduced the population to about 4,000, and when the proud town came under Florentine rule a decade or so later it was forced to topple most of its 72 towers. More than 800 structures fashioned on a 1:100 scale from a ton of clay show San Gimignano how it looked around 1300, with its looming towers intact, and the realistic craftsmanship is based on thorough archival research. The little street scenes showing snippets of daily medieval life, enhanced with sound and light effects, are especially enchanting, but you might ask yourself why you're inside looking at a model when the real town outside the door is just as fascinating.

Via Berignano 23. ℰ **327-4395165.** www.sangimignano1300.com. Admission 5€. Daily 10am–6pm (until 5pm Jan–Feb).

VOLTERRA ★★

29km (18 miles) SW of San Gimignano, 50km (31 miles) W of Siena

In the words of the writer D. H. Lawrence, Volterra is "on a towering great bluff that gets all the winds and sees all the world." Volterra seems to rear higher than any other Tuscan town, rising a precipitous 540m (1,772 ft.) above the valley below and drawn out thinly along a narrow ridge with a warren of medieval alleys falling steeply off the main piazza. You'll see the town long before you arrive, pointing a grimace at the world from way above the pastures of the Valdera.

Lawrence came here to study the Etruscans, who took the 9th-century-B.C. town established by the Villanovan culture and by the 4th century B.C. had turned it into Velathri, one of the largest centers in Etruria's 12-city confederation. Seeing their haunting bronzes and alabaster funerary urns is a compelling reason to venture over here, though fans of Stephanie Meyer's teen vampire trilogy, "Twilight," might come to see the town that is the home of the Volturi.

Essentials

GETTING THERE Driving is the easiest way to get here: Volterra is on the SS68 about 30km (19 miles) from where it branches off the Colle di Val d'Elsa exit on the Florence-Siena highway. From San Gimignano, head southwest on the secondary road to Castel di San Gimignano, which is on the SS68.

From **Siena,** there are 16 daily TRAIN **buses** (www.trainspa.it) that make the 20- to 30-minute trip to **Colle di Val d'Elsa,** from which there are four daily buses to Volterra (50 min.). From **San Gimignano,** you have to first take a bus to Poggibonsi (20 mvin.), four of which daily link up with buses to Colle di Val d'Elsa for the final transfer. From **Florence,** take one of five daily buses (three on Sun) to Colle di Val d'Elsa and transfer there (2½–3 hr. total). Six to 10 **CPT** (www.cpt.pisa.it) buses run there Monday through Saturday from **Pisa** (change in Pontedera; 2–2½ hr. total).

VISITOR INFORMATION Volterra's helpful **tourist office** (© **0588-87-257;** www.volterratur.it), at Piazza dei Priori 19–20, offers both tourist information and free hotel reservations; it's open daily from 9:30am to 1pm and 2 to 6pm.

Where to Stay

Staying within Volterra's city walls and having the city right outside your door, especially in the evening when residents regain their town, is one of Tuscany's better travel experiences. Choices are fairly limited, so book ahead if you're planning a visit in the busy period May through September.

Albergo Etruria ★★ The lounge and guest kitchen are homey touches, but the real attraction is the roof garden, a leafy retreat where the greenery is backed by the town's brick towers and tile rooftops. Parts of an Etruscan wall enhance the historic character of the old house, but rooms are charmingly up to date, filled with comfortable, attractive furniture hand-picked by the friendly owners. The Piazza dei Priori is only a few steps away from this stylish and cozy retreat.

Via Matteotti 32. © **0588-87377.** www.albergoetruria.it. 21 units. 69€–99€ double. Rates include buffet breakfast. **Amenities:** Wi-Fi (free).

Hotel San Lino ★ There's a slightly institutional ring to the hallways and some of the guest rooms here, probably because for many centuries the 13th-century *palazzo* served as a cloistered convent. The large enclosed gardens are still in place, and a little terrace at one end looks across miles of countryside; there's also a small pool, the only one within the city walls and reason enough to stay here in the heat of the summer. Some rooms seem rather functional, but others are nicely turned out with a mix of contemporary and traditional Tuscan furnishings; the best of them overlook the garden and the sweeping landscapes beyond.

Via San Lino 6 (near Porta San Francesco). © **0588-85250.** www.hotelsanlino.com. 44 units. 90€–110€ double. Rates include buffet breakfast. **Amenities:** Restaurant, bar, pool, Wi-Fi (free).

Volterra

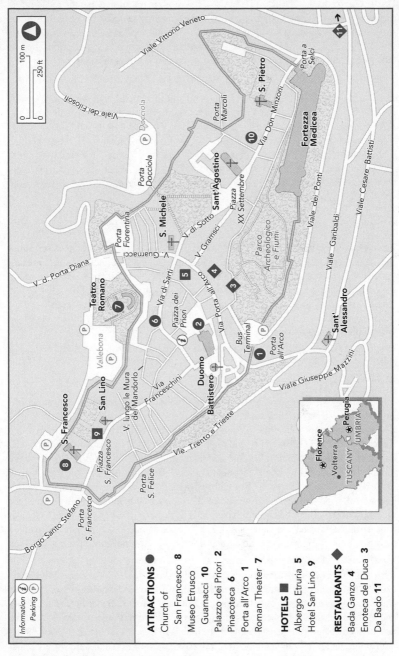

ATTRACTIONS ●
Church of
San Francesco **8**
Museo Etrusco
Guarnacci **10**
Palazzo dei Priori **2**
Pinacoteca **6**
Porta all'Arco **1**
Roman Theater **7**

HOTELS ■
Albergo Etruria **5**
Hotel San Lino **9**

RESTAURANTS ◆
Bada Ganzo **4**
Enoteca del Duca **3**
Da Bado **11**

Where to Eat

Bada Ganzo ★ MODERN TUSCAN   The room is traditional, but the menu offers a contemporary take on Volterran cuisine: *primi,* such as ravioli with *pecorino Volterrano e noci* (local sheep's milk cheese and hazelnuts), *pollo arrosto al vino e uvetta* (chicken roasted with wine and raisins), and often some specials with truffles. The few tables out front are especially atmospheric to dine on summer evening.

Via dei Marchesi 13. ☏ **0588-80508.** Main courses 8€–12€. Daily noon–3pm and 7:30–10:30pm.

Da Bado ★★ TUSCAN   Owner Giacomo's mom, Lucia, is in the kitchen of this neighborhood favorite in San Lazzero, just outside the walls a short walk from the Etruscan museum. She prepares a few daily choices that often include *zuppa volterrana* (bread and vegetable soup) and *"baccalà rifatto"* (pan-fried salted codfish stewed with tomatoes), along with *pappardelle alla lepre* (wide fettuccine with rabbit sauce) and other heart pastas well suited to homey, stone-arched surroundings. Lucia also makes the jams that fill her delicious homemade *tortes* (cakes). A cafe in front serves coffee and pastries all day.

Borgo San Lazzero 9. ☏ **0588-80402.** Main courses 8€–13€. Thurs–Tues 12:30–2:30pm and 7:30–10:30pm.

Enoteca del Duca ★★ MODERN TUSCAN   You'll have a choice of surroundings at Volterra's best, in the rather elegant high-ceilinged dining room, an arched, bottle-lined enoteca, or on a pretty patio out back. Wherever you choose to enjoy them, the offerings are innovative and refined takes on Tuscan classics: All the salamis and cheeses are from local producers, *lavagnette* (homemade egg pasta) comes with a sauce of celery and pecorino pesto, and local beef is grilled to perfection. Some of the wines come from the owners' vineyards.

Via di Castello 2. ☏ **0588-81510.** www.enoteca-delduca-ristorante.it. Main courses 15€–25€. Wed–Mon 12:30–3pm and 7:30–10pm (also Tues dinner in summer).

Exploring Volterra

The most evocative way to enter Volterra is through **Porta all'Arco,** the main 4th-century-B.C. gateway to the Etruscan city. Via die Priori leads steeply uphill to Volterra's stony medieval heart, the old and stony **Piazza dei Priori,** where the Gothic **Palazzo dei Priori** (1208–57) is said to be the first city hall in Tuscany and the model on which Florence's Palazzo Vecchio and many other civic buildings in Tuscany were modeled. The squat tower in the eastern corner is festooned with a little pig *(porcellino),* hence its name, **Torre del Porcellino.** Enjoy the view of the square with a coffee or glass of wine and a *panino* at one of the tables that front Bar Priori. Inside the modest-looking Duomo, behind the piazza, is a life-size wood group of the **"Deposition from the Cross,"** carved around 1228 by anonymous Pisan masters and painted in bright colors. With their fluidity and emotional expressiveness the figures look vaguely contemporary.

Church of San Francesco ★ CHURCH   Volterra's 13th-century Franciscan church, just inside the Porta San Francesco, has one overwhelming reason to visit: Halfway up the right aisle is the **Cappella Croce del Giorno,** frescoed with the "Legend of the True Cross" in medieval Technicolor by Cenni di Francesco in 1410. While not nearly as beautifully executed as Piero della Francesca's telling of the same story in the church of San Francesco in Arezzo (p. 183), Cenni's version of the wildly popular medieval tale of the miraculous cross is quite compelling, especially with his knack for reproducing the dress and architecture of his era. Though the artist worked for some of the most important families in Florence, this is his only remaining signed work and shows off a unique style: use of golden backgrounds, flattened space, and elongated figures with elegant features.

Piazza San Francesco. No phone. Free admission. Daily 8:30am–6:30pm.

Museo Etrusco Guarnacci ★★ MUSEUM   Volterra's remarkable collection of Etruscan artifacts is dusty, poorly lit, and devoid of a lot of English labeling but it is nonetheless a joyful celebration of this culture that flourished before the Golden Age of Greece and laid many of the foundations for the Roman Empire. The bulk of the holdings are on the ground floor, with row after row of 600 **Etruscan funerary urns,** most from the 3rd century B.C., but some from as early as the 7th century B.C. Ashes were placed in caskets topped with elaborately carved lids that show snippets of life from more than 2 millennia ago. Many of the finely dressed characters lounge as if at a banquet, holding cups in which they will offer wine to the gods. Some urns depict horse and carriage rides into the underworld. One of the finest, the **Urna degli Sposi,** is a striking bit of portraiture of a husband and wife, both very old, somewhat dour-faced and full of wrinkles, together in death as in life. The Etruscans also crafted bronze sculptures, and one of the finest is a lanky young man with a beguiling smile known as the **"Ombra della Sera" ("Shadow of the Evening")**—so called because the elongated shape looks so much like a shadow stretched in evening light.

Via Don Minzoni 15. ✆ **0588-86-347.** Admission by cumulative ticket with Pinacoteca 10€, or 8€. Summer daily 9am–7pm; winter daily 8:30am–1:45pm.

Pinacoteca ★ MUSEUM   While much of Volterra preserves the Etruscan, Roman, and medieval past, the town's worthy painting gallery transports you to the Renaissance with several standout paintings. Room 4 has a remarkably intact polyptych of the "Madonna with Saints" (1411), signed by Taddeo di Bartolo, who traveled throughout Tuscany and left works in Pisa, Montepulciano, and nearby San Gimignano, where he did a terrifying Last Judgment and a portrait of the town's namesake saint (see above). In this work the thin-elongated figures are typical of the Sienese school in which he trained and the fellow in the red cape and beard in the tiny left tondo is the original Santa Claus, St. Nicholas of Bari. In room 11 is a "Christ in Glory with Saints" (1492), the last great work of Florentine Domenico Ghirlandaio, one of the Florentine masters of the Renaissance and a favorite of the Medici and other aristocrats. The figures create a perfectly oval architectural frame for the Flemish-inspired landscape detailing of the background. If you look hard, you can spot a giraffe, recently acquired by the Medici for their menagerie, being led along the road. Ghirlandaio pleased his local audience with the two kneeling women who are actually Etruscan goddesses, Attinea and Greciniana, still venerated at the time.

In Room 12 hangs a remarkably colored Annunciation (1491) by Luca Signorelli (whose masterpiece is his "Last Judgment" in Orvieto; see p. 223) that is both solemn and spontaneous, with a great rush of feeling as the archangel seems to be bursting through the doorway to announce the news to Mary, who looks quite poised as she learns she's about to become the mother of Christ. A swirl of unruly putti float above the archangel's wings. A "Deposition" (1521) in the same room is by 26-year-old Rosso Fiorentino and is considered to be his masterpiece. The redheaded (and reportedly hot-headed) Florentine studied in Rome and worked here in Volterra and other small Italian cities before going off to France. He spent the rest of his short career working at the Chateau Fontainbleau and died there, allegedly a suicide, at age 46. His

Greek historian Herodotus reckoned that the Etruscans came from Turkey, but the more usual explanation is that they were simply farmers, seafarers and miners who lived around here and gave their name to "Tuscany." There are signs of Etruscan civilization in the area from about 800 B.C., and they had complex government structures, language, and artistic forms. At their peak they controlled the territory between the Tiber and the Arno, with lands as far north as the Po and south to Salerno. By 500 B.C. or so they appear to have settled into a fairly sophisticated way of life: They drained low-lying lands to farm, mined precious metals from which they fashioned exquisite jewelry, and sailed around the Mediterranean. Their frescoes portray show banquets where food and wine were plentiful and music accompanied the festivities. They'd more or less disappeared by A.D. 100, assimilated by the rise of Rome.

work here, an altarpiece originally done for the Duomo, shows his odd color palette of flat grays and reds and a similarly unusual approach to the subject. While the action of taking Christ from the cross, part of the repertoire of most Renaissance masters, is usually portrayed as a solemn occasion, here only the gray sky is somber. The rest of the canvas is a swirl of action, with sashes flapping in the wind, workers scurrying up and down precarious-looking ladders and along the cross beams, and the whole operation seeming rather frantic and disorganized.

Via del Sarti 1. ✆ **0588-87580.** Admission by cumulative ticket with Etruscan Museum 10€, or 6€. Daily 9–6:45 (until 1:45 Nov to mid-Mar).

Porta all'Arco ★★   As you approach Volterra, the city announces its greatest landmark right from the start, with this huge, magnificent gate that is the only round arch to come down to us from the Etruscans. On the outside are mounted three basalt heads—worn by well over 2,000 years of wind and rain to featurelessness—said to represent the Etruscan gods Tinia (Jupiter), Uni (Juno), and Menrva (Minerva). What fascinated the Romans was the keystone, from which they took inspiration for the arches that were such an essential part of their architecture. The gateway almost didn't survive World War II, when retreating German troops decided to blow it up to block the Allied advance through the city. Volterrans dug up the surrounding paving stones and plugged the opening, convincing the German command that it wasn't necessary to destroy the landmark since no one could pass through it anyway. The gate is still very much a part of everyday life in Volterra, and just beyond it is the Duomo and Palazzo die Priori.

Roman Theater ★ ARCHAEOLOGICAL SITE   A walk north in town along Via Guarnacci as it leads steeply down toward Porta Fiorentina takes you to Via Lungo le Mure, a walkway atop the medieval ramparts overlooking the impressive remains of Volterra's Roman theater and baths. These are some of the best-preserved Roman remains in Tuscany, dating back to the 1st century B.C., though parts of the theater were destroyed during the construction of the medieval walls. The view from up here is the best way to see it all, but if you do want to wander among the stones, there's an entrance down on Viale Francesco Ferrucci.

Viale Francesco Ferrucci. ✆ **0588-86050.** 3.50€. Summer daily 10:30am–5:30pm; winter Sat–Sun 10am–4pm.

The Etruscans made good use of the easily mined, watery, translucent calcium sulfate stone found around town in huge quantities to create the hundreds of **alabaster** sarcophagi you'll see in the Guarnacci museum. Alabaster became a major industry in Volterra again at the end of the 19th century, when the translucent material was well suited for lampshades, much in demand with the introduction of electric lighting. Today artisans work alabaster into a mind-boggling array of object from fine art pieces to some remarkable kitsch to lots of items that fall in the middle of the spectrum. The *comune* has put plaques at the workshops of some of the best traditional artisans, in whose shops you will find only hand-worked items. Via Porta all'Arco has several fine shops, including the showroom of internationally known **Paolo Sabatini**, at no. 45 (℡ **0588-87-594;** www.paolosabatini. com), whose alabaster sculptural pieces often combine wood and stone. The large shop of **Rossi Alabastri** (℡ **0588-86-133;** www.rossialabastri.com), at Piazzetta della Pescheria, at one end of the Roman theater panoramic walk, shows off some especially distinctive lighting pieces, as well as alabaster bowls, fruits, and all sorts of other easily portable items. At **alab'Arte** (℡ **0588-**

87-968; www.alabarte.com), at Via Orti S. Agostino 28, near the Guarnacci museum, Roberto Cini and Giorgio Finazzo create classical and contemporary sculptural pieces of museum quality—in fact, they are often called upon to help restore sculpture in churches and museums around Italy. You'll find the work of many other local artisans at the **Società Cooperativa Artieri Alabastro,** Piazza dei Priori 4–5 (℡ **0588-87-590**), a cooperative showroom and sales outlet for smaller workshops. To learn more about the town's alabaster industry, visit the **Ecomuseo dell'Alabastro,** Piazzetta Minucci (℡ **0588-87580**); admission costs 3.50€ and daily hours are 9:30am to 7:30pm in summer and 10:30am to 4:30pm in winter.

Alabaster isn't the only game in town. **Fabula Etrusca,** Via Lungo le Mura del Mandorlo 10 (℡ **0588-87401;** www. fabulaetrusca.it), sells intricate handmade jewelry cast using ancient goldsmith techniques and modeled after original Etruscan designs. Prepare your credit card before entering. Prints and lithographs created from hand-engraved zinc plates are another local artisan specialty, and you'll find especially fine work at **L'Istrice,** Via Porta all'Arco 23 (℡ **0588-85422;** www.labositrice.it), and **Bubo Bubo,** Via Roma 24 (℡ **0588-80307**).

A Side Trip to Massa Marittima

The road south from Volterra leads south over stark mountains to Massa Marittima, a high hill town 65km (40 miles) south of Volterra perched high above the coastal plain. Volterra is at the edge of the Maremma, a region that was once fertile farmland for the Etruscans but by the Middle Ages and for centuries afterward was so swampy and riddled with malaria that only *butteri*, cowboys, ventured across the empty landscapes. These stretches along the coast and inland hills are still more desolate than any other part of Tuscany and surround you with a forlorn beauty that is a stark contrast to the green forests and vineyard-clad hills often associated with the region.

ESSENTIALS   The only easy way to reach Massa Marittima is by car, a twisty-turny trip of at least an hour and a half from Volterra on SR439. From Siena, head southwest on the SS73 then the SS441 for 67km (42 miles).

The most convenient parking is in Piazza Mazzini, costing 1€ per hour. Massa Marittima doesn't have its own train station, but there's a stop at Follonica on the main line between Rome (11 daily; 2½ hr.) and Pisa (18 daily; 80 min.). Buses meet incoming trains for the ride to Massa.

The **tourist information office** (© 0566-902-756; www.altamaremmaturismo.it) is at Via Todini 3–5, down the right side of the Palazzo del Podestà. Hours are generally Tuesday to Sunday from 9:30am to 1pm and 2 to 6:30pm. Try to avoid a visit on Monday, when the town museums are all closed.

EXPLORING MASSA MARITTIMA

Massa Marittima looks quite stately atop its 356m (1,168-ft.) mount with a sweeping view over the farmland far below and Metalliferous Hills beyond. It's been a mining town since Etruscan times, and in the 14th century drew up the first mining code in European history, one of the most important legislative documents from the Middle Ages. It is a town divided, between the lower Città Vecchia (Old Town) and the upper half of town, the Città Nuova (New Town) that the Sienese established after they subdued Massa in 1335.

The **Città Vecchia** clusters around triangular Piazza Garibaldi, where the Duomo sits rather off kilter off to one side. Carved panels above the main door celebrate the life of St. Cerbonius, the town's 9th-century bishop and patron. Legend has it that Cerbonius, born in North Africa, was shipwrecked during a storm and washed up on the shores of Tuscany. He soon became bishop but was called to Rome when his flock complained that he said mass at irregular times. On the way he encountered a gaggle of wild geese, tamed them by making the sign of the cross over them, and brought the birds to Rome with him. One at St. Peter's, Cerbonius made the sign of the cross again and the birds flew off. He showed his way with animals again when invading Visigoths locked him in a pen with a ferocious bear; facing Cerbonius, maws agape, the beast suddenly slinked down onto its haunches and licked the saint's feet. The remains of Cerbonius are inside in the similarly carved Arca di San Cerbone.

From the narrow end of Piazza Garibaldi, Via Moncini branches steeply up from Via della Libertà toward the Porta alla Silici, part of the fortifications the Sienese built when they revamped the **Città Nuova** in 1337. An arch connects the fortress ramparts to the **1228 Torre del Candeliere** (© 0566-902289; www.massamarittimamusei.it), at Piazza Matteotti, still impressive at two-thirds of its original 60m (197 ft.). You can climb to the top for views over the ramparts. Admission is 3€ and the tower is open Tuesday through Sunday (Apr to mid-July and Sept Tues–Fri 10am–1pm and 3–6pm, Sat–Sun 10:30am–6pm; mid-July to Aug Tues–Fri 10:30am–1:30pm and 3:30–6:30pm, Sat–Sun 10:30am–6pm; Oct Tues–Sun 10am–1pm and 3–6pm; and Nov–Feb Tues–Sun 11am–1pm and 2:30–4:30pm).

The **Museo d'Arte Sacra** (© 0566-901-954; www.massamarittimamusei.it), Corso Diaz 36, houses the town's great art treasure, a "Maestà" painted in the late 1330s just after the Sienese takeover by Ambrogio Lorenzetti, who did the "Allegory of Good and Bad Government" in Siena (p. 131). Like that work, this painting is infused with humanity, and Mary is not portrayed as the remote figure as she is often is but gazes lovingly at her child, who clutches at her gown; it's one of the first great artistic representations of the maternal bond. Faith, Hope, and Charity sit at her feet, and among the saints looking on is black-robed St. Cerbonius, his tamed geese milling about his feet. During the baroque era, when Byzantine paintings were considered to be primitive, the painting was shoved aside and it wasn't rediscovered until 1867, by which point it had been divided into five pieces and nailed together to serve as an ash bin. The museum is

Massa Marittima

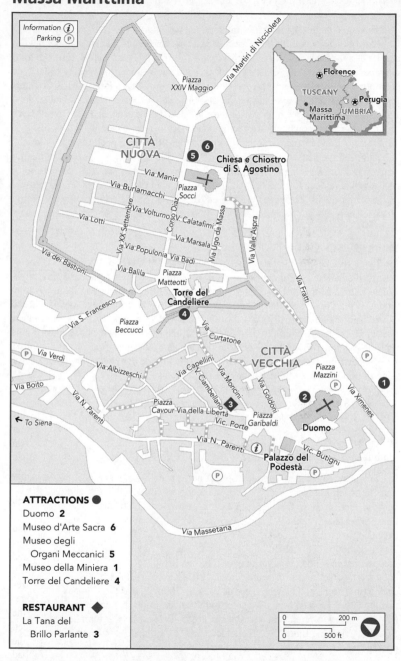

Information (i)
Parking (P)

Via Martiri di Niccioleta

Piazza
XXIV Maggio

Florence

TUSCANY

Massa
Marittima

Perugia

UMBRIA

CITTÀ
NUOVA

6

5

Chiesa e Chiostro
di S. Agostino

Via Manin

Via Burlamacchi

Piazza
Socci

Via Volturno

Corso Diaz

V. Calatafimi

Via Lotti

Via XX Settembre

Via Populonia

Via Badi

Via Marsala

Via Ugo da Massa

Via Valle Aspra

Via dei Bastioni

Via Balila

Piazza
Matteotti

Torre del
Candeliere

Via Fratti

Via S. Francesco

Piazza
Beccucci

4

Via Curtatone

CITTÀ
VECCHIA

P   Via Verdi

Via Albizzeschi

Via Capellini

V. Ciambelano

Via Moncini

Via Goldoni

Piazza
Mazzini

P

P

1

Via Ximenes

Via Boito

Via N. Parenti

Piazza
Cavour   Via della Libertà

3

Vic. Porte

Piazza
Garibaldi

2

Duomo

← To Siena

Via N. Parenti

(i)

Palazzo del
Podestà

Vic. Butigni

P

P

ATTRACTIONS ●

Duomo **2**
Museo d'Arte Sacra **6**
Museo degli
   Organi Meccanici **5**
Museo della Miniera **1**
Torre del Candeliere **4**

RESTAURANT ◆

La Tana del
   Brillo Parlante **3**

Via Massetana

0   200 m
0   500 ft

open Tuesday through Sunday from 10am to 1pm and 3 to 6pm (11am–1pm and 3–5pm Nov–Mar). Admission is 5€ adults and 3€ children 13 and under and seniors 60 and over.

The **Museo degli Organi Meccanici,** on the top floor of the 12th-century Chiesa e Convento di San Pietro all'Orto, Corso Diaz 28 (© **0566-940-282;** www.museodegliorgani.it), is a sanctuary for church organs, filled with instruments rescued from churches across Italy, some dating back to 1600 and restored to working order. The staff often performs impromptu concerts that are quite transporting as light filters through the stained-glass windows. Admission costs 4€, 3€ for children and seniors. From June through September the museum is open 10am to 1pm and 4 to 7pm; March through May afternoon hours are 4 to 6pm; and October through mid-January it's open 10:30am to 12:30pm and 3 to 6pm. From mid-January through February, it's closed.

Exhibits at the **Museo della Miniera** (© **0566-902-289;** www.massamarittimamusei.it), Via Corridoni, show off the town's long mining history, but the real reason for a visit is the guided, 45-minute tour (usually in Italian only) of 700m (2,300 ft.) of a reconstructed 1940s mineshaft. Tours run Tuesday to Sunday approximately hourly 10am to noon and 3 to 5:45pm (last tour 4:30pm Nov–Mar); 5€ adults; 3€ for children under 16.

WHERE TO EAT

La Tana del Brillo Parlante ★★★ TUSCAN/MEDITERRANEAN   The self-described smallest *osteria* in Italy seats only 10 diners at four tables in a tiny brick-walled room, and in good weather another six in the alley outside. You'll know you're among a privileged few the moment they hand you the parchment menu, and the exceptional preparations of local favorites made only from locally sourced products doesn't lessen the feeling. Offerings change all the time, but you can count on some typical Maremma favorites as *chicche al cinghiale* (chestnut-flour gnocchi with a sauce made from boar marinated in red wine), then *stinco di maiale sfumato alla birra* (shin of pork stewed with herbs and beer).

Vicolo Ciambellano 4. © **0566-901274.** Main courses 14€–18€. Cash only. Thurs–Tues noon–2:30pm and 6:30–11pm.

LUCCA ★

72km (45 miles) W of Florence

Lucca is often called the forgotten Tuscan town, since it's just far enough off the beaten track to be left out of itineraries. That's less and less true these days, and really never was the case entirely. Travelers have been waxing poetic about the place for a long time. Seventeenth-century British essayist John Evelyn said, "The inhabitants are exceedingly civil to strangers, above all places in Italy." In the 19th-century novelist Henry James called Lucca "a charming mixture of antique character and modern inconsequence"—the "inconsequence" bit referring to the fact that, completely enclosed by 16th- and 17th-century walls, Lucca is a beautifully preserved remnant of ages past. The Etruscans were here as early as 700 B.C., and the Romans after them, and the city flourished as a silk center in the Middle Ages. No doubt such a long and colorful history inspired Giacomo Puccini (1858–1924), who was born here and whose "Tosca," "Madame Butterfly," "Turandot," and "La Bohème" are some of the greatest operatic works of all times. Lucca can seem like a stage set, and it's easy to look at the icing-white, four-tiered facade of the church of San Michele in Foro (Victorian art

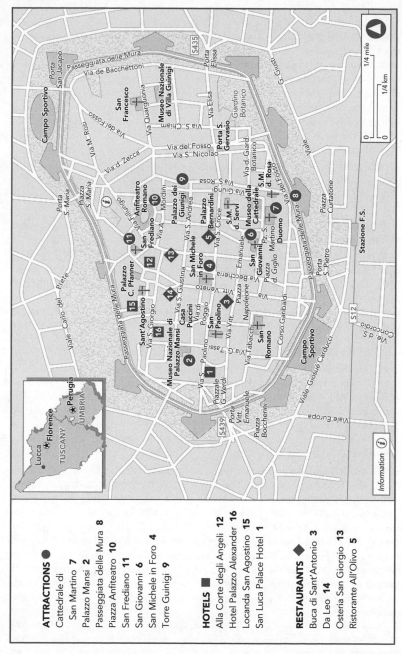

critic John Ruskin said it would be difficult to invent anything more noble) and hear the strains of "O Mio Bambino Caro."

Essentials

GETTING THERE Lucca is on the Florence-Viareggio **train** line, with about 30 trains daily (fewer on Sun) connecting with **Florence** (trip time: 75–90 min.). A similar number of trains make the short hop to/from **Pisa** (30 min.). The **station** is a short walk south of Porta San Pietro.

By **car,** the A11 runs from Florence past Prato, Pistoia, and Montecatini before hitting Lucca. Inside the walls, you'll usually find a pay-parking space underground at **Mazzini** (enter from the east, through the Porta Elisa, and take an immediate right).

A **VaiBus** (www.vaibus.it) service runs hourly from Florence (70 min.) and from Pisa (50 min.) to Lucca's Piazzale Verdi.

GETTING AROUND A set of *navette* (electric **minibuses**) whiz down the city's peripheral streets, but the flat center is easily traversable on foot.

To really get around like a Lucchese, though, you need to **rent a bike.** (See the box, "Get in the Saddle," later in this chapter, for rental recommendations.)

Taxis line up at the train station (② **0583-494-989**), Piazza Napoleone (② **0583-491-646**), and Piazzale Verdi (② **0583-581-305**).

VISITOR INFORMATION The main **tourist office** is inside the north side of the walls at Piazza Santa Maria 35 (② **0583-919-931;** www.luccaturismo.it; daily 9am–7pm, sometimes later in summer). The *comune* also has a small **local info office** on Piazzale Verdi (② **0583-442-944**), which keeps similar hours.

For **events** and theater, pick up the English-language monthly **"Grapevine"** for 2€ at most newsstands.

Where to Stay

Lucca has many B&B–style inns. Few top the large, stylish, and atmospheric rooms at the **Locanda San Agostino,** in a moody old palace at Piazza San Agostino 3 (② **0583-467884;** www.locandasantagostino.it). Four-poster beds and polished antiques provide a homey and fairly luxurious ambience, as does the raised hearth in the attractive lounge/breakfast room and the shady terrace. Doubles begin at 109€. For a complete listing of B&Bs in Lucca, ask the tourist board for the handy booklet "Extra Alberghiero."

Alla Corte degli Angeli ★★ Some of the most charming accommodations in Lucca flow across four floors of a beautifully restored and maintained, pink *palazzo* just off Via Fillungo, the main shopping street. It's hard not to fall for the gimmicky decor, which works brilliantly to provide just the right touch of playful ambience in the smallish but extremely tasteful rooms. In each, colorful murals incorporate a flower, and rich draperies and upholstered headboards pick up the theme. A scattering of antique pieces and excellent lighting enhance the air of stylish comfort, and some of the bathrooms have both showers and hydromassage tubs. Given the tightly packed medieval neighborhood, a room on an upper floor ensures an extra amount of sunlight—third-floor Paolina is an especially good choice because it has two exposures.

Via degli Angeli 23 (off Via Fillungo). ② **0583-469-204.** www.allacortedegliangeli.com. 10 units. 130€–210€ double. Rates include buffet breakfast. Garage parking 15€. Closed 2 weeks in Jan. **Amenities:** Bikes; concierge; Wi-Fi (free).

Hotel Palazzo Alexander ★ Stepping into this 12th-century palace tucked into medieval streets feels a bit like walking onto a regal operatic stage set, and the feeling certainly doesn't let up as you settle in amidst gilded and polished wood, reproduction antiques, old prints, and plush fabrics. You might have *putti* grinning down on your from the frescoed ceiling, but marble baths, Jacuzzi tubs in some rooms, excellent beds and fine linens, and other amenities are thoroughly up to date. The good-sized rooms are named after Puccini operas, and some of the especially charming suites have vaulted and beamed ceilings reminiscent of Rodolfo's "La Bohème" garret—well, that is, if the young poet had lived very, very well, which you will in this quirkily stylish little inn where service is as memorable as the surroundings.

Via Santa Giustina 28. ✆ **0583-47-615.** www.hotelpalazzoalexander.it. 9 units. From 80€ double. Rates include buffet breakfast. **Amenities:** Bar; Wi-Fi (free).

San Luca Palace Hotel ★★ A sense of tasteful, old world comfort begins in the downstairs hall and sitting room and continues into the large guest rooms, nicely done up with parquet floors, well-coordinated fabrics and draperies (green color schemes in some rooms, red in others), and many nice flourishes, like inviting and handy table-and-chair arrangements in all the rooms and small "reading" alcoves with day beds in many. This old palace just inside the walls also has plenty of practical conveniences, including an easy-to-reach location (parking is adjacent) and a short stroll from the sights and train station. The San Luca does not have an in-house restaurant, but an extremely pleasant bar off the lobby serves light snacks.

Via San Paolino 103 (off Piazza Napoleone). ✆ **0583-317-446.** www.sanlucapalace.com. 26 units. 85€ double. **Amenities:** Bar; Wi-Fi (free).

Where to Eat

Lucca's extra-virgin olive oil appears on every restaurant table. An atmospheric 19th-century pastry shop, **Taddeucci,** Piazza San Michele 34 (✆ **0583-494-933;** www. taddeucci.com), is famous for *buccellato,* a ring-shaped sweet bread flavored with raisins and fennel seeds and a Lucca specialty. For a fortifying (and addictive) snack stop by **Amedo Giusti,** Via Santa Lucia 18 (✆ **0583-496-285**), where focaccias with many different toppings constantly emerge piping hot from the oven to satisfy an appreciative crowd. The place to sample Lucca's excellent DOC wines is **Enoteca Vanni,** Piazza San Salvatore 7 (✆ **0583-491-902;** www.enotecavanni.com).

Antica Locanda di Sesto ★★★ LUCCHESE   The little community of Sesto di Moriano, just north of town, offers one of region's most pleasant dining experiences in a relaxed 300-year-old country dining room decorated with ceramics and antiques and where friendly staff preserves a welcome nod to old-fashioned service (just as the white linens suggest old-time elegance). Local and seasonal specialties permeate the menu, with plenty of choice from the grill and beautifully prepared game, and trout (fresh and local) has never tasted better. The oil that appears on the table and the wines that accompany meals are from family-owned groves and vineyards. Note that the restaurant has an unusual closing day, Saturday.

Via Ludovica 1660, Sesto di Moriano (signposted off S12, 11km/7 miles north of Lucca). ✆ **0583-578181.** www.anticalocandadisesto.it. Main courses 12€–18€. Sun–Fri 12:30–2:30pm and 8–10pm.

Buca di Sant'Antonio ★ LUCCHESE   Almost 3½ centuries old, Lucca's most famous and most venerable dining room relies a bit on its reputation these days, but sitting in the handsome tile-floored surroundings amid copper pots and brass instruments is a terribly pleasant experience—and usually requires a dinnertime reservation.

The popular way to get around Lucca, you'll soon learn, is on a bike. Enjoy the medieval lanes and squares on foot, but equip yourself with two wheels for a ride on the Passeggiata della Mura, atop the medieval walls. You can do so in style on one of the neon green or Barbie pink models from **Antonio Poli,** near the tourist office at Piazza Santa Maria 42 (ⓒ **0583-493-787;** www.biciclettepoli.com; daily 8:30am–7:30pm, closed Sun mid-Nov to Feb and Mon mornings year-round). Bikes are also available from **Cicli Bizzarri,** next door at Piazza Santa Maria 32 (ⓒ **0583-496-031;** www.ciclibizzarri.net; Mon–Sat 8:30am–1pm and 2:30–7:30pm, and same hours Sun Mar to mid-Sept). The going rates are 3€ an hour for a regular bike, 4€ to 4.50€ for a mountain bike, and 6.50€ for a tandem.

So is the nicely formal service of the waiters-in-bowties variety and welcoming glass of prosecco that launches a meal of traditional Lucchese dishes. The menu changes regularly, but usually includes such house specialties as *faro alla garfagnana* (spelt, or barley, soup) and *coniglio in umido* (rabbit stew). A house dessert is *buccellato,* a ring-shaped confection like a coffee cake named for the bread that sustained Roman legionnaires.

Via della Cervia 3 (a side alley just west of Piazza San Michele). ⓒ **0583-55-881.** Main courses 15€. Tues–Sat 12:30–3pm and 7:30–10:30pm; Sun 12:30–3pm.

Da Leo ★★ LUCCHESE/TUSCAN   It's a good sign when you have to veer off the well-beaten path to find a place, and even better when anyone you ask along the way knows exactly how to get there. The pleasantly old-fashioned room with plastic-draped tablecloths has been serving local classics for 50 years, and the *minestra di farro arrosto di maialino con patate* (roast piglet and potatoes), *cognilio* (rabbit) and other authentic Lucchese fare seems to improve with age. This is the place to try the typically Luccan *zuppa di farro,* a soup made with spelt, a barleylike grain cooked al dente.

Via Tegrimi 1 (just north of Piazza San Salvatore). ⓒ **0583-492-236.** www.trattoriadaleo.it. Main courses 9€–16€. Daily noon–2:30pm and 7:30–10:30pm.

Osteria San Giorgio ★ LUCCHESE/TUSCAN   A courtyard out front and comfortably informal, welcoming rooms decorated with old photos are a local favorite, tucked away on a quiet street near the Piazza Anfiteatro. The menu is geared to neighbors looking for a home-cooked meal: several soups, including a hearty *faro alla luchesse* (beans and barley), *coniglio stufato con olive taggiasche e uva* (rabbit stew with olives and grapes), and a local seafood favorite, *baccalà alla griglia cò ceci* (backed cod with chickpeas). Servers seem to know just about everyone who comes in the door and extend a warm welcome to newcomers as well.

Via San Giorgio 26. ⓒ **0583-953-233.** www.osteriasangiorgiolucca.it. Main courses 8€–13€. Daily noon–3pm and 7–10:30pm.

Ristorante All'Olivo ★ LUCCHESE/SEAFOOD   This is where the Lucchese come when they're in the mood for fish, and taking a seat in one of four comfortable and elegant little rooms—one with a fireplace, another like a covered garden—elevates a meal to a special occasion. The fish and seafood is brought in daily from Viareggio, the nearby Tuscan port, and appears in a bounty of seafood pastas, grilled seafood platters, a nice choice of *antipasti di mare,* and a simply prepared catch of the day. Meat lovers can venture over to the "terra" side of the menu for a selection of hearty roasts and grilled Tuscan steaks.

Piazza San Quirico 1. (© **0583-496-264.** www.ristoranteolivo.it. Main courses 12€–20€. Mon–Sat 12:30–2pm and 7:30–10pm.

Exploring Lucca

In your wanderings around Lucca you'll come upon many remarkable architectural landmarks. Most noticeable are the more than 4km (2½ miles) of walls, some 18m (59 ft.) wide and topped with the Passeggiata delle Mura. You can circumnavigate this tree-shaded avenue on foot or by bike, peering across Lucca's rooftops toward the hazy mountains and checking out the 11 bastions and six gates. The most curious feature of Lucca's street plan is Piazza Anfiteatro, near the north end of Via Fillungo, the main shopping street; this semicircle of handsome medieval houses stands atop what were once the grandstands of an A.D.-1st- or 2nd-century Roman amphitheater. Rising nearby is Torre Guinigi, sprouting from the 14th-century palace of Lucca's iron-fisted rulers and topped with a grove of ilex trees, one of many such gardens that once flourished atop the city's defensive towers; climb the 230 steps for a spectacular view of Lucca's skyline, the snowcapped Apuan Alps and the rolling green valley of the River Serchio (3.50€ adults, 2.50€ children 6–12 and seniors 65 and over; Apr–May daily 9am–7:30pm; June–Sept daily 9am–6:30pm; Oct and Mar daily 9:30am–5:30pm; Nov–Feb daily 9:30am–4:30pm). One of many surprises you will come across on narrow medieval lanes is the facade of **San Frediano,** Piazza San Frediano ((© **0583-493-627**), decorated with a glittering two-story-tall 13th-century mosaic that colorfully depicts the Apostles witnessing an ascending Christ. Another grace note is the presence of many storefronts with early-20th-century Art Nouveau signs etched in glass, imbuing the city's medieval atmosphere with a refined elegance, and the same could be said of the Lucchese themselves.

Cattedrale di San Martino ★★ CATHEDRAL Lucca's Duomo was completed in 1070 to house one of the most renowned artifacts in Christendom, the Volto Santo (more on that below), and the structure does justice to the prized procession. On the facade, three arches open to a deep portico sheathed in marble, and above it rises three tiers of arcaded loggias supported by several dozen little columns, each different. Legend has it that the Lucchese commissioned many artists to carve the columns, with the promise of hiring the best to do them all; they used all the entries and never paid anyone. A pair of binoculars will help you pick out the elaborate carvings of figures, animals, vines, and geometric patterns in the loggias and on the portico. St. Martin, the former Roman soldier to whom the cathedral is dedicated, figures prominently, and one statue shows the famous scene of him ripping his cloak to give half to a scantily clad beggar. A labyrinth is carved into the wall of the right side of the portico, intended for the faithful to make a figurative pilgrimage to the center of maze, as if to Jerusalem, before entering the church; faith is clearly a navigational aid on the road to salvation, as a Latin inscription makes the comparison, "This is the labyrinth built by Daedalus of Crete; all who entered therein were lost, save Theseus, thanks to Ariadne's thread."

Inside, the handsome sweep of inlaid pavement and altar are the 15th-century work of Lucca native Matteo Civitali, as is the Tempietto, an octagonal, freestanding chapel of white and red marble in the left nave built to house the Volto Santo. As the story goes, Nicodemus, the biblical figure who helped remove Christ's body from the cross, carved a crucifix but did not complete the face, fearing he could not do the holy visage

Nicodemus, medieval legend has it, stashed the Volto Santo in a cave for safekeeping, and an 8th-century Italian bishop discovered it while on pilgrimage to the Holy Land (the location came to him in a dream). He put the crucifix adrift in a boat, and it washed up on the shores of northern Italy. Once it again, the relic was set adrift, this time in a driverless wagon pulled by two oxen, and it arrived in Lucca. It was placed in the church of San Frediano but miraculously moved itself to the cathedral. The Volto Santo and the legends attached to it attracted medieval pilgrims from throughout Europe to Lucca, and on May 3 and September 13–14, the Lucchese walk in a candlelit procession from San Freidano to the cathedral, where the famous statue awaits them, dressed in gold and wearing a gold crown.

justice. He fell into a deep sleep, and when he awoke he discovered a beautiful face was miraculously in place (and that's just the beginning of the story; see box). The cathedral's other great treasure is the Tomb of Ilaria Carretto Guinigi, the wife of Lucca ruler Paolo Guinigi. Married in 1403, she died 2 years later at the age of 26; she lives on, accompanied by a little dog (a sign of her faithfulness) in a beautiful image carved by Jacopo della Quercia, the Sienese sculptor whose work so heavily influenced Michelangelo.

Piazza San Martino. (✆ **0583-957-068.** Admission to church free; transepts and Ilaria tomb 2€ adults, 1.50€ children 6–14. Cumulative ticket for tomb, Museo, and San Giovanni 6€ adults, 4€ children 6–14. Mon–Fri 9:30am–5:45pm (closes 4:45pm Nov–Mar), Sat 9:30am–6:45pm, Sun 9:30–10:45am and noon–6pm.

Palazzo Mansi ★ MUSEUM   Seeing the opulently decorated salons of the 16th-century palace of the Mansi clan of silk merchants is the real reason to come here, though some of the paintings deserve a close look, even if they are the lesser acclaimed efforts of mostly Italian and Flemish masters whose better works are on display elsewhere. Many are 16th and 17th Sienese works. A wildly colored "Temperance of Scipio" is by Domenico Beccafumi, who designed most of the panels on the floor of the cathedral in Siena (p. 130). The painting depicts an event in the Second Punic War during the siege of Carthage, when the Roman general Scipio released a beautiful virgin princess whom his troops had captured to her family.

Via Galli Tassi 43. (✆ **0583-55570.** www.luccamuseinazionali.it. 4€. Tues–Sat 8:30am–7:30pm.

San Michele in Foro ★ CHURCH   The magnificent facade of the Cattedrale di San Martino is matched, or even outdone for visual drama, by the delicately stacked arches and arcades on the exterior of this 12th-century church that rises above the site of Lucca's Roman forum. The show begins just above the main portal, where St. Michael slays a dragon as mythical creatures look on. Above that two lions flank a rose window, then begin four-soaring tiers of little columns; these are inlaid with intricate carvings and topped with human heads, flowers, and animals, and above each row is a frieze on which real and mythical animals jump and run. The two top tiers are narrow and freestanding, and topped with a statue of a bronze-winged St. Michael the Archangel flanked by two trumpeting cohorts. The interior is rather dull by comparison but enlivened with a lovely Madonna that Matteo Civitali, whose work you saw in the cathedral, sculpted to celebrate the city's deliverance from the plague in 1476, and a

You will discover another world beneath Lucca, in the bowels of the church of San Giovanni, the city's first cathedral across Piazza San Giovanni from the present-day cathedral. A well-marked route beneath the church leads you past layers of Roman-ear and early-Christian ruins: houses, cisterns, remnants of a 5th-century church and 6th-century cemetery, all jumbled together. Signage is not terribly illuminating, but you'll get the point—what you see in Lucca today is built atop a much-older place. 4€; open March to October daily 10am to 6pm, and November to mid-March Saturday and Sunday from 10am to 5pm.

painting of "Sts. Roch, Sebastian, Jerome, and Helen" by Filippino Lippi. The product of a notorious relationship between the painter Fra Filippo Lippi and a young nun, Lucrezia Buti, Filippino became one of the most accomplished painters of the late 15th century; his work shows the influence of his father as well as his teacher, Sandro Botticelli. Giacomo Puccini, one of Italy's greatest operatic composers, was born in 1858 down the block at Via Poggio no. 30 (a plaque marks the site) and sang in the church choir.

Piazza San Michele. © **0583-48-459.** Free admission. Summer daily 7:40am–noon and 3–6pm; winter daily 9am–noon and 3–5pm.

Entertainment & Nightlife

Every evening at 7pm, the **Chiesa di San Giovanni** hosts an opera recital or orchestral concert dedicated to hometown composer Giacomo Puccini, in a series called **Puccini e la sua Lucca** (Puccini and His Lucca; www.puccinielasualucca.com). Tickets are 17€ (13€ for those 22 and under) and can be purchased all day inside San Giovanni. Just try listening to "Nessun Dorma" in this lovely church in the composer's hometown without chills running up and down your spine. The shore of nearby Lago di Massaciuccoli provides the backdrop to the summer **Puccini Festival ★** (© **0584-359-322;** www.puccinifestival.it), the biggest annual date in a local opera lover's calendar. There's a seasonal ticket office at Viale Puccini 257a, in Torre del Lago, or book tickets online. Prices range from 35€ to 125€.

PISA ★★

85km (53 miles) south of Lucca, 76km (47 miles) W of Florence

It's ironic that one of the most famous landmarks in a country that has given Western civilization many of its greatest artistic and architecture masterpieces is an engineering failure. Built on sandy soil too unstable to support the weight of so much heavy marble, the city's famous tower began to lean even while it was still under construction. Eight centuries later, the Leaning Tower puts Pisa on the map, and seeing it, maybe climbing it, and touring other landmarks on the Campo dei Miracoli (Field of Miracles) is probably why you'll come to this city near the northwestern coast of Tuscany.

Pisa began as a seaside settlement around 1000 B.C. and was expanded into a naval trading port by the Romans in the 2nd century B.C. By the 11th century, the city had grown into one of the peninsula's most powerful maritime republics. In 1284, Pisa's battle fleet was destroyed by Genoa at Meloria (off Livorno), forcing Pisa's long slide into twilight. Florence took control in 1406 and despite a few small rebellions, stayed in charge until Italian unification in the 1860s. Today Pisa is lively and cosmopolitan, home to a university founded in 1343, one of Europe's oldest. Once away from the Campo die Miracoli, however, there's not a whole lot to see, so you may want to join the ranks of day-trippers who visit from Florence or nearby Lucca.

Essentials

GETTING THERE   There are around 25 runs between Lucca and Pisa every day (25–35 min.); from **Florence,** 50 daily trains make the trip (60–90 min.). On the Lucca line, day-trippers should get off at **San Rossore station,** a few blocks west of Piazza del Duomo and the Leaning Tower. All other trains—and eventually the Lucca one— pull into **Pisa Centrale** station. From here, bus no. 4 or the **LAM Rossa** bus will take you close to Piazza del Duomo.

There's a Florence-Pisa fast **highway** (the so-called FI.PI.LI) along the Arno valley. Take the SS12 or SS12r from Lucca. For details on parking locations and charges, see **www.pisamo.it**.

Tuscany's main international **airport, Galileo Galilei** (www.pisa-airport.com), is just 3km (2 miles) south of the center. Trains zip you from the airport to Centrale station in 5 minutes; the LAM Rossa bus departs every 9 minutes for Centrale station and then the Campo. A metered taxi ride will cost 10€ to 15€ (drivers accept credit cards).

GETTING AROUND   CPT (𝄐 **050-505-511** or 800-012-773 in Italy; www.cpt. pisa.it) runs the city's **buses.** Bus no. 4 and the LAM Rossa bus run to near the Campo dei Miracoli.

Taxis can be found on Piazza della Stazione and Piazza del Duomo. Call a radio taxi at 𝄐 **050-541-600** or 055-555-330.

VISITOR INFORMATION   The main **tourist office** is at Piazza Vittorio Emanuele II 16 (𝄐 **050-42-291;** www.pisaunicaterra.it; Mon–Sat 9am–7pm, Sun 9am–4pm). There's also a desk inside the arrivals hall at the airport (𝄐 **055-502-518;** daily 9:30am–11:30pm).

To find out what's going on in town, pick up a copy of the monthly **"ToDo"** (often in bars and cafes), or check it online at **www.todomagazine.it**.

Where to Stay

Most visitors come to Pisa on a day trip, which helps keep hotel prices down but also limits quality options. The low season for most hotels in Pisa is August.

Novecento ★   These small and simple rooms set around a courtyard in an old villa are strictly contemporary, not an antique armoire in sight. Instead, Philippe Starck chairs and upholstered contemporary headboards are set against handsomely colored accent walls. A lush garden is filled with lounge chairs and quiet corners, and off to one side is the best room in the house, a self-contained, cottagelike unit. For guests desiring a bit more greenery, Pisa's Botanical Garden is just up the street. The Campo Santo is a straightforward 10-minute walk away.

Via Roma 37. 𝄐 **050-500-323.** www.hotelnovecento.pisa.it. 14 units. 80€–120€ double. Rates include breakfast. Parking on street (10€ per day). **Amenities:** Wi-Fi (free).

Relais dell'Orologio ★★   Maria Luisa Bignardi provided Pisa with its only truly remarkable place to stay when she converted her family mansion into refined yet relaxing guest quarters. The large garden and cozy top floor "attic" lounge provide a

Pisa

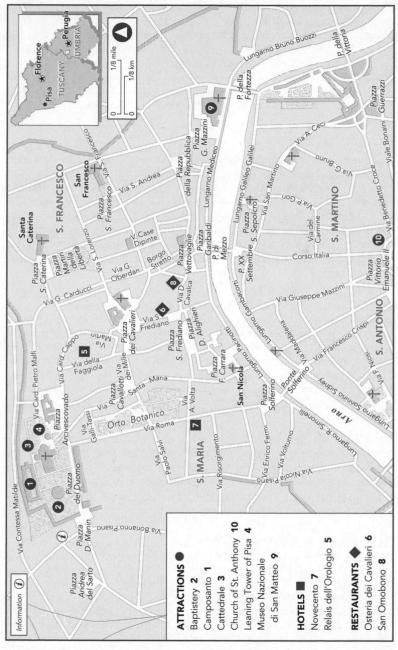

Florence
Pisa
TUSCANY
Perugia
UMBRIA

1/8 mile
1/8 km

Information (i)

Piazza Andrea del Sarto

Via Contessa Matilde

Via Bonanno Pisano

Piazza D. Manin

Piazza del Duomo

Piazza Arcivescovado

Via Galli-Tassi

Via Card. Pietro Maffi

Via Card. Cappo

Piazza S. C.

Piazza S. Caterina

Santa Caterina

S. FRANCESCO

San Francesco

Via S. Francesco

Piazza S. Francesco

Via S. Andrea

Via S. Lorenzo

Via G. Carducci

Via G. Oberdan

V. Case Dipinte

Borgo Stretto

Via G. Carducci

Martiri della Libertà

Via della Faggiola

Piazza Cavallotti

Via dei Mille

Santa Maria

Orto Botanico

Via Roma

Via A. Volta

Via Paolo Salvi

Via Risorgimento

S. MARIA

Via Nicola Pisano

Via Enrico Fermi

Via Volturno

Piazza dei Cavalieri

Via Martiri

Via S. Frediano

Piazza S. Frediano

Piazza D. Alighieri

F. Carrara

Santa Maria

San Nicola

Piazza Solferino

Ponte Solferino

Lungarno Pacinotti

Lungarno Gambacorti

Via Maddalena

Lungarno R. Simonelli

Lungarno Sonnino Sidney

Arno

Piazza Garibaldi

P. di Mezzo

Piazza Vettovaglie

Via D. Cavalca

Piazza della Repubblica

Piazza G. Mazzini

P. della Fortezza

Lungarno Mediceo

Lungarno Galileo Galilei

Piazza S. Sepolcro

P. XX Settembre

Corso Italia

Via Giuseppe Mazzini

Via del Carmine

Via San Martino

Via P. Gori

Via A. Ceci

Via G. Bruno

S. MARTINO

Piazza Vittorio Emanuele II

Via Francesco Crispi

S. ANTONIO

Via F. Niosi

Via Benedetto Croce

Viale Bonaini

Piazza Guerrazzi

P. della Vittoria

Lungarno Bruno Buozzi

ATTRACTIONS ●
Baptistery **2**
Camposanto **1**
Cattedrale **3**
Church of St. Anthony **10**
Leaning Tower of Pisa **4**
Museo Nazionale di San Matteo **9**

HOTELS ■
Novecento **7**
Relais dell'Orologio **5**

RESTAURANTS ◆
Osteria dei Cavalieri **6**
San Omobono **8**

relaxing refuge from the crowds in the Campo, just a 5-minute walk away, and guest rooms are filled with family heirlooms, some colorful architectural details, and lots of 21st-century conveniences, including excellent beds and marble bathrooms. Some of the rooms are quite small, though for a bit extra you can settle into a larger room or one overlooking the garden. Signora Bignardi also runs the 12-room **Relais dei Fiori,** Via Carducci 35 (© **050-556-054;** www.relaisdeifiori.com), where small but very attractive doubles start at 70€. At both, travelers 65 and older get a 20 percent discount in some periods.

Via della Faggiola Ugiccione 12–14. © **050-830-361.** www.hotelrelaisorologio.com. 21 units. 140€–200€ double. Rates include buffet breakfast. **Amenities:** Restaurant; bar; Wi-Fi (free in lobby).

Where to Eat

For pizza or *cecina* (a garbanzo-bean flour flatbread served warm), stop in at **Il Montino,** in the city center at Vicolo del Monte (© **050-598-695**), where Pisans go for a quick slice. If your wanderings take you to the banks of the Arno, an atmospheric place to sit awhile is **Caffè dell'Ussero,** one of Italy's oldest literary cafe-bars, installed in 1775 on the ground floor of Palazzo Agostini (Lungarno Pacinotti 27; © **050-581100**). Young men of the Risorgimento drank and plotted here as students. **Bottega del Gelato** (Piazza Garibaldi 11; © **050-575467**) serves Pisa's best ice cream, the perfect accompaniment for a stroll under the arcades of adjacent Borgo Stretto, Pisa's main shopping street.

Osteria dei Cavalieri ★ PISAN   The "Restaurant of the Knights" operates out of stone rooms off the Piazza die Cavalieri and a short stroll from the Campo that date to the 12th century, while the cooking is traditionally Tuscan but founded on the contemporary Slow Food principles of fresh and local. Being Pisa, this means seafood, including *tagliolini* with razor clams and a classic *baccala,* dried cod lightly battered and fried; some hearty meat choices, such as *pappardelle* with rabbit sauce and grilled steaks; and robust vegetable soups. You can get away with a one-dish meal here—in fact, it's encouraged at lunchtime, when a crowd of local office workers packs in.

Via San Frediano 16. © **050-580-858.** Main courses 10€–14€. Mon–Fri 12:30–2pm Mon–Sat 7:45–10pm.

San Omobono ★★ PISAN   The produce market in the piazza just outside the door provides some nice ambience (as does a column surviving from the medieval church that once stood here) along with plenty of ingredients for old-fashioned Pisan classics, such as *brachette alla renaiaola,* large pasta squares in a purée of turnip greens and smoked fish, and *trenette con rape e aringa,* narrow flat pasta with rape greens and herring. For the full Pisan experience move on to *baccalà alla livornese,* salt cod stewed with tomatoes and a side of *ceci* (garbanzo) beans. Prices and service are refreshing throwbacks to gentler times.

Piazza San Omobobo. © **050-540847.** Main courses 8€–10€. Mon–Sat 7:30–10pm.

Exploring Pisa

On a grassy lawn wedged into the northwest corner of the city walls, medieval Pisans created one of the most dramatic squares in the world. Dubbed the **Campo dei Miracoli (Field of Miracles),** Piazza del Duomo contains an array of elegant buildings that heralded the Pisan-Romanesque style. A subtle part of its appeal, aside from the beauty of the buildings, is its spatial geometry. If you were to look at an aerial photo of the square and draw connect-the-dot lines between the doors and other focal points, you'd come up with all sorts of perfect triangles and tangential lines.

Admission charges for the monuments and museums of the Campo are tied together in a complicated way. The Cattedrale alone costs 2€ (though it's free Nov–Feb). Any other single site is 5€; any two sites cost 6€. To access everything except the Leaning Tower costs 8€ between November and February and 10€ otherwise. Children 9 and under enter free. For more information, visit www.opapisa.it. Admission to the Leaning Tower is separate (see below).

Baptistery ★★ CHURCH   Italy's largest baptistery (104m/341 ft. in circumference), begun in 1153 and capped with a Gothic dome in the 1300s, is built on the same unstable soil as the Leaning Tower. The first thing you will notice is a decided tilt—not nearly as severe as that of the tower, but the round structure leans noticeably towards the cathedral. The unadorned interior is considered to be where the Renaissance, with its emphasis on classical style and humanism, began to flower, in the pulpit by Nicola Pisano (1255–60). The sculptor had studied sarcophagi and other ancient Roman works that the Pisan navy had brought back from Rome as booty, and the classic influence is obvious, nowhere more so than in the presence of a nude Hercules standing next to statues of St. Michael and St. John the Baptist. In scenes of the life of Christ, figures wear tunics and Mary wears the headdress of a Roman matron. If the baptistery is not too crowded, stand near the middle and utter something loudly; the sound will reverberate for quite a while, on account of the structure's renowned acoustics.

Piazza del Duomo. ℂ 050-835-011. www.opapisa.it. For prices, see above. Apr–Sept daily 8am–8pm; Mar daily 9am–6pm; Oct daily 9am–7pm; Nov and Feb daily 9am–5pm; Dec–Jan daily 9:30am–4:30pm. Bus: E, 4, LAM Rossa.

Camposanto ★ CEMETERY   Pisa's monumental cemetery, where the city's aristocracy was buried until the 18th century, was begun in 1278, when Crusaders began shipping back shiploads of dirt from Golgotha (the mount where Christ was crucified). Giovanni di Simone (architect of the Leaning Tower) enclosed the field in a marble cloister, and the walls were eventually covered by magnificent 14th- and 15th-century frescoes, mostly destroyed by Allied bombings in World War II; one of the few remaining, a "Triumph of Death," inspired the 19th-century composer Franz Liszt to write his Totentanz, "Dance of Death." Roman sarcophagi, used as funerary monuments, fared better, and 84 survive. So do the huge chains that medieval Pisans used to protect their harbor and now hang on the cemetery walls.

Piazza del Duomo. ℂ 050-835-011. www.opapisa.it. For prices, see above. Same hours as the Baptistery; see above. Bus: E, 4, LAM Rossa.

Cattedrale ★★ CATHEDRAL   Pisa's magnificent cathedral will forever be associated with Galileo Galilei (1564–1642), a native son and founder of modern physics. Bored during church services, he discovered the law of perpetual motion (a pendulum's swings always take the same amount of time) by watching the swing of a bronze chandelier now known as the "Lamp of Galileo." (It's also said, and the story is probably apocryphal, that Galileo climbed the adjacent Leaning Tower, dropped two wooden balls of differing sizes that hit the ground at the same time, proving that gravity exerts the same force on objects no matter what they weigh.) The exuberant structure, with its tiers of arches and columns, is quite remarkable in its own right; it was heavily influenced by Pisa's contact through trade with the Arab world and has come to be the prime example of Pisan Romanesque architecture. Giovanni Pisano, whose father, Nicola, sculpted the pulpit in the Baptistery (see above) created the pulpit here

(1302–11), covering it with intricate scenes from the New Testament. Considered to be among the great masterpieces of Gothic sculpture, the relief panels were deemed to be too old fashioned by the church's 16th-century restorers and packed away in crates until they were reassembled, rather clumsily, in 1926.

Piazza del Duomo. ⓒ **050-835-011.** www.opapisa.it. For prices, see above. Apr–Sept Mon–Sat 10am–8pm, Sun 1–8pm; Mar Mon–Sat 10am–5:30pm, Sun 1–5:30pm; Oct Mon–Sat 10am–6:30pm, Sun 1–6:30pm; Nov–Feb Mon–Sat 10am–12:45pm and 2–4:30pm, Sun 2–4:30pm. Bus: E, 4, LAM Rossa.

Leaning Tower of Pisa ★★★ ICON   Construction began on the bell tower of Pisa Cathedral in 1173, but three stories into the job architects Guglielmo and Bonnano Pisano called off the work when it became apparent the structure was leaning distinctly. A century later Giovanni di Simone resumed the job, having quite literally gone back to the drawing board and tried to compensate for the lean by making successive layers taller on one side than the other, creating a slight banana shape. Over the centuries engineers have poured concrete into the foundations and tried other solutions in vain, and by the late 20th century the tower was in serious danger of collapse. The tower was closed and braced with cables as crews removed more than 70 tons of earth from beneath the structure, allowing it to slightly right itself as it settled. With lean of just 4m (13 ft.), compared to a precarious 4.6m (15 ft.) before the fix, the tower has been deemed stable for now and safe to climb once again. Before you do, though, take time to notice just how lovely the multicolor marble tower is, with eight arcaded stories that provide a mesmerizing sense of harmony as you look up its height.

The only way to climb the arcaded tower is to book a visit in the office on the north side of the piazza—or for peak season, online well in advance. Visits are limited to 30-minutes, and you must be punctual for your slot or you'll lose your chance to climb the 293 steps. Children under 8 are not permitted to climb the tower, and those ages 8 to 18 need to be accompanied by an adult (8- to 12-year-olds must hold an adult's hand at all times). Leave bags at the cloakroom next to the ticket office behind the cathedral.

Piazza del Duomo. ⓒ **050-835-011.** www.opapisa.it. Admission 15€, or 17€ if you reserve a timed slot (essential in peak periods). Apr–Sept daily 8:30am–8pm (sometimes until 10:30pm June–Aug); Mar daily 9am–5:30pm; Oct daily 9am–7pm; Nov and Feb daily 9:30am–5pm; Dec–Jan daily 10am–4:30pm. Children 7 and under not permitted. Bus: E, 4, LAM Rossa.

Museo Nazionale di San Matteo ★ MUSEUM   An old riverside convent that was once a prison today houses sacred art and sculpture gathered from Pisa's holy places. The collection includes some moving ceramics and Crucifixes that decorated the city's early churches and is especially memorable largely because it shows off the works of so many Pisan masters. Masaccio's panel of St. Paul (1426) is the only piece of his much-studied "Pisa Altarpiece" still in Pisa; the enormous work was dismantled and dispersed around the world in the 18th century and only 11 pieces have been identified. Perhaps the most absorbing work is by Simone Martini (1284–1344), a Sienese painter who was part of that city's artistic flowering before it was decimated by the Black Death in 1348. He painted his polyptych of the "Virgin and Child with Saints" (also known as the "Pisa Polyptych") for the altar of Pisa's church of St. Catherine around 1320. He included more than 43 figures, with saints and angels surrounding the Madonna and Christ Child with Christ above them all. Among the saints is the church's namesake Catherine of Alexandria, a 4th-century princess, daughter of the governor of Alexandria, who was not only beautiful but well versed in the arts and sciences. She allegedly converted hundreds even while she was imprisoned and being tortured, and when she was finally put on the spiked breaking wheel, the device miraculously broke. Catherine was then beheaded and, legend has it, angels carried her corpse to Mt. Sinai.

Piazzetta San Matteo 1. © **050-541865.** 5€. Tues–Sat 8:30am–7pm, Sun 9am–1:30pm.

A MESSAGE ON THE WALL

One of many artists to leave their mark on Pisa is American Keith Haring. Shortly before his death from AIDS in 1989, Haring painted his Tottomondo mural on the south wall of the church of St. Anthony on Piazza Vittorio Emanuele. One of Haring's hallmark yellow figure walks across the bottom of the mural, on the same level as passersby, amid a swirl of figures representing various aspects of peace in the world: Mankind struggles with the serpent (evil), a woman cradles a baby (maternal love), and two men surround a dolphin (our relationship to nature). Haring once said, "My drawings don't try to imitate life, they try to create life," and his mural is a vital presence in Pisa. Piazza Vittorio Emanuele is on the other side of the river from the Campo Santo (about a 25-min. walk south, mostly along Via Santa Maria to the river, then along Via Francesco Crispi once you cross).

CENTRAL & EASTERN TUSCANY

The Tuscan lands that flank either side of Italy's big central valley, the Valdichiana, are first and foremost places of distinctive landscapes. Silvery olive groves sweep up and down hillsides, large swaths of otherwise barren-looking countryside are ablaze with sunflowers and punctuated with pointy cypresses, and vineyards produce two of the world's favorite red wines, Rosso di Montepulciano and Brunello di Montalcino. This part of the world, from Arezzo in the north to Montepulciano and a string of nearby towns in the south, welcomes you with an everyday beauty and unsophisticated, easy charm that leaves no doubt you are in a place apart.

You'll experience the region's warm hospitality in sun-drenched hill towns that are almost eponymous with everything that's good about Italy, from friendly little restaurants serving homemade pasta, to bright, warm-stoned piazzas that are the centers of town life, to masterpieces tucked away in dusty little museums. An overnight stay in any of the towns below introduces you to some memorable experiences of real, everyday Tuscan life, and a visit to any or all of them will fill as many pleasant days as you can spare.

MONTEPULCIANO ★★

67km (41 miles) SE of Siena, 124km (77 miles) SE of Florence, 186km (116 miles) N of Rome

Sipping a delicious ruby wine in a friendly hill town is a good reason to trek across beautiful Tuscan countryside. Few better places to aim for than Montepulciano, with its famous, violet-scented, orange-speckled Vino Nobile di Montepulciano. Wine that flows like water is a major attraction, but the beauty of this place is not to be found only at the bottom of a glass. Noble palaces, proud medieval gateways, and a jumble of enticing alleyways spread out below airy Piazza Grande at the very top of the town, and views over the surrounding hills and valleys are as intoxicating as the wine. Montepulciano is also a good base for exploring other hill towns, especially nearby Pienza and Montalcino, and for making excursions into the Val d'Orcia, that enchanting region of rolling green hills and stream-watered valleys.

Central & Eastern Tuscany

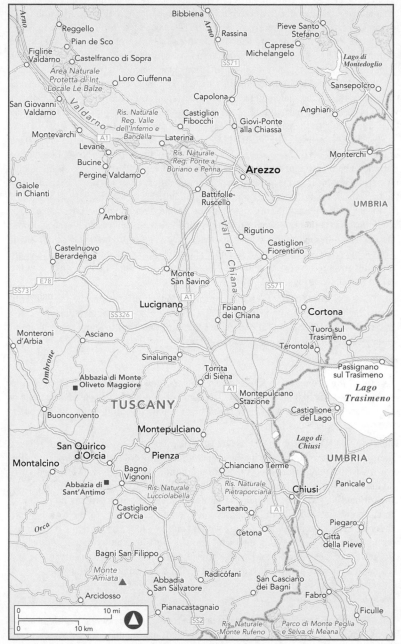

Bibbiena

Arno

Rassina

Pieve Santo Stefano

Caprese Michelangelo

Reggello

Pian de Sco

Figline Valdarno

Castelfranco di Sopra

Area Naturale Protetta di Int. Locale Le Balze

Loro Ciuffenna

Lago di Montedoglio

Sansepolcro

San Giovanni Valdarno

Ris. Naturale Reg. Valle dell'Inferno e Bandella

Capolona

Castiglion Fibocchi

Giovi-Ponte alla Chiassa

Anghiari

Montevarchi

A1

Levane

Laterina

Bucine

Pergine Valdarno

Ris. Naturale Reg. Ponte a Buriano e Penna

Arezzo

Monterchi

Gaiole in Chianti

Battifolle-Ruscello

UMBRIA

Ambra

Rigutino

Castiglion Fiorentino

Castelnuovo Berardenga

E78

SS73

SS326

Monte San Savino

A1

Lucignano

Foiano dei Chiana

SS71

Cortona

Monteroni d'Arbia

Asciano

Ombrone

Sinalunga

Tuoro sul Trasimeno

Terontola

Abbazia di Monte Oliveto Maggiore

Torrita di Siena

Passignano sul Trasimeno

Lago Trasimeno

TUSCANY

Montepulciano Stazione

A1

Buonconvento

Montepulciano

Castiglione del Lago

San Quirico d'Orcia

Pienza

Lago di Chiusi

Montalcino

Bagno Vignoni

Chianciano Terme

UMBRIA

Abbazia di Sant'Antimo

Ris. Naturale Lucciolabella

Ris. Naturale Pietraporciana

Chiusi

Panicale

Castiglione d'Orcia

Sarteano

A1

Orca

Cetona

Piegaro

Città della Pieve

Bagni San Filippo

Monte Amiata

Abbadia San Salvatore

Radicófani

San Casciano dei Bagni

Fabro

Ficulle

Arcidosso

Pianacastagnaio

SS2

Ris. Naturale Monte Rufeno

Parco di Monte Peglia e Selva di Meana

0   10 mi

0   10 km

Essentials

GETTING THERE Traveling by **car** is the easiest way, as bus and train connections are a bit slow and complicated. From Siena, the most scenic route is south on the SS2 to San Quirico d'Orcia, where you get the SS146 eastbound through Pienza to Montepulciano. Parking can be a bit daunting but the system is well organized and lots are well marked. Driving in town is off-limits and you are subject to a fine if you do (your hotel will issue a permit and parking instructions in advance). To park, follow the signs to the well-marked lots outside the city center. The most convenient are the several near the Porta al Prato gate and the nearby bus station; from the lower lots an elevator will take you to the piazza outside the gate, or you can board an orange shuttle bus (1.10€ for a ride to the gate or all the way up the Corso to Piazza Grande).

Six TRAIN **buses** (𝒞 **0577-204-111;** www.trainspa.it) run daily from Siena (1½ hr.). LFI (𝒞 **0578-31-174**) buses run three times daily (none on Sun) from Florence to Bettolle, where you transfer for the bus to Montepulciano (2¼ hr. total). Montepulciano's **train** station is in the valley about 12km (7 miles) from town; you can also use the Chiusi-Chinciano Terme Station, about the same distance away. The advantage of the former is that buses (2€) run up to Montepulciano throughout the day on weekdays and Saturdays (but beware, none on Sun), while the latter is on a main Florence–Rome line so there's frequent service from Florence. There's also train service on the small Siena–Chiusi line. A taxi trip from either station to Montepulciano costs about 20€ each way, for up to four passengers (if you're alone, try to find a fellow traveler at the station and share a ride).

VISITOR INFORMATION Montepulciano's **tourist office** is in the little parking lot just below Porta al Prato (𝒞 **0578-757-341;** www.prolocomontepulciano.it). It's open daily from 9:30am to 12:30pm and 3 to 6pm (until 8pm in summer); it's closed Sunday afternoons, but not for *riposo* in August.

Where to Stay

A stay in Montepulciano surrounds you with small-town Italian life and puts you in easy access to pastoral landscapes and any number of other hill towns. Even Siena is just a short trip away, as are Cortona and Arezzo, two appealing towns on the other, eastern side of the Valdichiana.

Meuble il Riccio ★★ This atmospheric 800-year-old *palazzo* near Piazza Grande, passed down through the innkeeper's family, just doesn't stop laying on the charm—in the arcaded, mosaic-filled courtyard; the vast, antiques-and-art-filled salon and breakfast room; the homey lounge; or the rooftop terrace that overlooks the checkerboard landscapes of the Valdichiana far below the town. Some rooms do justice to the surroundings with palatial expanses and view-filled terraces of their own, while others are simpler and viewless but not without charm—look for the replicas of carved wooden *ricci,* hedgehogs, that once emblazoned the 13th-century facade. Ivana and Giorgio Caroti are on hand to dispense advice and make restaurant reservations, and they serve delicious homemade pastries at breakfast and drinks throughout the day.

Via di Tolosa 21. 𝒞 **0578-757713.** www.ilriccio.net. 10 units. 100€–160€ double. Rates include buffet breakfast. **Amenities:** Bar; Wi-Fi (free).

Osteria del Borgo ★ Polished wood and exposed brickwork and arches and beams supply these bright, good-sized rooms and apartments with plenty of rustic Tuscan charm, but the comfortably stylish furnishings and modern baths lend them a

Montepulciano

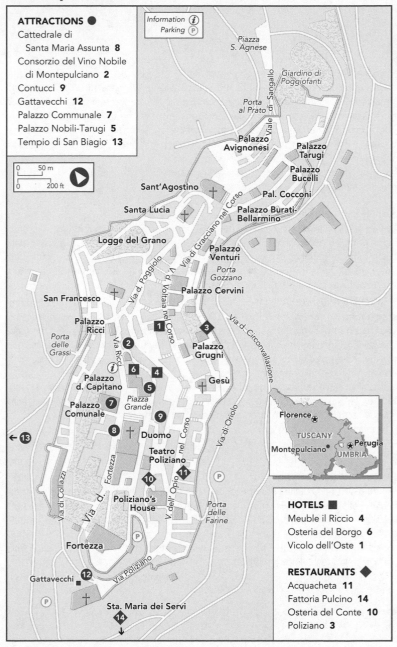

ATTRACTIONS ●

Cattedrale di
  Santa Maria Assunta **8**
Consorzio del Vino Nobile
  di Montepulciano **2**
Contucci **9**
Gattavecchi **12**
Palazzo Communale **7**
Palazzo Nobili-Tarugi **5**
Tempio di San Biagio **13**

Information ⓘ
Parking Ⓟ

Piazza
S. Agnese

Giardino di
Poggiofanti

Porta
al Prato

Palazzo
Avignonesi

Palazzo
Tarugi

Palazzo
Bucelli

Pal. Cocconi

Sant'Agostino

Palazzo Burati-
Bellarmino

Santa Lucia

Logge del Grano

Palazzo
Venturi

Porta
Gozzano

Palazzo Cervini

San Francesco

Palazzo
Ricci

Porta
delle
Grassi

Palazzo
Grugni

Palazzo
d. Capitano

Gesù

Palazzo
Comunale

Piazza
Grande

Florence ★

Duomo

TUSCANY

Montepulciano ● ★ Perugia

UMBRIA

Teatro
Poliziano

Poliziano's
House

Porta
delle
Farine

Fortezza

HOTELS ▪

Meuble il Riccio **4**
Osteria del Borgo **6**
Vicolo dell'Oste **1**

Gattavecchi

RESTAURANTS ◆

Acquacheta **11**
Fattoria Pulcino **14**
Osteria del Conte **10**
Poliziano **3**

Sta. Maria dei Servi

chic flair. The hilltop perch is right in the center of town, just off one side of Piazza Grande, so views from some rooms and the shared courtyard are expansive. A homey restaurant downstairs serves Tuscan specialties and spills out to a nice terrace in good weather.

Via Ricci. 𝄢 **0578-716799.** www.osteriadelborgo.it. 5 units. 90€–120€ double. Rates include buffet breakfast. **Amenities:** Restaurant; Wi-Fi (free); free parking.

Vicolo dell'Oste ★★ Tuscan chic prevails in this house on a narrow lane off the Corso, just below the top of the hill and Piazza Grande. Wood-beamed ceilings set off streamlined contemporary furnishings, while a lot of care has gone into such deluxe touches as large Jacuzzis tucked into the corners of some rooms and practical amenities that include streamlined kitchens in several. While there are no communal spaces, breakfast is served in a nearby cafe, and innkeepers Giuseppe and Luisa seem to always be near at hand to take care of your needs.

Via delle Oste. 𝄢 **0578-758393.** www.vicolodelloste.it. 5 units. 95€–100€ double. Rates include breakfast. **Amenities:** Wi-Fi (free).

Where to Eat

With a local wine that pairs especially well with hearty sauces and red meat, it's no accident that food in Montepulciano is typically Tuscan and relies heavily on game, beef from the Valdichiana, and thick pastas like hand-rolled *pici* topped with rich sauces. Aside from the town's many tasting rooms, you can also quaff the local wines and taste local salamis and cheeses in an atmospheric old cafe, the late-19th-century **Poliziano,** on the Corso (number 27; 𝄢 **0578-758615**).

Acquacheta ★★★ SOUTHERN TUSCAN/GRILL If you're craving steak, you'll want to work a meal in this cellar eatery where the emphasis is on local products into your Montepulciano wine-tasting visit. In a rustic dining room, long and narrow, seating is at shared tables and meat is sold by weight and brought to your table by a cleaver-wielding chef for your approval before it goes onto the grill. A choice of pastas and sauces (mix and match as you please) are also available, as are hearty salads. Please don't ask for a separate wine glass—drinking water and wine from the same glass is an age-old tradition in simple eateries in these parts.

Via del Teatro 22 (down right side of Palazzo Contucci from Piazza Grande). 𝄢 **0578-717-086.** www.acquacheta.eu. Reservations essential. Main courses 7€–18€. Wed–Mon noon–3pm and 7:30–10:30pm. Closed mid-Jan to mid-Mar.

Fattoria Pulcino ★ SOUTHERN TUSCAN/GRILL Several of the larger wineries around Montepulciano have rustic dining rooms, and this one is the most pleasant, because of the totally satisfying selection of grilled meats straight from the farm prepared to order and homemade pastas, and also because of the mesmerizing views of the rolling countryside and Montepulciano crowning its hilltop. *Pici di Montepulciano,* the local, thick, hand-rolled spaghetti, is topped with rich sauces, and anything you order is to be washed down with the estate's Vino Nobile.

Via SS146, 3km/2 miles SE of Montepulciano. 𝄢 **339-1403162.** www.pulcinoristorante.com. Main courses 8€–16€. Daily noon–10pm. Shorter hours in winter.

Osteria del Conte ★ SOUTHERN TUSCAN A trek to the top of town is well rewarded with a delicious meal in this simple room overseen by a mother-and-son team who are devoted to home cooking and warm hospitality. You can put yourself in their hands with the set menu, which includes several local specialties and wine, or choose from a nice a la carte selection—the *pici all'aglione* (handmade spaghetti with garlic sauce) is a memorable first, and most of the meats are grilled to order.

Via di San Donato 19. ✆ **0578-756062.** www.osteriadelconte.it. Main courses 9€–14€. Thurs–Tues 12:30–2:30pm and 7:30–9:30pm.

Exploring Montepulciano

It's all uphill from **Porta al Prato,** where the Medici balls above the gate hint at Montepulciano's long association with Florence. As the Corso begins its steep climb, just be glad you're not pushing a giant wine cask all the way up, as competing teams do the last week of August for the Bravio delle Botti, a competition that commemorates many years of back and forth between Florentine and Sienese rule, with Florence ultimately winning out. A short way beyond the gate is the Colona dell'Marzocco, a column topped with a lion holding the Medici shield. At one time this symbolic signage was a proclamation to all who walked beneath that Montepulciano belonged to Florence. Before 1390, though, passersby would have seen a she-wolf suckling human twins, the symbol of Siena. On Piazza Michelozzo in front of the church of Sant'Agostino stands the **Torre di Pulcinella,** a short clock tower on which a life-size Pulcinella strikes the hours. The black-and-white clown is a stock figure of the commedia dell'arte, a bumpkin from Naples with a beaklike nose. His presence in Montepulciano is attributed to a philandering and homesick Neapolitan bishop who was exiled here in the 16th century for his dalliances.

The climb up the Corso comes with a look at some impressive palaces. At no. 91 is the massive **Palazzo Avignonesi,** with grinning lions' heads, and across the street is the **Palazzo Tarugi** (no. 82). Both are by Vignola, the late Renaissance architect who designed Rome's Villa Giulia. The lower level of the facade of the **Palazzo Bucelli** (no. 73) is embedded with a patchwork of Etruscan reliefs and funerary urns—placed there by 18th-century antiquarian scholar and former resident Pietro Bucelli to show off his collection. Among the fragments you can make out Etruscan text and circles that symbols of libation cups that often appear on tombs, symbols of the last libation of life and the first libation on the journey to the beyond. As you continue up, look left down steep alleyways for some dizzying glimpses of the countryside far below. At the top of the street, the highest point in a very high town, is **Piazza Grande,** surrounded by 16th-century palaces. You might recognize the 14th-century **Palazzo Comunale** from the 2009 vampire movie "Twilight: New Moon"—filmed here, though set in Volterra. The **Palazzo Nobili-Tarugi,** with an arcaded loggia on the corner, facing a **well** topped by the Medici arms flanked by two Florentine lions and two Poliziani griffins. Both the palace and well, along with the **Palazzo Contucci** across from the Palazzo Comunale, are the work of Antonio Sangallo the Elder, who broke away from his usual specialty of fortress design to build these monuments and the Tempio di San Biagio below town. One side of the piazza is taken up by the rambling brick, never-completed 17th-century **Cattedrale di Santa Maria Assunta.**

A short and level walk north along Via Ricci brings you to Piazza San Francesco, where views extend south to Lago Trasimeno in Umbria and northeast across the golden folds of hills toward Siena.

Note: The Corso is very steep indeed. If you are unfit, or suffer from health problems, take the little orange *pollicini* buses that connect the junction just below the Porta al Prato and Piazza Grande in about 8 minutes. Tickets cost 1.10€ each way (buy them on the bus) and run every 20 minutes; you might want to take the bus up to the top of town and walk down.

Cattedrale di Santa Maria Assunta ★ CATHEDRAL   Montepulciano's bare-brick, homely cathedral was completed in 1680 on the site of a much earlier church pulled down (the relatively new 15th-c. bell tower was left in place) to make way for what was to have been a landmark worthy of the noble neighbors on Piazza Grande. The city was by then out of funds, however, and the exterior was never sheathed in marble as planned. Inside is Montepulciano's great work of art, a 1401 gold-hued altarpiece by Taddeo di Bartolo (1363–1422) of the "Assumption of the Virgin with Saints." Bartolo was one of the Sienese artists of the generation after the 1348 Black Death, and this is one of his greatest works; he must have been pleased with it, as he included his self-portrait among the apostles gathered around the tomb of Mary. You can't get too close to the massive triptych soaring above the high altar, which is a shame, because the charm lies in the detail of the many various panels. The main sections show the death of the Virgin, with the apostles miraculously summoned to her bedside; her assumption into Heaven, with most of the apostles also present, here surveying her empty tomb in amazement; and the Virgin's coronation, an extremely popular theme among 14th- and 15th-century Italian artists in which Christ crowns his mother as queen of Heaven. Surrounding these scenes are various adoring saints and, along the bottom, episodes from the life of Christ. One particularly charming vignette shows a child shinning up a tree to get a better view of Christ entering Jerusalem.

The cathedral's other masterpiece is a scattershot affair, the remnants of a marble sculptural group that the Florentine architect and sculptor Michelozzo (1396–1472) crafted between 1427 and 1436 for the tomb of papal secretary Bartolomeo Aragazzi, a humanist and prominent Poliziani. You've seen Michelozzo's light touch throughout Tuscany: He designed the outdoor pulpit for the showing of the Sacra Cintola (girdle of the Virgin) in Prato (p. 109); redesigned the Palazzo Vecchio and designed the Palazzo Medici in Florence; and sculpted the statue of St. John over the door of Florence's Duomo. You'll have to walk around the church to see the bits and pieces of his work here in Montepulciano, as the tomb was disassembled in the 17th century when the original church on this spot was demolished; some pieces were stolen and have eventually found their way to the Victoria and Albert Museum in London, while others are rather randomly distributed around the cathedral. A reclining, hooded statue of the deceased is to the right of the central entrance door, and figures of fortitude and justice stand on either side of the high altar; leaning against a nearby pillar is the figure of St. Bartholomew, after whom Aragazzi was named.

Piazza Grande. No phone. Daily 9am–12:30pm and 3:15–7pm. Free admission.

Tempio di San Biagio ★ CHURCH   This lovely church just outside the walls, completed in 1534, is the masterwork of Antonio da Sangallo the Elder and one of the treasures of High Renaissance architecture. Sangallo was best known for fortresses and other military defenses, but here he broke out of the mold to create a beautiful travertine church of classical proportions on the plan of a Greek cross, with the four arms of equal length radiating from a central dome. Since the church is in open countryside with no other buildings nearby, it's easy to admire the classical unity of the place, and that is all you need to do—the interior is as refined as the exterior but like many a great beauty, a bit dull at close inspection.

Via di San Biagio. No phone. Daily 9am–12:30pm and 3:30–7:30pm. Free admission.

Wine Tasting in Montepulciano

The **Gattavecchi** *cantine,* Via di Collazzi 74 (*C* **0578-757-110;** www.gattavecchi.it), burrow under Santa Maria dei Servi, with cellars that that have been in use since before 1200, originally by the friars of adjacent Santa Maria dei Servi. Older still is the tiny room at the bottom chiseled from the rock; it was probably an Etruscan tomb. Gattavecchi's Vino Nobile is top-notch, as is the 100 percent Sangiovese Parceto. Tasting is free. **Contucci** (*C* **0578-757006;** www.contucci.it), in the 11th-century cellars of a historic palace in Piazza Grande, has a fine range of Vino Nobile wines grown on four soil types, all between the magical numbers of 200m (656 ft.) and 400m (1,312 ft.) altitude. According to winemaker Adamo Pallecchi, this is crucial. The cantina is open for free tastings every day of the year. Opposite the Duomo, the Palazzo del Capitano del Popolo is another stop for the wine buffs. Turn right from the corridor for the **Consorzio del Vino Nobile di Montepulciano** (*C* **0578-757812;** www.consorziovinonobile.it), which offers a rotating menu of tastings for a small fee, and is open Monday through Friday 11:30am to 1:30pm and 2 to 6pm and Saturday 2 to 6pm, from week after Easter through October. Local wineries without a shop in town also sell by the bottle here, and if you're heading into the country for some wine touring, the staff here can provide maps and ideas—as can the **Strada del Vino Nobile** office (*C* **0578-717484;** www.stradavinonobile.it) across the corridor, who are the people to speak to if you want to arrange a local wine itinerary.

Side Trips from Montepulciano
PIENZA ★
14km (9 miles) west of Montepulciano, 55km (34 miles) southeast of Siena

Perched above the Val d'Orcia, Pienza was rebuilt in the mid–15th century by humanist Pope Pius II and architect Bernardo Rossellino to be the ideal Renaissance town. Rossellino's budget was 10,000 florins and he spent 50,000, but Pius was so pleased with the transformation of his birthplace that he scrapped the old name of Corsignano and named the town after himself. Even so, Pius died soon thereafter, leaving most of his plans for palaces, churches, piazzas and a grid of well-ordered streets he envisioned never realized.

Though only a piazza, Duomo, papal palace, and unfinished town hall attest to the grand scheme, they show off a refined and sophisticated Renaissance urban plan in which piazzas and palaces, spaces and perspectives, were designed to reflect Renaissance ideals of rationality and humanism. The town's physical unity was meant to instill the populace with the notions of peace and harmony, and though much of Pienza is for the most part just another lovely rustic Tuscan hill town, these notions are still re-enforced by the glorious, unspoiled landscapes of vineyards and wheat fields that roll away from the town in every direction.

GETTING THERE Pienza is on the SS146 between Montepulciano and San Quirico d'Orcia. From Siena, take the SS2 south to the SS146 (or the slower, but more dramatic SS438 south through Asciano and via Monte Oliveto Maggiore). You can park along the streets surrounding the walls, though some stretches are reserved for residents and others require that "park and display" (buy a ticket in a machine and display it in your windshield; see "Getting Around—By Car," in chapter 9). There's a large, well-marked lot at Piazza del Mercato. There are five daily TRAIN buses (1¼ hr., 3.60€; www.trainspa.it) from Siena on weekdays.

VISITOR INFORMATION   Pienza's **tourist office** is inside the Palazzo Vescovile on Piazza Pio II, Corso Rossellino 30 (✆ **0578-749-905;** www.pienza.info). From mid-March through October, it's open Wednesday to Monday 10am to 1pm and 3 to 6pm; the rest of the year, it's open on weekends only (10am–4pm).

Exploring Pieza

The main street, **Corso Rossellino,** goes in one end of town and out the other in less than 4 minutes at an easy stroll. In the middle of town is the splendid, city-worthy Piazza Pio II, a Renaissance stage set of architectural perfection that is as far as Pope Pius's town-planning dream ever got. A handful of narrow side streets within Pienza's proud little walls are lined with shops selling the town's famous pecorino (sheep's milk cheeses) and honey.

Duomo ★ CATHEDRAL   The light-drenched *domus vitrea* (literally "a house of glass") fulfilled Pius's notion that the structure should symbolize enlightenment. The exterior represents Renaissance ideals of unity with a facade of three blind arches, atop which the pope rather immodestly placed his coat of arms. The light-drenched interior was in part inspired by the pope's travels in Germany, where he admired hall churches lit by tall windows. For all of its perfection, the structure showed signs of a serious flaw almost as soon as it was completed—the hillside on which it is built is unstable, and the foundations are slowly shifting (as you walk toward the rear, you'll notice the floor slightly slopes).

Piazza Pio II. No phone. Daily 7am–1pm and 2:30–7pm. Free admission.

Palazzo Piccolomini ★ HISTORIC SITE   Pope Pius, of course, had to have a residence worthy of his lofty status, and his dining room, bedroom, library, and other chambers are appropriately and stuffily regal. Nothing in the cavernous salons, home to the pope's descendants until 1968, are going to incite much enthusiasm, nor will the dry-as-dust audioguide that steers you along an ordained route (the earnestly dull slog might make you yearn for a bit of mirth, a la Pee-wee Herman asking to see the basement at the Alamo). The bright spot is the *palazzo*'s hanging garden and triple-decked loggia, reached through the painted courtyard; you can linger a while to take in the devastating views south over the Val d'Orcia. With a setting like this it's easy to see why Silvio Piccolomini (he later added "Aeneas" as a first name out of love of the tales of Virgil), born into an impoverished branch of a noble Sienese family, wanted to return to this humble town of his birth after an event-filled life as a humanist scholar, gout sufferer, itinerant diplomat, and pope from 1458 to 1464.

Piazza Pio II. ✆ **0578-74392.** www.palazzopiccolominipienza.it. Admission 7€ adults, 5€ students and children 6–17, free for children under 5. Jan–Feb and Nov daily 2–4pm; Mar and Dec 1–4pm; Apr daily 11am–5pm; May–Oct daily 10am–6pm.

Where to Eat

Trattoria Latte di Luna ★   Just about everyone who's in Pienza at mealtimes seems to squeeze through the narrow door of this family-run trattoria, where home-cooked meals are prepared by mom in the kitchen and served by dad and daughter in the yellow-stucco dining room. *Pici all'aglione* (with spicy tomato-and-garlic sauce) or *zuppa di pane* (a local variant on *ribollita,* with more cabbage) are stellar starters, followed by wild boar or suckling pig in season or grilled steaks any time. The dessert of choice is the house-made *semifreddi* flavored with walnuts and seasonal fruits and berries.

Corso Rossellino, next to Porta al Ciglio. ✆ **0578-748606.** Main courses 7€–16€. Wed–Mon 12:15–2:15pm and 7:15–9:15pm.

MONTALCINO ★

23km (14 miles) west of Pienza; 28km (17 miles) west of Montepulciano; 40km (25 miles) south of Siena

Montalcino presents a warm welcome on the approach from the valley of the Ombrone River below, looking like yet another lovely Tuscan hill town where medieval houses cling higgledy-piggledy to precipitous alleys beneath prickly towers. Of course, if you know wine, you're aware that scenery is not the town's real calling card—that's Brunello di Montalcino, one of the world's most acclaimed reds, of which the town produces more than 3.5 million bottles a year, along with 3 million of its lighter-weight cousin Rosso di Montalcino.

For many centuries, Montalcino wasn't concerned with wine at all but was instead caught up with its changing allegiances to the constantly battling Florence and Siena. The little town was once known as the "Republic of Siena at Montalcino" for housing refuges who sought safe haven when Florence conquered Siena in 1555. Montalcino soon fell to Florence, however, and more or less languished until the 1960s, when the world began waking up to the fact that the local sangiovese grosso grapes—known as "Brunello" to the locals—yielded a wine to be reckoned with. Today Montalcino is flourishing, mostly because of the wine trade, and along with its famous beverages is also known for its fine honey.

GETTING THERE   Montalcino is about a 25-minute drive west of Pienza on SP146. From Siena, it's a straight, 50-minute shot down SR2. The most reliable place for parking spaces (1.50€/hour) is the town's western edge, along Viale Strozzi, or at the fortress (1.50€/hour). From Siena, Montalcino is served by regular TRAIN buses (𝒞 **0577-204246;** www.trainspa.it), six a day, taking 1¼ hours (line 114); there's also bus service to and from Pienza and Montepulciano, with a change in Torrenieri.

VISITOR INFORMATION   The **tourist office** (𝒞 **0577-849331;** www.prolocomontalcino.it), at Costa del Municipio, up a ramp in the shadow of the bell-tower, is open daily April through October from 10am to 1pm and 2 to 5:40pm (closed Mon Nov–Mar). Montalcino's hunting and game festivals, the **Sagra di Galletto** (first Sun in Oct in nearby Camigliano) and **Sagra del Tordo** (last Sun in Oct), celebrate roosters and thrushes by spit-roasting them by the thousand over fire-fed flames.

Exploring Montalcino

Though Montalcino once divided itself into four Siena-like *contrade* in keeping with its sympathies with that city, the center is small and can be crossed in an easy stroll. Via Mazzini cuts through the heart of town from Piazza Cavour to Piazza del Popolo and adjoining Piazza Garibaldi, and the Fortezza is just beyond.

La Fortezza ★ HISTORIC SITE   Built in 1361, this castle's moment arrived when the Sienese holed up here for 4 years after their city's final defeat by Florence in 1555 (ironically, the fortress had only recently been expanded and strengthened by Florence's Medici dukes). You can wander round the pentagonal walls and scale a ladder to the highest turret for a view across hills and dales all the way to Siena, but do so before you sample wine in the on-premised enoteca, perhaps the only tasting room in the world with ramparts.

Piazzale Fortezza. 𝒞 **0577-849211.** www.enotecalafortezza.it. Nov–Mar daily 10am–6pm, Apr–Oct daily 9am–8pm. Ramparts 4€ adults, 2€ children 6–17.

Museo di Montalcino ★ ART MUSEUM   Coming upon this small collection is a bit of a treat, as the cloisters of the church of Sant'Agostino house a trove of masterpieces that you wouldn't expect to find in such a small town. The painting galleries are devoted largely to Sienese artists, whose cold, Byzantine influences are not always immediately appealing. It's interesting to think, however, that many of these artists were the bold innovators of their times, belonging to the generations who worked in the years after the plague of 1348 killed more than half the population of Europe. The Virgin Mary, the favorite subject of early Renaissance painters, shows up in works of Bartolo di Fredi and Luca Tomme, who often collaborated and in the mid–14th century carried on the traditions of the Sienese school after the plague decimated their city; Fredi's multi-panel painting of the "Coronation of the Mary" and scenes from her life is considered to be his masterpiece. The "Madonna dell'Umiltà" ("Madonna of Humility"), by Sano di Pietro (1406–81), was quite radical in its time, showing Mary kneeling on a cushion rather than seated on her traditional throne, a departure that reflected an attempt among some religious to move away from corrupting worldly influences and portray humble acts of faith. Girolano di Benvenuto (1470–1524) shows the familiar scene of the apostle Thomas, who famously doubted the resurrection of Christ, witnessing the Virgin's empty, flower-filled tomb as she has ascends to Heaven and throws him her belt; you'll encounter this story again you visit Prato, just outside Florence (p. 106). Andrea della Robbia's terracotta statue of St. Sebastian, who looks rather boyish and calm considering he's about to be shot full of arrows, brings the collection into the full flowering of the Renaissance in the late 15th century. A corny, life-size model of an Etruscan warrior is the crowd-pleaser among the archaeological bits and pieces left behind by locals who have inhabited the region, as you'll learn, for more than 200,000 years.

Via Ricasoli 31. ℂ **0577-846014.** Tues–Sun 10am–1pm and 2–5:40pm. 4.50€ adults, children 3€. Joint ticket with Fortezza saves 2.50€.

Where to Eat

Fiaschetteria Italiana ★★ The town's most popular drinking spot, in the center of town on Piazza del Popolo, was founded in 1888 by Ferrucci Biondi Santi, a pioneer in the development of Brunello. He modeled his establishment on Caffe Florian in Venice, and locals pay homage to this history by referring to the Art Deco establishment with red velvet sofas and marble-top tables as "The Florian." The square out front may not be as grand as the Piazza San Marco but it's certainly picturesque in its own way. Prince Charles is among the famous patrons who have quaffed the excellent Brunellos and other wines on offer. Snacks and light meals are available, and the coffee, almost as treasured as the wines, is hands-down the best for miles around.

Piazza del Popolo 6. ℂ **0577-849-043.** www.caffefiaschetteriaitaliana.com. Main courses 8€–12€. Daily 7:30am–11pm, closed Thurs Nov–Mar.

The Abbeys

Montalcino is the jumping off point for two of Italy's most enticing abbeys. Both are within easy driving distance, and you can walk to one of them, Abbazia di Sant'Antimo.

Abbazia di Sant'Antimo ★★★ RELIGIOUS SITE Should the urge to lead a monk's life ever strike, or if you simply want to retreat from the world for an hour or two, you'd be hard-pressed to find a better place than Sant'Antimo. This exquisite Romanesque abbey of pale yellow stone nestles serenely in a valley amidst vines and silvery olive groves at the foot of the small village of Castelnuovo dell'Abate, 9km (6 miles) south of Montalcino. Adding to the allure of the scenic setting of the abbey is the luminous effect of light filtering through alabaster, the strains of Gregorian chant monks sing seven times a day, and the scent of incense wafting across the surrounding fields.

The first stone was allegedly laid on the order of Charlemagne in A.D. 781 when, as the story goes, the emperor was returning north from Rome along the Via Francigena. His party of courtiers and soldiers was felled by the plague, but an angel appeared to the emperor and told him to feed the stricken with an infusion made from a certain grass that grows in the valley to this day and is known as "Carolina." He did, the stricken returned to good health, and the emperor founded the abbey in thanksgiving. While any claim of a direct connection to the emperor is debatable, the monastery does date to the 8th century and may have once housed the relics of namesake Saint Anthimus, an early Christian priest. Saved by an angel when Romans threw him into the Tiber with a millstone tied around his neck, Anthimus was eventually beheaded, but not before converting many pagan priests and Roman officials.

Near the entrance, on one side of the campanile, is a charming medieval relief of the Madonna and Child, and carvings of mythological animals and geometric designs surround the doors. Inside the columned interior, the capitals are carved with a plethora of eagles and evangelists, sheep and medieval Christs; an especially intricate carving on the right side tells the story of Daniel in the lion's den, with Daniel peacefully praying between two lions while their mates devour his tormentors. Above these scenes a second-floor matroneum (women's gallery) runs above the nave. In the chapel, 15th-century frescoes by Giovanni di Asciano depict scenes from the Life of St. Benedict and are rich in earthy details; the animals that look on in the various scenes seem wonderfully oblivious to the holy events happening around them. (One scene features two blatantly amorous pigs.)

The French monks who have inhabited the abbey since 1992 fill Sant'Antimo with their haunting Gregorian chant during prayer services, open to the public, six times a day, usually at 7, 9, 11am, 12:45, 2:45, 7, and 8:30pm (9pm in the summer); you can also hear them from a respectful distance on the grounds. A small shop on the road that leads up toward Castelnuovo dell'Abate sells souvenirs and has washrooms. A walk to the monastery from Montalcino along a well-marked hiking trail through fields and vineyards, with refreshing views over the surrounding valleys, takes about 2 hours; ask for a return bus timetable from the abbey at Montalcino's tourist office.

Castelnuovo dell'Abate, 10km (6 miles) south of Montalcino on Via Della Badia di Sant'Antimo. ✆ **0577–835659.** www.antimo.it. Open for visits Mon–Sat 10:30am–12:30pm and 3–6:30pm; Sun 9:15am–12:45pm and 3–6pm; also open for prayer services with chanting at the times above. Free admission.

Monte Oliveto Maggiore ★★★ RELIGIOUS SITE The most famous of Tuscany's rural monasteries might also be the loveliest, set in the scarred hills of the Crete Senesi (see box) northeast of Montalcino and surrounded by glorious scenery that could easily inspire religious fervor. Founded in 1313 by a group of wealthy Sienese businessmen who wanted to devote themselves to the contemplative life, the red-brick monastic complex was built in the early 15th century. The Olivetans, still an active order within the Benedictines, were trying to restore some of the original simplicity and charity of the Benedictine rule, and the monks cared for victims during the 1340s Black Death. What draws most visitors today is the 36-scene fresco cycle by Luca Signorelli and Sodoma illustrating the Life of St. Benedict, one of the masterpieces of High Renaissance narrative painting and Sodoma's greatest work. After parking, walk under the gate tower with its small cafe and through the cool woods for about 5 minutes to the bulky brick heart of the complex. The entrance to the monastery is around to the right: A signed doorway leads into the Chiostro Grande.

Montepulciano

HEDGES & hot spots IN THE VAL D'ORCIA

If you're driving from Montalcino to Pienza, an easy side trip takes you to some rather extraordinary sights nestled in the rippling hills of the Val d'Orcia. First stop is San Quirico d'Orcia, about 15km (9 miles) east of Montalcino on SR2. The 12th-century, honey-colored **Collegiata dei Santi Quirico e Giulitta** assaults you with a wealth of carved stone: capitals composed of animal heads, friezes of dueling fantasy creatures, and columns rising from the backs of stone lions. The church was once a popular stop for pilgrims on the Francigena road from Canterbury to Rome, who paused to venerate its namesake saints, a mother and son; when 3-year-old Quircio inadvertently scratched the face of the pagan governor of Taurus, he was thrown down a flight of stairs; rather than being horrified, Giulitta was delighted that her little boy had become a martyr. Her calm acceptance of this show of might so angered the governor had her ripped apart with hooks and beheaded. Just down the block in the main square, Piazza della Libertà, is the entrance to the **Horti Leonini,** a Renaissance Italianate garden (1580) with geometric box-hedge designs and shady holm oaks, originally a resting spot for pilgrims. It's a surprisingly sophisticated spot, suggestive of worldly palaces, to come across in such a small, sleepy town and is open daily from sunrise to sunset. The town's tourist office is inside the Palazzo Chigi, Via Dante Alighieri (ⓒ **0577-897-211**); it's open April through

Signorelli started the job here in 1497. He finished nine of the scenes before skipping town the next year to work on Orvieto's Duomo, where he created his masterpiece, a Last Judgment (p. 223). Antonio Bazzi arrived in 1505 and finished the cycle by 1508. Bazzi is better known as "Il Sodoma," a derogatory nickname that is probably a reference to his predilection for young men. Sodoma was married at least three times, however, and may have had in the neighborhood of 30 children. You'll meet this eccentric character in scene 3, in which Benedict asks God to mend a broken earthenware sieve belonging to a poor woman and his prayers are answered—proof that God works his wonders in small ways. Sodoma incorporates a self-portrait into the scene, and appears with his flowing black hair, garbed in the fancy clothing that a nobleman had shed upon entering the abbey; he's accompanied by his two pet badgers, a chicken, and a tamed raven.

To follow the cycle's narrative, start in the back-left corner as you enter, with a scene of the young Benedict, astride a spirited white horse, leaving his parents' home to study in Rome. The scenes are especially appealing because of the precise details they provide of medieval life: In scene 11, showing Benedict founding monasteries, is a visual primer of medieval construction techniques: A workman atop scaffolding trowels plaster onto brick vaulting while a cohort applies whitewash with a brush on a long pole and a stonemason prepares the base of a column. Scene 19 shows Benedict sending away harlots that Florenzo, an evil monk, had smuggled into the monastery to tempt the brothers; allegedly, Sodoma painted the women in the nude for verisimilitude, but the abbot was so incensed that he made the artist put dresses on them. (Signorelli depicts Florenzo's death in scene 21.) In scene 6, Sodoma compresses several episodes of an act of mercy into one image, as he shows a priest taking bread out of the oven in the background, Christ appearing to him a vision (shown in a medallion) to tell him to share it with the hermit Benedict, the priest recoiling from the vision on

October Thursday to Tuesday from 10am to 1pm and 3:30 to 6:30pm

Five kilometers (3 miles) south and well signposted off the SR2 is **Bagno Vignoni,** little more than a group of houses surrounding one of the most memorable *piazze* in Tuscany. Instead of paving stones you'll find a steaming pool of mineral water, created when the Medici harnessed the naturally hot sulfur springs percolating from the ground; it's lined with stone walls and finished with a pretty loggia at one end. Even St. Catherine of Siena, when not performing religious and bureaucratic miracles, relaxed here with a sulfur cure. To see the springs in their more natural state, as Roman legionnaires did, take the second turnoff on the curving road into town

and pull over when you see the tiny sulfurous mountain on your right. The waters bubble up here in dozens of tiny rivulets, gathering in a pool at the bottom. Especially on misty days, there's a fairy-tale view of the **Rocca d'Orcia,** the 11th- to 14th-century stronghold and strategic watchtower of the Aldobrandeschi clan, formidable toll collectors along the Francigena pilgrim road through these parts.

Should you wish to partake of the waters, head to **Antiche Terme di Bagno Vignoni,** Piazza del Moretto 12 (*©* **0577-887635;** www.termedibagnovignoni.it) or **Piscina Val di Sole,** at the Hotel Posta Marcucci (www.piscinavaldisole.it; *©* **0577-887112**) to soak away your cares.

the right, and enjoying a meal with Benedict on the left. Signorelli shows us Benedict Receiving Mauro and Placido, depicting the arrival of two young boys of noble birth sent to Benedict to live a monastic life; one day when Placido began to drown in a lake, Mauro miraculously walked across the surface of the water to save him, and the two eventually spread the Benedictine order to far-flung corners of Europe. Inside the church are gorgeous choir stalls that Giovanni da Verona (1505), a monk who was trained in the art of woodcarving, crafted in intarsia, showing some riveting city scenes with remarkable perspective.

22km (13 miles) northeast of Montalcino and 9km (6 miles) northeast of Buonconvento on SP 451, Strada di Monte Oliveto. www.monteolivetomaggiore.it. 9:15am–noon and 3:15–6pm daily (until 5pm in winter). Free admission.

Sampling the Vino

Brunello di Montalcino is one of Italy's mightiest reds, a brawny wine that can hold its own with the rarest *bistecca alla fiorentina.* It's also the perfect accompaniment to game, pungent mushroom sauces, and aged cheeses. Brunello exudes the smell of mossy, damp earth and musky berries. It tastes of dark, sweet fruits and dry vanilla and as the deep ruby liquid mellows to garnet, the wine takes on its characteristic complex and slightly tannic aspect.

Although Montalcino has produced wine for centuries, its flagship Brunello is a recent development, born out of late-19th-century sangiovese experiments to concentrate the grapes through strict cultivation methods. Most Brunellos are drinkable after about 4 to 5 years in the bottle, and the complex ones are best after 10 years or so (few last beyond 30 years). Montalcino's wine consortium, **Consorzio del Vino Brunello di Montalcino** (*©* **0577-848246;** www.consorziobrunellodimontalcino.it) is at Piazza

Cavour 8, and staff members are happy to answer questions and provide information on the local wines.

In town, the most atmospheric place to taste the deep-red liquid is the **Enoteca La Fortezza** (© **0577-849-211;** www.enotecalafortezza.it), inside the ramparts of the town's medieval defenses. The stone-and-brick vaults of a medieval tower are filled with excellent wines and grappa, as well as prosciutto, salami, pecorino cheese, and Montalcino's famous honey. A range of Brunello di Montalcino is carefully selected from 205 registered producers and the staff is adept at helping you and the wine get better acquainted. Glasses of Brunello generally start at 7€; tasting samples of Brunello along with Rosso di Montalcino and Super Tuscans, began at 13€ and go up to 85€ for sessions with your own sommelier. There's free shipping on mixed dozens of selected labels.

If you prefer to go right to the source, quite a few Brunello estates welcome visitors. **Banfi** (© **0577-877-505;** www.castellobanfi.com) above Sant'Angelo Scalo, 10km (6¼ miles) south of Montalcino, is part of an American-owned exporting empire, an enormous ultramodern vineyard with a massive cantina. It's a little corporate, certainly, and bus tours pile in, but there's no arguing with the outstanding quality of the wines. Banfi also runs a small museum (4€ admission) on the history of glass and wine in its medieval castle. The huge enoteca (wine cellar) sells books, ceramics, packaged local foods, and all the Banfi wines and offers tastings beginning at 15€. The enoteca and museum are open daily from 10am to 7:30pm (until 6pm Nov–Feb). Call ahead for an appointment (best at least a week in advance) to take a free, 1-hour guided tour of the cellars at 4pm Monday through Friday (3:30pm Nov–Feb). At La Taverna, a handsome, vaulted room in the former barrel cellars of the castle, you can pair Montalcinese cooking with multiple wine tastings.

Fattoria dei Barbi (© **0577-841-111;** www.fattoriadeibarbi.it), 5km (3 miles) south of town on the road to Castelnuovo, makes a noted Brunello di Montalcino riserva, Vigna del Fiore, and also sells Moscadello and vin santo. A stop here comes with a chance to wander around the utterly charming but misleadingly named Brunello Museum—misleading because the emphasis is not only on wine but on local traditions. On display are old, handcrafted farm implements, 19th-century clothing, cobblers' and blacksmiths' tools, rustic farmhouse furnishings, and hundreds of photographs that chronicle the town when it was a sleepy backwater eking out a living from the land. True to the name, the museum also shows off bottles from more than 300 local producers of Brunello. The museum and tasting room are open Monday through Friday from 10am to 1pm and 2:30 to 6pm, weekends from 2:30 to 6pm. Cantina tours cost 5€ per person and are given Monday through Friday at noon and 3pm. A shop selling their delicious cheeses and salami is open weekdays from 8am to noon and 1 to 5pm (closed 4pm Fri). The refined **Taverna** (© **0577-841-200**) serves good meat and pasta dishes using their own farm products (olive oil, cheeses, and, of course, wine); it's open Thursday through Tuesday from 12:30 to 2:30pm and 7:30 to 9:30pm.

Smaller wineries around Montalcino also receive visitors, but often want advance notice. The Montalcino wine consortium (see above) can steer you to vineyards that are open to the public. For a full day of winery visits, without worrying about driving, you can board the **Brunello Wine Bus** (© **0577-846021;** www.lecameredibacco.com). From mid-June to November, the bus leaves Montalcino at 9am on Tuesday, Thursday, and Saturday for a trip through the countryside to six or so renowned wineries, returning at 8pm. The cost is 25€ a person, plus additional tasting fees.

Into the Crete Sienese

Montepulciano, Montalcino, and Pienza are in the Crete Sienese, literally the "Sienese Clay Hills." You've probably seen the iconic photographs of this terrain that stretches south from Siena—lone farmhouses and pointy cypress trees in a stark landscape of golden rolling hills. You'll get a nice sense of the Crete Sienese on the drive between the three towns on SP146. This is another face of Tuscany, quite different from the green, vineyard-clad hills of Chianti country, and at times the countryside seems forsaken, almost like the surface of the moon. Not that the landscapes aren't beautiful in their own way. The clay soil is planted with wheat, fava beans, and sunflowers, and, depending on the season, the expanses of golden grasses and yellow blooms enfold you in a most welcoming way.

AREZZO ★

53km (32 miles) NE of Montepulciano; 85km (53 miles) SE of Florence; 246km (153 miles) N of Rome

This lively little city on the eastern flanks of the Valdichiana is not nearly as well known or as often visited as its more famous Tuscan neighbors, but that doesn't mean that Arezzo doesn't have a lot to show off or that Aretines would have it any other way. Arezzo is a prosperous place, occupied with agriculture from the surrounding Valdichiana farmlands and vineyards, a goldsmithing tradition that goes back many centuries, and a lively, world-famous antiques trade.

Within a fairly unremarkable 20th-century perimeter (much of it is built atop the rubble left behind after Allied bombings in World War II) is an enticingly and dignified medieval city of cobbled streets that climbs a slope to the Piazza Grande, rather charmingly lopsided and built on an incline like the rest of the town. Piero della Francesca, from nearby Sansepolcro, is the famous name most associated with Arezzo, because of his sumptuous fresco cycle in the church of San Francesco. But Arezzo claims some famous natives of its own: The poet Petrarch (1304–74) was born here, as was Giorgio Vasari (1512–74), a mediocre painter, a much more talented architect, and, with his book "Lives of the Artists"—a collection of gossipy biographical sketches of Renaissance masters from Cimabue and Giotto through Michelangelo—the unwitting author of the first art history text. Another native son, actor and director Roberto Benigni, filmed parts of the 1999 Oscar-winning "La Vita è Bella" ("Life Is Beautiful") here.

Essentials

GETTING THERE   Arezzo is just off the A1 autostrada so is within easy reach of Florence and other places in Tuscany. Well-marked free parking lots lie just outside the city walls, and there's one near the train station. From the lot on Via Pietri, on the north side of town, a series of escalators whisk you straight up to the Duomo.

Arezzo is on a main Rome–Florence train line so there are as many 40 trains a day to and from Florence, less than an hour away. The train station (℃ **0575-20-553**) is just outside the old city on Piazza Repubblica and within an easy walk of the main sights. You can reach Siena and many other towns in Tuscany on **buses** operated by SITA (℃ **0575-749-818;** www.sitabus.it) and **LFI** (℃ **0578-324294;** www.lfi.it). Buses stop just outside the train station on Piazza Repubblica, and there's a ticket office on the square as well.

VISITOR INFORMATION There are several **APT information offices** (www. arezzoturismo.it) in the center: at Piazza della Repubblica 28, just outside the train station (© **0575-377-678;** Mon–Fri 9am–1pm); Palazzo Communale, Piazza Libertà 1 (© **0575-401-945;** Mon–Fri 2–4pm, Sat–Sun 11am–4pm); San Sebastiano Church, Via Ricasoli (© **0575-403-574;** daily 10:30am–5:30pm, winter Fri–Sun only); and inside the Logge Vasari, Piazza Grande 13 (© **0575-182-4358;** Thurs–Tues 10:30am–6:30pm).

Where to Stay

Antiche Mura ★ Arezzo's most atmospheric and comfortable little inn is just a few steps below the Duomo, enjoying an airy prospect off to one side of the town—in fact, it's tucked into the old walls and dates from the 1200s. Rock outcroppings, stone walls, glass walkways over ancient foundations, and an old olive press celebrate this heritage, while sleekly simple furnishings, bright white walls beneath old beams, and splashes of color add a distinctly contemporary flair; each room is named and styled after a famous woman in literature or the movies, from Madame Bovary's period decor to the sensual reds used in the Marilyn Monroe room. Breakfast is served is served in a nearby bar.

Piaggia di Murello 35. © **0575-20410.** www.antichemura.info. 6 units. 75€–95€ double. Rates include breakfast. Free parking nearby. **Amenities:** Wi-Fi (free).

Graziella Patio Hotel ★★ Decor in this old palace a stone's throw from the Piero della Francesco frescoes in the church of San Francesco is based on the travel essays of the late Bruce Chatwin. The gimmick actually works, adding romance and drama without sparing comfort, along with flourishes like huge bathtubs in the sitting/ sleeping areas and a pleasantly contemporary lounge and breakfast room. The colonial India room, with bright yellow walls and a four-poster bed, seems especially well suited to the palatial surroundings, and the Moroccan room, with beautiful glazed-tile walls, is as colorful as the town's famous frescoes. Three especially extravagant rooms are on a lower floor that opens to a hidden garden. One is equipped with a hot tub the size of a small swimming pool, and another has a huge sunken bathtub reached by a dramatic staircase behind the bed. Guests have use of a MacBook for the duration of their stay, and spa services are available.

Via Cavour 23. © **0575-401962.** www.hotelpatio.it. 10 units. 140€–240€ double. Rates include buffet breakfast. **Amenities:** Spa services; Wi-Fi (free).

Vogue Hotel ★★ With a name like this a hotel had better be stylish, and these good-sized and gracious rooms deliver on the promise, bringing flair (without sacrificing comfort) to centuries-old surroundings. Stone walls and beams accent rooms where huge soaking tubs are tucked behind glass headboards, enormous showers have windows, and sitting areas are set into alcoves. Plenty of nice traditional comforts include rich fabrics, fine carpets, and handsome wood furnishings, individually chosen for each room. Some rooms also provide a decidedly untrendy and timeless view of the town's towers and rooftops, and all the sights are just steps away.

Via Guido Monaco 54. © **0575-24361.** www.voguehotel.it. 26 units. 140€–230€ double. **Amenities:** Bar; Wi-Fi (free).

Arezzo

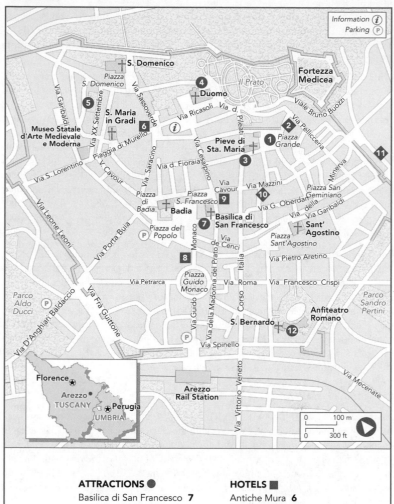

Information ⓘ
Parking ⓟ

S. Domenico

Piazza S. Domenico

Fortezza Medicea

Il Prato

Via Garibaldi

Via Sassoverde

Duomo

Viale Bruno Buozzi

S. Maria in Gradi

Via Ricasoli   Via d.

Via XX Settembre

ⓘ

Via Pelliceria

Museo Statale d'Arte Medievale e Moderna

Piaggia di Murello

Piazza Grande

Via Pileati

Pieve di Sta. Maria

Via Cesalpino

Via d. Fioraia

Via S. Lorentino

V. Cavour

Via Saracino

Via Minerva

Piazza San Geminiano

Via Mazzini

Via Cavour

Via della Garibaldi

Via S. Lorentino

Piazza di Badia

Piazza S. Francesco

Badia

Via G. Oberdan

Via Leone Leoni

Basilica di San Francesco

Sant' Agostino

Piazza del Popolo

ⓟ

Via Monaco

Piazza Sant'Agostino

Via de Cenci

Via Pietro Aretino

Via Porta Buia

Via Italia

Via Petrarca

Piazza Guido Monaco

Via Roma

Via Francesco Crispi

Parco Aldo Ducci

ⓟ

Via D'Anghiari Baldaccio

Via Frà Guittone

Via Guido

Via della Madonna del Prato

Via Corso Italia

Parco Sandro Pertini

Anfiteatro Romano

S. Bernardo

ⓟ

Via Spinello

Florence

Arezzo
TUSCANY

Perugia

UMBRIA

Via Vittorio Veneto

Arezzo Rail Station

Via Mecenate

0   100 m
0   300 ft

ATTRACTIONS ●

Basilica di San Francesco **7**
Casa di Vasari
   (House of Vasari) **5**
Cattedrale di Arezzo **4**
Piazza Grande **1**
Museo Archeologico
   G. C. Mercenate **12**
Santa Maria
   della Pieve **3**

HOTELS ■

Antiche Mura **6**
Graziella Patio Hotel **9**
Vogue Hotel **8**

RESTAURANTS ◆

Antica Osteria
   l'Agania **10**
La Torre di Gnicche **2**
Sottolemura **11**

Where to Eat

In all but the worst weather, Aretines turn out for the evening *passeggiata*. Two prime spots to sit on a terrace and enjoy a pre-dinner glass of wine or aperitif while watching the comings and goings are **Caffe dei Costanti** in Piazza San Francesco (✆ **0575-1824075**) and **Caffe Vasari** (✆ **0575-21945**) under the Loggia overlooking Piazza Grande, a good place to perch even in the rain.

Antica Osteria l'Agania ★ TUSCAN   On any given night half the town seems to be packing into these two floors of plain, brightly lit dining rooms, where the wait staff never seems daunted by the din or the crowds. All of the pastas are homemade from organic ingredients (five types are available, topped with a choice of five sauces), produce is market fresh, and the meats are from local farms. Daily specials usually include such local favorites as *trippa* (tripe) and *grifi e polenta* (chunks of veal stomach in polenta), but lighter fare is almost always available, too, and specials often include eggs topped with fresh asparagus or *tartufo* (dried truffles), especially tasty when accompanied with a Pinot Grigot. But the house wine is excellent, and very inexpensive, and the house grappa puts the perfect finish on a meal.

Via Mazzini 10. ✆ **0575-295381.** www.agania.com. Main courses 7€–9€. Tues–Sun 12:30–2:30pm and 7:30–10:30pm.

La Torre di Gnicche ★★★ TUSCAN/WINE BAR   The emphasis here is on wine, with more than 30 choices available by the glass and hundreds by the bottle, and it's accompanied by a tempting choice of small plates and meals that might have you coming back more than once. A huge selection of cheeses and salamis from local producers are available, as are many local favorites, such as *baccalà in umido* (salt-cod stew) and, in summer, *pappa al pomodoro* (a thick bread and tomato soup served at room temperature). The cluttered bottle-lined room just off Piazza Grande is a nice hideaway on a chilly evening, and a few tables in the narrow lane outside are a much-in-demand warm-weather spot. Reservations are essential.

Piaggia San Martino 8. ✆ **0578-717-086.** Main courses 7€–11€. Thurs–Tues noon–3pm and 6pm–1am. Closed 2 weeks in Jan.

Sottolemura ★ TUSCAN/PIZZERIA   Arezzo has several nice family-oriented restaurants like this, but many Aretines claim the pizza served here, in two big, friendly rooms and a large garden, is the best in town. Some of the other dishes are formidable as well, including hefty pastas that include a *rigatoni alla amatriciana* with a hearty and spicy tomato sauce, and a big choice of grilled meats. Even on a weeknight you'll be surrounded by boisterous families, and tables can be hard to get on weekends when Sottolemura is a big favorite for get-togethers.

Via A. Sansovino 18. ✆ **0575-21403.** www.sottolemura.it. Main courses 8€–12€. Tues–Sun 7–11pm.

Exploring Arezzo

Arezzo's appealing jumble of *palazzi,* towers, and churches spills down a gentle hillside, with the focal point, the Piazza Grande, near the top. An elegant loggia designed by Vassari anchors one side of the piazza, while the rest of the space seems to be rather casually draped across the slope, with slanting cobblestones and an irregular shape. Arezzo's famous antique fair takes over the square the first Sunday of each month and the preceding Saturday, and the Giostra del Saracino, a jousting contest between the eight districts of the town, turns the clock back to medieval times twice a year in June

WHO DID SHE THINK SHE WAS, THE queen of sheba?

The story Piero della Francesca chose to tell, the "Legend of the True Cross," is a real doozy, even when it comes to complex religious fables that were so popular among Renaissance artists. The artist based his fresco cycle on a story included in Jacopo da Varazze's 1260 "Golden Legend," a compilation of saintly lore that was a medieval best-seller and circulated as quickly as scribes could write out a manuscript; with the invention of the printing press in the 1450s, printers made fortunes selling copies in every European language.

As the story goes, Seth, son of Adam, planted the seeds from the apple tree that had so consequentially led his parents into sin on the grave of his father. Timbers from the tree were eventually made into a bridge and, while crossing it, the Queen of Sheba, the much-mythologized ruler of an Arabic kingdom, recognized the wood had special significance. She told King Solomon, king of Israel, that a savior would one day be hung from the timbers and in so doing usurp the kingdom of the Jews. So, Solomon had the wood buried, but Romans discovered the beams and used them to crucify Christ. Two centuries later Roman co-emperor Constantine the Great saw the cross in a vision, emblazoned the image on his army's shields, defeated his co-emperor Maxantius to become sole emperor, and converted to Christianity. His mother, Helen, went in search of the true cross in Jerusalem, where she had unbelieving Jews thrown into a pit to die of hunger until they revealed the location of the cross. One man was dragged from the pit and revealed the whereabouts, then converted. Step forward another few centuries and the cross was still working miracles, aiding what remained of the Eastern Roman Empire in its battles with the Persians. A tad convoluted and obscure? To us, certainly, but nonetheless riveting as told by Piero della Francesco.

and September. The Duomo, seeming a bit forlorn, crowns the hilltop, while next it to the green expanse of the Parco del Prato, with airy views of the countryside, surrounds a ruined, 16th-century fortress.

Basilica di San Francesco ★★★ RELIGIOUS SITE   The chance to spend 25 minutes (about what the well-organized admission system allots you) in front of Piero della Francesca's fresco of the "Legend of the True Cross" is reason enough to come to Arezzo. One of the greatest artists of the Renaissance painted one of the world's greatest fresco cycles, in a league with the Sistine Chapel, between 1452 and 1466. The 10 panels are remarkable for their grace, narrative detail, compositional precision, perfect perspective, depth of humanity, and dramatic light effects—["]the most perfect morning light in all Renaissance painting," wrote art historian Kenneth Clark. The full religious significance of the story may escape you (see box, below) but with stalwart knights and fair ladies, and their bloody battles and sense of adventure, the scenes seem like a medieval romance. The beauty is in the details: heaving bosoms, pouty lips, and dreamy eyes, along with some wonderful ancient and medieval finery— elaborate hats, clunky shoes, snazzy cloaks, hair shirts, and tight britches and revealing togas. Adam, now ancient, looks humanely frail as he lies beneath a sturdy oak with his children gathered around him; cross bearers wear disheveled clothing and bite their lips under the strain of their task; grooms gossip amiably off to one side while the

Queen of Sheba looks terribly regal, whether she's worshipping in the woods or meeting with Solomon in a royal pavilion; throat stabbing soldiers and hair-pulling thugs are suitably menacing, though the artist never seems able to render a human face without an aesthetic humanity that seems to call out to us from the plaster. For a preview of encountering these figures, watch the scene from the film "The English Patient" in which Kip hoists Hana past the frescoes by means of ropes and pulleys; we see her expressions of delight and wonder as she comes face to face with Piero's colorful ladies and gents, and you'll feel the same, even when earthbound and jostling for a good look with your co-viewers.

Piazza San Francesco. © **0575-352-727.** www.pierodellafrancesca.it. Church: Mon–Sat 8:30am–noon and 2:30–6:30pm, Sun 9:45–10:45am and 1–5pm. Piero cycle by 30-min. timed entry only, admission on the half-hour: Mon–Fri 9am–6:30pm, Sat 9am–5:30pm, Sun 1–5:30pm. Reservations for Piero cycle tickets required by phone, website, or in person. 8€ adults, 5€ students and children under 17.

Casa di Vasari (House of Vasari) ★★ HISTORIC SITE   Giorgio Vasari was born in Arezzo in 1511, just as the Renaissance was flowering all around him. Though he never achieved the greatness of many of the other artists working around him, Vasari helped define the period and may have even coined the name for the creative flowering that led Europe out of the Dark Ages. He was an architect as well an artist, and one of the buildings he designed, the Palazzo degli Uffizi in Florence, houses one of his most famous paintings, commissioned by the Medicis, a Portrait of Lorenzo the Magnificent. Vasari is best known for "Lives of the Most Excellent Painters, Sculptors and Architects," a rather juicy account of the great masters, many of whom Vasari knew and whom he observes with an opinionated contemporary's eye, giving us an invaluable account in what is considered to be the world's first art history text. He settled down here in his hometown in 1540 and set about frescoing the walls and ceilings of his gracious house with classical themes and portraits. Among his frescoes is a playful "Virtue, Envy, and Fortune" in which the three virtues appear to contend for top position and are painted in such a way that each of the threes figures appears to be prominent as you view the images from different perspectives. In the Room of Celebrities Vasari painted portraits of Michelangelo, Adrea del Sarto, and other notable contemporaries, surrounding himself with the cultural greats of his day. Vasari's copious correspondence, including 17 letters from Michelangelo, are also sometimes on view. While the original furnishings are no longer in place, part of the beautiful garden remains, and like the rest of the house provides a glimpse at a cultured Renaissance lifestyle.

Via XX Settembre 55. © **0575-409040.** Wed–Mon 8:30am–7:30pm. 2€. 9:15am–noon and 3:15–6pm daily (until 5pm in winter). Free admission.

Cattedrale di Arezzo ★ RELIGIOUS SITE   This big and austere Gothic barn, at the highest point in town, reveals some nice surprises once you step inside the coldly stark interior. First to catch your eye will be the stained-glass windows by Guillaume de Marcillat (1470–1529), a French master who was summoned to Rome to work for the popes and spend the last 10 years of his life in Arezzo, much of them creating these seven magnificent frescoes in glass—one of the few complete cycles of his work to survive the centuries (his rose window is in San Francesco, above). His colorful scenes here include the Calling of St. Matthew, the Baptism of Christ, the Expulsion of Merchants from the Temple, the Adulteress, and the Raising of Lazarus along the right wall; and Saints Silvester and Lucy in the chapel to the left of the apse; Lucy has a stunningly serene face, all the more remarkable considering she's about to have her eyes gouged out.

Another notable female presence is that of Mary Magdalene, portrayed in a fresco by Piero Della Francesco in an arch near the sacristy door. She's having a bad hair day, and a nest of straggly strands fall over her broad shoulders, but she is nonetheless a robust figure in colorful robes and holding a luminous jar of ointment. Her hair may look the way it does because she's just used it, as the Bible tells us, to dry the feet of Christ once she had washed them, then anointed them with the ointment. The artist, a passionate student of geometry and mathematics, captures the scene with his skillful use of perspective and he imparts his subject with his telltale serenity.

Quite riveting, on close inspection, are the stone-carved scenes on the tomb of Guido Tarlati, an Aretine bishop who died in 1327. Scenes show this man of the cloth constantly at war, clad in armor and besieging castles with glimpses of Arezzo in the background—acts of aggression that eventually got him excommunicated but, since his family chose to commemorate him at war, apparently his fall from favor with papal authorities didn't interfere with his plans for eternal salvation. A grace note in the chapel on the left near the entrance are the bright and pretty terra cottas of the Assumption, a Crucifixion, and Madonna and Child, all by Andrea della Robbia of the well-known Tuscan family who introduced terra-cotta sculpture to the Renaissance art scene.

Piazza del Duomo. ℂ **0575-23991.** Daily 7am–12:30pm and 3–6:30pm. Free admission.

Museo Archeologico G. C. Mercenate ★ MUSEUM As Arretium, Arezzo was an important member of the 12-city Etruscan confederation, and the town was quite famous in Roman times for its mass-produced *corallino* ceramics. This past comes to light with a few standout finds in the 14th-century Convento di San Bernardo, built atop the remains of a Roman amphitheater and well worth an hour of browsing. Among the Etruscan artifacts upstairs is an utterly charming urn with human arms as handles and a lid shaped like a human head—the piece could hold its own as pop art and manages to convey the sophistication and humanity of the Etruscans. Ground floor rooms house the remnants of the mass-produced *corallino* clay pottery that from 50 B.C. to A.D. 70 put Roman Arezzo on the map of the ancient world. Room 8 shows off the commercial weight of this enterprise with the remnants of the famed Ateius workshop, which at its height had branch ateliers in Pisa and Lyons. These clay vases of Arezzo were much less expensive than the silver vessels on which they were modeled, and they flooded the empire in the same way mass produced made-in-China plastic imitators have today usurped so many hand-crafted items. Plus, they were available in the same shapes as more finely wrought vessels, and decorated similarly. Not that Aretines didn't value quality: A wide-mouthed vase, the so-called crater of Euphronius, was made by namesake Greek master in the 6th century B.C. and used to mix wine and water. It would have been extremely precious even in its own time, a symbol of the great status of the Arezzo resident who had shipped from Greece through the Greco-Etruscan port of Spina, on the Po delta, and from there carted overland across the Apennine passes. Similarly exquisite is a highly refined tiny portrait of a toga-wearing man incised on gold and silver leaf and protected by a glass disk, dating from the A.D. early 3rd century and reflecting a goldsmithing tradition for which Arezzo is still well known.

Via Margaritone 10. ℂ **0575-20882.** Daily 8:30am–7:30pm. 4€ adults, 2€ 18–25, under 18 free.

Santa Maria della Pieve ★★ RELIGIOUS SITE Most great churches are intended to draw the eye heavenward, but few achieve the effect quite as dramatically and almost playfully as this 12th-century arched facade. Three stacked arcades of beige stone, one piled atop the other, become slightly narrower as they rise above a five-arched lower floor and the narrow street below, and above it all rises a bell towers with five rows of windows. The effect is all the more powerful since the church is built on a slope, so the towering facade is often viewed from below and seems all the higher for it. In the rear, three rounded tiers of arches face Piazza Grande.

Inside, beyond an entryway carved with the months of the year (with the two-faced pagan god Janus representing the month of January, named after him), is an altarpiece by Pietro Lorenzetti, a Sienese artist who would eventually perish when the Black Death devastated the city in 1348. His work here is multi-tiered like the church's facade, with figures getting smaller on each successive layer. The paintings are unusually vivacious for the typically remote Sienese school and show the Madonna draped in a luxurious ermine-lined robe, surrounded by a retinue of similarly well-attired saints; among them is St. Luke, recording the "Annunciation" in his Gospel. It is one of relatively few altarpieces that remain in situ in the church for which it was intended, as most have been broken into segments and scattered around the world. Some of the remains of the town's patron saint, Donato, are here, too, in a beautiful gold reliquary. Donato was a 4th-century bishop of Arezzo, and must have been a welcome presence: He could bring the dead back to life, restore sight, and exorcise demons, and he slew a dragon that was poisoning a well (the bones of this beast, along with other parts of Donato, are in the church of Santa Maria e San Donato on the island of Murano, near Venice). Donato met his end after pagans broke into a church where he was saying mass and smashed a chalice; Donato pieced the vessel back together save for one large fragment, but in his hands the chalice did not leak—a miracle that convinced 79 pagans to convert on this spot. This was too much for local authorities, who had the bishop beheaded soon afterwards.

Corso Italia 7. ✆ **0575-22629.** May–Sept daily 8am–7pm, Oct–Apr daily 8am–noon and 3–6pm. Free admission.

Side Trips from Arezzo
SANSEPOLCRO

37km (23 miles) NE of Arezzo

Around the year 1,000, two pilgrims, Arcanus and Aegidius, returned from the Holy Land with a few bits of the Holy Sepulcher. They housed the treasure in an oratory (since replaced by the cathedral) and their hometown soon became known as Borgo San Sepolcro. The name has stuck, though the namesake souvenirs are long lost and forgotten. These days attention focuses on Piero della Francesca, the monumentally important painter who was born Sansepolcro around 1412 or 1415. Seeing his works here and in nearby Monterchi is what brings most visitors across the green hills from Arezzo to the forest-shaded upper reaches of the Tiber Valley.

GETTING THERE By car from Arezzo, Sansepolcro is less than half an hour away via SS73. Buses operated by SITA (✆ **0575-749-818;** www.sitabus.it) and Baschetti (✆ **0575-749816;** www.baschetti.it) ply the route about six times a day.

Exploring Sansepolcro
Modern Sansepolcro is home to the Buitoni pasta empire, founded by Giulia Buitoni in 1827. Within the medieval walls, however, the narrow streets belong to earlier eras,

following a grid laid out by the Romans and lined with palaces and churches. A well-marked route follows cobbled lanes and arcaded loggias to the medieval town hall, where the Museo Civico houses the town's acclaimed works by Piero della Francesca.

Museo Civico ★★★ MUSEUM During World War II, the British officer commanding the heights over Sansepolcro remembered he'd read an essay by Aldous Huxley, "The Greatest Picture," about Piero della Francesca's 1468 "Resurrection of Christ," in the town hall. He ordered shelling to cease lest a masterpiece be lost, maybe saving Sansepolcro in the process. The painting that saved a town is upstairs at the far end of Room 4. Painted in 1463, the fresco-and-tempera work shows Christ rising from his tomb as four guards doze unaware. We see Christ in an unusually earth-bound pose, face on, staring directly out of the painting at us, his heavy, peasantlike features suggesting God in human form. Even so, the way he stands above the sleeping soldiers implies he is a Divine presence elevated above his human subjects. Christ has placed his leg on the parapet of the classic-looking sarcophagus, suggesting he is just in the act of climbing out. The soldier in brown with his head against the same parapet is thought to be a self-portrait of the artist; the soldier next to him, holding a lance, is positioned in such a way that he appears to have no legs—technically, we should see them, so obviously the artist abandoned anatomical veracity for the sake of a good composition. The landscape behind Christ is significant, too, mostly barren but just beginning to bud, a harbinger of springtime resurrection.

Piero appears again in room 1, in a 19th-century terra-cotta bust, and Room 3 house his "Polyptych della Misericordia" (1445–62), reassembled without its frame. The Mary of Mercy spreads her cloak around kneeling donors, who are dwarfed by her towering figure. The one to the left of her, in red and looking up, is believed by some to be another self-portrait of Piero. A sleepy-eyed St. John the Baptist, St. Sebastian (who seems more consumed by the ecstasy of being pierced by arrows than with his holy company), and other saints look on. By Piero's contract with the Compagnia della Misericordia, the co-fraternity that commissioned the work, he was to deliver the finished product within 3 years, but he did not finish until 17 years later. Piero was a notoriously slow worker, and his father was tasked with mollifying patrons and apologizing to them for his son's lateness. Failing eyesight made the situation even worse. Even so, had the brothers kept better tabs on their artist, they would have known that during the time he was under contract with them he also accepted commissions in Ferrara and Rimini, as well as closer to home, from other churches in Sansepolcro and Arezzo.

At least one other works by the artist, and possibly two, are in the museum: a much-deteriorated fresco fragment of "San Giuliano" (1455–58), who even in this rather sorry state looks quite beatific, and a much-disputed "San Ludovico da Tolosa" (1460), often attributed to Piero's student Lorentino.

Via Aggiunti 65. 📞 **0575-732218.** June 15–Sept 15 daily 9:30am–1:30pm and 2:30–7pm; Sept 16–June 14 9:30am–1pm and 2:30–6pm. 6€.

Museo "Madonna del Parto" ★★★ MUSEUM Art lovers detour to the village of Monterchi, about 15km (9 miles) south of Sansepolcro, for one reason: to see Piero's "Madonna del Parto" ("Parto" meaning birth). The work is almost unique in Italian art in that it depicts the Virgin Mary heavily pregnant, one eyelid dropping and a hand on her belly. She's revealed to us by two angels who hold back the flaps of a tent, as if we're catching her in a private moment. It was painted sometime after 1459

The Greatness of Piero

What is it about the work of Piero della Francesca that is so enduringly appealing? Critics have long been trying to answer that question, and over the centuries have managed to come up with a compelling list of qualities that make Piero stand out among other Renaissance artist, and what you will want to look when viewing his paintings. The effete and erudite Victorian critic John Addington Symonds commented that "by dignity of portraiture, by loftiness of style, and by a certain poetical solemnity of imagination, [Piero] raised himself above the level of the mass of his contemporaries." His artistic mastery, along with his mathematical, geometric perceptions, are considered to represent a perfect union of art and science. Late in life, when his failing eyesight made it impossible for him to paint, Piero wrote about his views of proportion and perspective in a treatise, "On Perspective in Painting," that influenced generations of artists. He is unquestionably a master of light and color. Most of all, perhaps, his paintings are unemotional and hauntingly inexpressive, tranquil and serene, and his subjects are immobile and constrained, and for that reason timeless—as much a part of the present-day as of their own distant times.

(dating Piero is notoriously tricky), for a church in a cemetery where, it's been suggested, the artist's mother may be buried, making the fresco her son's tribute to her. The painting has long been popular with pregnant women, who still travel from afar to pay homage to the image of the uncomfortably pregnant Madonna and pray for an easy birth (pregnant women get free admission to the museum). If you are driving from Arezzo to Sansepolcro to see the Pieros, it's easy to add a stop in Monterchi to the itinerary—it's right on the way, just off S78.

Via Reglia1, Monterchi. ℂ **0575-70713.** Apr–Oct Tues–Sun 9am–1pm and 2–7pm; Nov–Mar 9am–1pm and 2–5pm. 3.50€, free for pregnant women.

Where to Eat

Pasticceria Chieli, Via Vittorio Veneto 35A (ℂ **0575-742026;** www.pasticceriachieli.it), is the best pastry shop in town; you'll want to stock up on the pine-nut-studded ricotta tart.

Da Ventura ★ TUSCAN   Service is mix and match in these three unpretentious wood-beamed and arched rooms, where hearty Tuscan cooking takes center stage. You can select from an assortment of salamis, cheeses, and crostini for an antipasta, then move on to homemade tagliatelle and other pastas where you have a choice from a cart filled with an assortment of sauces. Waiters will also roll up to your table with carts laden with beef stew (swimming in Chianti Classico) and herb-laced roast pork, and excellent steaks are also available, cooked to order.

Via Niccolò Aggiunti 30. ℂ **0575-75900.** www.albergodaventura.it. Main courses 8€–15€. Tues–Sat 12:30–3pm and 7–10:30pm, Sun 12:30–3:30pm.

CORTONA ★★

34km (22 miles) S of Arezzo; 105km (63 miles) SE of Florence; 194km (120 miles) N of Rome

Cortona cuts a rather austere figure, draped across the upper reaches of a green mountainside above terraced olive groves, stony and austere. It's a steep medieval city where cut-stone staircases take the place of many streets, and views extend far away into the

Cortona

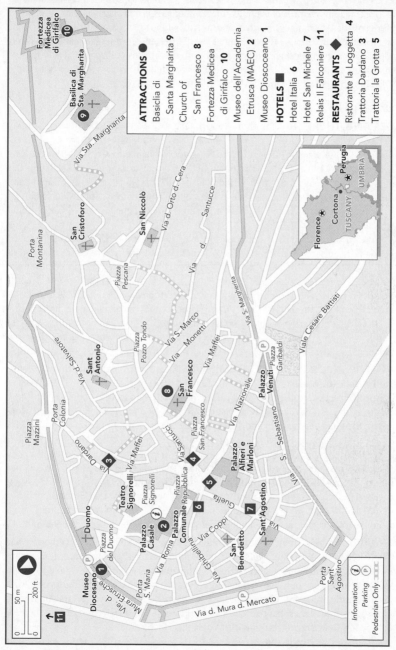

ATTRACTIONS ●

Basiclia di
Santa Margharita **9**

Church of
San Francesco **8**

Fortezza Medicea
di Girifalco **10**

Museo dell'Accademia
Etrusca (MAEC) **2**

Museo Dioscoceano **1**

HOTELS ■

Hotel Italia **6**

Hotel San Michele **7**

Relais Il Falconiere **11**

RESTAURANTS ◆

Ristorante la Loggetta **4**

Trattoria Dardano **3**

Trattoria la Grotta **5**

Florence ✪
Cortona ✪ Perugia ●
TUSCANY
UMBRIA

Fortezza
Medicea
di Girifalco **10**

Basilica di
Sta. Margharita **9**

Via Sta. Margharita

San
Cristoforo

San Niccolò

Via d. Orto d. Cera

Porta
Montanina

Piazza
Pescaria

Via d. Santucce

Via S. Marco

Piazza
Pozzo Tondo

Via — Monetti

Sant
Antonio

Via d. Salvatore

Via Maffei

Porta
Colonia

San
Francesco **8**

Via Nazionale

Via S. Margharita

Palazzo
Venuti

Piazza
Garibaldi

Viale Cesare Battisti

Piazza
Mazzini

Via Dardano

Teatro
Signorelli

Via Maffei

Piazza
Signorelli

Via Maffei

3

Piazza
San Francesco

Via Santucce

4

Palazzo
Alfieri e
Marloni

Via S. Sebastiano

Piazza
Comunale Repubblica

5

Guelfa

6

Palazzo
Casale

2

Via Roma

i

Via Guelfa

7

Sant'Agostino

Via Coppi

San
Benedetto

Via Ghibellini

Duomo

Piazza
del Duomo

1

Museo
Diocesano

Vie. d.
Mura Etrusche

Porta
S. Maria

Porta
Sant'
Agostino

Via d. Mura d. Mercato

11 ←

Information **i**

Parking **P**

Pedestrian Only ▪▪▪▪

0 — 50 m
0 — 200 ft

189

mists over the wide Valdichiana. The town shed a bit of its remoteness in recent years when the book and film "Under the Tuscan Sun" brought appreciative fans to town, but Cortona has survived the onslaught—the somber streets and stage-set piazzas are a bit more crowded in summer than they once were, but the town's appeal—including some significant art treasures—is as strong as ever. After all, Cortona has witnessed many comings and goings over its long history and was already a thriving city by the 6th century B.C., when it was 1 of 12 cities that formed the Etruscan confederation, and it was a prosperous art city under Medici rule.

Essentials

GETTING THERE By **car** from Arezzo, take the SS71 and follow the signs up to Cortona when you get to Sodo or Camucia, two communities in the valley beneath town. From Florence or Rome, take the A1 to the Valdichiana exit and follow the Raccordo Perugia–A1 (direction: Perugia) until the Cortona exit; you would also take this highway from Siena. You'll find parking just outside the walls, but read the signs carefully—some spaces require payment, others don't, and some are for residents only. A sure bet is the well-marked lot on Via Cesare Battisti, beneath Piazza Garibaldi, to which you can ascend via escalators.

Cortona's **train** station, Camucia/Cortona (✆ 0575-603-018), is 5km (3 miles) below town in the workaday town of Camucia, where many services are located as well. It's about a 25-minute ride from Arezzo (26 trains daily), 1 hour (2 hr. on the slowest line) from Florence (24 trains daily), and 2 to 3 hours from Rome (15 trains daily). Camucia is served only by slower regional trains, while more and faster trains serve Terontola station (✆ 0575-67-034), 11km (7 miles) south, and on a direct north–south rail line. From both stations, buses run up to Cortona, but not as frequently as you'll wish—only once an hour at some periods during the day. You can buy your ticket on the bus, 1.60€; for schedules, go to www.lfi.it/servizi_linee_lfi_et-mob.asp.

VISITOR INFORMATION The **APT office** is at Piazza Signorelli 9, in the courtyard beyond the Museo dell'Accademia Etrusca ticket office (✆ 0575-637-223; www.cortonaweb.net). October through mid-May, it's open 9am to 1pm and 3 to 6pm Monday to Friday, 9am to 1pm only on Saturdays. Mid-May to November it's open Monday to Saturday 9am to 1pm and 3 to 6pm, and Sunday 9am to 1pm.

Where to Stay

Some of Cortona's most reasonably priced accommodations are in two convents just outside the city walls: **Casa Betania,** Via Gino Severini 50 (✆ 0575-630423; www.casaperferiebetania.com), and **Instituto Santa Margherita,** Viale Cesare Battisti 17 (✆ 0575-1787203; www.santamargherita.smr.it). They are just a few minutes' walk from the town center, and Spartan but pleasant doubles at both begin at about 60€.

Hotel Italia ★ This 15th-century palace is not as grand as the neighboring San Michele, but the hospitality hits the same high notes, Piazza Signorelli is just steps away, and the relaxed ambiance seems to come naturally and is well-suited to small-town Cortona. The spacious high-ceiling rooms are plain but nicely atmospheric, with tasteful rustic wood furnishings, beamed ceilings, and other architectural flourishes. Only a few have views, but to enjoy those you can linger over your coffee in the panoramic top-floor breakfast room or relax on the roof terrace.

Via Ghibellina 5–7. ✆ **0575-630254.** www.hotelitaliacortona.com. 17 units. 70€–90€ double. **Amenities:** Wi-Fi (free).

Hotel San Michele ★★ Many hotels in Italy occupy palaces, but few do so as seamlessly and comfortably as these accommodations in a 15th-century *palazzo* right in the center of town. The gracious salons and high-ceilinged guest rooms, a few frescoed and paneled, are reminders of Cortona's long past as a prosperous and noble town. Tile-floored rooms are furnished in what might be described as "fading grandeur" style, and are quite appealing for it, and some have views over the valley below, while a choice few, including tower suites, have their own terraces. A rooftop terrace with the same panoramic outlook is open to all guests, as is a decidedly medieval-looking courtyard. The San Michele also operates **Residence Borgo San Pietro** (✆ **0575-612-402;** www.borgosanpietro.com), 4km (2½ miles) outside town in San Pietro a Cegliolo, with a countrified take on grand living in the 14 rooms and 5 apartments, each with a kitchenette; a pool is set amid the 7 acres of olive trees and lavender.

Via Guelfa 15. ✆ **0575-604348.** www.hotelsanmichele.net. 42 units. 79€–89€ double. Rates include buffet breakfast. Parking 20€. **Amenities:** Bar; Wi-Fi (free).

Relais Il Falconiere ★ When Riccardo Baracchi inherited a farm from his grandmother, he and his wife, Sylvia, created a stylish and sophisticated retreat where antiques-filled rooms are scattered among a villa and several stone farmhouses. As comfortably luxurious as the furnishings are, timbered ceilings and terracotta floors suggest the rural surroundings, where a pool and gardens are set amid 20 acres of olive groves and vineyards on the flanks of the Valdichiana. A luxurious spa with a walled garden enhances the sense of relaxation. Sylvia oversees one of the best restaurants in the area, serving refined Tuscan food in the refitted lemon house (daily 1–2pm and 8–10pm; closed Mon–Tues afternoon Jan–Feb).

San Martino (3km/2 miles north of Cortona). ✆ **0575-612616.** www.ilfalconiere.it. 15 units. 250€–350€ double. Rates include buffet breakfast. **Amenities:** Restaurant; bar; 2 swimming pools; spa; free Wi-Fi in public areas.

Where to Eat

With a local wine that pairs especially well with rich sauces and meats, it's no accident that food in Montepulciano is typically Tuscan and relies heavily on game, beef from the Valdichiana, and thick pastas like hand-rolled *pici* to support rich sauces.

Ristorante la Loggetta ★★★ TUSCAN/GRILL You would probably be happy eating canned spaghetti while savoring the view over the stage-set Piazza della Repubblica from the namesake loggia—or for that matter, under the enchanting stone-and-brick vaults inside. It's a moot point as the food is very well done and nicely, if rather stiffly, served, and the kitchen is acclaimed for its preparations of beef from the Valdichiana, often served with a rich, red-wine reduction.

Piazza di Pescharia. ✆ **0575-95395.** www.laloggetta.com. Main courses 9€–28€. Thurs–Tues 12:15–2:30pm and 7:15–9:30pm.

Trattoria Dardano ★ TUSCAN/GRILL Cortonans come to this simple, single, brightly lit room for meat—roasted here over a charcoal fire, all from local butchers, with the emphasis on *bistecca alla fiorentina* from cattle raised in the valley below town and considered to be the best beef in Italy. *Pollo* (chicken), *anatra* (duck), *miale* (pork), and *faraona* (guinea hen) also go onto the flames, and the heaping platters are usually preceded by *crostini neri,* with chicken liver, some local salamis, and often *ribollita,* the thick Tuscan soup, all accompanied by local wine.

Via Dardano 24. ✆ **0575-601944.** www.trattoriadardano.com. Main courses 8€–13€. Thurs–Tues noon–2:45pm and 6:40–10pm.

Trattoria La Grotta ★ TUSCAN   For many regulars, any meal in the medieval, brick-vaulted dining room or in the tiny courtyard just off Piazza della Repubblica must include the house gnocchi, made with a perfect touch and light as a feather. All the pastas are house made, and topped with rich, sweet sauces, while fresh, locally grown zucchini and artichokes are a light antidote for the deftly grilled steaks. The house wine is delicious and very reasonably priced.

Piazza Baldelli 3. © **0575-630271.** www.trattorialagrotta.it. Main course 8€–18€. Wed–Mon noon–2 and 7:30–11.

Exploring Cortona

Via Nazionale, known as the Rugapiana ("flat street," since it's the only one in town that even comes close to fitting that description), is the setting for the evening *passeggiata.* The street sets off on its easterly course through the medieval town from Piazza della Repubblica, where the stern City Hall is a romantic-looking conglomeration of towers, a stone staircase, and wooden balconies. On the northern corner the square opens into Piazza Signorelli, another lovely expanse that is named for the town's famous 15th- and 16th-century artist and was once the headquarters of Cortona's Florentine governors, whose coats of arms adorn the Casali Palace (now home to the excellent Etruscan museum). From the square streets lead down to the Piazza del Duomo and a treasure trove of art in the Museo Diosceano and climb steeply uphill to the Basiclia di Santa Margherita and, even higher, the hilltop fortress. You can stay on level ground, as many strollers choose to do, and walk east along Via Nazionale to Piazza Garibaldi. This airy balcony at the edge of town extends into public gardens where views look south to Lago Trasimeno in Umbria and west across the Valdichiana to Montepulciano.

Basiclia di Santa Margherita ★ RELIGIOUS SITE   High above the town, this somber 19th-century church with a red-and-white striped interior would be quite forgettable if it were not for the presence of Margaret of Cortona (1247–97), a humble follower of St. Francis. Margaret had a bit of a past by the time she sought refuge with the Franciscan friars of Cortona in her late twenties—she had been a promiscuous teenager then the mistress of the lord of a castle near Montepulciano, with whom she lived and bore a son. When she found her lover murdered in the forest, she saw the light and devoted her life to fasting and caring for the sick and poor, establishing a hospital and order of nursing sisters. Her life of prayer involved direct conversation with God, who once famously asked her, "What is your wish, *poverella* ("little poor one?"), to which she replied, "I neither seek nor wish for anything but You, my Lord Jesus." The 13th-century crucifix through which Margaret carried on this dialogue with God hangs in the church. Margaret died in 1297 and her embalmed body, to which the intervening centuries have not been terribly kind, lies in full view in a lavish 14th-century Gothic tomb above the main altar.

Piazza Santa Margherita. © **0575-603116.** Apr–Oct daily 8–noon and 3–7pm; Nov–Mar 9am–noon and 3–6pm. Free admission.

Church of San Francesco ★ RELIGIOUS SITE   The second Franciscan church ever built, after the one in Assisi—and dramatically altered over the centuries but still showing signs of its original beams and some fresco fragments—was begun around 1247 on orders of Brother Elias, the closest companion of St. Francis. Elias, whom Francis chose to administer the Franciscan Order upon his death in 1226, is buried here, and the contemplative space houses three precious relics of St. Francis—his tunic, his manuscript of the New Testament, and a cushion he often used. On the high altar is the Reliquary of the Holy Cross, an ornate 10th-century ivory tablet containing a fragment of Christ's cross, presented to Elias by the Byzantine Emperor in 1244. The artist Luca Signorelli, who died in Cortona in 1523, is believed to be buried in the crypt.

Via Berrettini. ℂ **0575-603205.** Daily 9am–5:30pm. Free admission.

Fortezza Medicea di Girifalco ★ HISTORIC SITE

It's all uphill to Cortona's defenses, built in 1556. Handily, or ironically, the torturous, stepped ascent is enlivened by 15 mosaics depicting the Stations of the Cross by Cortonese Futurist Gino Severini (1883–1966). By the second time Christ falls, you'll feel like doing the same, though you can pause for a restorative drink at the bar by the Basilica Santa Margherita. The views from the four surviving bastions reward the climb, extending all the way across the Valdichiana to Montepulciano, south into Umbria toward Lago Trasimeno, and north toward Arezzo and the colossal Monte Amiata.

Viale Raimondo Bistacci. ℂ **0575-637235.** Hours vary but usually Sat–Sun 10am–7pm. 3€.

Museo dell'Accademia Etrusca (MAEC) ★ MUSEUM

Cortona was 1 of the 12 cities of the Etruscan confederation, and the proliferation of artifacts discovered in the area led to the founding of an Etruscan Academy in 1727. Their illuminating collections are now housed in the Palazzo Casali, a 13th-century mansion built for the city's governors; the original upper floors evoke the medieval period, while the lower galleries have received a smart, contemporary overhaul. The lower galleries tackle the Etruscan and Roman history of Cortona, with lots of gold from excavated tombs and the enigmatic Cortona Tablet, a 200-word document inscribed in bronze. Archaeologists are still puzzling over the text, with some vocabulary never before encountered before. Some more Etruscan finds are housed on the sprawling upper floors. The most spectacular find is a one of a kind, an oil lamp chandelier from the late 4th century B.C. decorated with human heads, allegorical figures, and a few virile Pans playing their pipes, all surrounding a leering Gorgon's head on the bottom.

Piazza Signorelli 9. ℂ **0575-637235.** www.cortonamaec.org. Apr–Oct daily 10am–7pm (closed Mon Nov–Mar). 12€.

Museo Dioscoceano ★ MUSEUM

Almost every work in this small collection hanging in the former church of the Gesu is a masterpiece, with pride of place belonging to Fra' Angelico and Luca Signorelli. Fra Angelico, who was known during his life as Fra Giovanni, trained as an illuminator, joined the convent of San Domenico in Fiesole, outside Florence, sometime around 1420, and had been elevated in parlance as the Angelic Painter by the time of his death in 1455. He did several Annunciations, and the one here, an altarpiece from 1436, shows his command of minute detail (obviously the hallmark of his training as an illustrator) in the delicate feathers on Gabriel's wings, the angel's precious garment embroidered in gold, the Virgin's elaborate robes, and the carpet of wildflowers (the new Eden) on which her house sits. The artist's astute mastery of perspective is evident in the way the picture extends in spaces beyond the bed chamber and into the garden beyond the loggia.

Luca Signorelli was born in Cortona around 1450. He is best known for his terrifying depiction of the "Last Judgment," with its scores of nude figures, in the cathedral of Orvieto (p. 223). He painted the "Deposition" on view here for the cathedral in Cortona in 1502, and instilled Christ with so much realism and passion that a legend soon began to circulate that he modeled the figure on his son, who died of the plague that year. As Vasari wrote, "overwhelmed with grief as he was, he had the body

etruria IN CORTONA

The countryside around Cortona is dotted with so-called "Meloni," Etruscan burial-mounds. Most are looked after by the Museo dell'Accademia Etrusca under the collective heading Parco Archeologico di Cortona; three of the most intriguing tombs are located on the slopes just below the Cortona walls. You could walk to all of them, but the exploration would be a lot easier by car or taxi. Closest to town, heading down the hill on the main road to Camucia, you'll come upon a well-marked turnoff to the right for the Tanella di Pitagora. This 2nd-century-B.C. tomb (misnamed by someone who mistakenly thought Cortona was the ancient home of Pythagorus, who is from Crotone, in Calabria) is on a circular plan with a vaulted roof no longer covered with earth as it once was and open to the elements. It's open all day; free admission.

Farther down follow the signs to the hamlet known as Il Sodo (just off the SS71 to Arezzo), and the Tumulo I del Sodo, open April to October Tuesday, Friday, and Sunday 9:30am to 12:30pm, admission 2€. The passage and chambers inside this 6th-century-B.C. structure are in excellent condition, as the brickwork was put back in place during a restoration a century ago. The walls are made of tufa imported from Orvieto (the 200km/125 miles were a very long distance 2,500 years ago), and they are punctuated with a small passage between two of the burial chambers—the final resting places of a husband and wife, who could use the passage through eternity to visit each other.

From tomb 1 a signposted footpath leads to the Tumulo II del Sodo, from the late 7th century B.C. and open Tuesday to Sunday from 8:30am to 1:30pm; free admission. This is a fairly monumental structure, with an altar that is reached by a monumental stairway flanked by two sphinxes biting the heads off warriors who are simultaneously stabbing the animals in the side, thought to represent the battle between life and death. At least 17 more tombs surround the tumulus. For more information on these and other Etruscan remains around Cortona, ask at the Museo dell'Accademia Etrusca.

stripped, and with the greatest fortitude of soul, without tears or lamentation, he made a drawing of it, to have always before his eyes what Nature had given him . . . and what cruel fate had snatched away." The story is unfounded, though there's no doubt about Signorelli's telltale style. As in his works in Orvieto, the painting is packed with action, detail, and complex medieval symbolism: the crucifixion, the resurrection, and a surreal city by a lake all in the background, and in the foreground a swooning Mary, a blonde Christ, and a saint pocketing a crucifixion nail and the crown of thorns—presumably destined for numerous Italian reliquaries. Signorelli's "Communion of the Apostles" (1512) is in the same room, showing the artist's strong sense of perspective and architectural space; notice Judas in the foreground, hiding the host in his purse—ashamed of his imminent betrayal, he can't swallow it.

Piazza del Duomo. ✆ **0575-4027268.** Daily 10am–6pm. 5€

Side Trips from Cortona
CASTIGLION FIORENTINO
12km (7 miles) N of Cortona

You can't miss it: As you approach, the Torre del Cassero, a pronglike tower built in the 1330s by the Perugians, looms over the skyline of this quiet, unassuming town on

THE BIG valley

Cortona, Arezzo, and to the west, Montepulciano, nestle on the flanks of the Valdichiana (or Val di Chiana), a wide swath of farmland running north–south for some 100km (62 miles) through central Italy, roughly between Arezzo and Lago Trasimeno in Umbria. Etruscans settled the valley 2,500 years ago, leaving behind remnants of their sophisticated civilization in Cortona, Chiusi, and other centers of their 12-city confederation. These early residents and subsequent settlers were plagued by malaria, spread by mosquitoes breeding in the low-lying wetlands. Leonardo da Vinci was among the medieval and Renaissance architects who set about draining the malaria swamps, a task not completed until the middle of the 19th century. These days the valley supplies some of Italy's most prized beef, *bistecca alla fiorentina,* from Chianina cattle, along with no end of stunning views from Cortona and the other hill towns that overlook the green and golden folds of the landscape. You'll shoot through the valley on the A1 *autostrada* and the fast trains between Rome and Florence, and you'll get a nice close-up look on the 33km (20-mile) drive between Cortona and Montepulciano.

a hill rising out of the Valdichiana. With some stately *palazzi* and quiet squares, this is a place for some aimless wandering, and it's a short and easy excursion by car from nearby Cortona.

GETTING THERE Castiglion Fiorentino is just 20 minutes north of Cortona on SR71. Parking is available in a parking lot (1€ for 1 hr.) near the 13th-century Porta Fiorentina. The tourist office (© **0575-658278;** www.prolococastiglionfiorentino.it), at Piazza Risorgimento 19, is open Monday from 9:30 to 11:30am and Tuesday through Saturday from 9:30 to 11:30am and 4 to 6pm.

Exploring Castiglion Fiorentino

Wandering into the little hill town takes you through a medieval girdle of fortified walls, leading to its hub, Piazza del Municipio, on the site of the Roman forum. Dominating the square is the now somewhat tattered Loggia di Vasari, reputedly designed by Renaissance man Giorgio Vasari from nearby Arezzo in the 16th century.

The town's museum, the Pinacoteca Comunale, occupies the deconsecrated church of Sant'Angelo al Cassero, directly uphill from Piazza del Municipio. It houses a 13th-century Umbrian Crucifix and a painting of "St. Francis Receiving the Stigmata," by Bartolomeo della Gatta—unusual because another monk looks on, while in legend Francis was alone in prayer when the seraph appeared and pierced him with wounds similar to those Christ received on the cross. Francis was thus the first person to receive the stigmata, though legions of medieval saints followed suit (skeptics have attributed the sores to malaria, malnutrition, and self-mutilation). In any case, the painting is a haunting presence in this quiet little town. There's also access to the church's atmospheric crypt. The museum (© **0575-659457**) is open Tuesday through Sunday from 10am to 12:30pm and 4 to 6:30pm (closes 6pm Nov–Mar). Admission is 3€. You can climb the Torre del Cassero, surrounded by the ruins of a Perugian fortress, for a satisfying look over the Valdichiana, on weekends from May to September 10am to 12:30pm and 4 to 6:30pm; admission is 1.50€.

LUCIGNANO

40km (25 miles) W of Cortona

This quiet little hill town will have you walking around in circles, literally, as the street plan is follows four concentric circles. As a result Lucignano, small as it is, can be a rather confusing place, but that was the point: The simplified maze was intended to thwart invaders.

GETTING THERE Driving is the only practical way to reach Lucignano. From Cortona, follow SR71 and SP25 north and west to Lucignano; the trip takes about 40 minutes.

Exploring Lucignano

Aside from the pleasure of becoming disoriented amid the mazelike streets and finding yourself in a sunny little piazza, the town's main attraction is the tiny Museo di Lucignano, Piazza del Tribunale (✆ **0575-838001**), with its Albero della Vita (Tree of Life). Sienese goldsmiths fashioned this complex reliquary, about 6 feet tall, from copper and silver in the 14th century. Six branches on each side sprout gold-plated leaves studded with dazzling gems and coral. A Christ figure tops the tree, and at his feet a bird pecks at its own breast, drawing blood to feed its young. This show of selfless devotion to family has made the piece somewhat of a national symbol of familial fidelity, and Italian couples often come to Lucignano to pray and renew their marriage vows. The town promotes the practice and has declared the first Sunday in September as Couple's Day, inviting the untied to flock to Lucignano and declare their undying love in front of the famous little bird. The frescoed Sala di Buon Governo that houses the reliquary is also a popular spot for wedding vows. The museum is open mid-March to October Thursday to Sunday from 10am to 1pm and 2:30 to 6pm; November to February Friday to Sunday from 10am to 1pm and 2:30 to 5:30pm; admission is 5€.

CHIUSI

50km (31 miles) S of Cortona; 21km (13 miles) SE of Montepulciano

One of southern Tuscany's smaller hilltop cities doesn't transport you to the Middle Ages or wow you with the Renaissance. Instead, the town was such powerful member of the Etruscan 12-city confederation, alternately spelled Camars or Clevsins, that in the late 500s B.C. the lucumo (king) Lars Porsenna launched an attack on Rome. Remnants of these early inhabitants make Chiusi a major stop on the Etruscan trail—in fact, seeing a bit if Etruria is about the only reason to come to this pleasant but otherwise unremarkable farm town, unless you're changing trains (it's a major stop on the north south lines).

GETTING THERE By **car,** the fastest route from Cortona takes you down the A1 autostrada in just 45 minutes. From Montepulciano, take SP 146 for a trip of about half an hour. You'll find well-marked and free parking just outside the historic center.

If you're traveling by train, you may end up in Chiusi even if you don't want to, as you may well transfer here as you travel around Tuscany or are traveling between a smaller town and Siena, Florence, or Rome, all of which have direct service to and from Chiusi. The train station is below the old town, about 3km (2 miles) away; buses run with inconvenient infrequency (buy tickets for 1.10€ at the newsstand in the station).

VISITOR INFORMATION The tourist office is in the old town at Via Porsenna 79 (✆ **0578-22766;** www.prolocochiusi.it) and is open daily in spring and summer (9am–1pm and 3–6pm), with shorter hours the rest of the year.

Museo Archeologico Nazionale ★★ MUSEUM   Although a huge portion of Chiusi's rich Etruscan patrimony was carried off by early archaeologists, a good share remains in these well displayed collections. As you've seen elsewhere, Etruscan artisans devoted much of their energy to funeral pottery, typically topped by lids carved with the man or woman's reclining likeness. A particularly dramatic 7th-century-B.C. piece shows the deceased, perched on the lid, apparently orating and surrounded by stylized griffins whose heads are raised high, crying out. Many of the urns here are done in the town's distinctive bucchero ware, with a very dark glaze that imitates metal. Others are carved from a local limestone called *pietra fetida,* as well as travertine and alabaster. Not all the pottery was buried with the dead. The Sella Caccatoia is a terracotta pot that residents used to toilet train their toddlers, while a ghirarium is a large terra-cotta pot used to breed dormice, a popular Etruscan delicacy.

Your ticket is good for entry to two Etruscan tombs 3km (2 miles) north of Chiusi: the Tomba del Leone and Tomba della Pellegrina. Tell the staff when you leave the museum and they'll make sure someone's there to unlock the tombs for you. Hours are the same as the museum. The Tomba della Scimmia (Tomb of the Monkey, so called for its frescoes) can be visited Tuesday, Thursday and Saturday only (11am and 4pm, or 2:30pm winter). The 2€ fee is not included in the museum fee, but you can book a place at the museum desk.

Via Porsenna 93. ⓒ **0578-20177.** www.archeotoscana.beniculturali.it. Daily 9am–8pm. 6€ adults, 3€ 18–25, under 18 free.

Labirinto di Porsenna (Labyrinth of Porsenna) ★ HISTORIC SITE   A 120m (394-ft.) section of this subterranean labyrinth, cut from the sandstone, is part of a system of defensive tunnels and aqueducts that underpin the entire town and is open to guided tours. They were rediscovered in the 1920s and slowly cleared of refuse, and another good stretch of the *cunicoli* (water sewers) was opened to the public in 1995. The narrow passages apparently once supplied the Etruscan city, as well as medieval firefighters, from a huge underground lake; the firefighters were apparently less than altruistic and demanded payment in advance before dousing flames from their underground source. An atmospheric half-hour tour leads you through this ancient Etruscan cave system before arriving at a giant Roman cistern, 6m (19-ft.) high with a vaulted ceiling right under Chiusi's Piazza Duomo; you can climb all the way up the 140 steps to the top of the bell tower inside the campanile of San Secondiano for views over Chiusi and the Tuscan and Umbrian countryside. The half-hour tours are in Italian, with an English handout.

Museo della Cattedrale, Piazza Duomo. ⓒ **0578-226490.** June to mid-Oct 9:45–12:45 and 4–6:30pm, mid-Oct to May 9:45am–12:45pm. 3€.

THE BEST OF UMBRIA

Umbria is often called a land apart, a reference to its remove from its more famous neighbor to the north as well as to its gentle, almost otherworldly landscapes—some observers go so far as to call the rolling green hills "mystical" and call Umbria *"la terra dei santi"* (land of the saints), of whom St. Francis of Assisi is the world favorite. Umbria certainly holds its own against Tuscan scenery with its hillsides covered with vineyards and olive groves, forests, golden, checkerboard valleys, rugged mountains, and noble hill towns that have been the strongholds of everyone from the Etruscans to medieval dynasties. The region also contributed its fair share to wine and gastronomy, and its art and architecture takes in a wealth of treasures that include the glorious Basilica di San Francesco in Assisi, the Gothic Upper Church of which houses Giotto's 28-part fresco, "The Life of St. Francis"; Orvieto's garish and glorious Duomo; and Todi's heavily medieval Piazza del Popolo. It's not that Umbria is a land apart as much as "a land in addition to"— another region of Italy to be discovered and savored in conjunction with your explorations of Tuscany.

PERUGIA ★★

164km (102 miles) SE of Florence, 176km (109 miles) N of Rome

Perugia is Umbria's capital, but it's most appealing in its guise of medieval hill town. Ancient alleys drop precipitously off Corso Vannucci, the cosmopolitan shopping promenade, and Gothic palaces rise above stony piazzas. The city produced and trained some of Umbria's finest artists, whose works fill the excellent art gallery. For all appearances today, Perugia is a mellow and sophisticated town, home to one of Italy's largest state universities as well as the Università per Stranieri, the country's most prestigious school teaching Italian language and culture to foreigners. All these students impart the old streets with a youthful energy, and Perugia's other pursuits are pleasingly benign. The town is home to Perugina, purveyor of Italy's famous Baci chocolates, stages an urbane and stylish *passeggiata* stroll every evening, and hosts one of Europe's most celebrated jazz festivals every summer, Umbria Jazz (see below).

Essentials

GETTING THERE   Two **rail** lines serve Perugia. The state railway connects with **Rome** (2–3 hr.; most trains require a change at Foligno) and

Umbria

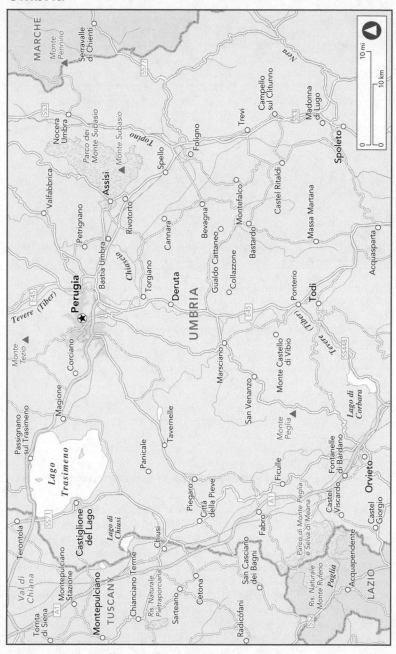

plotting & poisoning IN PERUGIA

Perugia most recently gained world attention when American Amanda Knox and her Italian boyfriend, Raffaele Solle-cito, were implicated in the murder of a British student, Meredith Kercher. While the press expressed surprise that such a gentle place could foster such violence, Perugia was once known for such intrigues.

In the Middle Ages especially, when Perugia was a thriving center of trade, the Perugini had quite a reputation for being warlike and ferocious and became known for their bellicose tendencies, vicious tempers, and violent infighting. The Oddi and Baglioni were just two of the noble families who waged secret vendettas and vied with the middle-class burghers for absolute power. Burgher Biordo Miche-lotti, egged on by the pope, managed to seize power in 1393 by murdering a few rivals from the Baglioni family. Five years later, his despotic rule ended with a knife in the back. A period of relative calm came in 1416 with the stewardship of Braccio Fortebraccio ("Arm Strongarm"), under whose wise and stable rule the city's small empire expanded over the Marches region. In the end, he was done in by a fellow Perugian while he was besieging L'Aquila in 1424. And then there were the Baglioni.

When their rivals, the Oddi, were run out of town in 1488, the field was more or less clear for the Baglioni to reign in all their horrible glory. The family turned assassination, treachery, and incest into gruesome art forms. When not poisoning their outside rivals, they killed siblings on their wedding nights, kept pet lions, tore human hearts out of chests for lunch, and married their sisters. In a conspiracy so tangled it's almost comic in its ghastli-ness, the bulk of the family massacred one another on a single day in August 1500.

The last of the surviving Baglioni, Rodolfo, tried to assassinate a papal leg-ate in response to his uncle's murder at the hands of the pontiff. All that did was anger Pope Paul III, who beheaded Rodolfo and upped the salt tax a year after promising otherwise. The rebellion Paul was trying to provoke ensued, giv-ing the pope the excuse he needed to subdue the city. Papal forces quickly quashed the city's defenses and leveled the Baglionis' old neighborhood. After riding triumphantly into town, the pope had all Perugia's nuns line up to kiss his feet, an experience he reported left him "very greatly edified."

The enormous Rocca Paolina fortress he built to keep an eye on the city quelled most rebellious grumblings for a few hundred years, during which time the Perugini slowly mellowed.

Florence (2¼ hr.; most trains require a change at Terontola) every couple of hours. There are also hourly trains to **Assisi** (20–30 min.) and **Spoleto** (1¼ hr.). The station is a few kilometers southwest of the center at Piazza Vittorio Veneto (✆ **147-888-088**), but well connected with buses to/from Piazza Italia (1€); Perugia's new seven-stop, 3km (2-mile) long "minimetro" also makes the run from the station up to stops in the town center (1.50€, buy tickets in machines). The station for the **Umbria Mobilità–operated regional railway** (✆ **800/512-141**), Sant'Anna, is in Piazzale Bellucci (near the bus station). These tiny trains serve **Todi** every couple of hours.

Perugia is connected by three fast, and free, roads. The Raccordo Perugia-A1 runs east-west between the A1, Lago Trasimeno, and Perugia, bypassing the city to link with the E45 (aka SS3bis). The E45 runs south to Todi and Terni (for Rome). Heading southeast, the SS75bis connects the E45 at Perugia with Assisi and Spoleto.

Perugia

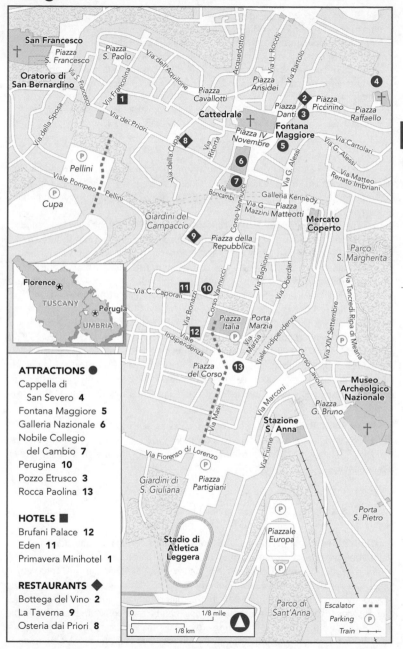

ATTRACTIONS ●

Cappella di
  San Severo **4**
Fontana Maggiore **5**
Galleria Nazionale **6**
Nobile Collegio
  del Cambio **7**
Perugina **10**
Pozzo Etrusco **3**
Rocca Paolina **13**

HOTELS ■

Brufani Palace **12**
Eden **11**
Primavera Minihotel **1**

RESTAURANTS ◆

Bottega del Vino **2**
La Taverna **9**
Osteria dai Priori **8**

Escalator ▪▪▪
Parking Ⓟ
Train ├──┤

Perugia is a chocoholic's paradise. **Perugina** has been making candy here since 1907 and now pumps out 120 tons of the brown stuff a day, including 1½ million Baci (kisses), its gianduja-and-hazelnut bestseller. You can buy them and other products at the Perugina shop at Corso Vannucci 101 (© **075-573-4760**). Perugia hosts a weeklong **Eurochoco-** **late Festival** (www.eurochocolate.com) every year from mid- to late October. The highlight is the chocolate-carving contest, when the scraps of 1,000-kg (455-lb.) blocks are handed out for sampling. **Umbria Jazz** (www.umbriajazz. com), one of Europe's top jazz festivals, draws top international names to town for 2 weeks in mid-July.

Parking is fairly abundant, with the most convenient being the underground pay lots at Piazza Partigiani, from which escalators take you up to Piazza Italia (with some amazing underground scenery along the route; see box). For information about parking in Perugia, visit www.sipaonline.it.

SULGA bus lines (© 075-500-9641; www.sulga.it) also has one bus (Mon and Fri) from Florence (6pm; 2 hr.), six or seven daily from Assisi (30 min.) and Todi (40 min.), and around six a day from Rome (2½ hr.); the morning buses usually stop at the airport; the station is in Piazza Partigiani and connected to Piazza Italia by escalator. Umbria Mobilità (© 800/512-141; www.umbriamobilita.it) buses connect Perugia with Assisi (six buses daily; 50 min.), Gubbio (six buses daily; 1 hr., 10 min.), and Todi (six buses daily; 1 hr., 15 min.).

There's also a regional airport: Six weekly Ryanair (© 0871/246-0000; www. ryanair.com) flights connect London Stansted with Perugia's Aeroporto Internazionale dell'Umbria (© 075-592141; www.airport.umbria.it), 10km (6 miles) east of the city at San Egidio. Flights are usually met by a minibus outside the terminal, taking you to Perugia train station and Piazza Italia (30–40 min.; 3.50€), but heading back there are just three buses per day, so check times in advance (just one Sat–Sun). Taxis cost around 25€.

VISITOR INFORMATION The **tourist office** is at Piazza Matteotti 18 (© **075-573-6458;** www.regioneumbria.eu). It's open daily from 8:30am to 6:30pm. You can also pick up a copy of **"Viva Perugia"** (1€) at newsstands to find out what's going on around town.

Where to Stay

Most Perugian hotels are flexible about rates, which dive 40 to 50 percent below posted prices in the off-season, so it always pays to ask.

Brufani Palace ★★ Perugia's bastion of luxury commands one side of Piazza Italia, looming proudly over the valley below. Built in 1883 to host English travelers on the Grand Tour, the premises have not changed too much in the intervening years, except that the large, traditionally furnished rooms (most with sweeping views) are now equipped with lavish marble bathrooms and lots of other amenities that include extremely comfortable lounge chairs and sofas and good reading lamps. Despite the grand surroundings, the real pleasures here are in the details: Fires burn in big old stone hearths in the dining room and lounges; a swimming pool has been carved out of subterranean brick vaults, with see-through panels exposing Etruscan ruins beneath; and a large rooftop terrace is a perfect spot of a glass of wine at sunset.

Piazza Italia 12. ℂ **075-573-2541.** www.brufanipalace.com. 94 units. From 140€ double. **Amenities:** Restaurant/bar (tables on the piazza in summer); babysitting; concierge; small exercise room; indoor pool; room service; Wi-Fi (free with most rates).

Eden ★ This comfortable little inn occupies the top floor of a 13th-century building in the city center (an elevator takes you up), and the airy accommodations seem a world removed from the medieval city below. Furnishings are contemporary, with colorful accent walls and modern art; the compact, shower-only bathrooms are up to date; and a pleasant breakfast room that doubles as a lounge is sleek and functional. Outside the tall windows are an enticing jumble of rooftops, towers, and narrow stone lanes, and when you're ready to go down and explore the sights, the friendly management supplies an insightful, self-guided itinerary of their own design.

Via Cesare Caporali 9. ℂ **075-572-8102.** www.hoteleden.perugia.it. 12 units. 65€–95€ double. Rates include breakfast. MC, V. Garage parking 25€. **Amenities:** Wi-Fi (free).

Primavera Minihotel ★★ It's well worth the climb up the three flights of stairs to reach this aerielike retreat atop a house just down some twisty streets from Piazza della Repubblica. The rooftop locale means all the tall windows frame views of the green valleys spread out below the town. Best are from a room one additional flight up, with its own large terrace, though there's not a bad room in the house. All are different, some with Art Nouveau pieces, some with traditionally rustic furnishing and Deruta pottery, others quite contemporary. All have warm hardwood floors and lots of timber, stone, and other architectural details, and all surround a welcoming lounge/breakfast room.

Via Vincioli 8. ℂ **075-572-1657.** www.primaveraminihotel.it. 8 units. 65€–90€ double. Breakfast extra. Garage parking 15€ per day. **Amenities:** Wi-Fi (free).

Where to Eat

Plenty of cheap *pizzerie* feed the student population. The best is **Il Segreto di Pulcinella,** Via Larga 8, off Via Bonazzi and a short walk from Piazza della Repubblica (℗ **075-573-6284**). Pizzas cost 4€ to 7€. It's open Tuesday through Sunday from noon to 2:30pm and 8:30pm to midnight.

Bottega del Vino ★ UMBRIAN A snug, vintage-photo-lined room right off piazza IV Novembre dispenses wines by the glass and accompanies them with a nice assortment of Umbrian hams and cheeses—perfect for an evening *aperitivo* at one of the tables out front as all of Perugia promenades by. Small lunch and dinner menus include salads and a couple of pastas, as well as a dish or two of the day, which might be a steak or roasted leg of lamb. Live jazz often continues into the small hours, making this a popular after-dinner spot, too.

Via del Sole 1. ℂ **075-571-6181.** Main courses 13€. Tues–Sun noon–3pm and 7pm–midnight. Closed Jan.

La Taverna ★★ UMBRIAN For many Perugians, a tiny courtyard down a flight of steps from Corso Vannucci is the epicenter of good dining, filled in warm weather with tables of this venerable institution. Inside, the barrel-vaulted ceilings shimmer with candlelight in evening, and the service and the cooking are similarly warm and down to earth. Everything, from bread to pasta to desserts are made in house and are typically Umbrian: *Papardelle* is sauced with a hearty Umbrian ragù, *caramelle rosse* *al gorgonzola* (beet ravioli with Gorgonzola) is made with beets from a local farm, and the grilled and roasted meats are seasoned with fresh herbs from the surroundings hillsides. Chef Claudio will make his way to your table at some point to ensure that everything is *tutto bene.*

Via delle Streghe 8 (near Corso Vannucci's Piazza Repubblica). © **075-572-4128.** Reservations recommended. Main courses 9€–16€. Tues–Sun 12:30–2:30pm and 7:30–11pm.

Osteria dai Priori ★ UMBRIAN   You'll pass through a wine shop downstairs and climb a flight of stairs to reach this welcoming brick, vaulted room with contemporary blonde furnishings where the emphasis is on local ingredients and age-old Umbrian recipes. A portion of slowly cooked small beans *(fagioloina)* is paired with eggs and onions and bread salad; *gnoccconi* (large potato dumplings) are stuffed with fresh ricotta; slow-roasted pork shank *(stinco di mialale)* is served with crisp potatoes. The staff will eagerly walk you through the ever-changing menu and pair wines with each course.

Via dei Priori 39. © **075-572-7098.** Main courses 9€–12€. Wed–Mon noon–3pm and 7:30–10:30pm.

Exploring Perugia

Piazza Italia is like a balcony hanging over the hillside at one end of town. From this airy square, sophisticated Corso Vannucci flows through the massive Palazzo dei Priori to Piazza IV Novembre, where the cathedral is a backdrop for the Fontana Maggiore, with elaborate panels and figures that Nicola Pisano and his son Giovanni carved between 1278 and 1280. Also overlooking the square is the Palazzo dei Priori, one of the largest town halls in Italy, started in the 1290s and expanded in 1443. The noble structure still serves as City Hall and houses the Galleria Nazionale and Collegio del Cambio (see below). An especially entertaining time to stroll up the *corso* is in the early evening, when it becomes the stage set for one of Italy's most lively and decorous evening *passeggiate.*

Cappella di San Severo ★ CHURCH   Before young Raphael Sanzio made a name for himself in Florence and Rome, he settled briefly in Perugia, where in 1504 he painted the first of the many frescoes that would make him famous in his own lifetime and establish for him a place alongside Leonardo da Vinci and Michelangelo in the triumvirate of great Renaissance masters. Only the upper half of his "Holy Trinity" remains, and that is damaged, and the work seems touchingly modest compared to the complex and engagingly humane "School of Athens" and other works he did for the Vatican palaces and chapels. As energetic in life as he was in his work, Raphael ran a huge workshop, had dozens of wealthy patrons, was in line to be a cardinal, and died on his 37th birthday, allegedly after a long, lustful session with his mistress. After Raphael's death, his then-septuagenarian teacher, Perugino, painted the six saints along the bottom of the fresco.

Piazza Raffaello. © **075-573-3864.** Admission 3€ adults, 2€ seniors 65 and over, 1€ children 7–14, free for children 6 and under; includes admission to Pozzo Etrusco, valid 1 week. May–July and Sept–Oct Tues–Sun 10am–1:30pm and 2:30–6pm; Nov–Mar Tues–Sun 11am–1:30pm and 2:30–5pm; Apr and Aug daily 10am–1:30pm and 2:30–6pm.

Galleria Nazionale ★★★ ART MUSEUM   The world's largest repository of Umbrian art covers 7 or so fruitful centuries and showcases dozens of artists, among whom two stand out in particular. Pride of place belongs to the altarpieces by Perugino, who was born nearby in Città della Pieve and spent much of his career working

PERUGIA'S MEDIEVAL pompeii

Beneath Piazza Italia is some remarkable underground scenery. Around 1530 the Perugians rebelled against Pope Paul III over a tax on salt—to this day, Perugian bread is salt-free. In retribution, the pope demolished more than one-quarter of the city, and built his **Rocca Paolina** atop the ruins. After Italian unification in 1860, locals ripped the castle to pieces and built Piazza Italia on top. Today the vaults of the fort and the remains of medieval dwellings and streets it was built atop are in full view beneath the piazza. You can clamber through door-less entrances, climb the remains of stairways, walk through empty rooms, and wander at will through the brick maze. Enter the underground city daily (no admission fee) from the escalators that connect the lower town's Piazza Partigiani, with its car park and bus station, and Piazza Italia (daily 6:15am–1:45am).

Another underground experience takes you to the bottom of a well, and the excursion (popular with children) is as anticlimactic as it sounds—even though the Pozzo Etrusco (Etruscan Well) is almost 2,500 years old and topped with impressive marble beams fashioned by ancient craftsmen. The descent down the dank, 35m-deep (115-ft.) shaft past mossy, dripping stone walls brings you a quaint bridge across the original source. Enter at Piazza Dante (📞 **075-573-3669** for information). Hours are April to October Tuesday to Sunday 10am to 1:30pm and 2:30 to 6:30pm and November to March Tuesday to Sunday 11am–1pm and 2:30–5pm. Admission is 3€ for adults, 1€ for children 7 to 14, and free for children 6 and under; the ticket includes admission to Cappella di San Severo, so be sure to walk up the street to see the wonderful Raphael fresco (see above).

in Perugia, between time in Florence, where he studied alongside Leonardo da Vinci, and in Rome, where he executed frescoes in the Sistine Chapel. Among his works in Rooms 22–26 are delicate landscapes, sweet Madonnas, and grinning Christ childs that reveal his spare, precise style. They are all the more ironically transcendent given that Perugino was openly anti-religion, and they certainly reveal nothing of the artist's fairly turbulent life—he was arrested in Florence for assault and battery and barely escaped exile; sued Michelangelo for defamation of character; and more than once was censored for reusing images and lacking originality. He persevered, however, and worked prodigiously until his death at age 73 and left a considerable fortune.

The museum's other showpiece is by a Tuscan, Piero della Francesca, who completed his "Polyptych of Perugia" for the city's church of Sant'Antonio in 1470. The symmetry, precise placement of figures and objects, and realistic dimensions of interior spaces reveal the artist's other occupation as a mathematician, though his figures are robustly human, real flesh and blood. The artist works sheer magic at the top of the piece, in a scene of the Annunciation, when an angel appears to Mary to tell her she will be the mother of the Son of God. She's standing in a brightly lit cloister, and the illusion of pillars leading off into the distance is regarded as one of the greatest examples of perspectives in Renaissance art.

Palazzo dei Priori, Corso Vannucci 19. 📞 **075-574-1247.** www.gallerianazionaleumbria.it. Admission 6.50€ adults, 3.25€ ages 18–25 (EU citizens only), free for children 17 and under and seniors 65 and over (EU citizens only). Mon 9:30am–7:30pm; Tues–Sun 8:30am–7:30pm.

Nobile Collegio del Cambio ★★ ART MUSEUM   The cubicles and fluorescent lighting of modern office life will seem all the more banal after a visit to the frescoed and paneled meeting rooms of Perugia's Moneychanger's Guild, one of the best-preserved "office suites" of the Renaissance. Perugino was hired in 1496 to fresco the Sala dell' Udienza (Hearing Room), perhaps with the help of his young student Raphael. The images merge religion, with scenes of the Nativity and Transfiguration; classical references, with female representations of the virtues; and most riveting of all, glimpses of 15th-century secular life that provide a fascinating look at Perugians of the time and their sartorial tastes.

Palazzo dei Priori, Corso Vannucci 25. (© **075-572-8599.** Admission 4.50€ adults, 2.50€ seniors 65 and over, free for children 12 and under. Dec 20–Jan 6 Tues–Sat 9am–12:30pm and 2:30–5:30pm, Sun 9am–1pm; Mar 1–Oct 31 Mon–Sat 9am–12:30pm and 2:30–5:30pm, Sun 9am–1pm; Nov 1–Dec 19 and Jan 7–Feb 28 Tues–Sat 8am–2pm, Sun 9am–12:30pm.

Shopping

One of Italy's great centers of ceramics, Deruta, is just 20km (12 miles) south of Perugia. Dozens of artisans have workshops and streets of shops sell an overwhelming array of wares in traditional and contemporary designs, fashioned from terracotta that is fired and glazed. The traditional Deruta design in bright orange and yellow hues appears on ceramics sold all over town (and throughout Tuscany and Umbria) and includes a Renaissance-era dragonlike motif set amid flowers. Workshops also turn out contemporary designs, and you can buy the wares on the spot or place orders for custom made place settings and other pieces. Among the highly regarded traditionalists is **Deruta Placens,** Via Unberto I 16 (© **075-9724027;** www.derutaplacens.com). **Ubaldo Grazia,** the largest operation in town, at Via Tiberina 181 (© **075-9710201;** www.ubaldograzia.it), carries on a 500-year-old family tradition and turns out traditional and contemporary pieces. Just about all shops will pack your purchases and ship them.

The town's long ceramics tradition comes to the fore in the Museo Regionale della Ceramica (Regional Ceramics Museum), where pieces from the Middle Ages through contemporary times are on display. Hours vary slightly throughout the year, but the museum is generally open Wednesday through Sunday, June through September 10am to 1pm and 3 to 6pm, March and October 10:30 to 1pm and 2:30 to 5pm, April through May 10:30am to 1 and 3 to 6pm, and November through February 10:30 to 1pm and 2:30 to 4:30pm. Admission is 7€.

A Side Trip to Gubbio

39km (24 miles) NE of Perugia

Gubbio is hands-down the most medieval-looking town in Umbria, with a crenelated skyline backed by a tree-covered mountain. At its stony heart is Piazza Grande, where the harsh expanse is softened from the south side by views of misty hills and the wide valley that spreads beneath them.

GETTING THERE   By **car,** the SS298 branches north from Perugia, off the E45, through rugged scenery. Gubbio is not served by train, but there are eight or nine daily **Umbria Mobilità buses** (© **800/512-141;** www.umbriamobilita.it) from **Perugia** (4.60€; 5.50€ if you pay on board) to Piazza 40 Martiri (1 hr., 10 min.), named for citizens killed by the Nazis for aiding partisans during World War II.

EXPLORING GUBBIO

If you want to avoid the climb up to Piazza Grande, take the free elevator at the junction of Via Repubblica and Via Baldassini (daily 7:45am–7pm). The tourist office is nearby at Via della Repubblica 15 (© **075-922-0693** or 075-922-0790; www.comune.

GO jump IN THE LAKE

Lago Trasimeno, Italy's fourth-largest lake, washes up against the Tuscany–Umbria border between Cortona and Perugia. The shallow waters aren't quite a match for the romance and beauty of Como and the other lakes in the north, but Trasimeno is nonetheless a refreshing splash of blue amid olive groves and sunflower fields. The lakeshore was the site of a big moment in history, too—in 271 B.C., when Hannibal, having just breached the Alps, lured 16,000 Roman soldiers into an ambush and massacred them. A well-equipped spot from which to enjoy the lake is Castiglione del Lago, 50km (30 miles) west of Perugia, where you can swim from a pebbly beach or do a bit of biking on shoreline paths; you can rent bikes for about 10€ a day at

Cicli Valentini, Via Firenze 68/B (*©* **333-9678327;** www.ciclivalentini.it); it's open Saturday to Sunday 9am to 1pm and 3:30 to 8pm. Hourly ferry trips of about half an hour cross the lake to the picturesque island of Isola Maggiore, an especially nice place to take a dip in the relatively uncrowded waters. You can also buy lace from the increasingly few local women who carry on a long-standing island craft tradition, and just stepping ashore you'll be following in the footsteps of St. Francis, who spent Lent of 1213 here. Allegedly, the saint even charmed the local fish—when Francis threw a pike given to him by a fisherman back into the lake, the grateful creature swam alongside his savior until the saint have him a special blessing.

gubbio.pg.it). It's open Monday through Friday from 8:30am to 1:45pm and 3:30 to 6:30pm, Saturday from 9am to 1pm and 3:30 to 6:30pm, and Sunday from 9:30am to 1pm and 3 to 6pm; October through March, all afternoon hours are 3 to 6pm.

Museo del Palazzo dei Consoli ★★ MUSEUM   The former home of the town government is a solidly Gothic-looking palace, almost improbably so, with crenellations, a tower, and an imposing stone staircase that seems to demand you climb up from Piazza Grande. The main hall, where the medieval commune met, houses the sleep-inducing town museum, where one prize stands out amid the old coins and bits of pottery. The seven Eugubine Tables, inscribed on bronze from 200 to 70 B.C., provide the only existing record of the Umbri language transposed in Etruscan and Latin letters, ancient Umbria's Rosetta Stone. The tablets mainly detail the finer points of animal sacrifice and divination through watching the flight patterns of birds. A local farmer turned up the tablets while he was plowing his fields in 1444, and the city convinced him to sell them for 2 years' worth of grazing rights. In your explorations be sure to find the secret corridor that leads from the back of the ceramics room to the Pinacoteca upstairs, via the medieval toilets.

Piazza Grande. *©* **075-927-4298.** Admission 5€ adults, 2.50€ children 7–25, free for children 7 and under and seniors. Apr–Sept daily 10am–1pm and 3–6pm; Oct–Mar daily 10am–1pm and 2–5pm.

Monte Igino ★ PARK/GARDEN   An open-air funicular whisks you to the top of this 908m (2,980-ft.) summit in about 5 minutes for yet more stupendous Umbrian views. On the ascent you can be glad you are not taking part in the May 15 **Corso dei Ceri,** when teams race up the mountainside carrying 15-foot-long wooden battering ram–like objects called *ceri,* or "candles." The race is part of festivities honoring St. Ubaldo, the bishop who allegedly smooth-talked Frederick Barbarossa out of sacking the town in the 1150s and was sainted for his efforts. The Basilica di Sant'Ubaldo, a

5-minute walk from the top station of the funicular, houses the saint's corpse, looking the worse for wear in a glass casket. The **Funivia Colle Eletto** (© 075-927-3881) runs Monday through Friday 10am to 1:15pm and 2:30 to 6:30pm and Saturday and Sunday 9:30am to 1:15pm and 2:30 to 7pm. Round-trip tickets are 5€ adults, 4€ children 4 to 13; one-way tickets are 4€ adults, 3€ children.

WHERE TO EAT

Grotta dell'Angelo ★ ITALIAN/UMBRIAN   A long barrel-vaulted dining room where locals have been gathering for the past 700 years or so is the place to sit in winter, while warm-weather dining is on a vine-shaded terrace. Wherever you eat, enjoy homemade gnocchi and other pastas, followed by flame-grilled sausages and other meats roasted over the open fire—the whole roast chicken stuffed with fennel is especially delicious.

Via Gioia 47. © **075-927-3438.** www.grottadellangelo.it. Main courses 9€–14€. Wed–Mon 12:30–2:30pm and 7:30–11pm. Closed Jan 7–Feb 7.

ASSISI ★★★

27km (17 miles) E of Perugia

St. Francis is still working miracles: His birthplace remains a lovely Umbrian hill town, despite a steady onslaught of visitors. Many pilgrims come to pay homage to Francis at the Basilica di San Francisco, and almost as many are drawn by the frescoes celebrating the saint's life with which the painter Giotto decorated the church. You'll also find a blend of romance and magic in Assisi's honey-colored stone, the quiet back lanes, and the mists that rise and fall over the Val di Spoleto below the town. With its saintly presence and pleasant ambiance, Assisi an essential stop on any Umbrian tour.

Essentials

GETTING THERE   From **Perugia,** there are about 20 **trains** daily (25–30 min.). From **Florence** (2–3 hr.), there are trains every 2 hours or so, though some require a transfer at Terontola. The station is in the modern valley town of Santa Maria degli Angeli, about 5km (3 miles) from Assisi, with bus connections to Assisi every 20 minutes (1€), or you can take a **taxi** for about 15€ to 20€.

By car, Assisi is 18km (11 miles) east of Perugia, off the SS75bis. The center's steep streets are off-limits to non-resident drivers. The best strategy is to park in Piazza Matteotti (1.15€/hour), keep walking west, and finish at the basilica; it's all downhill. A dependable alternative is the Mojano multistory garage (1.05€ first 2 hr., 1.45€/hour thereafter) halfway up the hill from Piazza Giovanni Paolo II to Porta Nuova. Escalators whisk you into the center of town.

Eight Umbria Mobilità buses (© 800/512-141; www.umbriamobilita.it) run seven times daily (Mon–Fri) between Perugia and Assisi's Piazza Matteotti (50 min.; 3.20€; 4€ if you pay on the bus). They also run about five buses from Gubbio (13/4 hr.). SULGA (© 075-500-9641; www.sulga.it) runs two buses daily from Rome's Tiburtina station, taking about 3 hours, and one daily trip from Piazza Adua in Florence, which takes about 21/2 hours.

VISITOR INFORMATION   The **tourist office** (© **075-812-534;** www.comune. assisi.pg.it) is in the Palazzo S. Nicola on Piazza del Comune, 06081 Assisi. It's open summer daily from 8am to 6:30pm, winter Monday through Saturday from 8am to

Assisi

1/8 mile
1/8 km

Information (i)

Rocca Minore

Anfiteatro Romano **6**

Porta Cappuccini
Via Carceri

1

Porta Nuova

Porta Perlici

Via Villamena

Via Padre A. Giorgi

Piazza Matteotti

Viale Umberto I

Viale Valentin Muller

Porta di...

Duomo

Via S. Gabriele dell'Addolorata

Via Borgo Aretino

Vicolo D. Castello

Piazza S. Rufino

Via S. Rufino

Corso Mazzini

Piazza S. Chiara

Santa Chiara

5

Rocca Maggiore **4**

V. di S. Rufino

Piazza del Comune

Ch. Nuova **2**

3

V. Sant'Agnese

V. Sant'Antonio

Porta Moiano

S. Maria Minerva (i)

Via A. Cristofani

Via Apollinare

Porta del Sementone

Perugia
Assisi
Florence
TUSCANY
UMBRIA

Via S. Paolo

Via Fortini

V. Seminario

V. Brizi

Via Ancaiani

Via Metastasio

Via San Francesco

Via Fontebella

Via del Fosso Cupo

Via Borgo San Pietro

San Pietro

Via Vittorio Emanuele II

Tescio

Porta S. Giacomo

Piazza Sup. di San Francesco

San Francesco **1**

Piazza Inf. di San Francesco

Via Frate Elia

Porta S. Francesco

Piazza Unità d'Italia

Piazza S. Pietro

Porta S. Pietro

8

SS147

ATTRACTIONS ●

Basilica di
San Francesco **1**

Basilica di Santa Chiara **5**

Basilica di Santa
Maria degli Angeli **8**

Rocca Magiore **4**

HOTELS ■

NUN Assisi Relais
& Spa Museum **6**

Umbra **2**

RESTAURANTS ◆

La Fortezza **3**

La Stalla **7**

THE WORLD'S FAVORITE saint

For Christian pilgrims the magic of Assisi is all about **St. Francis,** one of the patron saints of Italy (along with Catherine of Siena), founder of one of the world's largest monastic orders, and generally considered to be just about the holiest person to walk the earth since Jesus. Born to a wealthy merchant and a spoiled young man of his time, Francis did an about turn in his early twenties and dedicated himself to a life of poverty. His meekness, love of animals, and invention of the Christmastime crèche scenes have all helped ensure his popularity. Though Francis traveled as far as Egypt (in an unsuccessful attempt to convert the sultan and put an end to the Crusades) he is most associated with the gentle countryside around Assisi, where he spent months praying and fasting in lonely hermitages. You can visit one of

them, the **Eremo delle Carceri,** 4km (2½ miles) above Assisi in a gorge on the oak- and ilex-covered slopes of **Mt. Subasio,** where Francis often withdrew to meditate and pray with his followers. This is where he caused water to gush from the rocks and preached his sermons to the birds (the spots are well marked on the grounds). Within the stone complex, home to a community of monks, some tiny, rock-hewn passages lead to the rocky bed where Francis slept. From Assisi, follow the Via Eremo delle Carceri (reached through the Porta Cappuccini). The Eremo delle Carceri (✆ **075-812301**) is open daily from 6:30am to 7pm Easter to October, and the rest of the year 6:30am to 6pm; the sanctuary is open daily 8:30am to 5:30pm. Admission is free.

2pm and 3 to 6pm, Sunday from 9am to 1pm. The private websites www.assisionline.com and www.assisiweb.com also have good info.

Where to Stay

Never show up in Assisi, especially from Easter to fall, without a hotel reservation. Don't even think of showing up without a reservation on pilgrim-thronged **church holidays** or the **Calendimaggio,** a spring celebration, the first weekend (starting Thurs) after May 1, when the town divides itself into "upper" and "lower" factions that date to the 1300s and celebrates with processions, medieval contests of strength and skill, and late-night partying—all in 14th-century costume, of course. At these times you'll search in vain and find yourself stuck overnight in one of the bus-pilgrimage facilities 4km (2½ miles) away in Santa Maria degli Angeli. The official central booking office is **Consorzio Albergatori ed Operatori Turistici di Assisi,** Via A. Cristofani 22a (✆ **075-816-566;** www.visitassisi.com).

St. Anthony's Guesthouse, Via G. Alessi 10 (✆ 075-812-542; atoneassisi@tiscali net.it), is run by the Franciscan Sisters of Atonement, an American order of nuns. They offer hotel-like rooms with bathrooms from 60€ for a double with breakfast (singles are 40€). They're open March through October, have a 2-night minimum stay, and usually require a deposit in advance (parking is 5€ a day).

NUN Assisi Relais & Spa Museum ★★   A dramatic change of pace from Assisi's heavily medieval aura is in full force at this contemporary redo of a centuries-old convent. Handsome guest quarters are all white surfaces and bursts of bright colors, accented with stone walls and arches, and boldly turned out with Eames chairs, laminate tables, and high-tech lighting. A two-level suite with a hanging sleeping loft is focused on a massive 13th-century fresco of saints in the wilderness, bound to instill nighttime visions. A lavish breakfast buffet and other meals are served in a stark, white-vaulted, hi-tech version of the refectory, and downstairs are hedonistic pleasures the former veiled tenants could never have dreamed of—two pools, a series of saunas and steam rooms, and a state-of-the-art spa.

Eremo delle Carceri 1A. ℂ **075-815-5150.** www.nunassisi.com. 18 units. From 260€ double. Rate includes breakfast. **Amenities:** Restaurant; bar; concierge; indoor pools; room service; sauna; steam room; spa; Wi-Fi (free).

Umbra ★★ Assisi lodgings don't get any homier than they do at the Laudenzi family's welcoming little inn down a tiny alley from Piazza del Commune. A gate opens into a shady patio and beyond it are welcoming, if a bit outdated, guest rooms with vaulted ceilings, fresco fragments, and other historic remnants here and there and nicely furnished with old-fashioned armoires and dressers. Views over rooftops to the valley below unfold through the tall windows, from the private terraces off the choicest rooms, and the one on the roof for all guests to enjoy. The dining room is one of the most pleasant places to eat in town and extends into a lovely garden in good weather.

Via Delgli Archi 6 (off the west end of Piazza del Comune). ℂ **075-812-240.** www.hotelumbra.it. 24 units. 110€ standard double; 125€ superior double. Rates include breakfast. Garage parking 10€ per day. Closed mid-Jan to Easter. **Amenities:** Restaurant; bar; babysitting; bikes; concierge; room service; Wi-Fi (free).

Villa Zuccari ★ If you have a car, you can easily visit Assisi from any number of smaller nearby towns. The little wine village of Montefalco, about 20 minutes south, is especially appealing, given the presence of dozens of wineries and all the more so since it's home to this old family estate where you will feel like a guest in a gracious Italian home. You will also be within easy reach of Spello, Trevi, Spoleto, Todi, and other hill towns that spill down the Umbrian hillsides. But you might be tempted to stay put on your own large terrace or in the palm-shaded garden surrounding a pool. Inside, the airy, light-filled bedrooms are especially large and homily equipped with soft armchairs, king-sized beds, and some nice antiques, and the big bathrooms are sheathed in marble. Welcoming lounges are filled with books and pottery, and dinners are served in a vaulted room that glistens with terracotta tiles.

Locanda San Luca (just east of Montefalco). ℂ **742-399-402.** www.villazuccari.com. 34 units. From 110€ double. **Amenities:** Restaurant; bar; pool Wi-Fi (free).

Where to Eat

Several of Assisi's restaurants and bars serve a local flatbread called *torta al testa,* usually split and stuffed with cheeses, sausages, and vegetables (spinach is popular). It's a meal in itself and a fast and cheap lunch.

La Fortezza ★★ UMBRIAN You don't have to veer far off the beaten track to find the Chiocchetti family's plain, stone-walled dining room, where the focus is on authentic Umbrian home cooking. You'll discover that both body and soul benefit from their specialties, such as *cannelloni all'Assisiana* (fresh pasta sheets wrapped around a veal *ragù,* all baked under parmigiana) and *cognilio in salsa di mele* (rabbit roasted in a sauce of wine and apples).

Vicolo della Fortezza/Piazza del Comune (up the stairs near the Via San Rufino end). ℂ **075-812-993.** www.lafortezzahotel.com. Main courses 10€–13€. Fri–Wed 12:30–2:30pm and 7:30–9:30pm. Closed Feb and 1 week in July.

La Stalla ★★ GRILL/UMBRIAN It's not often that the term "old barn" is associated with good dining, but a meal in these rustic and rather raucous converted livestock stalls, with stone walls and low ceilings, can be the highlight of a trip to Assisi (even the servers seem to be having a good time). The pleasant, 15-minute walk out here will work up an appetite, so begin with the *assaggini di torta al testo*, small samplers of Assisian flatbread stuffed with cheese, meat, and vegetables, then move through the hearty selection of pastas to the simple servings of steak, pork and sausage skewers, chicken, even potatoes that come off the grill. Palatable house wines compliment the meals, which you can enjoy on a terrace in good weather.

Santuario della Carceri 24 (1½km/less than 1 mile from centre, direction Eremo). ✆ **075-812-317.** Main courses 8[eu–13€. Tues–Sun noon–2:30pm and 7–10:30pm.

Exploring Assisi

The geographical and civic heart of Assisi is Piazza del Comune with its 13th-century Palazzo del Capitano and the stately Corinthian columns of the Roman Tempio di Minerva guarding its northern fringe. The most atmospheric route to the basilica goes downhill from here along medieval Via Portica, which becomes Via Fortini and Via San Francesco before arriving at the main event.

Basilica di Santa Maria di Angeli ★ RELIGIOUS SITE This massive church, built between 1569 and 1679, dominates the valley below Assisi. While the imposing and pompous monument seems out of keeping with the saint's humble ways, inside are three sites of great interest to followers of Francis (and are often overrun with bus loads of Catholic pilgrims): the **Porziuncola,** a tiny 9th-century church within the basilica where he established his order in 1209; the **Cappella del Transito,** built around the primitive room where he died in 1226; and the **Cappella delle Rose,** built on the site of the mud hut where the saint often retreated.

Via Protomartiri Francescani, S.M. degli Angeli. ✆ **075-8051430.** Daily 6:15am–12:30pm and 2:30–7:30pm. Free admission; Museo della Porziuncola 2.50€ adults, 1.50€ children 11–18, free for children 10 and under.

Basilica di San Francesco ★★★ RELIGIOUS SITE One of the most popular pilgrimage sites in Christendom combines homage to eternally popular St. Francis, masterworks of medieval architecture, and some of the favorite works of Western art. The basilica is actually two churches, lower and upper; the lower church is dark and somber, a place of contemplation, while the upper church soars into Gothic vaults and is light-filled and colorful, instilling a sense of celebration. This assemblage was begun soon after the saint's death in 1226, under the guidance of Francis's savvy and worldly colleague, Brother Elias. The lower church was completed in 1230, and the upper church in 1280. The steeply sloping site just outside the city walls was until then used for executions and known as the Hill of Hell. The presence of the patron saint of Italy, in spirit as well as in body, now makes this one of Italy's most uplifting sights. His kindness, summed up in his saying, "For it is in giving that we receive," seems to permeate the soft gray stones, and the frescoed spaces move the devout to tears and art lovers to fits of near-religious ecstasy.

THE LOWER CHURCH Entered off Piazza Inferiore di San Francesco (the lower of the two squares abutting the church), the basilica's bottom half is a cryptlike church that is indeed, first and foremost a crypt, housing the stone sarcophagus of St. Francis, surrounded by four of his disciples. An almost steady stream of faithful files past the monument, many on their knees. Inside is the saint's remarkably intact skeleton. Most saints of the Middle Ages fell victim to the purveyors of relics, who made enormous profit dispensing bones, a finger here, a toe there. It's said that Brother Elias, Francis' savvy colleague, had the foresight to seal the coffin in stone, and it remained undetected until 1818. The dimly lit atmosphere is greatly enlivened with the presence of many rich frescoes, including Simone Martini's action-packed depictions of the life of St. Martin in the Cappella di San Martino (1322–26). Martini amply displays his flare for boldly patterned fabrics and his familiarity with detailed manuscript illumination (many examples would have passed through his native Siena, on the pilgrimage route from northern Europe to Rome). He was also, like Martin, a knight, and these influences show up in several richly detailed scenes, including those of the saint, a Roman soldier, ripping his cloak to share it with a beggar; being investitured; and renouncing chivalry and weaponry in favor of doing good deeds. The imagery is not out of keeping with Francis, who as a youth dreamed of being a soldier.

Giotto and his assistants frescoed the Cappella della Santa Maria Maddalena, with the "Life of St. Mary Magdalene" (1303–09). An incredibly moving cycle of "Christ's Passion" (1316–19) by Pietro Lorenzetti includes a hauntingly humane "Deposition," in which the young Sienese artist imparts his scene with a gaunt Christ and sorrowful Mary with naturalism and emotion not before seen in painting.

THE UPPER CHURCH Entering the light-filled Gothic interior of the Upper Church you'll first encounter scenes of the New Testament by Cimabue, the last great painter of the Byzantine style; some critics say only the "Crucifixion" (1277) is his, and the rest of the scenes are by his assistants. In any case, it's rather ironic he's here at all. The artist was infamous for his stubbornness and difficult personality, and in the "Divine Comedy," Dante places him in Purgatory among the proud, adding the comment, "Cimabue thought to hold the field of painting, and now Giotto hath the cry." It's Giotto who famously holds court in the church, with his 28-part fresco cycle on "The Life of St. Francis," completed in the 1290s. Even nonreligious viewers know and love these scenes of the saint removing his clothing to renounce material processions, marrying poverty (symbolized by a woman in rags), and preaching to the birds (the perennial favorite and the subject of ubiquitous postcards for sale around town).

Piazza Superiore di San Francesco. ℂ **075-819-001.** www.sanfrancescoassisi.org. Free admission. Lower Church daily 6am–6:45pm; Upper Church daily 8:30am–6:45pm. You may visit church for Mass on Sun morning (before 2pm), but purely touristic visits at this time are frowned on.

Basilica di Santa Chiara ★ RELIGIOUS SITE   One of the first followers of St. Francis was a young woman, Chiara (Clare, in English), daughter of a count and countess who was so swept away by the teachings of the young zealot that she allowed him to cut her hair and dress her in sackcloth. She founded the order of the Poor Dames (now known as Poor Clares), whose members continue to renounce material processions, and she lies on view in this vast, stark church on full view, with her face covered in wax. The Oratorio del Crocifisso preserves the venerated 12th-century crucifix from which the figure of Christ allegedly spoke to St. Francis and asked him to rebuild his church (the reference was to the organization, which had by then become mired in politics, corruption, and warfare). As Clare lay ill on Christmas Eve 1252, she allegedly voiced regrets that she would not be able to attend services in the then-new Basilica di San Francisco. Suddenly, in a vision, she saw and heard the mass clear as a bell and in Technicolor, a miracle for which she was named the patron saint of television in 1958.

Piazza Santa Chiara. ℂ **075-812-282.** Free admission. Daily 6:30am–noon and 2–7pm (6pm in winter).

San Francesco and Santa Chiara have a strict dress code. Entrance is forbidden to those wearing shorts or miniskirts or showing bare shoulders. You also must remain silent and cannot take photographs in the Upper Church of San Francesco.

Rocca Maggiore ★★ CASTLE   A show of might is built of bleached yellow stone atop a steep hillside very high above the city. Some view enthusiasts claim that a sharp-eyed observer can see all the way to the Mediterranean on a clear day, but that's probably an oxygen-deprivation vision induced by the hearty climb through narrow medieval lanes and up the pine-scented hillside. Hyperbole aside, views across the Umbrian plain below are wonderful and quite a bit more exhilarating than the dull displays of costumes and weapons in the restored keep and soldiers quarters; save the admission fee for a glass of wine when you get back down.

Piazzale delle Libertà Comunali, at the top of town, at the ends of Via della Rocca, Via del Colle, and the stepped Vicolo San Lorenzo off Via Porta Perlici. ℭ **075-815-292.** Admission 5€ adults; 3.50€ students, children 8–18, and seniors 65 and over; free for children 7 and under; joint ticket with Foro Romano and Pinacoteca Comunale 8€ and 5€. June–Aug daily 9am–8pm; Apr–May and Sept–Oct daily 10am–6:30pm; Nov–Feb daily 10am–4:30pm; Mar 10am–5:30pm.

SPOLETO ★

63km (39 miles) SE of Perugia

Spoleto can seem to be the center of the cultured world in June, when the Festival dei Due Mondi (aka Spoleto Festival) brings performers and audiences from all over the world to town. For most of the year, though, Spoleto is a just another lovely Umbrian hill town, sweeping up a steep hillside. The pleasant warren of steep streets and airy piazzas are lined with artifacts from the Roman past and prosperous Middle Ages, and include one of Italy's most beautifully situated cathedrals.

Essentials

GETTING THERE   Spoleto is a main **rail** station on the Rome-Ancona line, and 16 daily trains from **Rome** stop here (about 11/2 hr.). From **Perugia,** take one of the 20 daily trains to Foligno (25 min.) to transfer to this line for the final 20-minute leg. From outside the station, take bus A, B, or C to Piazza Carducci on the edge of the old town.

By car, the town sits on the old Roman Via Flaminia, now the SS3. There's usually plenty of parking, but the easiest option is to make for the Spoletosfera parking garage, signposted from the SS3's Spoleto Sud exit (1€ per hour). Escalators from the lot run up the hillside to the top of town, allowing you to get off at well-signposted levels (for Piazza della Libertà, the Duomo, and so forth)

VISITOR INFORMATION   The **information center** at Piazza della Libertà 7 (ℭ **0743-220-773;** www.visitspoleto.it) hands out heaps of info and an excellent map. It's open Monday to Friday from 9am to 1:30pm and 2 to 7pm, Saturday 9am to 1pm, and Sunday 10am to 1pm and 3:30 to 6:30pm.

Spoleto

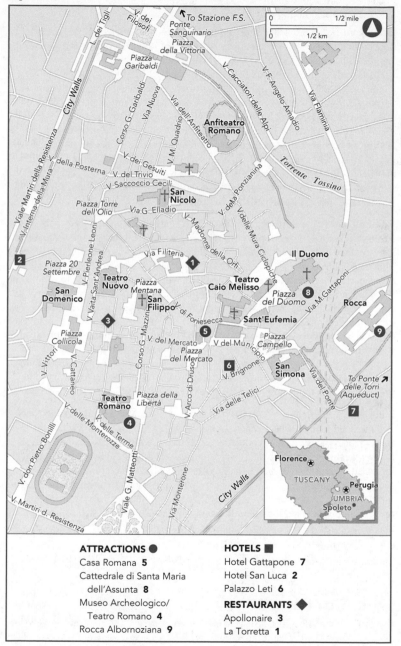

To Stazione F.S.
Ponte
Sanguinario
Piazza
della Vittoria

L. dei Tigli
V. dei Filosofi
Piazza Garibaldi
City Walls
Corso G. Garibaldi
Via Nuova
Via dell'Anfiteatro
V. M. Quadrio
V. Cacciatori delle Alpi
V. F. Angelo Amadio
Via Flaminia
Anfiteatro Romano
Viale Martiri della Resistenza
V. Interna della Mura
V. della Posterna
V. dei Gesuiti
V. del Trivio
V. Saccoccio Cecili
Piazza Torre dell'Olio
Via G. Elladio
San Nicolò
Torrente Tossino
V. della Ponzianina
V. Madonna della Orfi
V. delle Mura Ciclopiche
Il Duomo
Via Filiteria
Piazza 20 Settembre
V. Pierleone Leoni
V. Vaita Sant'Andrea
Teatro Nuovo
Piazza Mentana
San Filippo
San Domenico
Teatro Caio Melisso
Piazza del Duomo
Via M. Gattaponi
Rocca
V. di Foniesecca
Corso G. Mazzini
V. del Mercato
Piazza Collicola
V. Vittori
V. Cattaneo
Piazza del Mercato
Sant'Eufemia
Piazza Campello
V. del Municipio
V. Brignone
San Simona
V. del Ponte
To Ponte delle Torri (Aqueduct)
Teatro Romano
V. delle Terme
V. delle Monterozze
Piazza della Libertà
V. Arco di Druso
Via delle Telici
V. don Pietro Bonilli
Viale G. Matteotti
Via Monterone
City Walls
V. Martiri d. Resistenza

0 — 1/2 mile
0 — 1/2 km

Florence
TUSCANY
Perugia
UMBRIA
Spoleto

ATTRACTIONS ●
Casa Romana **5**
Cattedrale di Santa Maria
  dell'Assunta **8**
Museo Archeologico/
  Teatro Romano **4**
Rocca Albornoziana **9**

HOTELS ■
Hotel Gattapone **7**
Hotel San Luca **2**
Palazzo Leti **6**

RESTAURANTS ◆
Apollonaire **3**
La Torretta **1**

Where to Stay

Accommodations are tight during the Spoleto Festival; reserve by March if you want to find a good, central room.

Gattapone ★   From the street, this completely unexpected retreat beneath the Rocca Albornozina seems like a relatively modest 19th-century villa. But step inside, and it's all polished wood, curved, free-floating staircases, and leather couches facing window walls overlooking the Ponte dei Torre and green Montulco hillsides. There's a cinematic, 1960s Antonioni-film quality to the place, including the guest rooms, where slightly dated but well maintained contemporary furnishings mix with traditional pieces and surround huge bay windows hanging over the same stunning views; rooms in the newer wing have sitting areas facing the views. Some guests comment that the air-conditioning is vintage, too, and anyone with mobility issues should keep in mind that there's no elevator and rooms and lounges flow for several floors down the hillside. But a flowery terrace at the bottom is one of many quirky charms.

Via del Ponte 6. © **0743-223-447.** www.hotelgattapone.it. 15 units. From 90€ double. Rates include buffet breakfast. **Amenities:** Bar; Wi-Fi (free).

Palazzo Leti ★★   An entrance through a Renaissance garden that opens at one side to the Tessino gorge announces the air of enchantment that pervades this beautifully restored 13th-century palace of the Leti family. Views of the gorge and green Monteluco hills are the focal point of most of the guest rooms, though a few overlook a medieval alley that has a charm all its own; all have handsome period furnishings and rich fabrics, as well as welcoming couches and arm chairs in the larger rooms, and exposed beams, granite hearths, and vaulted ceilings throughout enhance the historic surroundings. Anna Laura and Giampolo, who restored the palace from a dilapidated pile, are a friendly presence and provide all sorts of advice, including how to negotiate the narrow surrounding lanes in a car and where to find a good meal.

Via degli Eremiti 10. © **0743-224-930.** www.palazzoleti.com. 12 units. 130€–200€ double. Rates include breakfast. Free parking. **Amenities:** Bar; babysitting; bikes; spa; Wi-Fi (free).

San Luca ★★   A 19th-century tannery at the far edge of the city next to the Roman walls lends itself well to its current incarnation as an atmospheric and gracious hotel. A book-lined lounge, where canaries chirp in an antique cage and a fire crackles in colder months, faces a large courtyard, as do many of the rooms—others overlook a rose garden to the side. The unusually large quarters are all different and individually furnished with a mix of traditional and contemporary pieces and a smattering of antiques chosen by the owner—whose experience in the bath fixture business accounts for the extremely large and well-equipped windowed marble bathrooms. Sights and restaurants are about a 5-minute walk away, and the attentive staff will map out a route that involves the least amount of climbing. Among the many amenities is an easy-to-reach in-house garage, a real rarity in Spoleto.

Via Interna delle Mura 21. © **0743-223-399.** www.hotelsanluca.com. 35 units. From 100€ double. Rates include buffet breakfast. Garage parking (13€ per day). **Amenities:** Bar; babysitting; bikes; concierge; room service (bar); Wi-Fi (fee).

Where to Eat

For some gastro-shopping, visit **Bartolomei Orvieto** at 97 Corso Cavour (© **0763-344550;** www.oleificiobartolomei.it), where you can taste and drink the products before buying. **Colder Gelateria** (© **0743-235-015**) serves some of the best gelato

Spoleto's be-all and end-all annual event bridges the end of June and early July. The **Spoleto Festival** (www.festivaldispoleto.it) offers 3 weeks of world-class drama, music, and dance held in evocative spaces like an open-air restored Roman theater and the pretty piazza fronting the Duomo. A secondary **Spoleto Estate** season of music, art, and theater runs from just after the festival ends through September.

(notably the "bread and chocolate" flavor) in Umbria, created by local artisans Crispini; it's open daily from 12:30pm to midnight.

Apollonaire ★ UMBRIAN   The low wood ceilings, stone walls, and beams are traditional holdovers from a 12th-century Franciscan monastery, but the menu is innovative and adventurous—contemporary Spoletan, if the food world has invented such a term, would well describe dishes that rely on fresh local ingredients and traditional Umbrian recipes but have that extra twist: *Strangozzi* (local long, rectangular wheat pasta) is topped with a pungent sauce of cherry tomatoes and mint, herb-roasted rabbit is served with black olive sauce, and pork filet mignon is topped with a house-invention, a sauce of pecorino cheese and pears soaked in Rosso di Montefalco.

Via Sant'Agata 14 (near Piazza della Libertà). ✆ **0743-225-676.** www.ristoranteapollinare.it. Main courses 12€–24€. Thurs–Tues noon–3pm and 7pm–midnight. Closed Feb.

La Torretta ★★ UMBRIAN   Two welcoming rooms in a medieval tower converted to a wine cellar, just off an airy little piazza in a quiet corner of the old town, is the place to settle in for a relaxed meal. Brothers Stefano and Elio Salvucci extend a genuine welcome and present a nice selection of Umbrian dishes with a focus on truffles, beginning with the *tris di antipasti al tartufo estivo* (trio of truffle-based appetizers) and working up to a choice of extremely well-seasoned pork and beef grilled over a wood fire. The kitchen also makes a light-as-air truffle omelet, a memorable break from heavier *secondis*. Outdoor seating is available in summer.

Via Filitteria 43. ✆ **0743-44-954.** www.trattorialatorretta.com. Main courses 9€–16€. Wed–Mon 12:30–2:30pm and 7:45–10:45pm (closed Sun evening).

Exploring Spoleto

You won't spend much time in the Lower Town, but a highlight is the 11th-century Romanesque **San Gregorio di Maggiore,** Piazza della Vittoria (✆ **0743-44-140**), which replaced an earlier oratory here in a cemetery of Christian martyrs. The church's namesake saint was killed in a spectacle at the nearby amphitheater in A.D. 304, as were a supposed 10,000 lesser-known martyrs whose bones symbolically reside beneath the altar. It opens daily from 8am to noon and 4 to 6pm, and admission is free. Once you settle into town, with the aid of a map you'll be able to figure out ways to use handy **escalators** to avoid steep uphill climbs; hotel staff will also usually help you plot a level course. **Piazza del Mercato,** the probable site of the old Roman forum, is a bustling spot in the Upper Town lined with grocers and fruit vendors' shops.

Casa Romana ★ HISTORIC HOME   As a stop on the busy Via Flaminia and an important supplier of wine, Spoletium was fairly prosperous in the Roman world. Enough of this patrician's home remains, including frescoes and mosaics, to give an idea of what the good life was like for a Roman occupant in the A.D. 1st century. The resident was obviously well to do, though there's no proof for the claim that she was Vespasia Polla, the mother of the Emperor Vespasian.

Via di Visiale. © **0743-234-350.** Admission 2.50€ adults, 2€ ages 15–25 and seniors 65 and over, 1€ children 7–14, free for children 6 and under. Daily 10:30am–5:30pm.

Cattedrale di Santa Maria dell'Assunta ★★ CATHEDRAL Spoleto's
almost playfully picturesque cathedral was consecrated in 1098, barely 40 years after Frederick Barbarossa, Holy Roman Emperor, razed the entire town in retaliation for the citizens' lack of support in his ongoing wars against the papacy. The church they built seems to defy the brutality of that catastrophe and is serenely set in a broad piazza at the bottom of a flight of monumental steps, with the white marble and golden mosaics on the dazzling facade framed against a gentle backdrop of a forested hill. Inside, the apse is graced with frescoes of the "Life of the Virgin" that are largely from the brush of Filippo Lippi, one of the more colorful characters of his time. An ordained priest, Filippo shirked his duties to draw and was eventually given permission to paint full time. Though he worked frequently and was a favorite of the Medicis, he was chronically impoverished, supposedly because he spent so much money on women. The commission to come to Spoleto must have been a plum for the artist, then close to 60. His delicate and engaging scenes of the elegant Virgin being visited by the Archangel and holding her very sweet-looking infant betray nothing of the turbulence in his life, as he was fighting to get dispensation to marry a young nun, Lucrezia Buti, whom he had seduced and who had bore his son, Filippino Lippi (who would soon match his father's greatness as a painter). Both Lippis appear in the Domition of the Virgin scene, Filippo wearing a white habit with young Filippino, as an angel, in front of him. Filippo died before he completed the frescoes, and his assistants finished the task. The cause of his death was suspected to be poison, perhaps administered by Lucrezia's family or yet another paramour. He is buried beneath a monument that Filippino would design at the request of Lorenzo de' Medici, Filippo's patron, who tried in vain to get the body back to Florence. In the Cappella delle Reliquie (Reliquary Chapel), on the left aisle, is a rare treasure—a letter written and signed by St. Francis. (Assisi has the only other bona fide signature.)

Piazza del Duomo. © **0743-231-063.** Free admission. Daily 8:30am–12:30pm and 3:30–5:30pm (until 7pm Apr–Oct).

Museo Archeologico/Teatro Romano ★ MUSEUM/RUINS Spoleto had the
good fortune to more or less flourish through the Dark Ages and the Middle Ages, and as a consequence most of the Roman city was quarried or built over. The monastery of St. Agata was built atop this splendid theater that wasn't recognized until 1891. After a thorough restoration in the 1950s, the theater is the evocative venue for performances during the Spoleto Festival. Much of the original orchestra flooring is intact, as is an elaborate drainage system that was allegedly quite efficient in flushing out the blood of slain animals and martyrs. Busts and statuary that once adorned the theater are on display in the adjoining Museo Archeologico.

Via di Sant'Agata 18A. © **0743-223-277.** Admission 4€ adults, 2€ ages 18–25, free for children 17and under and seniors 65 and over. Daily 8:30am–7:30pm.

Rocca Albornoziana ★★ CASTLE Cardinal Albornoz, a power-hungry zealot
tasked with rebuilding and strengthening the papal states, arrived in Spoleto in the

mid–14th century and commissioned the Umbrian architect Matteo Gattapone to build a fortress. The site was perfect—atop a high hill above the town and, as history would prove, virtually impregnable. The walled-and-moated castle became famous in the 20th century as one of Italy's most secure prisons, where members of the Red Brigades terrorist organization were routinely incarcerated. The fortunate ones might have had a view through their cell windows of the majestic Ponte delle Torri, a 232m-long (760-ft.) aqueduct built in the 13th century on Roman foundations. Its arches span a deep, verdant gorge, 90m (295 ft.) above the Tessino river, a scene that so impressed Wolfgang von Goethe on a 1786 visit to Spoleto that he dedicated an entire page of his "Italian Travels" to the spectacle.

The current occupant of the fortress is the Museo Nazionale del Ducato di Spoleto (℃ 0743-223-055), with a benumbing collection of sarcophagi, mosaics, and religious statuary that you needn't feel guilty about not seeing (and it's very expensive as well). The views of the town and Umbrian countryside from the grounds are free and well worth the ride up, via a series of escalators and elevators.

Piazza Campello. ℃ **0743-224-952.** Admission 7.50€ adults, 6.50€ ages 15–25, 3.50€ children 7–14, free for children 6 and under. Tues–Sun 8:30am–7:30pm (last ticket 6:45pm).

A Side Trip to Todi

45 km (28 miles) northwest of Spoleto

For sheer picturesque quotient, few Umbrian hill towns can match somber and proud Todi. What's more, at the top of the town is the finest square in Umbria, the Piazza del Popolo, a remarkable assemblage of 12th- to 14th-century palaces, the Duomo, and belvederes providing eagle's-eye views of the rolling Umbrian countryside and the Tiber Valley below. Standing in this square and exploring the little lanes that run off it is the reason to be in Todi, where there's not much to see but a lot of ambience to soak in.

GETTING THERE It's easy by **car,** following scenic S418 west out of Spoleto to Acquasparta, where you then take E45 northwest to Todi. By train, travel north from Spoleto to Perugia and change there for Todi; but you'll have to switch from the main station to Sant'Anna, in Piazzale Bellucci, and be sure to time the trip carefully so you don't wait hours for a connection.

EXPLORING TODI

The central **tourist office** is under the arches of the Palazzo del Capitano at Palazzo del Popolo 38/39 (℃ **075-894-2526;** www.comune.todi.pg.it/fap). It's open Monday through Saturday from 9:30am to 1pm and 3:30 to 7pm, Sunday 10am to 1pm and 3:30 to 7pm (in winter it closes at 6pm and is not open Sun afternoons). The *palazzo* is one of three harmonious public buildings from the 13th and 14th centuries that lend the square its austere dignity; the others are the Palazzo dei Priori, with its curious trapezoidal tower, and oldest of the three, the Palazzo del Popolo from 1213. Todi's Duomo is simple and elegant, graced with a rose window added to the 12th-century structure in 1500.

These medieval stones are quite recent in the scheme of the town's past, which is said to stretch to at least the 7th century B.C., though legend has it that Hercules founded the town a century or so before, and it was here that he killed Cacus, the fire-breathing dragon. It's known that the Romans usurped an Etruscan outpost sometime around 217 B.C., and their walls are still part of the town's massive fortifications.

WHERE TO EAT & STAY

Ristorante Umbria ★ UMBRIAN   For many visitors, the main reason to come to Todi is to enjoy a meal at this decades-old dining room just off Piazza del Popolo. *Palombaccio* (a type of wild dove), steaks, and other meats are grilled over an open fire, and often accompanied by truffles. The other pleasure of dining here is to sit on the terrace, from which all of Umbria seems to unfold at your feet like a vast green checkerboard (be sure to reserve an outside table in advance).

Via San Bonaventura 13. ℂ **075-894-2737.** Main courses 10€–18€. Wed–Mon 11am–3pm and 7–10:30pm.

Castello di Castiglione ★★   For an authentic Umbrian experience, it's hard to beat this medieval castle and its walled hamlet in the countryside outside Todi. Part of the business here is an excellent restaurant, the **Il Re Beve** (the King Quaffs), one of the region's best, where meals are served in front of a roaring fire in winter (meats are roasted over the coals) and on a geranium-filled terrace overlooking fields of sunflowers in warm weather; you can also dine on request in some subterranean chambers reached through secret tunnels. A vast, vaulted suite in the castle keep is the most atmospheric accommodation, exuding medieval atmosphere in every brick and stone, except in the luxurious 21st-century bathroom with a hydromassage shower for two. Rustic yet extremely comfortable apartments scattered throughout the attached hamlet are multilevel, sleep as many as six, and face the well-kept gardens and small pool or overlook the countryside. Weekly rates are available, as are nightly rates with dinner included.

Piazza Corsini 1A. Casiligiano Terni (16km/10 miles south of Todi off E45). ℂ **0744-943-428.** www.castellodicasigliano.com. 8 units. 80€–96€ double; 150€–180€ suite. Rates include breakfast. **Amenities:** Restaurant; bar; pool; Wi-Fi (free).

ORVIETO ★★

87km (54 miles) W of Spoleto, 86km (53 miles) SW of Perugia

Walking through the streets of Orvieto you might be delighted to discover that nothing much has changed in the past 500 years. Adding to the magic is that off to one side of town is what might be Italy's most beautiful cathedral, covered in dazzling mosaics and statuary and rising above an airy piazza. The final coup de grace is the fact that the entire town is set atop a volcanic outcropping some 315m (1,033 ft.) above the green countryside. This impenetrable perch ensured that Etruscan "Velzna" was among the most powerful members of the *dodecapoli* (Etruscan confederation of 12 cities) and the aerielike positioning continues to make Orvieto seem a world apart.

Essentials

GETTING THERE   Fourteen **trains** on the main Rome-Florence line stop at Orvieto daily (1 hr., 45 min. from Florence; 1 hr., 20 min. from Rome). From **Perugia,** take the train to Terontola (16 trains daily) for this line heading south toward Rome (11/4 hr. total train time).

Orvieto's station is in Orvieto Scalo in the valley. To reach the city, cross the street and take the funicular (every 10 min. 7:20am–8:30pm; www.atcterni.it).

Orvieto is straightforward to reach by **car,** especially from southern Tuscany: It's right by the A1. The main link to the rest of Umbria is the SS448 to Todi (40 min.).

Orvieto

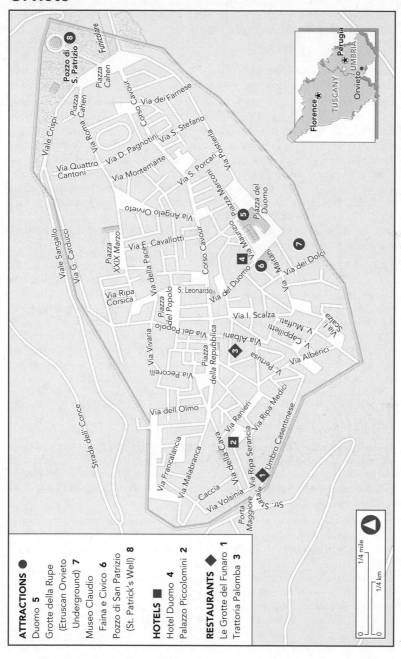

ATTRACTIONS ●
Duomo **5**
Grotte della Rupe
(Etruscan Orvieto
Underground) **7**
Museo Claudio
Faina e Civico **6**
Pozzo di San Patrizio
(St. Patrick's Well) **8**

HOTELS ■
Hotel Duomo **4**
Palazzo Piccolomini **2**

RESTAURANTS ◆
Le Grotte del Funaro **1**
Trattoria Palomba **3**

VISITOR INFORMATION The **tourist office** is opposite the Duomo at Piazza Duomo 24 (© **0763-341-772;** www.comune.orvieto.tr.it). It's open Monday through Friday from 8:15am to 1:50pm and 4 to 7pm, Saturday from 10am to 1pm and 3:30 to 7pm, and Sunday from 10am to noon and 4 to 6pm.

Where to Stay

The upper town does not have many places to stay, so be sure to book ahead—especially on weekends, when many Romans come up to Orvieto for a small-town getaway.

Hotel Duomo ★★ These snug quarters just a few steps from Duomo (viewable from some rooms with a lean out of the window) are not only extremely comfortable—with lots of built in modern, rich wood furnishings and excellent lighting (a rarity in Italian hotels in this price range)—but are also surprisingly quirky. A local artist, Livio Orazio Valentini, did the decor and hung his surrealistic paintings in the hallways, lounges, and rooms, and complemented them with colorful upholstery and carpets to match the tones. He also created sculptural light fixtures that hang over many of the desks. The effect is slightly bohemian and quite homey, and the ambiance is topped off nicely with a pleasant garden to one side of the hotel.

Vicolo dei Maurizio 7. © **0763-341-887.** www.orvietohotelduomo.com. 18 units. 80€ double. Rates include breakfast. **Amenities:** Wi-Fi (free).

Palazzo Piccolomini ★★ Orvieto's most luxurious and character-filled accommodations are in a 16th-century *palazzo* that was resurrected from a dilapidated wreck 25 years ago. The stone and vaulted subterranean breakfast room and a couple of frescoed salons whisk you into the past, but most of the guest rooms are done in contemporary Umbrian chic—wood and tile floors, dark, simple furnishings, and crisp white walls with neutral-tone accents here and there, all very soothing. Some rooms have sitting areas, or open to terraces, or are two-level, though the real prize here is a room of any size with a countryside view (only those on the upper floors have them).

Piazza Ranieri 36 (2 blocks down from Piazza della Repubblica). © **0763-341-743.** www.palazzo piccolomini.it. 32 units. From 154€ double. Rates include breakfast. Parking 15€ in main public lot next door. **Amenities:** Restaurant; babysitting; concierge; room service; Wi-Fi (free in public areas).

Where to Eat

Orvieto's unofficial pasta is *umbrichelli,* simple flour-and-water spaghetti rolled out unevenly by hand and somewhat chewy—similar to the *pici* of southern Tuscany, but not as thick. To sample a glass (or buy a bottle) of Orvieto Classico (accompanied by a *panino*), drop by the **Cantina Foresi,** Piazza Duomo 2 (© **0763-341-611**). Ask to see the small, moldy cellar carved directly into the *tufo.*

Le Grotte del Funaro ★ UMBRIAN A *funaro* (rope maker) had his workshop in these grottoes carved into the tufa in a cliffside at the edge of town almost a thousand years ago, and you can almost see him at work in the shadowy recesses of the multilevel, cavelike rooms. You can sit outside in front and enjoy the sweep of green countryside far below the town, or better yet—so you don't miss all the atmosphere inside—ask for one of the few window seats. Wherever you sit, you'll dine simply and well on grilled meats, the house specialty (including a *grigliata mista* of suckling pig, lamb, sausage, and yellow peppers), as well as excellent pizzas.

Via Ripa Serancia 41 (at the west end of town near Porta Maggiore; well signposted). © **0763-343-276.** www.grottedelfunaro.it. Main courses 10€–13€; pizza 5.50€–8.50€. Tues–Sun noon–3pm and 7pm–midnight. Closed 1 week in July.

Trattoria Palomba ★★ UMBRIAN   This pleasant white-walled room is the kind of place you'll want to linger, so settle in for a long lunch after a morning of seeing the sights or a comfy evening if you're spending the night in town—meal here deserves long, leisurely appreciation. Black Umbrian truffles top many of the house made pastas, most notably *umbrichelli al tartufo,* tossed with egg yolk and parmigiano. The house signature dish (*palomba,* Italian for wild dove) is roasted in a memorably delicious sauce of capers, rosemary, olives, and a hint of anchovies. Any of the meat dishes, including beef is a red wine sauce, are similarly satisfying, and accompanied by a nice selection of wines.

Via Cipirano Menente 16. ℂ **0763-343-395.** Main courses 10€–16€. Thurs–Tues noon–2pm and 7:30–10pm.

Exploring Orvieto

Duomo ★★ CATHEDRAL   Orvieto's pièce de résistance is a mesmerizing assemblage of spikes and spires, mosaics and marble statuary—and that's just the facade. The rest of the bulky-yet-elegant church is banded in black and white stone and seems to perch miraculously on the edge of the cliffs that surround the town. You might notice that it is wider at the front than at the back, designed so to create the optical illusion upon entering that it is longer than it actually is. The facade has been compared to a medieval altarpiece, and it reads like an illustrated Catechism. On the four broad marble panels that divide the surface, Sienese sculptor and architect Lorenzo Maitani (who also more or less designed the church) and others carved scenes from the Old and New Testament. On the far left is the story of creation, with Eve making an appearance from Adam's rib; on the far left, Christ presides over the Last Judgment, as the dead shuffle out of their sarcophagi to await his verdict. Prophets and the Apostles surround a huge rose window, and Mary appears in lush mosaics inlaid in fields of gold; she ascends to heaven in a triangular panel above the main portal, and she is crowned Queen of Heaven in the gable at the pinnacle of the facade.

CAPELLA DEL CORPORALE   In 1263, a Bohemian priest, Peter of Prague, found himself doubting transubstantiation, the sacrament in which the host is transformed into the body of Christ during mass. He went to Rome to pray on St. Peter's tomb that his faith be strengthened and, stopping in Bolsena, just below Orvieto, was saying mass when the host began to bleed and dampened the corporal, or altar cloth. Pope Urban IV, who was in Orvieto at the time, had the cloth brought to him, and a few decades later, Pope Nicholas IV ordered the cathedral built to house the relic. Frescoes in the chapel tell the story of the miracle, and the exquisite enamel reliquary that once held the cloth remains in place.

CAPPELLA SAN BRIZIO   The cathedral's other treasure is one of the Renaissance's greatest fresco cycles. The themes are temptation, salvation, damnation, and resurrection, though the scenes are rich in everyday humanity and allegedly inspired Michelangelo, who came to Orvieto and filled sketchbooks before beginning work on the Sistine Chapel. (In subsequent centuries church authorities had workers scramble over the frescoes and put sashes on the male nudes that Michelangelo so admired, though subsequent restorations have removed most of them.) Fra Angelico (the "Angelic Friar," who learned his craft illuminating manuscripts) began the series in 1447 and Luca Signorelli completed the works that have come to be considered his masterpiece in 1504. Both artists appear in a magnificent panel of the "Sermon of the Antichrist," in which the devil coaxes a Christ impostor to lure the faithful to damnation. Signorelli looks handsome and proud, with his long blonde hair, and he gets a bit of revenge on the mistress who had jilted him, portraying her as the worried recipient of funds from a moneylender (or, according to some interpretations, she's a prostitute being paid for her services).

To the right of the altar is "The Entrance to Hell and The Damned in Hell," in which devils torment their victims, a man raises his fists to curse God as he sees Charon rowing across the Styx for him, and bodies writhe and twist for eternity. Signorelli gets his revenge again in his depiction of a winged devil leering toward a terrified blonde on his back—the ex-mistress, of course. Should a bit of relief be in order after all this misery, you need only look at the "Elect in Heaven," where those who have been saved look quite content, even smug, in their assurance of eternal salvation.

Piazza del Duomo. ✆ **0763-341-167.** www.museomodo.it. Admission 3€ including Cappella di San Brizio, free for children 10 and under. Apr–Oct Mon–Sat 9:30am–7pm, Sun 1–5:30pm (to 6:30pm July–Sept); Nov–Mar Mon–Sat 9:30am–1pm and 2:30–5pm (Sun to 5:30pm).

Grotte della Rupe (Etruscan Orvieto Underground) ★★ HISTORIC

SITE   More than 1,200 artificial and natural caverns have been found in the *pozzolana* (a volcanic stone powdered to make cement mix) and tufa rock upon which Orvieto rests. Guided tours take in just two, 15m (45 ft.) below Santa Chiara convent, reached by a steep climb up and down 55 steps, along a narrow rock-hewn passage. The caverns have variously been used as Etruscan houses, water wells, ceramic ovens, pigeon coops, quarries and cold storage (the temperature is a constant 58°F/14°C). Residents took shelter in them during World War II Allied bombings, but most unwisely—a direct hit would have annihilated the soft rock.

To look at Orvieto's tufa foundations from the outside, take a hike along the rupe, a path that encircles the base of the cliff. A landmark along the way is the Necropoli Etrusca di Crocifisso del Tufo (Etruscan Necropolis), where tombs are laid in a street-like grid in subterranean caverns (3€, daily 8:30am–5:30pm). The tourist office can supply a map, Anello delle Rupe.

Grotte della Rupe: Piazza Duomo 23 (next to the tourist info office; daily 10:30am–5:30pm). ✆ **0763-344-891.** www.orvietounderground.it. Admission (by guided tour only, 45 min.–1 hr.) 6€ adults, 5€ students and seniors. Tours daily at 11am and 12:15, 3, 4, and 5:15pm (other times can be arranged); tours only Sat–Sun in Feb. English tours usually at 11:15am, but check in advance.

Pozzo di San Patrizio (St. Patrick's Well) ★ HISTORIC SITE   Orvieto's

position atop a rocky outcropping made it a perfect redoubt in time of siege, easy to defend but with one big drawback—a lack of water. When Pope Clement VII decided to hole up in Orvieto in 1527 to avoid turbulence in Rome, he hired Antonio Sangallo the Younger to dig a new well. Sangallo's design was unique: He dug a shaft 175 feet deep and 45 feet wide, accessible via a pair of wide spiral staircases that form a double helix and are lit by 72 internal windows. Mule-drawn carts could descend on one ramp and come back up the other without colliding. You can climb down, too, though it's a trek up and down 496 steps, and there's nothing to see at the bottom but, well, a well. A few steps up and down will introduce you to the concept, and give you time to contemplate the name. It's a reference to St. Patrick's Purgatory, a pilgrimage site in Ireland where Christ allegedly showed St. Patrick a cave and told him it was an entrance to hell.

Viale San Gallo (near the funicular stop on Piazza Cahen). ✆ **0763-343-768.** Admission 5€ adults, 3.50€ students. May–Aug daily 9am–7:45pm; Mar–Apr and Sept–Oct daily 9am–6:45pm; Nov–Feb daily 10am–4:45pm.

Orvieto's Liquid Gold

The plains and low hills around Orvieto grow the grapes—*verdello, grechetto,* and Tuscan varietals *trebbiano* and *malvasia*—that go into one of Italy's great wines, a pale straw-colored DOC white called simply Orvieto Classico. The Romans built a special port on the Tiber below town just to ensure a steady supply of the delicious wine to the capital. A well-rounded and judiciously juicy white (often with a hint of crushed almonds), it goes great with lunch. Most Orvieto Classico you'll run across is secco (dry), but you can also find bottles of the more traditional abboccato (semidry/semisweet), amabile (medium sweet), and dolce (sweet) varieties. To visit a vineyard, pick up a copy of the Strada dei Vini brochure at the tourist office; it lists the wineries along with the hours of tours and contact numbers.

Museo Claudio Faina e Civico ★ MUSEUM   A palace next to the cathedral houses what began as private collection in 1864. Interestingly, some of the most stunning pieces are not Etruscan at all, but Greek—Attic black-figure (6th-c.-B.C.) and red-figure (5th-c.-B.C.) vases and amphorae from Athenian workshops (including some by Greek master Exekias from 540 B.C.) that were bought by discriminating Etruscan collectors. You'll see the resemblance to Etruscan black *bucchero* ware from the 6th and the 5th century B.C.

Piazza del Duomo 29. ℂ **0763-341-511** or 0763-341-216. www.museofaina.it. Admission 4.50€ adults; 3€ ages 7–12, seniors 65 and over, and families of 4 or more. Apr–Sept daily 9:30am–6pm; Oct–Mar daily 10am–5pm (closed Mon Nov–Mar).

PLANNING YOUR TRIP TO FLORENCE & TUSCANY

T his chapter provides a variety of planning tools, including information on how to get there, how to get around, and the inside track on local resources.

If you do your homework on special events, pick the right transport options, and pack for the climate, preparing for a trip to Florence and Tuscany should be uncomplicated. See also "When to Go," p. 22.

9

GETTING THERE
By Plane
If you're flying direct to Italy across an ocean, you'll most likely land at Rome's **Leonardo da Vinci–Fiumicino Airport** (FCO; www.adr.it/fiumicino), 40km (25 miles) from the center, or **Milan Malpensa** (MXP; www.milanomalpensa-airport.com), 45km (28 miles) northwest of central Milan. Rome's much smaller **Ciampino Airport** (CIA; www.adr.it/ciampino) serves low-cost airlines connecting with European cities and other destinations in Italy. It's the same story with Milan's **Linate Airport** (LIN; www.milanolinate-airport.com). For information on getting to Tuscany from Rome or Milan, see "Getting Around," below.

FLYING TO FLORENCE, PISA, OR PERUGIA
Carriers in Europe fly direct to several small Italian cities, including 3 within the regions of Tuscany and neighboring Umbria. Florence's major airport is **Amerigo Vespucci** (FLR; www.aeroporto.firenze.it), in the suburb of Peretola, 5km (3 miles) west of central Florence. It's partly a domestic airport—**Alitalia** (www.alitalia.it) connects daily with Rome and **Volotea** (www.volotea.com) with Sicily. **CityJet** (www.cityjet.com) flies several days a week to London City Airport. **Vueling** (www.vueling.com) also flies direct from London's Gatwick Airport, Madrid, and Barcelona; **Lufthansa** (www.lufthansa.com) connects daily to Frankfurt.

To reach the center of Florence, take the half-hourly "Vola in bus" service (6€) operated by **ATAF** (℃ **800-424500;** www.ataf.net). It terminates next to Santa Maria Novella, the city's main rail station. A **taxi** (℃ **055-4242;** www.socota.it) from the air terminal to any hotel in the center (or vice versa) costs 20€ during the day, 22€ on Sundays and holidays, and 23€ at night (plus 1€ per bag).

For reaching Florence from **Pisa Airport,** see p. 45.

Perugia Airport (PEG; www.airport.umbria.it), in Umbria, serves a limited range of destinations, including a **Ryanair** (www.ryanair.com) connection with London Stansted Airport. Local buses connect the airport directly with central Perugia (3€) and Assisi (3€).

By Train

Florence is fairly well connected to Europe's rail hubs. You can arrive in Milan on direct trains from France—Nice, Paris, and Lyon—by TGV, or from Switzerland, and connect speedily from there to Florence (see "Getting Around," below). Direct trains from central and Eastern Europe arrive at Verona and Venice, where you can change and connect onward to Tuscany.

Thello (www.thello.com) also operates an overnight service connecting Paris with northern Italy. After crossing the Alps in the dead of night, the train calls at Milan, Brescia, Verona, Vicenza, and Padua, before arriving in Venice around 9:30am. For Florence and points south, alight at Milan (around 6am) and switch to Italy's national high-speed rail lines; see below. Accommodation on the Thello train is in sleeping cars, as well as in six- and four-berth couchettes. Prices range from 35€ per person for the cheapest fare in a six-berth couchette to a maximum of 275€ for sole occupancy of a sleeping car.

It pays to book any long-distance rail travel in advance, with **Rail Europe** (© 800/622-8600; www.raileurope.com) or **International Rail** (© 0871/231-0790; www.internationalrail.com).

GETTING AROUND
By Car

Much of Tuscany is accessible by public transportation, but to properly explore vineyards, countryside, and smaller hill towns, a car is essential. You'll get the **best rental rate** if you book your car before arriving. Try such websites as **Kayak.com, CarRentals.co.uk,** and **Momondo.com** to compare prices across multiple rental companies and agents. Car rental search companies usually report the lowest rates being available between 6 and 8 weeks ahead of arrival. Rent the smallest car possible, and request a diesel rather than a petrol engine, to minimize fuel costs.

You must be 25 or older to rent from many agencies (although some accept ages 21 and up, at a premium price).

The legalities and contractual obligations of renting a car in Italy (where accident rates are high) are more complicated than those in almost any other country in Europe. You must have nerves of steel, a sense of humor, and a valid driver's license or **International Driver's Permit.** Insurance on all vehicles is compulsory. *Note:* If you're planning to rent a car in Italy during high season, you should **book in advance.** It's not unusual to arrive at the airport in June or July to find that every agent is all out of cars, perhaps for the whole week.

It can sometimes be tricky to get to the *autostrada* (fast highway) or the city center from the airport, so consider renting or bringing a GPS-enabled device or having an offline GPS app, with preloaded Italy maps, on your smartphone.

The going can be slow almost anywhere, especially on Friday afternoons leaving Florence and Sunday nights on the way back into town, and an urban rush hour any day of the week can be epic. Long-distance driving for a day or so either side of the busy *ferragosto* (Aug 15) holiday is to be avoided *at all costs.* See **www.autostrade. it** for live traffic updates and a road-toll calculator.

Autostrada tolls can get expensive, costing approximately 1€ for every 15km (10 miles), which means that it would cost about 4.60€ for a trip from Rome to Lucca. Add in the high price of fuel (averaging over 1.70€ *per liter* at time of writing) plus car rental, and it's often cheaper to take the train, even for two people.

Before leaving home, you can apply for an **International Driving Permit** from the American Automobile Association (www.aaa.com). In Canada, the permit's available from the Canadian Automobile Association (ⓒ **416/221-4300;** www.caa.ca). Technically, you need this permit and your actual driver's license to drive in Italy, though in practice your license itself often suffices. Visitors from within the EU need only take their domestic driver's license.

Italy's equivalent of AAA is the **Automobile Club d'Italia** (**ACI;** www.aci.it). They're the people who respond when you place an emergency call to ⓒ **803-116** (ⓒ 800-116-800 from a non-Italian cellphone) for road breakdowns, though they do charge for this service if you're not a member.

DRIVING RULES Italian drivers aren't maniacs; they only appear to be. Spend any time on a highway and you will have the experience of somebody driving up insanely close from behind while flashing his headlights. Take a deep breath and don't panic: This is the aggressive signal for you to move to the right so he (invariably, it's a "he") can pass, and until you do he will stay mind-bogglingly close. On a two-lane road, the idiot passing someone in the opposing traffic who has swerved into your lane expects you to veer obligingly over into the shoulder so three lanes of traffic can fit—he would do the same for you. Probably. Many Italians seem to think that blinkers are optional, so be aware that the car in front could be getting ready to turn at any moment.

Autostrade are toll highways, denoted by green signs and a number prefaced with an *A,* like the A11 from Lucca to Florence. A few fast highways aren't numbered and are simply called a *raccordo,* a connecting road between two cities (such as Florence–Siena and Florence–Pisa–Livorno).

Strade statali (singular is *strada statale*) are state roads, sometimes without a center divider and two lanes wide (although sometimes they can be a divided four-way highway), indicated by blue signs. Their route numbers are prefaced with an *SS,* as in the SS75 from Perugia to Assisi. On signs, however, these official route numbers are used infrequently. Usually, you'll just see blue signs listing destinations by name with arrows pointing off in the appropriate directions. It's impossible to predict which of all the towns that lie along a road will be the ones chosen to list on a particular sign. Sometimes the sign gives only the first minuscule village that lies past the turnoff. At other times it lists the first major town down that road. Some signs mention only the major city the road eventually leads to, even if it's hundreds of kilometers away. It pays to study the map before coming to an intersection, to carry a GPS device, or to download an offline GPS app for your smartphone. The *strade statali* can be frustratingly slow due to traffic, traffic lights, and the fact that they bisect countless towns: When available, pay for the autostrada.

The **speed limit** on roads in built-up areas around towns and cities is 50kmph (31 mph). On two-lane roads it's 90kmph (56 mph) and on the highway its 130kmph (81 mph). Italians have an astounding disregard for these limits. However, police can ticket you and collect the fine on the spot. The blood-alcohol limit in Italy is .05 percent, often achieved with just two drinks; driving above the limit can result in a fine of up to 6,000€, a driving ban, or imprisonment. The blood-alcohol limit is set at zero for anyone who has held a driver's license for under 3 years.

Safety belts are obligatory in both the front and the back seats; ditto child seats or special restraints for minors under 1.5m (5 ft.) in height—though this latter regulation is often ignored. Drivers may not use a handheld cellphone while driving—yet another law that locals appear to consider optional.

PARKING On streets, **white lines** indicate free public spaces, **blue lines** are pay public spaces, and **yellow lines** mean only residents are allowed to park. Meters don't line the sidewalk; rather, there's one machine on the block where you punch in coins corresponding to how long you want to park. The machine spits out a ticket that you leave on your dashboard.

If you park in an area marked *parcheggio disco orario,* root around in your rental car's glove compartment for a cardboard parking disc (or buy one at a gas station). With this device, you dial up the hour of your arrival and display it on your dashboard. You're allowed *un'ora* (1 hr.) or *due ore* (2 hr.), according to the sign. If you do not have a disk, write your arrival time clearly on a sheet of paper and leave it on the dash.

Parking lots have ticket dispensers, but exit booths are not usually manned. When you return to the lot to depart, first visit the automated payment machine to exchange your ticket for a paid receipt or token. You then use this to get through the exit gate.

ROAD SIGNS A **speed limit** sign is a black number inside a red circle on a white background. The **end of a speed zone** is just black and white, with a black slash through the number. A red circle with a white background, a black arrow pointing down, and a red arrow pointing up means **yield to oncoming traffic,** while a point-down red-and-white triangle means **yield ahead.**

Many city centers are closed to traffic and a simple white circle with a red border, or the words *zona pedonale* or *zona traffico limitato,* denotes a **pedestrian or restricted zone** (you can sometimes drive through to drop off baggage at your hotel); a white arrow on a blue background is used for Italy's many **one-way streets;** a mostly red circle with a horizontal white slash means **do not enter.** Any image in black on a white background surrounded by a red circle means that image is **not allowed** (for instance, if the image is two cars next to each other, it means no passing; a motorcycle means no Harleys permitted; and so on). A circular sign in blue with a red circle-slash means **no parking.**

KEY TUSCAN tourist offices

Arezzo: Palazzo Comunale, Piazza della Libertà (*C* **0575-401-945**)

Chiusi: Via Porsenna 79 (*C* **0578-227-667;** www.prolocochiusi.it)

Colle Val d'Elsa: Via del Castello 33 (*C* **0577-922-791**)

Cortona: Palazzo Casali, Piazza Signorelli 9 (*C* **0575-637-223**)

Florence: Piazza della Stazione 4 (*C* **055-212-245;** www.firenzeturismo.it); Via Cavour 1R (*C* **055-290-832**); Loggia di Bigallo, Piazza del Duomo (at Via dei Calzaiuoli)

Lucca: Palazzo Ducale, Cortile Carrara (*C* **0583-919-931;** www.luccaturismo.it)

Massa Marittima: Via Todini 3–5 (*C* **0566-902-756;** www.altamaremma turismo.it)

Montalcino: Costa del Municipio 1 (*C* **0577-849-331;** www.prolocomon talcino.com)

Montepulciano: Piazza Don Minzoni 1 (*C* **0578-757-341;** www.prolocomonte pulciano.it)

Pienza: Palazzo Vescovile, Corso Il Rossellino 30 (*C* **0578-749-905**)

Pisa: Piazza Vittorio Emanuele II 16 (*C* **050-42-291;** www.pisaunicaterra.it)

Pistoia: Via Roma 1 (at Piazza del Duomo; *C* **0573-374-401;** www.turismo.pistoia.it)

Prato: Piazza Buonamici 7 (*C* **0574-24-112;** www.pratoturismo.it)

San Gimignano: Piazza del Duomo 1 (*C* **0577-940-008;** www.sangimignano.com)

Sansepolcro: Via Matteotti (*C* **0575-740-536;** www.lavalledipiero.it)

Siena: Santa Maria della Scala, Piazza del Duomo 1 (*C* **0577-280-551;** www.terresiena.it)

Volterra: Piazza dei Priori 19–20 (*C* **0588-87-257;** www.volterratur.it)

Gasoline (gas or petrol), *benzina,* can be found in pull-in gas stations along major roads and on the outskirts of town, as well as in 24-hour stations along the autostrada. Almost all stations are closed for the *riposo* and on Sundays (except for those on the autostrada), but the majority have a machine that accepts cash. Unleaded gas is *senza piombo.* Diesel is *gasolio.*

By Train

The train is an excellent option if you're looking to visit Tuscan cities and large towns without the hassle of driving, or just to get to Florence from Milan or Rome. The vast majority of rail lines are run by the state-owned **Ferrovie dello Stato,** or **FS** (*C* **89-20-21;** www.trenitalia.com). A private operator, **Italo** (*C* **06-07-08;** www.italotreno.it) operates on the high-speed line that connects Florence with Milan and Bologna (to the north) and Rome and Naples (south).

The travel times and the prices of the tickets vary considerably depending on what type of train you are traveling on. The country's principal north–south, high-speed line links Turin, Milan, and Bologna to Florence, then runs on through Rome and Naples, to Salerno. Milan to Florence, for example, takes around 1½ hours on the quick train, and costs 50€—though you can find tickets as low as 20€ if you buy ahead and travel in off-peak hours. If you want to bag the cheapest fares on high-speed trains, aim to book around 100 to 120 days before your travel dates.

The speed, cleanliness, and overall quality of trains vary. High-speed trains usually have four classes: Standard, Premium, Business, and Executive on the state railway;

Smart, Smart XL, First, and Club on Italo. The cheapest of these, on both operators, is perfectly comfortable, even on long legs of a journey. These are Italy's premium trains.

The **Frecciarossa,** along with Italo's rival high-speed service, is the fastest of the fast (Italy's bullet train). These operate on the Turin–Milan–Bologna–Florence–Rome–Naples line, and run up to 300kmph (186 mph). The **Frecciargento** uses similar hardware, but is a bit slower; it links Naples and Rome, via Florence, with Verona and Venice at speeds of up to 250kmph (155 mph). Speed and cleanliness come at a price, with tickets for these high-speed trains usually costing around three times a slower regional train. On high-speed services, you **must make a seat reservation** when you buy a ticket. If you are traveling with a rail pass (see below), you must pay a 10€ supplementary fee to ride them and reserve a seat.

Within Tuscany itself, slower *Regionale* **(R)** and *Regionale Veloce* **(RV)** trains do all the work. These services make many stops and can sometimes be on the grimy side of things, but they are also very cheap: A Florence–Arezzo second-class ticket will set you back only 7.90€. Old *Regionale* rolling stock is slowly being replaced, and not before time. On these local trains, *prima* (first class) is usually only a shade better than *seconda* (second class), and the only real benefits of first class come if the train is overcrowded and there are seats available only in first class. Several *Regionale* trains don't even have a first-class section, however. There is no benefit to booking *Regionale* train tickets ahead of travel—prices are fixed.

Overcrowding is often a problem on standard services (that is, not the prebookable high-speed trains) on Friday evenings, weekends, and holidays, especially in and out of big cities, or just after a strike. In summer, the crowding escalates, and any train going toward a beach in August bulges like an overstuffed sausage. The Florence–Viareggio link—which passes Lucca and Pistoia en route—is one.

When buying a **regular ticket,** ask for either *andata* (one-way) or *andata e ritorno* (round-trip). If the train you are targeting on the departures board is marked with an IC prefix, ask for the ticket *con supplemento rapido* (with speed supplement) to avoid on-train penalty charges—though IC trains are increasingly rare. The best way to avoid presenting yourself on the train with the wrong ticket is to tell the person at the ticket window exactly what train you are going to take, for example, "the 11:30am train for Pisa."

If you don't have a ticket with a reservation for a particular seat on a specific train, then you must **validate you ticket by stamping it in the little yellow box** on the platform before boarding the train. If you board a train without the correct ticket, or without having validated your ticket, you'll have to pay a hefty fine on top of the ticket or supplement, which the conductor will sell you. If you knowingly board a train without a ticket or realize once onboard that you have the wrong type of ticket, your best bet is to search out the conductor who is likely to be more forgiving because you found him and made it clear you weren't trying to ride for free.

Schedules for all trains leaving a given station are printed on yellow posters tacked up on the station wall (a similar white poster lists all the arrivals). These are good for getting general information, but keep your eye on the electronic boards and television screens that are updated with delays and track *(binario)* changes. You can also get official schedules (and more train information, also in English) and buy tickets at **www.trenitalia.com**. (Or download Trenitalia's ProntoTreno app.)

In Florence especially, ticketing lines can be dreadfully long. There is a solution though: **automatic ticket machines.** They are easy to navigate, allow you to follow instructions in English, accept cash and credit cards, and can save your life by cutting down on the stress that comes with waiting on an interminably slow line. *Note:* You can't buy international tickets at automatic machines.

Stations tend to be well run, with luggage storage facilities at all but the smallest and usually a good bar attached that serves surprisingly palatable food, and of course a decent cup of coffee. If you pull into a dinky town with a shed-size station, find the nearest bar or *tabacchi,* and the man behind the counter will most likely sell tickets.

SPECIAL PASSES & DISCOUNTS   To buy the **Eurail Italy Pass,** available only outside Italy and priced in U.S. dollars, contact **Rail Europe** (www.raileurope.com). You have 2 months in which to use the train a set number of days; the base number of days is 3, and you can add up to 7 more. For adults, the first-class pass costs $307, second class is $250. Additional days cost $30 to $35 more for first class, roughly $25 for second class. For youth tickets (25 and under), a 3-day pass is $204 and additional days about $20 each. Saver passes are available for groups of two to five people traveling together at all times, and amount to a savings of about 15 percent on individual tickets.

There are also Italy–Greece, Italy–Spain, and Italy–France rail pass combinations. However, if your travels will mostly be within Tuscany—with perhaps a return trip to an air hub in Milan or Rome tacked on—a rail pass probably does not represent good value. Buy individual tickets.

If you're **25 and under,** you can buy a 40€ **Carta Verde (Green Card)** at any Italian train station. This gets you a 10 percent discount for non-prebooked domestic trips and 25 percent off international connections for 1 year. Present it each time you buy a ticket. An even better deal is available for anyone **61 and over** with the **Carta d'Argento (Silver Card):** 15 percent off domestic and 25 percent off international rail tickets, for 30€ (the Carta d'Argento is free for those 76 and over). Children 11 and under ride half-price while kids 3 and under don't pay, although they also do not have the right to their own seat.

By Bus

Although trains are usually quicker and easier, you can get just about anywhere on a network of local, provincial, and regional bus lines. Keep in mind that in smaller towns, buses exist mainly to shuttle workers and schoolchildren, so the most runs are on weekdays, early in the morning, and usually again in midafternoon.

In a city, the **bus station** is usually near the main train station. A small town's **bus stop** is usually either in the main square, on the edge of town, or the bend in the road just outside the main town gate. You should always try to find the local ticket vendor—if there's no office, it's invariably the nearest newsstand or *tabacchi* (signaled by a sign with a white T), or occasionally a bar—but you can usually also buy tickets on the bus. You can sometimes flag down a bus as it passes on a country road, but try to find an official stop (a small sign tacked onto a pole). Tell the driver where you're going and ask him courteously if he'll let you know when you need to get off. When he says, *"È la prossima fermata,"* that means yours is the next stop. *"Posso scendere?"* (*Poh*-so *shen*-dair-ay?) is "Can I get off?"

A number of regional bus companies provide the best links between rail hubs like Florence or Pisa, and the smaller towns of Tuscany. Among the most useful are: **CPT** (Pisa–Volterra link; ✆ **050-884-111;** www.cpt.pisa.it); **LFI** (Arezzo; ✆ **0575-39-881;** www.lfi.it); **ACV** (Florence–Chianti link; ✆ **055-47-821;** www.acvbus.it); **Siena Mobilità** (Florence–Siena and around; ✆ **0577-204-111;** www.sienamobilita.it); and **VaiBus** (Lucca and around; www.vaibus.it). Most have downloadable timetables online. Tickets are usually sold at newsstands, small general stores, and the bus travel office.

[FastFACTS] FLORENCE & TUSCANY

Area Codes The **country code** for Italy is **39.** Former **city codes** (for example, Florence 055, Siena 0577) are incorporated into the numbers themselves. Therefore, you must dial the entire number, *including the initial zero,* when calling from *anywhere* outside or inside Italy and even within the same town. For example, to call Florence from the United States, you must dial **011-39-055,** then the local phone number. Phone numbers in Italy can range anywhere from 5 to 12 digits in length.

Business Hours, Banks & ATMs General open hours for **stores, offices,** and **churches** are from 9:30am to noon or 1pm and again from 3 or 3:30pm to 7:30 or 8pm. The early afternoon shutdown is the *riposo,* the Italian siesta (in the downtown area of Florence and Siena, stores don't close for the *riposo*). Outside Florence and Siena, most stores close all day Sunday and many also on Monday (morning only or all day). Some services and business offices are open to the public only in the morning.

Traditionally, **state museums** are closed Mondays. Most of the large museums stay open all day long otherwise, though some close for

riposo or are only open in the morning (9am–2pm is popular). Some churches open earlier in the morning, and the largest often stay open all day, though the last hour or so of opening is usually take up with a service, and tourist visits are frowned upon. **Banks** tend to be open Monday through Friday 8:30am to 1:30pm and 2:45 to 4:15pm.

The easiest and best way to get cash away from home is from an ATM (automated teller machine), referred to in Italy as a *bancomat.* ATMs are very prevalent in Tuscan cities and while every small town usually has one, it's good practice to fuel up on cash before traveling to villages or rural areas.

Be sure to confirm with your bank that your card is valid for international withdrawal and that you have a four-digit PIN. (Some ATMs in Italy will not accept any other number of digits.) Also, be sure you know your daily withdrawal limit before you depart. **Note:** Many banks impose a fee every time you use a card at another bank's ATM, and that fee can be higher for international transactions (up to $5 or more) than for domestic ones. In addition, the bank from which you withdraw cash may charge

its own fee, although this is not common practice in Italy.

If at the ATM you get an on-screen message saying your card isn't valid for international transactions, don't panic: It's most likely the bank just can't make the phone connection to check it (occasionally this can be a citywide epidemic). Try another ATM or another town.

Customs Foreign visitors can bring along most items for personal use duty-free, including merchandise up to $800.

Disabled Travelers A few of the top museums and churches have installed ramps at their entrances, and several hotels have converted first-floor rooms into accessible units—**Il Guelfo Bianco** (p. 55), in Florence, for example, has 2 fully equipped disabled rooms. Other than that, you may not find parts of Tuscany easy to tackle. Builders in the Middle Ages and the Renaissance didn't have wheelchairs or mobility impairments in mind when they built narrow doorways and spiral staircases, and preservation laws keep Italians from being able to do much about this in some areas.

Some buses and trains can cause problems as well,

with high, narrow doors and steep steps at entrances—though the situation on public transportation is improving. For those with disabilities who can make it on to buses and trains, there are usually seats reserved for them and Italians are quick to give up their space for somebody who looks like they need it more than them.

Accessible Italy (✆ **011-378-0549-941-111** from U.S.; www.accessibleitaly. com) provides travelers with info about accessible tourist sites and places to rent wheelchairs, and also sells organized "Accessible Tours" around Italy. **Trenitalia** has a special number that disabled travelers should call for assistance on the rail network: ✆ **199-303-060.**

Doctors & Hospitals

See individual chapters for details of emergency rooms and walk-in medical services.

Drinking Laws

People of any age can legally consume alcohol in Italy, but a person must be 16 years old in order to be served alcohol in a restaurant or a bar. Noise is the primary concern to city officials, and so bars generally close around 2am, though alcohol is commonly served in clubs after that. Supermarkets carry beer, wine, and spirits.

Electricity

Italy operates on a 220-volt AC (50 cycles) system, as opposed to the U.S. 110-volt AC (60 cycles) system. You'll need a simple adapter plug to

make the American flat pegs fit the Italian round holes and, unless your appliance is dual-voltage (as some hair dryers, travel irons, and almost all laptops are), an electrical currency converter. You can pick up the hardware at electronics stores, travel specialty stores, luggage shops, and airports.

Embassies & Consulates

The **U.S. Embassy** is in Rome at Via Vittorio Veneto 121 (✆ **06-46-741;** http://italy.usembassy.gov). The **U.S. consulate** in Florence—for passport and consular services but not visas—is at Lungarno Vespucci 38 (✆ **055-266-951;** http://florence.usconsulate. gov), open to emergency drop-ins Monday through Friday from 9am to 12:30pm. Afternoons and for nonemergencies, the consulate is open by appointment only; call ahead or book online.

The **U.K. Embassy** is in Rome at Via XX Settembre 80a (✆ **06-4220-2431;** http://ukinitaly.fco.gov.uk), open Monday and Friday from 9am to noon and 2 to 3pm. There is no longer a U.K. consulate in Florence.

Of English-speaking countries, only the U.S. has a consulate in Florence. Citizens of other countries must go to Rome for help: The **Canadian Embassy** in Rome is at Via Zara 30 (✆ **06-85444-3937;** www. italy.gc.ca). **Australia**'s Rome embassy is at Via Bosio 5 (✆ **06-852-721;** www.italy.embassy.gov.au).

The consular section is open Monday through Friday from 9am to 5pm. **New Zealand**'s Rome representation is at Via Clitunno 44 (✆ **06-853-7501;** www. nzembassy.com/italy), open Monday through Friday from 8:30am to 12:30pm and 1:30 to 5pm. The embassy for **Ireland** is at Villa Spada, Via Giacomo Medici, Rome (✆ **06-585-2381;** www.ambasciata-irlanda.it), open weekdays 10am to 12:30pm and 3 to 4:30pm.

Emergencies

The best number to call in Italy (and the rest of Europe) with a **general emergency** is ✆ **112,** which connects you to the *carabinieri* who will transfer your call as needed. For the **police,** dial ✆ **113;** for a **medical emergency** and to call an **ambulance,** the number is ✆ **118;** for the **fire department,** call ✆ **115.** If your car breaks down, dial ✆ **116** for **roadside aid** courtesy of the Automotive Club of Italy. All are free calls, but roadside assistance is a paid-for service for nonmembers.

Family Travel

Italy is a family-oriented society. A crying baby at a dinner table is greeted with a knowing smile rather than a stern look. Children almost always receive discounts, and maybe a special treat from the waiter, but the availability of such accoutrements as child seats for cars and dinner tables is more the exception than the norm. (The former, however, is a legal requirement: Be sure to ask a rental car company to provide them.) Restaurants will almost always do a *"mezza porzione"* (half-portion) of a dish if physically possible.

There are plenty of parks, offbeat museums, markets, ice-cream parlors, and vibrant streetlife to amuse even the youngest children. In Florence, for example, see "Especially for Kids," p. 95. Child discounts apply on public transportation, and at public and private museums. **Prénatal** (www. prenatal.it) is the premier toddler and baby chain store in Italy.

Health There are no special health risks you'll encounter in Italy. The country's public health care system is generally well regarded. Italy offers universal health care to its citizens and those of other European Union countries (UK nationals should remember to carry an EHIC; see **www. nhs.uk/ehic**). Others should be prepared to pay medical bills upfront. Before leaving home, find out what medical services your **health insurance** covers. *Note:* Even if you don't have insurance, you will always be treated in an emergency room.

Pharmacies offer essentially the same range of generic drugs available in the United States and internationally. Pharmacies are ubiquitous (look for the green cross) and serve almost like miniclinics, where pharmacists diagnose and treat minor ailments, like flu symptoms and general aches and pains, with

over-the-counter drugs. Carry the generic name of any prescription medicines, in case a local pharmacist is unfamiliar with the brand name. Pharmacies in cities take turns doing the night shift; normally there is a list posted at the entrance of each pharmacy informing customers which pharmacy is open each night of the week.

Insurance Italy may be one of the safer places you can travel in the world, but accidents and setbacks can and do happen, from lost luggage to car crashes. For information on traveler's insurance, trip cancellation insurance, and medical insurance while traveling, please visit **www. frommers.com/tips**.

Internet Access Internet cafes are in healthy supply in most Italian cities, though don't expect to find them in every small town. If you're traveling with your own computer or smartphone, you'll find wireless access in most hotels, but if this is key for your stay make sure you ask before booking and certainly don't expect to find a connection in every rural *agriturismo* (disconnecting from the 21st c. is part of their appeal, after all). In a pinch, hostels, local libraries, and some bars will have some sort of terminal for access. Several spots around Florence are covered with free Wi-Fi access provided by the local administration, but at these and any other Wi-Fi spots around Italy,

anti-terrorism laws make it obligatory to register for an access code before you can log on. Take your passport or other photo I.D. when you go looking for an Internet point. Florence's discount **Firenze Card** (p. 71) comes with 72 hours of free city Wi-Fi included.

Internet Train (www. internettrain.it) is a national franchise chain with Internet points in Florence, Pisa, and elsewhere in Italy.

LGBT Travelers Italy as a whole is gay-friendly. Homosexuality is legal, and the age of consent is 16. Italians are generally more affectionate and physical than North Americans in all their friendships, and even straight men occasionally walk down the street with their arms around each other—however, kissing anywhere other than on the cheeks at greetings and goodbyes will draw attention. As you might expect, smaller towns tend to be less permissive than cities, and beach resorts such as Viareggio.

Italy's national associations and support networks for gays and lesbians are **ARCI-Gay and ArciLesbica.** The national websites are **www.arcigay.it** and **www. arcilesbica.it**, and most cities have a local office. See **www.arcigay.it/comitati** for a searchable directory.

Mail & Postage Sending a postcard or letter up to 20 grams, or a little less than an ounce, costs .85€ to other European countries, 2€ to North America, and a whopping 2.50€ to Australia and New Zealand. Full details on Italy's postal services are available at **www.poste.it** (some in English).

Mobile Phones GSM

(Global System for Mobile Communications) is a cellphone technology used by most of the world's countries that makes it possible to turn on a phone with a contract based in Australia, Ireland, the U.K., Pakistan, or almost every other corner of the world and have it work in Italy without missing a beat. (In the U.S., service providers like Sprint and Verizon use a different technology—CDMA—and phones on those networks won't work in Italy unless they also have GSM compatibility.)

Also if you are coming from the U.S. or Canada, you may need a multiband phone. All travelers should activate "international roaming" on their account, so check with your home service provider before leaving.

But—and it's a *big* but—using roaming can be very expensive, especially if you access the Internet on your phone. Much cheaper, once you arrive, is to buy an Italian SIM card (the fingernail-size removable plastic card found in all GSM phones that is encoded with your phone number). This is not difficult, and is an especially good idea if you will be in Italy for more than a week. You can **buy a SIM card** at one of the many cellphone shops you will pass in every city. The main service providers are TIM, Vodafone, Wind, and 3 *(Tre)*. If you have an Italian SIM card in your phone, local calls may be as low as .10€ per minute, and incoming calls are free. Prepaid data packages are available for each, as are micro- and nano-SIMs, as well as prepaid deals for iPads and other tablets. If you need 4G data speeds, you will pay a little more. Not every network allows **tethering**—be sure to ask if you need it. Deals on each

network change regularly; for the latest see the website of one of this guide's authors: **www.donaldstrachan.com/dataroamingitaly**. **Note:** Contract cellphones are often "locked" and will only work with a SIM card provided by the service provider back home, so check to see that you have an unlocked phone.

Buying a phone is another option, and you shouldn't have too much trouble finding one for about 30€. Use it, then recycle it or eBay it when you get home. It will save you a fortune versus alternatives such as roaming or using hotel room telephones.

Money & Costs
Frommer's lists exact prices in the local currency. The currency conversions quoted below were correct at press time. However, rates fluctuate, so before departing, consult a currency exchange website, such as **www.oanda.com/currency/converter**, to check up-to-the-minute rates.

THE VALUE OF THE EURO VS. OTHER POPULAR CURRENCIES

€	Aus$	Can$	NZ$	UK£	US$
1	A$1.49	C$1.53	NZ$1.61	£0.82	$1.38

Like many European countries, Italy uses the euro as its currency. Euro coins are issued in denominations of .01€, .02€, .05€, .10€, .20€, and .50€, as well as 1€ and 2€; bills come in denominations of 5€, 10€, 20€, 50€, 100€, 200€, and 500€.

The aggressive evolution of international computerized banking and consolidated ATM networks has led to the triumph of plastic throughout the Italian peninsula—even if cold cash is still the most trusted currency, especially in small towns and mom-and-pop

joints, where credit cards may not be accepted. Traveler's checks have gone the way of the Stegosaurus.

You'll get the best rate if you **exchange money** at a bank or one of its ATMs. The rates at "Cambio/change/wechsel" exchange booths are invariably less favorable but still better than what you'd get exchanging money at a hotel or shop (a last-resort tactic only). The bill-to-bill changers have largely disappeared from touristy places, and anyway existed solely to rip you off.

WHAT THINGS COST IN FLORENCE (HOTEL PRICES ARE HIGH SEASON)

Bus ticket (from/to anywhere in the city)	1.20€
Double room at Continentale (expensive)	400.00€
Double room at Antica Dimora Johlea (moderate)	180.00€
Double room at Locanda Orchidea (inexpensive)	75.00€
Continental breakfast (cappuccino and croissant standing at a bar)	2.30€
Dinner for one, with wine, at Ora d'Aria (expensive)	80.00€
Dinner for one, with wine, at Osteria Pastella (moderate)	35.00€
Dinner for one, with wine, at GustaPizza (inexpensive)	12.00€
Small gelato at Gelateria della Passera	2€
Glass of wine at a bar	2.50€–7.00€
Coca-Cola (standing/sitting in a bar)	2.50€/4.50€
Cup of espresso (standing/sitting in a bar)	1.00€/2.50€
Admission to the Uffizi	6.50€–11.00€

Credit cards are widely accepted in urban Italy, especially in hotels and large establishments. However, it is always a good idea to carry some cash, as small businesses may accept only cash or may claim that their credit card machine is broken to avoid paying fees to the card companies.

Visa and **MasterCard** are almost universally accepted. Some businesses also take **American Express,** especially at the higher end and in Florence. **Diners Club** tends not to be accepted at most places in Tuscany.

Finally, be sure to let your bank know that you will be traveling abroad to avoid having your card blocked after a few days of big purchases far from home. **Note:** Many banks assess a 1 to 3 percent "transaction fee" on **all** charges you incur abroad (whether you're using the local currency or your native currency).

Newspapers & Magazines The "International New York Times" and "USA Today" are available at many newsstands in the cities, and sometimes even in smaller towns. You can find the "Wall Street Journal Europe," European editions of "Time," the "Economist," and most of the major European newspapers and magazines at the larger kiosks in Florence.

Police For emergencies, call ℂ **112** or ℂ **113.** Italy has several different police forces, but there are only two you'll most likely ever need to deal with. The first is the Carabinieri (ℂ **112**), who normally only concern themselves with serious crimes but will point you in the right direction. The Polizia (ℂ **113**), whose city headquarters is called the questura, is the place to go for help with lost and stolen property or petty crimes.

Safety Italy is a remarkably safe country. The worst threats you'll likely face are the pickpockets who sometimes frequent touristy areas and public buses; keep your hands on your camera at all times and your valuables in an under-the-clothes money belt or inside zip-pocket. Don't leave anything valuable in a rental car overnight, and leave nothing visible in it at any time. If you are robbed, you can fill out paperwork at the nearest police station (questura), but this is mostly for insurance purposes and perhaps to get a new passport issued—don't expect them to spend any resources hunting down the perpetrator.

In general, avoid public parks at night. The areas around rail stations are sometimes unsavory, but rarely worse than that. Otherwise, there's a real sense of personal security for travelers in Tuscany.

Senior Travel   Seniors and older people are treated with a great deal of respect and deference, but there are few specific programs, associations, or concessions made for them. The one exception is on admission prices for museums and sights, where those ages 60 or 65 and older will often get in at a reduced rate or even free: **Carry I.D.** There are also special train passes and reductions on bus tickets and the like in many towns (see "Getting Around," p. 227). As a senior in Italy, you're un anziano or if you're a woman, un'anziana, "elderly"—it's a term of respect, and you should let people know you're one if you think a discount may be in order.

Smoking   Smoking has been eradicated from restaurants, bars, and most hotels. Many smokers

remain, and they tend to take outside tables at bars and restaurants. If you're keen for an al fresco table, you are essentially choosing a seat in the smoking section, and requesting that your neighbor not smoke may not be politely received.

Student Travelers   An **International Student Identity Card (ISIC)** qualifies students for savings on rail passes, plane tickets, entrance fees, and more. The card is valid for 1 year. You can apply for the card online at **www.myisic.com** or in person at **STA Travel** (© **800/781-4040** in North America; www.statravel.com). If you're no longer a student but are still 26 and under, you can get an **International Youth Travel Card (IYTC)** and an **International Teacher Identity Card (ITIC)** from the same agency, which entitles you to some discounts.

In Italy, students will find many university cities that offer ample student discounts and inexpensive youth hostels.

Taxes   There's no sales tax added onto the price tag of purchases in Italy, but there is a 22 percent value-added tax (in Italy: IVA) automatically included in just about everything except basic foodstuffs like milk and bread. Entertainment, transport, hotels, and dining are among a group of goods taxed at a lower rate of 10 percent. For major purchases, you can get IVA refunded. Several cities also

recently introduced an **accommodation tax.** For example, in Florence, you will be charged 1€ per person per night per government-star rating of the hotel, up to a maximum of 10 nights. Children 9 and under are exempt. Siena other localities also operate taxes. This tax is not usually included in any published room rate. Each operates slightly differently; see destination chapters for details.

Tipping   In **hotels,** a service charge is usually included in your bill. In family-run operations, additional tips are unnecessary and sometimes considered rude. In fancier places with a hired staff, however, you may want to pay the bellhop or porter 1€ per bag. In **restaurants,** a 1€ to 3€ per person "cover charge" is automatically added to the bill and occasionally in tourist-oriented places, another 10 to 15 percent is tacked on (this will be noted on the menu somewhere; to be sure you can ask, è incluso il servizio?). It is not necessary to leave any extra money on the table, though it is not uncommon to leave up to 5€, especially for good service. Locals generally leave nothing. At **bars and cafes,** you can leave something very small on the counter for the barman (maybe 1€ if you have had several drinks), though it is not expected; there is no need to leave anything extra if you sit at a table, as they are probably already charging you double or triple the price you'd have paid standing at the bar. It is not necessary to tip **taxi** drivers, though it is common to round up the bill to the nearest euro or two.

Toilets   Aside from train stations, where they cost about .50€ to use, and gas/petrol stations, where they are free (with perhaps a basket seeking donations), public toilets are few and far between. Standard procedure is to enter a cafe, make sure the bathroom is not *fuori servizio* (out of order), and then order a cup of coffee before bolting to the facilities. It is advisable to always make use of the facilities in the hotel, restaurant, museum, or bar before a long walk around town.

USEFUL ITALIAN PHRASES

BASIC VOCABULARY

English	Italian	Pronunciation
Thank you	Grazie	*graht-tzee-yey*
You're welcome	Prego	**prey-go**
Please	Per favore	**pehr** fah-**vohr**-eh
Yes	Si	**see**
No	No	**noh**
Good morning or Good day	Buongiorno	**bwohn**-*djor*-noh
Good evening	Buona sera	*bwohn*-ah **say**-rah
Good night	Buona notte	*bwohn*-ah **noht**-tay
It's a pleasure to meet you.	Piacere di conoscerla.	pyah-**cheh**-reh dee *koh*-nohshehr-lah
My name is ____.	Mi chiamo ____.	mee *kyah*-moh
And yours?	E lei?	**eh lay**
Do you speak English?	Parla inglese?	*pahr*-lah een-*gleh*-seh
How are you?	Come sta?	*koh*-may **stah**
Very well	Molto bene	*mohl*-toh *behn*-ney
Goodbye	Arrivederci	ahr-ree-vah-*dehr*-chee
Excuse me (to get attention)	Scusi	*skoo*-zee
Excuse me (to get past someone)	Permesso	pehr-*mehs*-soh

GETTING AROUND

English	Italian	Pronunciation
Where is . . . ?	Dovè . . . ?	*doh*-vey
the station	la stazione	lah stat-tzee-*oh*-neh
a hotel	un albergo	oon ahl-*behr*-goh
a restaurant	un ristorante	oon reest-ohr-*ahnt*-eh
the bathroom	il bagno	eel *bahn*-nyoh
I am looking for . . .	Cerco . . .	*chehr*-koh
the check-in counter	il check-in	eel check-in
the ticket counter	la biglietteria	lah beel-lyeht-teh-ree-ah

English	Italian	Pronunciation
arrivals	l'area arrivi	*lah*-reh-ah ahr-*ree*-vee
departures	l'area partenze	*lah*-reh-ah pahr-*tehn*-tseh
gate number	l'uscita numero	loo-*shee*-tah *noo*-meh-roh
the men's restroom	la toilette uomini	lah twa-*leht woh*-mee-nee
the women's restroom	la toilette donne	lah twa-*leht dohn*-neh
the police station	la stazione di polizia	lah stah-*tsyoh*-neh dee poh-lee-*tsee*-ah
a security guard	una guardia di sicurezza	*ooh*-nah *gwahr*-dyah dee see-koo-*ret*-sah
the smoking area	l'area fumatori	*lah*-reh-ah foo-mah-*toh*-ree
the information booth	l'ufficio informazioni	loof-*fee*-choh een-*fohr*-mah-*tsyoh*-nee
a public telephone	un telefono pubblico	oon teh-*leh*-foh-noh *poob*-blee-koh
an ATM/cashpoint	un bancomat	oon *bahn*-koh-maht
baggage claim	il ritiro bagagli	eel ree-*tee*-roh bah-*gahl*-lyee
a luggage cart	un carrello portabagagli	oon kahr-*rehl*-loh *pohr*-tah-bah-*gahl*-lyee
a cafe	un caffè	oon kahf-*feh*
a restaurant	un ristorante	oon ree-stoh-*rahn*-teh
a bar	un bar	oon bar
a bookstore	una libreria	*oo*-nah lee-breh-*ree*-ah
To the left	A sinistra	ah see-*nees*-tra
To the right	A destra	ah *dehy*-stra
Straight ahead	Avanti (or sempre diritto)	ahv-*vahn*-tee (*sehm*-pray dee-*reet*-toh)

DINING

English	Italian	Pronunciation
Breakfast	Prima colazione	*pree*-mah coh-laht-tzee-*ohn*-ay
Lunch	Pranzo	*prahn*-zoh
Dinner	Cena	*chay*-nah
How much is it?	Quanto costa?	*kwan*-toh *coh*-sta
The check, please	Il conto, per favore	eel kon-toh *pehr* fah-*vohr*-eh

A MATTER OF TIME

English	Italian	Pronunciation
When?	Quando?	*kwan*-doh
Yesterday	Ieri	ee-*yehr*-ree
Today	Oggi	*oh*-jee
Tomorrow	Domani	doh-*mah*-nee
What time is it?	Che ore sono?	kay *or*-ay *soh*-noh
It's one o'clock.	È l'una.	eh *loo*-nah

English	Italian	Pronunciation
It's two o'clock.	Sono le due.	*soh*-noh leh *doo*-eh
It's two-thirty.	Sono le due e mezzo.	*soh*-noh leh *doo*-eh eh *mehd*-dzoh
It's noon.	È mezzogiorno.	*eh* mehd-dzoh-*johr*-noh
It's midnight.	È mezzanotte.	*eh* mehd-dzah-*noht*-teh
in the morning	al mattino	ahl maht-*tee*-noh
in the afternoon	al pomeriggio	ahl poh-meh-*reed*-joh
at night	alla notte	dee *noht*-the

DAYS OF THE WEEK

English	Italian	Pronunciation
Monday	Lunedì	loo-nay-*dee*
Tuesday	Martedì	mart-ay-*dee*
Wednesday	Mercoledì	mehr-cohl-ay-*dee*
Thursday	Giovedì	joh-vay-*dee*
Friday	Venerdì	ven-nehr-*dee*
Saturday	Sabato	*sah*-bah-toh
Sunday	Domenica	doh-*mehn*-nee-kah

MONTHS & SEASONS

English	Italian	Pronunciation
January	gennaio	jehn-*nah*-yoh
February	febbraio	fehb-*brah*-yoh
March	marzo	*mahr*-tso
April	aprile	ah-*pree*-leh
May	maggio	*mahd*-joh
June	giugno	*jewn*-nyo
July	luglio	*lool*-lyo
August	agosto	ah-*gohs*-toh
September	settembre	seht-*tehm*-breh
October	ottobre	oht-*toh*-breh
November	novembre	noh-*vehm*-breh
December	dicembre	dee-*chehm*-breh
spring	la primavera	lah pree-mah-*veh*-rah
summer	l'estate	lehs-*tah*-teh
autumn	l'autunno	low-*toon*-noh
winter	l'inverno	leen-*vehr*-noh

NUMBERS

English	Italian	Pronunciation
1	uno	*oo*-noh
2	due	*doo*-ay
3	tre	tray

English	Italian	Pronunciation
4	quattro	*kwah*-troh
5	cinque	*cheen*-kway
6	sei	say
7	sette	*set*-tay
8	otto	*oh*-toh
9	nove	*noh*-vay
10	dieci	dee-ay-chee
11	undici	*oon*-dee-chee
20	venti	*vehn*-tee
21	ventuno	vehn-*toon*-oh
22	venti due	*vehn*-tee *doo*-ay
30	trenta	*trayn*-tah
40	quaranta	kwah-*rahn*-tah
50	cinquanta	cheen-*kwan*-tah
60	sessanta	sehs-*sahn*-tah
70	settanta	seht-*tahn*-tah
80	ottanta	oht-*tahn*-tah
90	novanta	noh-*vahnt*-tah
100	cento	*chen*-toh
1,000	mille	*mee*-lay
5,000	cinque milla	*cheen*-kway *mee*-lah
10,000	dieci milla	dee-ay-chee mee-lah

ITALIAN MENU & FOOD TERMS

Acciughe or Alici   Anchovies.

Acquacotta   "Cooked water," a watery vegetable soup thickened with egg and poured over stale bread.

Affettato misto   Mix of various salami, prosciutto, and other cured meats; served as an appetizer.

Agnello   Lamb.

Agnolotti   Semicircular ravioli (often stuffed with meat and/or cheese).

Anatra   Duck.

Anguilla   Eel.

Antipasti   Appetizers.

Aragosta   Lobster.

Arista di maiale   Roast pork loin, usually served in slices, flavored with rosemary, garlic, and cloves.

Baccalà (alla livornese)   Dried salted codfish (cooked in olive oil, white wine, garlic, and tomatoes).

Bistecca alla fiorentina   Florentine-style steak, made with Chianina beef, grilled over wood coals, and then brushed with olive oil and sprinkled with pepper and salt.

Bocconcini   Small veal chunks sautéed in white wine, butter, and herbs. (Also the word for ball-shaped portions of any food, especially mozzarella.)

Braciola   Loin pork chop.

Branzino   Sea bass.

Bresaola   Air-dried, thinly sliced beef filet, dressed with olive oil, lemon, and pepper—usually an appetizer.

Bruschetta   A slab of bread grilled and then rubbed with garlic, drizzled with olive oil, and sprinkled with salt; often served *al pomodoro* (with tomatoes).

Bucatini   Fat, hollow spaghetti. Classically served *all'amatriciana* (with a spicy hot tomato sauce studded with pancetta [bacon]).

Cacciucco   Seafood soup-stew of Livrono in a spicy tomato base poured over stale bread.

Cacio or Caciotto   Southern Tuscan name for pecorino (sheep's-milk) cheese.

Cannellini   White beans, the Tuscan's primary vegetable.

Cannelloni   Pasta tubes filled with meat and baked in a sauce (cream or tomato). The cheese version is usually called *manicotti* (although either name may be used for either stuffing).

Cantuccini   Twice-baked hard almond cookies, vaguely crescent-shaped and best made in Prato (where they're known as *biscotti di Prato*).

Capocollo   Aged sausage made mainly from pork necks.

Caprese   A salad of sliced mozzarella and tomatoes lightly dressed with olive oil, salt, and pepper.

Capretto   Kid goat.

Caprino   Soft goat's-milk cheese.

Carciofi   Artichokes.

Carpaccio   Thin slices of raw cured beef, pounded flat and often served topped with arugula (rocket) and parmesan cheese shavings.

Casalinga   Home cooking.

Cavolo   Cabbage.

Ceci   Chickpeas (garbanzo beans).

Cervelli   Brains, often served *fritti* (fried).

Cervo   Venison.

Cibrèo   Stew of chicken livers, cockscombs, and eggs.

Cinghiale   Wild boar.

Cipolla   Onion.

Coniglio   Rabbit.

Cozze   Mussels.

Crespelle alla fiorentina   Thin pancakes wrapped around ricotta and spinach, covered with tomatoes and cheese, and baked in a casserole.

Crostini   Small rounds of bread toasted and covered with various pâtés, most commonly a tasty liver paste.

Dentice   Dentex; a fish similar to perch.

Fagioli   Beans, almost always white cannellini beans.

Faraona   Guinea hen.

Farro   Emmer or spelt, a barleylike grain (often in soups).

Fave   Broad (fava) beans.

Fegato   Liver.

Focaccia   Like pizza dough with nothing on it, this bready snack is laden with olive oil, baked in sheets, sprinkled with coarse salt, and eaten in slices plain or split to stuff as a sandwich. In Florence, it's also popularly called *schiacciato*.

Formaggio   Cheese.

Frittata   Thick omelet stuffed with meats, cheese, and vegetables; sometimes eaten between slices of bread as a sandwich.

Fritto misto   A deep-fried mix of meats, often paired with fried artichokes. By the coast, usually a mixed fry of seafood.

Frutte di mare   A selection of shellfish, often boosted with a couple of shrimp and some squid.

Funghi   Mushrooms.

Fusilli   Spiral-shaped pasta; usually long like a telephone cord, not the short macaroni style.

Gamberi (gamberetti)   Prawns (shrimp).

Gelato   Dense version of ice cream (*produzione propria* means homemade).

Gnocchi   Pasta dumplings usually made from potato.

Granchio   Crab.

Granita   Flavored ice; *limone* (lemon) is the classic.

Involtini   Thinly sliced beef or veal rolled with veggies (often celery or artichokes) and simmered in its own juices.

Lampreda   Lamprey (an eel-like fish).

Lenticchie   Lentil beans; Italy's best come from Castellúccio, in Umbria.

Lepre   Wild hare.

Lombatina di vitello   Loin of veal.

Maiale   Pork.

Manzo   Beef.

Mascarpone   Technically a cheese but more like heavy cream, already slightly sweet and sweetened more to use in desserts like tiramisù.

Melanzana   Eggplant (aubergine).

Merluzzo   Cod.

Minestrone   A little-bit-of-everything vegetable soup, usually flavored with chunks of cured ham.

Mortadella   A very thick mild pork sausage; the original bologna (because the best comes from Bologna).

Mozzarella   A nonfermented cheese, made from the fresh milk of a buffalo (but increasingly these days from a cow), boiled and then kneaded into a rounded ball; served as fresh as possible.

Oca   Goose.

Orata   Sea bream.

Orecchiette   Small, thick pasta disks (literally, "little ears").

Osso buco   Beef or veal knuckle braised in wine, butter, garlic, lemon, and rosemary; the marrow is a delicacy.

Ostriche   Oysters.

Paglio e fieno   Literally, "hay and straw," yellow (egg) and green (spinach) tagliatelle mixed and served with sauce.

Pancetta   Salt-cured pork belly, rolled into a cylinder and sliced—the Italian bacon.

Panforte   Any of a number of huge barlike candies vaguely akin to fruitcake; a dense, flat honey-sweetened mass of nuts, candied fruits, and spices.

Panino   A sandwich.

Panna   Cream (either whipped and sweetened for ice cream or pie; or heavy and unsweetened when included in pasta sauce).

Panzanella   A cold summery salad made of stale bread soaked in water and vinegar, mixed with cubed tomatoes, onion, fresh basil, and olive oil.

Pappa al pomodoro   A bready tomato-pap soup.

Pappardelle alle lepre   Wide, rough pasta tossed in hare sauce.

Parmigiano   Parmesan, a hard salty cheese usually grated over pastas and soups but also eaten alone; also known as *grana*.

Pecorino   A rich sheep's-milk cheese; in Tuscany it's eaten fresh and soft, or *stagionato* (aged, sometimes with truffle or chilli).

Penne strascicate   Hollow pasta quills in a creamy ragù (meat-and-tomato sauce).

Peperonata   Stewed peppers and onions under oil; usually served cold.

Peperoncini   Hot chili peppers.

Peperoni   Green, yellow, or red sweet peppers.

Peposo   Beef stew with peppercorns.

Pesce al cartoccio   Fish baked in a parchment envelope.

Pesce spada   Swordfish.

Piccione   Pigeon.

Pici or Pinci   A homemade pasta made with just flour, water, and olive oil, rolled in the hands to produce lumpy, thick, chewy spaghetti to which sauce clings. This local name is used around Siena and to its south.

Piselli   Peas.

Pizza   Comes in two varieties: *rustica* or *al taglio* (by the slice) and *al forno* in a pizzeria (large, round pizzas for dinner with a thin, crispy crust). Specific varieties include *margherita* (plain pizza of tomatoes, mozzarella, and basil), *napoletana* (tomatoes, oregano, mozzarella, and anchovies), *capricciosa* (a naughty combination of prosciutto, artichokes, olives, and sometimes egg or anchovies), and *quattro stagioni* (four seasons of fresh vegetables, sometimes also with ham).

Polenta   Cornmeal mush, ranging from soupy to a dense cakelike version related to cornbread; often mixed with mushrooms and other seasonal fillings, served plain alongside game, with a stew, or sometimes sliced and fried.

Pollo   Chicken; *alla cacciatore* is huntsman style, with tomatoes and mushrooms cooked in wine; *alla diavola* is spicy hot grilled chicken; *al mattone* is cooked under a hot brick.

Polpette   Small veal meatballs.

Polpo   Octopus.

Pomodoro   Tomato (plural *pomodori*).

Porcini   Large, wild bolete mushrooms, what the French call *cèpes*.

Porri   Leeks.

Ribollita   A thick, almost stewlike vegetable soup made with black cabbage, olive oil, celery, carrots, and whatever else *Mamma* has left over, all poured over thick slabs of bread.

Ricotta   A soft, fluffy, bland cheese made from the watery whey (not curds, as most cheese) and often used to stuff pastas. *Ricotta salata* is a salted, hardened version for nibbling.

Risotto   Rice, often arborio, served sticky.

Rombo   Turbot fish.

Salsa verde   Green sauce, made from capers, anchovies, lemon juice and/or vinegar, and parsley.

Salsicce   Sausage.

Saltimbocca   Veal scallop topped with a sage leaf and a slice of prosciutto and simmered in white wine.

Salvia   Sage.

Sarde   Sardines.

Scaloppine   Thin slices of meat, usually veal.

Scamorza   An air-dried (sometimes smoked) cheese similar to mozzarella; often sliced and grilled or melted over ham in a casserole, giving it a thin crust and gooey interior.

Schiacciata   See "Focaccia."

Scottiglia   Stew of veal, chicken, various game, and tomatoes cooked in white wine.

Semifreddo   A cousin to *gelato* (ice cream), it's a way of taking nonfrozen desserts (tiramisù, zuppa inglese) and freezing and moussing them.

Seppia   Cuttlefish (halfway between a squid and small octopus); its ink is used for flavoring and coloring in some pasta and risotto dishes.

Sogliola   Sole.

Spezzatino   Beef or veal stew, often with tomatoes.

Spiedino   A shish kebab (skewered bits of meat, onions, and slices of tomato or peppers grilled).

Spigola   A fish similar to sea bass or grouper.

Stracciatella   Egg-drop soup topped with grated cheese; also a flavor of ice cream (vanilla with chocolate ripple).

Stracotto   Overcooked beef, wrapped in bacon and braised with onion and tomato for hours until it's so tender it dissolves in your mouth.

Strozzapreti   Ricotta-and-spinach dumplings, usually served in tomato sauce; literally "priest chokers." Also called *strangolaprete.*

Stufato   Pot roast, usually in wine, broth, and veggies.

Tagliatelle   Flat pasta.

Tartufo   (1) Truffles; (2) An ice-cream ball made with a core of fudge, a layer of vanilla, a coating of chocolate, and a dusting of cocoa; order it *affogato* (drowning), and they'll pour brandy over it.

Tonno   Tuna.

Torta   A pie. *Alla nonna* is Grandma's style and usually is a creamy lemony pie; *alle mele* is an apple tart; *al limone* is lemon; *alle fragole* is strawberry; *ai frutti di bosco* is with berries.

Torta al testo   A flat, unleavened bread baked on the hearthstone and often split to be filled with sausage, spinach, or other goodies.

Tortellini   Rings or half-moons of pasta stuffed with ricotta and spinach or chopped meat (chicken and veal). Sometimes also called *tortelli* and *tortelloni.*

Trippa   Tripe (cow's stomach lining). Served *alla fiorentina* means casseroled with tomatoes and onions, topped with grated Parmesan cheese.

Trota   Trout.

Vermicelli   Very thin spaghetti.

Vitello   Veal. A *vitellone* is an older calf about to enter cowhood. *Vitello tonnato* is thinly sliced veal served cold and spread with tuna mayonnaise.

Vongole   Clams.

Zabaglione/zabaione   A custard made of whipped egg yolks, sugar, and Marsala wine.

Zampone   Pig's feet, usually stewed for hours.

Zuccotto   A tall liqueur-soaked sponge cake, stuffed with whipped cream, ice cream, chocolate, and candied fruits.

Index

See also Accommodations and Restaurant indexes, below.

General Index

A

Abbazia di Sant'Antimo (Montalcino), 174–175
Abbey of San Galgano (near Chiusdino), 4, 135
Accommodations, 3. *See also* Accommodations Index
Air travel, 226–227
  Florence, 44
Alabaster, Volterra, 147
Amedo Giusti (Lucca), 153
Amici degli Uffizi (Florence), 71
Amici della Musica (Florence), 99
Antica Macelleria Cecchini (Panzano in Chianti), 118
Antiche Terme di Bagno Vignoni, 177
Apartment rentals and alternative accommodations, Florence, 60
Aperitivo, 2
Appartamenti Reali (Florence), 91
Archaeological Museum (Florence), 87–88
Area codes, 233
Arezzo, 27, 34, 42, 179–186
Arezzo, Cattedrale di (Arezzo), 184–185
Art and architecture, 17–22
Assisi, 6, 34, 36, 208–214

B

Babele (Florence), 98
Badia a Coltibuono (near Gaiole), 120
Badia a Passignano, 118
Bagno Vignoni, 177
Banfi, 178
Banks and ATMs, 233
Bardini Garden (Florence), 91
Bargello Museum (Florence), 79
Baroni Ricasoli, 120
Bartolomei Orvieto (Spoleto), 216
Basilica di San Francesco (Arezzo), 183–184
Basilica di San Francesco (Assisi), 212–213
Basilica di Santa Chiara (Assisi), 213
Basilica di Santa Margherita (Cortona), 192
Basilica di Santa Maria di Angeli (Assisi), 212
Battistero (Baptistery)
  Florence, 71, 74
  Pisa, 161
Beer House Club (Florence), 100
Benincasa, Catherine, 134

Biblioteca delle Oblate (Florence), 96
Biblioteca Laurenziana (Florence), 85
Biking, 6–7
  the Chianti, 116
  Florence, 50, 95
  Lucca, 152, 154
Boboli Garden (Florence), 92
Bottega d'Arte (Siena), 135
Botticelli, 76, 77, 118
Box Office (Florence), 99
Bravio delle Botti (Barrel Race; Montepulciano), 24
Brunelleschi, Filippo, 79, 84, 85, 86, 89, 90
  Dome (Florence), 6, 74–75
Brunello di Montalcino, 177–178
Brunello Wine Bus, 178
Business hours, 233
Bus travel, 232

C

Caffè Sant'Ambrogio (Florence), 100
CAF Tours, 82, 94
Calcio Storico (Florence), 24
Calendar of events, 24–25
Calendimaggio (Assisi), 210
Campanile di Giotto (Florence), 74
Campo dei Miracoli (Pisa), 160–161
Camposanto (Pisa), 161
Cantinetta dei Verrazzano (Florence), 100
Capella del Coporale (Orvieto), 223
Capella di Sacra Cintura (Prato), 109
Cappella Barbadori-Capponi (Florence), 93
Cappella Bardi (Florence), 90
Cappella Baroncelli (Florence), 90
Cappella Brancacci (Florence), 93
Cappella Castellani (Florence), 90
Cappella Croce del Giorno (Volterra), 144
Cappella dei Magi (Florence), 85
Cappella dei Principi (Florence), 84
Cappella del Cardinale del Portogallo (Florence), 93
Cappella della Santa Maria Maddalena (Assisi), 213
Cappella dell'Assunzione (Prato), 109–110
Cappella delle Rose (Assisi), 212
Cappella del Transito (Assisi), 212
Cappella de Tau (Pistoia), 112, 114
Cappella di San Severo (Perugia), 204
Cappella Peruzzi (Florence), 90
Cappella Rucellai (Florence), 85–86
Cappella San Brizio (Orvieto), 223–224
Cappella Sassetti (Florence), 83
Cappelle Medicee (Florence), 84–85

Carnevale, 24
Car travel and rentals, 227–230
  Florence, 45–46
Casa di Santa Caterina (Siena), 134
Casa di Vasari (Arezzo), 184
Casa Romana (Spoleto), 217–218
Castello di Brolio (near Gaiole in Chianti), 119–120
Castello di Verrazzano (near Gretti), 116
Castello di Volpaia, 119
Castiglion Fiorentino, 194–195
Catherine, St., 134
Cellphones, 236
Cenacolo di Sant'Apollonia (Florence), 86–87
Ceramiche Artistiche Santa Caterina (Siena), 134
Chapel of the Assumption (Prato), 109–110
Chapel of the Girdle (Prato), 109
Chapel of the Princes (Florence), 84
Chiana Valley, 30
The Chianti, 27, 32, 38, 40, 115–120
Chianti Classico Expo (Greve in Chianti), 24
Chiesa di San Giovanni (Lucca), 157
Children, families with, 000m
Chiostro dei Morti (Florence), 86
Chiostro dei Voti (Florence), 88
Chiostro Verde (Florence), 86
Chiusdino, 135
Chiusi, 196–197
Churches and cathedrals, terminology, 18
Church of Sant'Andrea (Pistoia), 114
Città Nuova (Massa Marittima), 148
Città Vecchia (Massa Marittima), 148
Cloister of the Dead (Florence), 86
Collegiata (San Gimignano), 139
Collegiata dei Santi Quirico e Giulitta, 176
Consorzio del Vino Brunello di Montalcino, 177–178
Consorzio del Vino Nobile di Montepulciano, 171
Consulates, 234
Context Travel, 82, 94, 98
Convent of San Domenico (Fiesole), 104, 106
Corridoio Vasariano (Florence), 82
Corso dei Ceri (Gubbio), 207
Corso Rossellino (Pienza), 172
Cortona, 7, 30, 34, 188–194
Crete Senesi, 5, 30, 175
Crete Sienese, 179

D

Deruta, 206
Deruta Placens, 206
Disabled travelers, 233–234